Women Make Horror

Women Make Horror

Filmmaking, Feminism, Genre

EDITED BY ALISON PEIRSE

Rutgers University Press

New Brunswick, Camden, and Newark, New Jersey, and London

Library of Congress Cataloging-in-Publication Data

Names: Peirse, Alison, editor.
Title: Women make horror : filmmaking, feminism, genre / edited by Alison Peirse.
Description: New Brunswick : Rutgers University Press, 2020. | Includes bibliographical refer-
ences and index.
Identifiers: LCCN 2020004481 (print) | LCCN 2020004482 (ebook) | ISBN 9781978805118
(paperback) | ISBN 9781978805125 (hardcover) | ISBN 9781978805132 (epub) | ISBN
9781978805149 (mobi) | ISBN 9781978805156 (pdf)
Subjects: LCSH: Horror films—History and criticism. | Horror films—Production and direction.
| Women motion picture producers and directors. | Women in the motion picture industry. |
Feminism and motion pictures.
Classification: LCC PN1995.9.H6 W625 2020 (print) | LCC PN1995.9.H6 (ebook) | DDC
791.43/6522—dc23
LC record available at https://lccn.loc.gov/2020004481
LC ebook record available at https://lccn.loc.gov/2020004482

A British Cataloging-in-Publication record for this book is available from the British Library.

∞ The paper used in this publication meets the requirements of the American National Standard for Information Sciences—Permanence of Paper for Printed Library Materials, ANSI
Z39.48-1992.

www.rutgersuniversitypress.org

Manufactured in the United States of America

For Edith Fairclough,
a book of your own, at last, my love

Contents

Women Make Horror

1

Women Make (Write, Produce, Direct, Shoot, Edit, and Analyze) Horror

ALISON PEIRSE

In 2008, I secured my first academic post at the University of Hull and designed a new module, "The Horror Film." I began with *Island of Lost Souls* (1932), then *Cat People* (1942), *Horror of Dracula* (1958), *Les yeux sans visage* (1960), *Night of the Living Dead* (1968), *Suspiria* (1977), *Halloween* (1978), *The Evil Dead* (1981), and *The Lost Boys* (1987). I followed this with a series of national case studies: Canadian *Ginger Snaps* (2000), British *Dog Soldiers* (2002), Japanese *Ju-On: The Grudge* (2003), and South Korean *A Tale of Two Sisters* (2003). The selection process was straightforward: the 1930s was my PhD research; *Cat People*, *The Lost Boys*, and *Les yeux sans visage* were my favorites; the case studies reflected the then-academic preoccupation with national cinemas; and everything in between was (what I then considered to be) the key texts of the horror genre. This module was the ur-canon: the emergence of the genre in the American studio system in the 1930s and 1940s, British horror in the 1950s, independent American film-making and the development of European horror in the 1960s and 1970s, and the

1

rise of the slasher and video nasties in the 1970s and 1980s, and then the genre (more or less) goes under for most of the 1990s before returning globally in the new millennium.

Reflecting on those choices, I now realize that all the films were by male directors. In the cases of *Island of Lost Souls, Cat People, Horror of Dracula, Les yeux sans visage, Dog Soldiers,* and *Ju-On: The Grudge,* the writing, producing, directing, cinematography, and editing team was all men. Despite having written a PhD thesis on queer gender and sexuality in horror film, the gender of the filmmakers wasn't something I even considered while creating the module. Indeed, it was a number of years before I even thought about this at all. That moment came in 2014, in the Cinematek bar in Brussels, where I was waiting to give a public lecture at the Offscreen Film Festival. I was idly perusing the film posters on the wall, and my eyes were drawn to a bold, minimal poster. The background was a brilliant blood-red; at its center was a chador-wearing vampire; and across the chador, written in block capitals, was "A GIRL WALKS HOME ALONE AT NIGHT." I wrote down the title and, with Ana Lily Amirpour's vampire film as my gateway drug, I began devouring contemporary women-made horror films. I worked my way through *American Mary* (Jen and Sylvia Soska, 2012), *Soulmate* (Axelle Carolyn, 2013), *Honeymoon* (Leigh Janiak, 2014), *Inner Demon* (Ursula Dabrowsky, 2014), *The Babadook* (Jennifer Kent, 2014), *The Lure* (Agnieszka Smoczyńska, 2015), and *The Invitation* (Karyn Kusama, 2015). From 2016, references to women horror filmmakers achieved critical mass across multiple international media platforms. I read profiles of *Prevenge* (Alice Lowe, 2016), *The Love Witch* (Anna Biller, 2016), *Egomaniac* (Kate Shenton, 2016), *Raw* (Julia Ducournau, 2016), and *XX* (Jovanka Vuckovic, Annie Clark, Roxanne Benjamin, and Karyn Kusama, 2017) in articles proclaiming "The Rise of the Modern Female Horror Filmmaker" (*Rolling Stone*), "Welcome to the Golden Age of Women-Directed Horror" (*Vice*), and "The Female Directors Bringing New Blood to Horror Film" (*Observer*). And then the *Los Angeles Times* declared that *Revenge* (Coralie Fargeat, 2017) offered "the first horror heroine of the Time's Up era."[1]

I questioned my own work as an academic. Given my research in horror film frequently engaged with gender and sexuality and involved interviewing industry practitioners, why hadn't I considered women filmmakers in particular? This really bothered me. The most important academic writers *on* horror were women: Linda Williams, Carol J. Clover, Barbara Creed, Rhona J. Berenstein, Brigid Cherry, Isabel Pinedo, and Joan Hawkins.[2] But what about women as makers of horror? In the popular press that I was reading, critics always had the caveat "*of course* women were making horror films before now" and throwing out the same kind of examples: *Buffy the Vampire Slayer* (Fran Rubel Kuzui, 1992), *Ravenous* (Antonia Bird, 1999), and *Twilight* (Catherine Hardwicke, 2008). Where was this history of women horror filmmakers written? In a *Hollywood Reporter* profile, writer-director Jovanka Vuckovic explained that the making of *XX* was "a direct response to the lack of opportunities for women in the horror genre in particular . . . an area where women have been historically misrepresented onscreen and underrepresented behind the camera."[3] I excelled in the analysis of representation of gender on screen, and I'd read all the women writers on the genre, but in terms of understanding the underrepresentation of women in production roles . . . who? What? Where? When? In the 2010s, it was as if women horror filmmakers had emerged en masse for the first time, all shiny and new.

During this period, there was a major upswing in publications on women filmmakers in the academy. The research focused on four key areas: silent cinema, individual practitioners, national cinemas, and intersectional identities.[4] I realized there was an appetite for reading about horror films made by women and a growing body of academic literature on women filmmakers. This appeared to be a timely opportunity to think about how and why women make horror films. However, I quickly discovered that critical studies of horror were ill equipped to explore this subject further.

Let me explain to you how horror film critics write about filmmakers. In *Hollywood Horror: From the Director's Chair*, all the interviewees are men. In *The Anatomy of Fear: Conversations with Cult Horror and Science Fiction Film Creators*, all twenty-one filmmakers are men. In his 867-page compendium *Horror Film Directors, 1931–1990*, Dennis Fischer lists fifty-two "major" directors (all men) and forty-eight "promising, obscure or hack" directors. From these one hundred directors, Fischer lists just one woman, Stephanie Rothman, and places her in the obscure/hack category. Fischer's categorization of almost exclusively white North American or European men as horror film directors is typical of how our horror film histories are written. From Fischer's point of view, a self-proclaimed "exhaustive study," women have made a 1 percent contribution to the genre.[5] In *Voices in the Dark: Interviews with Horror Writers, Directors and Actors*, all directors featured are men, and all but one of the writers are men.[6] Do note the "actors" in this title. Women often *do* feature in these books, but they are usually reminiscing about the "great" man they knew, or they are discussing their on-screen work as actors. In these collections, women are objects of representation, a position that achieves its zenith in Marcus Hearn's *Hammer Glamour*, a "lavish, full colour celebration of Hammer's female stars."[7]

If interview collections are predicated upon white male directors, what about the theorization of horror? In the 1970s, Robin Wood inaugurated the academic study of the genre. While predominantly studying those male directors popular at the time, including Wes Craven, George Romero, and Brian De Palma, Wood offers a hugely helpful, feminist model for thinking through how to analyze horror film. In "Return of the Repressed" (1978), Wood argued that horror films can radically undermine the status quo of bourgeois capitalism (explored through Marxist dominant ideology) and the patriarchal, heterosexual nuclear family (explored through Freudian psychoanalysis). In particular,

he argued that "central to the effect and fascination of horror films is their ful-
filment of our nightmare wish to smash the norms that oppress us and which
our moral conditioning teaches us to revere."[8] While his demanding theoretical
framework may alienate a more general readership, Wood's primary belief was
that horror film is a space to rebel against dominant norms that oppress us
and that it can be a place to explore social and cultural change, particularly in
relation to (what was then called) the Gay Liberation Front and the women's
liberation movement. This proposition is hugely powerful for helping us to
understand horror film, yet it was Wood's psychoanalytic material that proved
to be most popular with feminist film critics and horror film analysts alike.

Psychoanalytically grounded feminist readings of horror films began to be
published, including Williams's "When the Woman Looks" (1984), Creed's
"Horror and the Monstrous-Feminine: An Imaginary Abjection" (1986), and
Clover's "Her Body Himself: Gender in the Slasher Film" (1987).[9] The readings predominantly focused on films made by men, exploring the representation
of gender on screen and the relationship between the image and the imagined
(usually male) audience member, theorized as the "spectator." In the 1980s and
1990s, these ideas dominated horror film criticism specifically and feminist film
criticism more generally (which focused on film noir and melodrama). There
were outliers during this period though, primarily Cherry, who interviewed real
women fans of horror film. While Williams argued that when women watch
horror, they often refuse to look at the screen "with excellent reason . . . not the
least of which is that she often asked to bear witness to her own powerlessness
in the face of rape, mutilation and murder," Cherry points out that "whether
most female spectators actually behave like this is another question. . . . There
are female viewers who do take pleasure in viewing horror films and who . . .
refuse to refuse to look."[10] Cherry's research is a significant influence on many of
the contributors to this book, and it is a clear indication of the ongoing value
of her work at a time when empirical studies were not highly valued in horror
film studies.

Throughout the 1990s and 2000s, critics began to raise problems with psychoanalysis as a feminist tool of film analysis. Author bell hooks, among many
others, pointed out that psychoanalysis was ahistorical and privileged (binary)
sexual difference, while suppressing "the recognition of race, reenacting and
mirroring the erasure of black womanhood that occurs in films, silencing any
discussion of racial difference—of racialized sexual difference . . . many feminist film critics continue to structure their discourse as though it speaks about
'women' when in actuality it speaks only about white women."[11] We return to
psychoanalysis in this collection to explore this important point further. In
chapter 14, Lindsey Decker works through the criticisms of canonical texts on
psychoanalytic film theory and suggests that a different kind of gaze theory
might be useful for thinking through the work of Iranian American director
Amirpour. In chapter 15, in her study of Mexican Canadian filmmaker Gigi Saul

Guerrero, Valeria Villegas Lindvall argues for the usefulness of psychoanalysis as a recognition of "the relevance of its call to rewrite a language within which the ontological constitution of the self is always gauged against a universal male subject" and then argues that its limitations can be overcome by grounding it in "decolonial thought and its revision by decolonial feminists as a critical tool to address racialized female monstrosity."

In the 1990s and 2000s, horror film studies slowly began to turn away from gender and sexuality to focus on affect, trauma, and national cinemas. At the same time, neoliberalism and postfeminism were on the rise in popular culture. For Imogen Tyler, neoliberalism is "packaged as concerned with individual freedom, choice, democracy and personal responsibility" while systematically stripping "assets from the poor (including welfare provisions) and concentrat[ing] wealth within a tiny global elite (individuals and corporations)," while postfeminism is, for Angela McRobbie, "the thorough dismantling of feminist politics and the discrediting of the occasionally voiced need for its renewal."[12] Rosalind Gill and Christina Scharff reveal the relationship between postfeminism and neoliberalism, suggesting that "both appear to be structured by a current of *individualism* that has almost entirely replaced notions of the social or political, or any ideas of individuals as subject to pressures, constraints or influence from outside themselves."[13] Looking back now at this period, as a fledgling academic doing my MA and PhD in the 2000s, it is no wonder that I'd never considered women horror filmmakers. Feminism was over, activism was unfashionable, filmmakers were white male directors, women were actors, and psychoanalysis, the primary methodological tool for analyzing gender in horror film, was proven to be lacking.

This brings me back to my module design for Hull. There were women working on those films, I just didn't know about them. Edna Ruth Paul edited *Night of the Living Dead*. Daria Nicolodi cowrote *Suspiria*. Debra Hill cowrote and produced *Halloween*. Janice Fisher was cocreator and cowriter of *The Lost Boys*. Karen Walton wrote *Ginger Snaps*. *A Tale of Two Sisters* was produced by Oh Jeong-wan and edited by Lee Hyeon-mi. I realized there was no point waiting around for someone to write this account of women horror filmmakers for me, and in 2017, I decided to write a call for papers for an edited book collection. I did not have a publisher, and I wasn't sure about the shape or structure of the book. At this point, my goal was to collect a marvelous group of like-minded academics to explore this unknown territory with me.

Cinefeminism Meets Horror Film

Writing the call for papers was difficult. I struggled to articulate the framing of a project on women horror filmmakers: I knew it was a political, feminist book, but in what way? I was overwhelmed with all the different possibilities for exploration. Thankfully, I was rescued by Annette Kuhn's *Women's Pictures* (1982).

Kuhn defines feminism as "a set of political practices founded in analyses of the social/historical position of women as subordinated, oppressed or exploited either within dominant modes of production (such as capitalism) and/or by the social relations of patriarchy or male domination."[14] This made sense, as did the idea of women's films as those not just about or addressed to women but *made by* women. What was more important though was Kuhn's conviction that "conditions now exist for feminist film criticism and feminist filmmaking to share some common concerns and goals," and they are interconnected "either explicitly in their politics, or implicitly in the kinds of thinking that underlie them."[15] This approach offered a feminist way of exploring both women filmmakers and the films they made.

Kuhn's work, like that of E. Ann Kaplan, Claire Johnston, and Pam Cook, is part of the 1970s "cinefeminism" movement that emerged from women's film festivals and women's liberation as "well as from the intellectual and ideological lessons of the New Left."[16] However, cinefeminism eventually transformed into feminist film criticism, which focused more on representation as opposed to women making films. As a result, "by the mid-1980s the artist behind the camera was barely in the picture. The near-symbiotic relationship between feminist film theory and women's film practice that characterized ... *Women's Pictures* ... was no longer sustainable."[17]

What happens if we take those initial, radical ideas about the relationship between women's filmmaking and film criticism and align them with the spirit of Wood's reading of horror as a place of potential political change? There is a natural synergy here between film theorization and the realities of film practice; as Wood argues, his model "enables us to connect theory closely with the ways we actually think and feel and conduct our lives."[18] By bringing together cinefeminism and Wood's work on horror this way, I offer a model for doing horror film studies that engages with women practitioners and resonates with the increased need for activism given our contemporary political climate. Having established the parameters of the project, I then wrote three questions for my contributors, designed to provide a coherent, intellectual underpinning for the collection.

The first question is *Can horror cinema be women's cinema?* If by women's cinema we mean cinema made by women, then yes, of course horror cinema can be women's cinema. But what I am digging at here is the long-standing assumption, explored academically, that horror is a misogynistic genre.[19] Really, the question is (how) can horror cinema be women's cinema? Critics have historically shared a similar point of view. In 1982, Janet Maslin published a *New York Times* article on (what we now call) slasher films, which she describes as a new form of "violent pornography" against women. She takes to task Debra Hill, producer of *Halloween III: Season of the Witch* (1982), and Amy Holden Jones and Rita Mae Brown, director and writer, respectively, of *The Slumber Party Massacre* (1982), for making these films, saying of the latter, it is "no less bloody, sexist or ugly than comparable films made by men. But it's a little more reprehensible, because its creators ought to know better."[20] For Maslin, the films are made even more dreadful because they were helmed by women. Nearly forty years later, it is still considered weird to be a woman and a horror fan or filmmaker. Sylvia Soska has commented, "Every time we said we were horror directors, people would look at us and go, 'Oh, honey, you don't have to do that.' It was almost like they were talking about how I clean up roadkill for the city, and it was this weird preconceived notion that horror movies and women don't mix."[21]

This has never made sense to me. Like many fans, many of my formative memories of my family and home life revolve around horror. When I was about seven, we watched *Legend* (1985) one Sunday afternoon. I remember being utterly terrified by Tim Curry as the Lord of Darkness while my mother grumbled through the ironing. When I was eleven, Chris, my younger brother, and I rented a VHS of *Tremors* (1990) from the corner shop. Just as a giant worm monster plowed through the desert after Kevin Bacon, my dad burst into the living room and threw the tumble dryer hose extension at us. We screamed, and he laughed his head off and went back into the kitchen to cook dinner. In between being a thoroughly revolting teenager, I bonded with my mother over a viewing of *The Lost Boys*; when my mother explained that she knew Max was the head vampire because he had to be invited into Lucy's house, I was really impressed with her, probably for the first time in years. Horror has always been in my family; it has always been communal, interactive, scary, and exciting. Why wouldn't I want to study it when I grew up?

Kier-La Janisse has noted that as a horror fan, she is often questioned about what she gets out of it: "I give them the stock answers: catharsis, empowerment, escapism and so on. Less easy to explain is the fact that I gravitate toward films that devastate me and unravel me completely—a good horror film will more often make me cry than make me shudder."[22] For those people who can't understand the relationship between women and horror, I wonder why it isn't enough of an explanation that we are simply drawn to a genre with the concomitant emotions and experiences (multiple, varied, distinct to individual fans) offered to us. We don't demand similar in-depth psychological explanations of fans of action films or comedy. The opposition we face here comes out of multiple sources: our gender as fans and filmmakers, the "low" cultural perception of the genre, and then the widespread beliefs about how this genre represents our gender. But there are plenty of gendered parallels in "high" cultural forms that don't attract this disapprobation. Take for example Greek tragedies like Sophocles's *Oedipus Rex* (429 BCE) and Aeschylus's *Agamemnon* (458 BCE) or Shakespeare's plays *Titus Andronicus* (1593 CE) and *King Lear* (1606 CE). These plays all feature significant amounts of emotional and physical violence enacted upon male bodies, including blinding, cannibalism, madness, and murder. Yet when male audience members leave the theater, we don't ask of them, confused, "But what do *you* get out of this?"

So rather than the question *Can horror cinema be women's cinema?* the perhaps more pertinent question to replace it with is *Why do women make the kinds of horror films that they have?* This book explores a variety of reasons for women's choices. A number of writer-directors initially got their break collaborating with Roger Corman across the 1960s–1980s, including Stephanie Rothman (discussed in chapter 2 by Alicia Kozma), Barbara Peeters, Katt Shea, Amy Holden Jones, and producer Gale Ann Hurd. Given its traditionally low budget and wide appeal, horror has also been a pragmatic choice for many women, including Karen Arthur (discussed in chapter 3 by Alexandra Heller-Nicholas) and Roberta Findlay, who worked across grindhouse, pornography, and horror, depending on where the money was.[23]

In the 1980s and early 1990s, franchises were also a place where women could work their way up through the ranks. Both *Slumber Party* sequels were also written, produced, and directed by women. Kristine Peterson worked on *A Nightmare on Elm Street* (1984) before directing *Critters 3* (1991). Hope Perello worked on *Puppetmaster* (1989) before directing *Howling VI: The Freaks* (1991). Rachel Talalay (discussed in chapter 6 by Tosha R. Taylor) cut her teeth collaborating with John Waters before working on the *Nightmare on Elm Street* series, eventually directing *Freddy's Dead: The Final Nightmare* (1991).

Some women had already developed good careers in related disciplines—in Mary Lambert's case, directing music videos such as Madonna's "Like a Prayer" before directing *Pet Sematary* (1989) for Paramount Pictures. With domestic box office receipts of more than $57.4 million, *Pet Sematary* remains not only the highest-grossing U.S. horror film directed by a woman but also in the top one hundred highest-grossing horror films of all time.[24] However, even Lambert still lacked creative control in the commercial studio system. When she made the sequel *Pet Sematary 2* (1992), she wanted to tell the story of Ellie, the one surviving member of the Creed family, but her idea was blocked by the studio, who insisted she made the protagonist an adolescent boy. She commented, "My career is littered with the projects I wanted to do that were about women—not, like, 'girl movies' but crazy, baby-killer psychopath women, or women in combat movies. They all got thrown back at me. Most of the time it was like, 'We can't do this with a female protagonist.' 'We have to make the male part bigger.' 'When she goes into combat, the guy's got to save her.' I'm like, that's not the movie!"[25]

For a new generation of filmmakers, horror film festivals have functioned as vital training, networking, and promotional sites. In chapter 12, Donna McRae examines the support networks offered by the Stranger With My Face International Film Festival in Australia, while in chapter 18, Sonia Lupher interviews women filmmakers at horror festivals in America and discovers that festivals play "a pivotal role in the transition between fandom and practice within the horror community." While festivals support women filmmakers working now, they also play an important part in rewriting and reconstructing our histories of women in the genre. The Fantastic Fest in Austin, Texas, collaborates regularly with the American Genre Film Archive (AGFA), and their screening strands—onstage Q&As and AGFA's subsequent home releases—have been instrumental in bringing to light little-known women horror filmmakers and their films, including Sarah Jacobsen and her *I Was a Teenage Serial Killer* (1993) and Tina Krause's shot-on-video *Limbo* (1999).

The next major question that *Women Make Horror* explores relates to the politics of storytelling. *What kinds of stories are told in women-made horror films? How do they represent women? Are they distinctive from, or similar to, stories told in horror films made by male teams?* This is representative of the broader questions asked about women filmmakers. In a 1975 *Village Voice* article, Molly Haskell asked, "Are women directors different"? And is there "such a thing as a 'woman's point of view,' a distinctly 'feminine' approach to filmmaking?"[26] But what is specifically interesting to us here is how these questions concern even destabilize—notions of gender and genre. As Christine Gledhill notes, "Does thinking about the constructedness and performativity of gender and sexual identity enable us to approach the production of film genres and the cultural-textual work of generic convention differently . . . how does gender get into genre, and what does genre do with it?"[27] Horror is a particularly valuable way of exploring these kinds of questions, given that the genre thoroughly explores (and often deconstructs) received notions of gender, sexuality, identity, and the body. In chapter 11, Molly Kim offers the first English-language study of women horror filmmakers in South Korea and argues that Lee Soo-yeon and Kim Mi-jeong address the experiences and concerns of women in contemporary Korean society, while in chapter 17's analysis of *Prevenge*, Amy C. Chambers argues that the then-heavily pregnant director, writer, and actor Alice Lowe "offers visibility of the lived experience that is biologically unavailable to male directors."

These questions of genre and gender then raise issues about how we conceptualize working through the films of "women." Writing on women's literary history, Margaret Ezell points out that her direction is "fundamentally interested in the historically specific, in the particularity of the past, rather than an essentialist one searching for 'the' woman."[28] Similarly, I argue that there is no specific "woman" to find, no universal experience applicable to all. And in using "women" in the title of this collection, I'm signaling that I'm working with contributors and filmmakers who self-identify as women. This is in line with E. Ann Kaplan's stance that "being 'female' or 'male' does not signify any *necessary* social stance vis-à-vis dominant cultural attitudes. We have learned that biological women are not necessarily more progressive or forward-looking than are biological men, and the terms 'male' and 'female' do not automatically link biological sex to masculine or feminine behaviors or to certain film genres."[29] But if this is the case, why bother to analyze women filmmakers at all?

In 1983, Joanne Russ explored the suppression of women's writing in society, culture, and academia. She argues that "a mode of understanding life which will-fully ignores [half the human consciousness] can do so only at the peril of thoroughly distorting the rest. A mode of understanding literature which can ignore the private lives of half the human race is not 'incomplete'; it is distorted through and through."[30] Similarly, what *Women Make Horror* proposes then is not that a woman director necessarily will make a woman-centered film, nor that *this* woman's experience will make sense for another woman per se, nor that directors must be feminist, nor that we need to create feminist readings of genre texts. To go even further, when we do have women filmmakers that explicitly identify as feminist, this doesn't mean that their films will necessarily contain this political content. For example, Barbara Peeters requested that her name was removed from directing credits for *Humanoids of the Deep* (1980) after executive producer Roger Corman arranged for the shooting of explicit nude rape scenes, but her request was refused. In 2019, she commented, "I don't talk about that film. . . . I've always—since a small, little girl—been a feminist."[31]

Instead, this book simply suggests that there are a vast number of women filmmakers completely absent from our written horror histories and that by not including the outputs from "half the human race," our histories are faulty. As Aislínn Clarke, director of *The Devil's Doorway* (2018), points out, "Female stories can and should be seen as human stories, rather than niche."[32] This is a long-standing sentiment, one echoed by actor/director Lee Grant, star of *The Mafu Cage* (Karen Arthur, 1978) over forty years earlier: "There is a sensibility, a back-log of experiences that have not been put on film and when they are, people will say, 'Oh my God, I know that. I was there.' It's not something limited to women, but all people who have been forced out of the mainstream."[33]

There is still value in thinking about who is telling the stories though. This brings us to authorship, explored in chapter 4 in Martha Shearer's study of Daria Nicolodi, in chapter 8 in Laura Mee's analysis of director Mary Harron and writer Guinevere Turner's *American Psycho* (2000), and in chapter 9 in Katarzyna Paszkiewicz's exploration of screenwriter Karen Walton's authoring of *Ginger Snaps*. Authorship is tricky, not only because filmmaking is a collaborative process but also because of its long-standing male connotations.[34] In *Genre, Authorship and Contemporary Women Filmmakers*, Paszkiewicz reconsiders women's authorship as a "complex network of discourses," including "What expectations did her gender bring to bear on the kinds of films she made? How did she negotiate these expectations in relation to her public persona? How did reviewers interpret women's films?"[35] Given Paszkiewicz's useful framework, I've left my contributors to assign authorship as and where they will, in the same way that I have not demanded the designation of either "woman" or "female" across the book. There are no simple solutions to thinking through authorship, but in accordance with Sue Thornham, this book makes the case that it remains important. Thornham explains, "When access to the signature, the 'authorizing function,' has been so lately granted to women it is important politically that it is not simply given up. But that signature is also important because it makes women, and their marginality, visible, and regenders male writing, so that it can no longer claim universality."[36]

This brings us to the third and final set of questions that underpins this collection. In *Women's Pictures*, Kuhn asks, "Is the feminism of a piece of work there because of attributes of its author (cultural interventions by women), because of certain attributes of the work itself (feminist cultural interventions), or because of the way it is 'read'?"[37] In writing my call for papers, I paraphrased this, pointing out that *a horror film made by a woman may not be feminist, and men may make feminist horror films. So what makes a horror film a feminist film? Is it the attributes of the author, attitudes in the work, or because of the way the film can be read?* Many women filmmakers do not identify as feminist. Ida Lupino, director of horror/noir hybrid *The Hitch-Hiker* (1953), said on set, "I retain every feminine trait. Men prefer it that way. They're more co-operative if they see that fundamentally you are of the weaker sex. . . . I assume no masculine characteristics, which can often be a fault of career women rubbing shoulders with their male counterparts, who become merely arrogant or authoritative."[38] In 1975, Karen Arthur also repudiated the feminist label, saying, "I am not part of the Woman's Movement as such: it's so bloody boring the way they talk, endless dreary polemics nothing to do with people." But she does concede, "I was brought up in a very sexist society. . . . Women have a lot of reason to scream. Bigotry and chauvinism in the film world is bad; and the industry has been notorious for poor handling of women, both in the projection of the image and in behind the scenes participation."[39] Some women have refused to engage with the gendered implications of filmmaking at all. Kathryn Bigelow, director of vampire western *Near Dark* (1987), not only rejects "the 'feminist' tag, she has also consistently resisted any attempt to categorize her as a 'female' director—whether in relation to her films, her position in the industry, or audiences."[40]

However, it is never just about the filmmaker's intent or academic readings. Katt Shea wrote and directed *Stripped to Kill I* (1987), *Stripped to Kill II* (1989), and *Dance of the Damned* (1989) for Roger Corman's Concorde Pictures and then cowrote and directed *Poison Ivy* (1992) for then-independent New Line Cinema. At the Seattle International Festival of Women Directors screening of *Poison Ivy*, curator Mary Brennan reported, "Most of the audience was furious that a female director would create something as politically incorrect. . . . Shea was bombarded with hostile questions at the postfilm Q&A," while the *New York Times* review described *Poison Ivy* as "a B movie with a vengeance, one that offers a wickedly feminine (though hardly feminist) view of nominally happy life and its failings."[41] This reflects Paszkiewicz's point about the inscription of authorship with the politics of gender. If you are a woman filmmaker, you are ascribed a political position regardless of personal belief. As Lizzie Francke notes, once feminism took root in the 1960s, "women in creative professions would find themselves and their work perused as feminist or not. 'Feminism,' with its multifold meanings, became something that women writers could espouse, distance themselves from, or claim to have never come across. It was a knot in the background fabric, there to be unraveled or ignored."[42] As such, this collection is feminist in its determination to illuminate the work and lives of women filmmakers in the horror genre. It explores some avowedly feminist filmmakers but also offers feminist readings: in chapter 10, Maddi McGillvray rereads Marina de Van's and Claire Denis's films as a "feminist art horror" model of the New French Extremity. Similarly, in her analysis of Talalay's work on *Freddy's Dead*, Taylor argues for the importance of audiences creating their own feminist analyses, noting, "Jane Gaines cautions us not to overlook the audience as another contributor to a film's meaning."

As a feminist collection though, this book also has one more really important point to make. In 2017, Wiley-Blackwell published Benshoff's "cutting-edge" collection *A Companion to the Horror Film*, a six-hundred-page book featuring "many of the finest academics working in the field" and "many exciting younger scholars." There are thirty chapters, and three are written by women. Given the centrality of women academics to the study of the genre, there is something truly terrible about the fact that we have to get to chapter 20 before we see a woman author. Of these three women contributors, two are Hawkins and Pinedo, two of the most preeminent international scholars on horror. As a woman, do you have to have transformed the field in order to be a contributor to this book? The same level of gatekeeping does not apply to all the male contributors. As with our filmmakers, effectively leaving out the opinions of half the population can only contribute to a flawed collection. We know that women write, produce, direct, shoot, and edit horror, but let's not forget that they analyze it too.

Books such as *A Companion to the Horror Film* are just one reason all *Women Make Horror*'s contributors identify as women. While this fact alone makes the book unique in horror film studies, it was not done to be distinctive. In the same way that some people might argue that the existing horror film histories don't address a wider range of women filmmakers because women were not making films (something we prove wrong), it's not good enough to assume that there are no women out there to contribute to these projects. I secured the majority of my contributors through a single posting to a Gothic Feminism Conference blog and was inundated with responses from all over the world. When I posted, I did not specify women contributors, and I did not plan to reject any outstanding abstracts on the basis of the writer's gender. But the response from women was so strong, I did not need to look any further. I then selected contributors at different stages of their careers, including four women who are still undertaking doctoral study. Mentoring new women academics is important: If, as women, we are only let into the major collections when we have transformed the discipline, what does that mean for most of us? And so, when we do secure that prestigious book contract with an eminent academic publisher (thank you,

Rutgers University Press), what stance should we take over the structure, content, and development of the collection?

The *Women Make Horror* Manifesto

In February 2010, Hannah Neurotica, creator of *Ax Wound* zine, created Women in Horror Recognition Month (WiHM). Inspired by the "girls to the front" ethos of Riot Grrrl, her aim was to bring about awareness of the women "writers, directors, producers, artists, eerie musicians, creepy doll makers, FX artists," and audiences involved in horror and "how we can ALL TAKE ACTION to bring AWARENESS to women in the industry."[43] WiHM went viral and has grown from a blog into a sustained, international initiative; in 2019, it celebrated its tenth year as "a Decade of Blood." In the spirit of WiHM, I offer you my six-point manifesto, a declaration of my intentions for this book, used to select, organize, and edit the material from my contributors. You'll notice each point is defined in opposition to an existing way of doing horror film studies or studying women filmmakers. This standpoint, while appearing negative, is designed to draw attention to and then deconstruct the natural and inevitable way women practitioners and/or horror film are analyzed and, in so doing, break open a much wider range of opportunities for future work on gender and genre.

The first principle is that *horror films do not need to be contemporary to be worthy of study*. At the beginning of this chapter, I referenced a number of recent film releases, and readers may be disappointed there are not more references to women filmmakers working now—where is the full chapter on the Soska sisters? On Anna Biller? On Jennifer Kent? On Kimberly Peirce's *Carrie* remake (2013)? And believe me, you don't know the pain I feel over the lack of space to write a chapter on *Jennifer's Body* (Karyn Kusama, 2009). However, for contemporary women filmmakers, there is an active network of online fan communities and horror film festivals that showcase women horror filmmakers, including Etheria Film Night, Sick Chicks Film Festival, and Women in Horror Film Festival (all in the United States); We Are the Weirdos touring program (United Kingdom); Final Girls Berlin (Germany); Stranger With My Face International Film Festival (Australia); and the Bloody Mary Film Festival (Canada). This isn't to say that the current system is perfect or by any means enough. Blogs and festivals are precarious entities, vulnerable to funding shortages and often dependent on volunteers. However, despite these ongoing difficulties, exposure for new filmmakers can and does occur.

So instead, *Women Make Horror* grounds its subject in history. Discussing *Raw* in 2016, Ducournau commented, "I really hope nobody thinks this is just a trend or something. That would be horrible."[44] Ducournau was commenting on the press's perception of the new "golden era" of women's horror filmmaking, but we can take her comment further. Women making horror is not a trend because they have always been doing this. Chapters 2, 3, and 4 explore women's filmmaking across the 1950s to the 1970s, while chapters 5, 6, and 7 focus on the 1980s and 1990s. The selection and organization of these chapters is the first step in piecing together stories of women working in the genre.

But we could go even further back in time. We could consider the work of Ardel Wray, Irene Kuhn, Ruth Rose, Lillie Hayward, Dodie Smith, or Leigh Brackett, all women screenwriters working in 1930s and 1940s American studio horror. Or further back still, to Edla Hansen, the Danish editor of *Häxan* (1922), or even back to the origins of cinema: in 1913, French-born Alice Guy-Blaché directed and produced a three-reeler adaptation of Edgar Allen Poe's *The Pit and the Pendulum*, of which one reel remains in the Library of Congress. So please keep looking further back into our histories to find women working at all points in genre cinema. These women may often be editors or screenwriters rather than directors, and at certain periods in history, there is literally just a handful of them working in above-the-line roles. But this doesn't mean they are not worth discussing. Until we fully engage with historical materials, our understanding of women's contributions to genre cinema remains faulty and incomplete. And we'll keep making the same mistakes as I did a few years ago when I enthusiastically greeted the work of women horror filmmakers as if they were all "shiny and new."

The second principle is that *horror films do not need to be feature length to be worthy of study*. This is important given that women filmmakers (and particularly women of color) historically have had far less access to funding for feature-length productions. Short films are a vital form for understanding women horror filmmakers, not least because a screenplay written by a woman can have a tangible impact on the hiring of women in other key creative roles. As a recent Writers Guild of Great Britain report revealed, "Female written films are far more likely to have female heads of both their creative and production teams, resulting in far greater female influence over both hiring down the line, and the eventual content of the project."[45] We can see this trickle-down effect in action on *Suicide by Sunlight* (2019), written by Nikyatu Jusu and R. Shanea Williams. The short film was then directed by Jusu, produced by Nikkia Moulterie, shot by Daisy Zhou, and edited by Marina Katz. As such, while we do cover features in *Women Make Horror*, we also consider a range of narrative and experimental short films in chapters 5, 12, 15, and 18; in addition, in chapter 13, Erin Harrington takes horror omnibuses and anthologies to task, arguing that "despite their self-professed eclecticism, [they] offer an inconvenient cultural barometer of horror that exposes the limits of a frustrating, male-dominated status quo."

The third principle is *horror films do not need to have a commercial narrative to be worthy of study*. A chapter on avant-garde Czech filmmaker Vera Chytilová's teen slasher *Vlci bouda* (*Wolf's Hole*; 1987) would have been fantastic, and I would have loved to have read a study of Germaine Dulac's *La Coquille et le clergyman* (1923) or Maya Deren's *The Witch's Cradle* (1944) and *Meshes of the Afternoon* (1943). However, tensions between fine art and filmmaking are still explored in chapter 7 in Dahlia Schweitzer's study of artist Cindy Sherman's *Office Killer* (1997); in chapter 16, Janice Loreck considers how Lucile Hadžihalilović's *Évolution* (2015) offers a hybrid of art cinema and genre filmmaking; while in chapter 5, the relationship between fine art, experimental video, and genre filmmaking are beautifully synthesized in Katia Houde's study of the fine artist videos of Cecelia Condit and Ellen Cantor.

The fourth principle is *horror filmmakers do not need to be directors to be worthy of study*. As a scriptwriter and script editor, I am fascinated by story, so I asked my contributors to focus on key above-the-line roles that have a major impact on story as a way of establishing voice and point of view. So while the collection does study a number of directors, we also look at screenwriters, including Daria Nicolodi, Karen Walton, Alice Lowe, and Guinevere Turner. I would have liked to have seen work on more writer-directors, including Jackie Kong, Shimako Sato, and Mari Asato, and case studies of Louise Sherrill's one-and-done *Ghosts of Hanley House* (1968) and Marina Sargenti's fabulous teen horror *Mirror, Mirror* (1990). There's also room for more work on multihyphenated filmmakers, covering multiple roles on low-budget independent productions, such as Gloria Katz, who codirected, produced, and wrote *Messiah of Evil* (1973); Kei Fujiwara, who wrote, directed, shot, and starred in *Organ* (1996); and Denisse Arancibia Flores, who codirected, coproduced, cowrote, and edited Bolivia's first feature-length horror film, *Casting* (2010). I'd also love to see future work on the (apparently) newly discovered version of splatter film *A Night to Dismember* (1983), directed, produced, and coedited by Doris Wishman.

Given the length of this book, I didn't push for work on editors or directors of photography (DoPs), but these are becoming increasingly rich roles to mine for future projects. Editing case studies could include Louise Ford, Amy Jump, Plummy Tucker, or Jennifer Lame, while DoPs in just the last few years include Ari Wegner on *In Fabric* (2019), Charlotte Bruus Christensen on *A Quiet Place* (2018), and Natasha Braier on *The Neon Demon* (2016). I had also hoped for work on specific producers, which didn't materialize; for example, a chapter on *You ling ren jian* (*Visible Secret*; 2001), produced and directed by Ann Hui, would have been welcome. I'm unclear why producer case studies are unpopular; are producers less well known, their names less familiar outside the film industry? Studies of producers are crucial for better understanding women's filmmaking practices. As Stacy L. Smith, Katherine Pieper, and Marc Choueiti have noted in their study of independent women filmmakers, "Across all behind-the-camera positions, females were most likely to be producers."[46] Thanks to Christopher Meir, Anthony McKenna, and Andrew Spicer's recent book, we now have a methodology for studying producers, and I hope that future writers are emboldened to explore the careers of women such as Jenn Wexler, Jennifer Handorf, Roxanne Benjamin, and Catherine Cyran.[47]

The fifth principle is that *horror films do not need to be demarcated as either national cinemas or Hollywood to be worthy of study*. This statement addresses the fact that historically, horror film studies have predominantly focused on anglo-phone cinema. Second, it then follows that when academics *did* start to write about nonanglophone horror, predominantly post-2000, films and filmmakers were frequently siloed into "national cinemas" (I'm also guilty of this one). In this collection, we study films and filmmakers from all over the world, one country of origin next to another, without comment. My decision to avoid a center-periphery model is influenced by Lucia Nagib, who proposes that we consider "the cinema of the world. It has no center. It is not the other, but it is us"; it is "not a discipline, but a method, a way of cutting across film history according to waves of relevant films and movements."[48] Nagib in turn inspires Patricia White, who argues that "women's cinema should always be seen as world cinema," a sentiment that this book embraces.[49]

Relatedly, *Women Make Horror* has a global remit that examines corporate for-profit cinema, grant-supported art cinema, and no/low-budget indie film-making and, in terms of chapter organization, makes little distinction between these monetary sources. This isn't to say that funding is not important. It impacts every stage of the filmmaking process and is the basis for decisions on distribution, exhibition, and intended audiences, which in turn controls how fans discover, access, and enjoy films. And indeed, academic engagement with audiences is crucial, not least because, as Lupher points out in chapter 18, fan audiences can and do become the next generation of women horror filmmakers. However, in this collection, all categorizations—short/feature, narrative/experimental, country of origin, and funding revenue—are purposefully fluid, a fluidity that reflects the intertextuality of the creative process for the above-the-line storytellers we explore. Creativity does not recognize these kinds of distinctions: consider the way that a major-studio American feature filmmaker can be influenced by an experimental European filmmaker like Dulac or how a fine artist such as Aïda Ruilova chooses to rework Italian *giallo* in *Goner* (2010).

Moving toward our final manifesto principle and reviewing this book as a whole, I hope that future research better foregrounds a range of identities. Darren Elliott–Smith engages with "male directors/producers who self-identify as gay, bi, queer or transgendered" in horror film, but this leaves us with plenty of space to illuminate the queer women in horror through films such as *Make a Wish* (Sharon Ferranti, 2002), *Lyle* (Stewart Thorndike, 2014), *Women Who Kill* (Ingrid Jungermann, 2016), and *Release the Bats* (Michelle Tea, 2018).[50] At the moment, critical studies of identity politics occur at the grassroots level, through blogs, podcasts, and social media. As Alex Hall, creator of the Lezzie Borden "dyke/lez/bi" horror Instagram, explains, she set up the account because she "was . . . experiencing this thriving queer horror community, mostly focused through the lens of male subjectivities," and she "was desperate for the kind of horror analysis that's so intrinsic to queer women; this lesbian lens to horror."[51]

Similarly, while this book addresses the experiences of a range of East Asian, black, and Latin American filmmakers, it is worth noting that many of the book's chapters, particularly the earlier ones, focus on white women. As Maya Montañez Smukler points out in her study of women directors in the 1970s, "that this is a white woman's history reflects the institutionalized gendered racism within the film and television industries during the 1960s and 1970s."[52] Black women were in horror in the 1970s, as Robin R. Means Coleman has explored, but they were predominantly on screen as actors.[53] The institutional problems highlighted by Smukler remain today: the majority of the filmmakers of black, East Asian, and Latin American descent discussed here work in short form, suggesting that whiteness is one barrier that many of our women feature filmmakers have not had to overcome. At the moment, blogs such as Ashlee Blackwell's *Graveyard Shift Sisters* are undertaking this valuable coverage of short form filmmaking, creating the "28 Black Women Horror Filmmakers" series in honor of Black History Month and WiHM.

However, this book is not simply about inclusion. This brings us to the final manifesto principle: *This book is not a correction of the existing canon.* As Anna Cooper argues, "politics of inclusion" are "ultimately quite limited" in terms of creating a more progressive or diverse canon because of how they "re-center white masculinity" and allow "inequalities to be concealed or to be made nondisruptive."[54] Instead, *Women Make Horror* is the beginning of a radical reappraisal of the genre. It demonstrates that the old, single model for horror film history is no longer viable and then rejects the correction of that history or of the creation of a counterhistory. Instead, this book offers you a plurality of *histories* that cut across form, content, country, and funding sources. So forget inclusion or correction, and instead, let's tear up the ur-canon so lovingly outlined in my Hull module guide.

Conclusion

Women Make Horror is not just the first all-woman edited collection on horror film; it is also the first book-length study to focus on women horror filmmakers.[55] As a foundational publication, it is the starting point in creating a multivoiced, global history of women in genre filmmaking. It offers a plurality of contributors and case studies from across the globe and in so doing demonstrates international and intercultural breadth. It comprehensively overturns commonly held beliefs about the lack of women working in horror film, a misapprehension still in circulation today, given the comments of Jason Blum (founder of powerhouse horror studio Blumhouse) that "there are not a lot of female directors period, and even less who are inclined to do horror."[56]

However, we could argue that to consider these horror filmmakers as "women" is to isolate them from their peers. As Mary Lambert has said "It's always a little annoying to be labelled a female film director because men are just 'directors,' then there's the double whammy of 'female' horror director. How many boxes can you be put into?"[57] Does it reduce the filmmaker by considering her as a "woman"? Existing horror film histories are not badged as histories of men or male filmmakers, so why should women's film be considered in this way? In short, why should you care about this project?

This project matters for two reasons. The first is visibility. Drama, comedy, and romance have long been considered the appropriate genres for women filmmakers, and women wanting to work in genres coded "male"—for example, horror, thriller, and action—can encounter a great deal of difficulty.[58] After cowriting and directing *Urban Ghost Story* (1998), her third feature film, British filmmaker Geneviève Jolliffe was invited out to Hollywood by MGM to interview for a teen horror film. After many boardroom meetings, she "sat down with the head of the studio where I was asked 'What makes you think anyone will listen to you, a woman director?'" Undeterred, she went for further horror directing roles, and she said, "It would come down to me and another person who was always a guy. Every single time the guy was picked . . . perhaps I was just unlucky, but after [a while,] you realise that perhaps something else is at play here." Jolliffe also found that women working in positions of power hewed closely to this line: "They were more comfortable taking a risk on a male director than a female director in the horror/thriller genre as otherwise they would have to fight a much bigger fight." Time and again, Jolliffe's chosen genre was an unsurmountable hurdle: "Studio execs would more easily give rom-com directing gigs to women because their audience is women and they've had a history of women rom-com directors doing well."[59]

Given experiences such as Jolliffe's, we can see why the "women" in this book title is important. By revealing that women have worked in horror since the inception of cinema, we can overturn this faulty assumption that women and horror do not mix. When women filmmakers then go for a key creative role on a horror film, we can then hope not only that these women are more confident of their lineage in the genre but also that those in positions of power consider hiring a woman to be less going against the grain and less of a risky prospect. Indeed, within months of Blum's comments and the ensuing online backlash, Blumhouse hired Sophia Takal to cowrite and direct the reboot of *Black Christmas* (2019) and signed Gigi Saul Guerrero to a first-look film and television deal. Since then, Blumhouse signed Zoe Lister-Jones to write and direct the reboot of *The Craft* (forthcoming) and Issa López to adapt and direct *Our Lady of Tears* (forthcoming) and announced the development of an untitled *Dracula* movie with Karyn Kusama. Here's hoping that this book is published at the start of major changes in gendered hiring practices for genre film.

Inspiration is the other reason that this project matters. R. Shanea Williams, multiaward-winning director of *Paralysis* (2015), explains, "If you don't see yourself often represented in something, it's hard to see yourself as a creator of that very thing."[60] As such, unearthing these invisible histories can have a positive impact on future generations of women genre filmmakers. In her biography of Milicent Patrick, creator of the Creature from *Creature of the Black Lagoon* (1954), Mallory O'Meara describes a transformative moment in her life. Teenage

O'Meara discovered a photograph of Patrick working on set. Patrick was not bringing the coffee, was not assisting the men, nor was she "being helplessly carried away in the arms of a monster. She was creating it. It was the first time in my life I had ever seen a picture of a woman like that."[61] Now a horror film writer and producer, O'Meara explains that as she worked her way into the film business, she thought of all the girls "who love monsters, girls who love film. These girls are sitting on the sidelines, not content to watch, but filled with a frustrated desire for momentum and creation. All these girls are potential artists, designers and filmmakers. It's so difficult to be something if you cannot envision it. To see no way in, to see the world you love populated exclusively with those who are not like you is devastating."[62] An encounter like Patrick's photograph—or, I hope, the discovery of a film or filmmaker among these pages—has so much potential power. As a horror fan, when you do see your like in the production credits, it is a validation of your creative ambition. It is a hand reaching out to you, an encouraging whisper that says, "Yes, you can."

As such, this book is for all those people (regardless of gender) who love horror but don't see themselves represented, either in the industry gatekeepers, or in the filmmakers discussed in the standard horror histories, or in the critics who write about the genre. This book is for everyone who still feels that they have to create their own horror histories from scratch and are exhausted by the prospect. You do not have to feel alone anymore. My contributors have much to share with you, and we hope that they will inspire you to write, produce, direct, shoot, or edit your own stories or even make your own monsters. Maybe this book will inspire you to be a critic; to follow this collection with your own zine, blog, article, or book on the genre; or to become a programmer, showcasing women filmmakers at your own film festival. "Women" horror filmmakers *ought* to be an oxymoron, and I do wish, like Debra Hill, that "someday there won't be a need for Women in Film. That it will be People in Film."[63]

But as this book evidences, we are not there yet.

Notes

1   Phoebe Reilly, "From *Babadook* to *Raw*: The Rise of the Modern Female Horror Filmmaker," *Rolling Stone*, October 26, 2016, https://www.rollingstone.com/ movies/movie-features/from-babadook-to-raw-the-rise-of-the-modern-female -horror-filmmaker-120169/; Evelyn Wang, "Welcome to the Golden Age of Women-Directed Horror," *Vice*, April 14, 2017, https://www.vice.com/en_us/article/zmbnd5/ welcome-to-the-golden-age-of-women-directed-horror; Kathryn Bromwich, "The Female Directors Bringing New Blood to Horror Films," *Observer*, March 19, 2017, https://www.theguardian.com/film/2017/mar/19/the-female-directors-bringing -new-blood-horror-films-babadook-raw-prevenge; Jan Yamato, "Pushed to Her Limits, the First Horror Heroine of the Time's Up Era Is Born in the Gutsy *Revenge*," *Los Angeles Times*, May 3, 2018, https://www.latimes.com/entertainment/movies/la -ca-mn-revenge-coralie-fargeat-matilda-lutz-20180503-story.html.

2   Linda Williams, "Film Bodies: Gender, Genre and Excess," *Film Quarterly* 44, no. 4

(1991): 2–13; Carol J. Clover, *Men, Women, and Chain Saws: Gender in the Modern Horror Film* (Princeton, N.J.: Princeton University Press, 1992); Barbara Creed, *The Monstrous Feminine: Film, Feminism, Psychoanalysis* (London: Routledge, 1993); Rhona J. Berenstein, *Attack of the Leading Ladies: Gender, Sexuality and Spectatorship in Classic Horror Cinema* (New York: Columbia University Press, 1996); Brigid Cherry, "Refusing to Refuse to Look: Female Viewers of the Horror Film," in *Horror, the Film Reader*, ed. Mark Jancovich (London: Routledge, 2002), 169–178; Isabel Cristina Pinedo, *Recreational Terror: Women and the Pleasures of Horror Film Viewing* (New York: State University of New York Press, 1997); Joan Hawkins, *Cutting Edge: Art-Horror and the Horrific Avant-Garde* (Minneapolis: University of Minnesota Press, 2000).

3   Quoted in Mia Galuppo, "Director Karyn Kusama on Sundance Horror Movie: 'Women Have a Lot to Be Really F-ing Afraid Of,'" *Hollywood Reporter*, January 22, 2017, https://www.hollywoodreporter.com/heat-vision/director-karyn-kusama -sundance-horror-movie-women-have-a-lot-be-f-ing-afraid-965251.

4   Jennifer M. Bean and Diane Negra, eds., *A Feminist Reader in Early Cinema* (Durham, N.C.: Duke University Press, 2002); Jane M. Gaines, *Pink-Slipped: What Happened to Women in the Silent Film Industries?* (Champaign: University of Illinois Press, 2018); Therese Graham and Julie Grossman, *Ida Lupino, Director: Her Art and Resilience in Times of Transition* (New Brunswick, N.J.: Rutgers University Press, 2017); Deborah Jermyn, *Nancy Meyers* (London: Bloomsbury, 2017); Frances Smith and Timothy Shary, eds., *ReFocus: The Films of Amy Heckerling* (Edinburgh: Edinburgh University Press, 2016); Rebecca Hillauer, *Encyclopedia of Arab Women Filmmakers* (Cairo: American University in Cairo Press, 2005); Stella Hockenhull, *British Women Film Directors in the New Millennium* (Basingstoke, U.K.: Palgrave Macmillan, 2017); Susan Liddy, ed., *Women in the Irish Film Industry: Stories and Storytellers* (Cork, Ireland: Cork University Press, 2020); Traci-Roberts Camps, *Latin American Women Filmmakers: Social and Cultural Perspectives* (Albuquerque: University of New Mexico Press, 2017); Lingzhen Wang, *Chinese Women's Cinema: Transnational Contexts* (New York: Columbia University Press, 2011); Christina N. Baker, *Contemporary Black Women Filmmakers and the Art of Resistance* (Columbus: Ohio State University Press, 2018); Yvonne Wellbon and Alexandra Juhasz, eds., *Sisters in the Life: A History of Out African American Lesbian Filmmaking* (Durham, N.C.: Duke University Press, 2018).

5   Simon A. Wilkinson, *Hollywood Horror: From the Director's Chair* (Jefferson, N.C.: McFarland, 2007); Chris and Kathleen Fernandez-Vander Kaay, *The Anatomy of Fear: Conversations with Cult Horror and Science Fiction Film Creators* (Bedford, Ind.: Norlights, 2014); Dennis Fischer, *Horror Film Directors, 1931–1990* (Jefferson, N.C.: McFarland, 2011).

6   Paul Kane and Marie O'Regan, *Voices in the Dark: Interviews with Horror Writers, Directors and Actors* (Jefferson, N.C.: McFarland, 2011).

7   Marcus Hearn, *Hammer Glamour: Classic Images from the Archive of Hammer Films* (London: Titan Books, 2009).

8   Robin Wood, "Return of the Repressed," *Film Comment* 14, no. 4 (1978): 27–28.

9   Linda Williams, "When the Woman Looks," in *Re-vision: Essays in Feminist Film Criticism*, ed. Mary Ann Doane, Patricia Mellencamp, and Linda Williams (Los Angeles: AFI, 1984), 83–99; Barbara Creed, "Horror and the Monstrous-Feminine: An Imaginary Abjection," *Screen* 27, no. 1 (1986): 44–71; Carol J. Clover, "Her Body, Himself: Gender in the Slasher Film," *Representations* 20 (1987): 187–228.

10 Williams, "When," 83; Cherry, "Refusing," 169.

11 bell hooks, "The Oppositional Gaze: Black Female Spectators," in *Movies and Mass Culture*, ed. John Belton (1992; repr., New Brunswick, N.J.: Rutgers University Press, 1996), 255.

12 Imogen Tyler, "Pregnant Beauty: Maternal Femininities under Neoliberalism," in *New Femininities: Postfeminism, Neoliberalism and Subjectivity*, ed. Rosalind Gill and Christina Scharff (Basingstoke, U.K.: Palgrave Macmillan, 2011), 22; Angela McRobbie, "Post-feminism and Popular Culture," *Feminist Media Studies* 4, no. 3 (2004): 255.

13 Rosalind Gill and Christina Scharff, "Introduction," in Gill and Scharff, *New Femininities*, 7 (my emphasis).

14 Annette Kuhn, *Women's Pictures: Feminism and Cinema* (1982; repr., London: Verso, 1994), 4.

15 Kuhn, x.

16 B. Ruby Rich, *Chick Flicks: Theories and Memories of the Feminist Film Movement* (Durham, N.C.: Duke University Press, 1998), 1–2.

17 Patricia White, *Women's Cinema, World Cinema: Projecting Contemporary Feminisms* (Durham, N.C.: Duke University Press, 2015), 11.

18 Robin Wood, "An Introduction to the American Horror Film," in *The American Nightmare: Essays on the Horror Film*, ed. Andrew Britton, Richard Lippe, Tony Williams, and Robin Wood (Toronto: Festival of Festivals, 1979), 7.

19 See Peter Hutchings, *The Horror Film* (London: Routledge, 2013), 52.

20 Janet Maslin, "Bloodbaths Debase Movies and Audiences," *New York Times*, November 21, 1982, H1.

21 Quoted in Wang, "Welcome."

22 Kier-La Janisse, *House of Psychotic Women: An Autobiographical Topography of Female Neurosis in Horror and Exploitation Films* (Godalming, U.K.: FAB, 2012), 7.

23 See Alexandra Heller-Nicholas, "Anti-auteur: The Films of Roberta Findlay," in *The Routledge Companion to Cult Cinema*, ed. Ernest Mathijs and Jamie Sexton (London: Routledge, 2019), 402–410.

24 April A. Taylor, "10 Most Important Horror Films Directed by Women," Bloody Disgusting, June 22, 2017, https://bloody-disgusting.com/editorials/3443101/10 -important-horror-movies-directed-women/.

25 Quoted in Jen Yamato, "Q&A: Original *Pet Sematary* Director Mary Lambert on Madonna and Stephen King Meetings at Denny's," *Los Angeles Times*, April 4, 2019, https://www.latimes.com/entertainment/movies/la-et-mn-pet-sematary-mary -lambert-director-stephen-king-madonna-20190404-story.html.

26 Molly Haskell, "Are Women Directors Different?," *Village Voice*, February 3, 1975, 73.

27 Christine Gledhill, "Introduction," in *Gender Meets Genre in Postwar Cinemas*, ed. Christine Gledhill (Champaign: University of Illinois Press, 2012), 1.

28 Margaret Ezell, *Writing Women's Literary History* (Baltimore: Johns Hopkins University Press, 1993), 14.

29 E. Ann Kaplan, "Women, Film, Resistance: Changing Paradigms," in *Women Filmmakers: Refocusing*, ed. Jacqueline Levitin, Judith Plessis, and Valerie Raoul (Vancouver: University of British Columbia Press, 2003), 25.

30 Joanne Russ, *How to Suppress Women's Writing* (London: Woman's Press, 1983), 111.

31 Quoted in Maya Montañez Smukler, "Liberating Hollywood: Women Directors | Barbara Peeters," UCLA Film and TV Archive, January 26, 2019, https://www .youtube.com/watch?v=9S7GviGxwc4.

32 Michael Jones, "Deadly Beauty: Aislínn Clarke," Morbidly Beautiful, February 18, 2018, http://morbidlybeautiful.com/deadly-beauty-aislinn-clarke/.

33 Quoted in Kirk Honeycutt, "Women Film Directors: Will They, Too, Be Allowed to Bomb?," *New York Times*, August 6, 1978, D1.

34 Shelley Cobb, *Adaptation, Authorship and Contemporary Women Filmmakers* (Basingstoke, U.K.: Palgrave Macmillan, 2015), 1.

35 Katarzyna Paszkiewicz, *Genre, Authorship and Contemporary Women Filmmakers* (Edinburgh: Edinburgh University Press, 2018), 261.

36 Sue Thornham, *What If I Had Been the Hero? Investigating Women's Cinema* (London: BFI, 2012), 28.

37 Kuhn, *Women's Pictures*, 8.

38 Quoted in Alicia Malone, *The Female Gaze: Essential Movies Made by Women* (Coral Gables, Fla.: Mago, 2018), Kindle.

39 Quoted in Suzanne Lowry, "The Champagne Legacy," *Guardian*, November 28, 1975, 11.

40 Katarzyna Paszkiewicz, "Hollywood Transgressor or Hollywood Transvestite? The Reception of Kathryn Bigelow's *The Hurt Locker*," in *Doing Women's Film History: Reframing Cinemas, Past and Future*, ed. Christine Gledhill and Julia Knight (Champaign: University of Illinois Press, 2015), 167.

41 Laurie Halperin Benenson, "How *Poison Ivy* Got Its Sting," *New York Times*, May 3, 1992, 13, 16; Janet Maslin, "She Joins a Family and Leaves It Well and Truly Wrecked," *New York Times*, May 8, 1992, C16.

42 Lizzie Francke, *Script Girls: Women Writers in Hollywood* (London: BFI, 1994), 86.

43 Hannah Neurotica, "Revolution Horror Grrrl Style, Now!!," Women in Horror Month, February 2010, https://womeninhorrormonth.wordpress.com/wih-manifesto/.

44 Quoted in Reilly, "From *Babadook* to *Raw*."

45 Alexis Kreager with Stephen Follows, *Gender Inequality and Screenwriters: A Study of the Impact of Gender on Equality of Opportunity for Screenwriters and Key Creatives in the UK Film and Television Industries* (London: Writers Guild of Great Britain / Authors' Licensing and Collecting Society, 2018), 146.

46 Stacy L. Smith, Katherine Pieper, and Marc Choueiti, *Exploring the Barriers and Opportunities for Independent Women Filmmakers* (Los Angeles: Sundance Institute, 2013), 10.

47 Christopher Meir, Anthony McKenna, and Andrew Spicer, eds., *Beyond the Bottom Line: The Producer in Film and Television Studies* (London: Bloomsbury, 2014).

48 Lucia Nagib, "Towards a Positive Definition of World Cinema," in *Remapping World Cinema: Identity, Culture and Politics in Film*, ed. Stephanie Dennison and Song Hwee Lim (London: Wallflower, 2006), 35.

49 White, *Women's Cinema*, 4.

50 Darren Elliott-Smith, *Queer Horror Film and Television: Sexuality and Masculinity at the Margins* (London: I.B. Tauris, 2016), intro., Kindle.

51 Quoted in Mariam Bastani, "Lez Is More: Discussing Critical Analysis of Queerness in Horror with Lezzie Borden," *Rue Morgue*, June 14, 2019, https://rue-morgue.com/lez-is-more-discussing-critical-analysis-of-queerness-in-horror-with-lezzie-borden/.

52 Maya Montañez Smukler, *Liberating Hollywood: Women Directors and the Feminist Reform of 1970s American Cinema* (New Brunswick, N.J.: Rutgers University Press, 2019), 5.

53 Robin R. Means Coleman, *Horror Noire: Blacks in American Horror Films from the 1890s to Present* (London: Routledge, 2011), 118–144.

54 Anna Cooper, "A New Feminist Critique of Film Canon: Moving beyond the

Diversity/Inclusion Paradigm in the Digital Era," *Quarterly Review of Film and Video*, May 3, 2019, https://doi.org/10.1080/10509208.2019.1590175.

55 See Alexandra Heller-Nicholas, *1000 Women in Horror* (Albany: Bear Manor Media, forthcoming), for a comprehensive study of women actors and filmmakers alike, and Patricia Pisters, *New Blood in Contemporary Cinema: Women Directors and the Poetics of Horror* (Edinburgh: Edinburgh University Press, forthcoming), a valuable addition to this growing body of work on women horror filmmakers.

56 Quoted in Matt Patches, "Blumhouse Has Never Produced a Theatrically Released Horror Movie Directed by a Woman—but Hopes To," Polygon, October 18, 2018, https://www.polygon.com/2018/10/17/17984162/halloween-blumhouse-female -director.

57 Quoted in Lisa Marks, "The Horror, the Horror: Women Gather in LA for Viscera Film Festival," *Guardian*, July 12, 2012, https://www.theguardian.com/film/2012/jul/ 12/viscera-festival-los-angeles.

58 Smith, Pieper, and Choueiti, *Exploring the Barriers*, 28.

59 Geneviève Jolliffe, email to the author, October 31, 2019.

60 R. Shanea Williams, "Black Woman, Why the Hell Did You Make a Horror Film?," Graveyard Shift Sisters, September 21, 2016, https://www.graveyardshiftsisters.com/ 2016/09/black-woman-why-hell-did-you-make.html.

61 Mallory O'Meara, *The Lady from the Black Lagoon: Hollywood Monsters and the Lost Legacy of Milicent Patrick* (New York: Hanover Square Press, 2019), 17.

62 O'Meara, 17.

63 Quoted in Myrna Oliver, "Debra Hill, 54; Pioneering Woman in Hollywood, Co-produced *Halloween*," *Los Angeles Times*, March 8, 2005, https://www.latimes.com/ archives/la-xpm-2005-mar-08-me-hill8-story.html.

2

Stephanie Rothman and Vampiric Film Histories

ALICIA KOZMA

In 1990, distributor On Line Cinema released a VHS of the film *The Velvet Vampire* (1971). On the front cover, a woman in an Elvira-like dress seductively stares out from the sleeve. To her right appears text that reads, "Starring Stephanie Rothman." The problem? Stephanie Rothman is the director, not the star. This particular VHS sleeve isn't alone in its incorrect attribution of authorship. Seven years earlier, distributors Entertainment Prime Time released a VHS of the same film under the title *The Waking Hour*.[1] The back of the VHS box art boldly declared the contents of the tape: "A film by Roger Corman—master of the macabre." Much later, a 2007 obituary for digital film pioneer Charles Swartz named him as the film's director: "Early in his career, Swartz collaborated with his wife on several features. He wrote and directed several B movies, including *It's a Bikini World* and *The Velvet Vampire*."[2] Swartz's unnamed wife? Stephanie Rothman.

By 1974, Rothman had directed seven feature films and had been an executive at Dimension Pictures, an independent production and distribution company. Her films were generally well reviewed and played everywhere from hardtop urban art theaters to suburban drive-ins. While VHS sleeves from now-defunct distribution companies are not standard bearers of cinema knowledge, these anecdotes do demonstrate the depth of Rothman's marginalization in film histories. Although Rothman was not an obscure figure when she was working, she is today. Nearly a decade ago, I encountered my first Stephanie Rothman film by chance. That happenstance triggered five years of research to first uncover and then compile Rothman's film history because it simply did not exist anywhere else.

Rothman's historical lack is partly due to the fact that she was a woman working in second-wave exploitation, an independent production paradigm that ran from 1960 to 1980. Second-wave exploitation films are hallmarked by an emphasis on a narrative that combines social zeitgeist with sensationalized sex, violence, or both; low production budgets; amateur acting; and a focus on catering to audiences in their teens, twenties, and thirties. Second-wave exploitation films appear minimally in cinema histories, often footnoted as immature economic products rather than alternative filmmaking. Additionally, the films' focus on spectacularized sex and violence codes them as particularly masculine. As a result, when they and their associated creative professionals are archived, it is primarily the men associated with the paradigm who are remembered.[3] Men like director Jack Hill, producer Roger Corman, and those members of New Hollywood that got their start in the "Corman school" of second-wave exploitation filmmaking, Martin Scorsese, Peter Bogdanovich, Jack Nicholson, and John Sayles among them.

This trend is not unique to Rothman; it extends to other women who directed second-wave exploitation films. Rothman's contemporaries like Barbara Peeters, Joan DeAnda and Marci Silver, and Marilyn Tenser are also conspicuously absent. Second-wave exploitation director Doris Wishman is perhaps most well known among cinephiles, but she is certainly not a household name like Scorsese.[4] The inclusion of men associated with second-wave exploitation and the exclusion of women defies coincidental logic. Cinema history does not simply appear as the eventual teleological outcome of the evolution of the form and the accumulation of time. As Lisa Gitelman notes, "History comes freighted with a host of assumptions about what is important and what isn't—about who is significant and who isn't."[5] The assumption yoked to Rothman and her female contemporaries is clear: they are unimportant. Resulting, it falls to feminist film scholars like the contributors to this volume to correct this inaccurate designation by actively writing women back into film histories.

Women working behind the screen are an integral part of the history and development of film as an industrialized art form. Deleting them from said history disserves the past, present, and future of filmmaking by constructing women working behind the screen as exceptions rather than the rule. Unsurprisingly then, women are severely underrepresented in behind-the-scenes creative positions today. The 2018 *Celluloid Ceiling* report produced by the Center for the Study of Women in Television and Film found that women account for only 8 percent of working Hollywood directors.[6] These disturbing ways in which women are and are not represented in the production of the contemporary film landscape have inspired groups like the Representation Project and the Women's Media Center, among others, to call for more women to become involved in film production. This is a much-needed effort. Yet elided from these calls for participation are deeper and broader understandings of the ways in which women *have already* participated in filmmaking. Expanding our collective understanding of women's role in film provides historical context and successful examples for women in the industry today and tomorrow. The impossible becomes possible once we know it's already been done. As a result, propagating the history of women in film and holding cinema histories to task for overlooking them are critical contemporary endeavors.

This chapter, then, offers a historical corrective and active feminist archival intervention into the construction of Rothman's subject marginality within film histories through an examination of her film *The Velvet Vampire*. I've chosen this film as an example of Rothman's filmmaking style and authorship because film histories have, in the most vampiric of ways, feasted on Rothman's career in service of a normative and patriarchal process of cinematic memory. She was drained of her place in film histories, her body of work depleted by a historical blind eye, and it is time to pump the blood back in.

Blood, Sex, and Sand

Stephanie Rothman was born in 1936 in Paterson, New Jersey. After earning a degree in sociology from the University of California, Berkeley, she entered film school at the University of Southern California (USC) in 1962. There she became the first woman to win the Directors Guild of America student award. At USC, she met her husband and longtime collaborator/producer, Swartz. Corman, then working with American International Pictures, hired Rothman as his assistant in 1964. Under Corman, Rothman began her professional directorial efforts, receiving her first credit for *Blood Bath* (a.k.a. *Track of the Vampire*, 1966) and her second for *It's a Bikini World* (1967). In 1970, Rothman and Swartz joined Corman in his new production/distribution company, New World Pictures, where she directed *The Student Nurses* (1970) and *The Velvet Vampire*.

The Velvet Vampire is Rothman's only horror film. She pitched the film to Corman as *Through the Looking Glass*, a title that evokes Rothman's interest in the human psyche and reveals literary inspiration. Indeed, Lewis Carroll's book by the same name is an apt guide for the film, particularly in its focus on reflection and reversal. Rothman expressed an interest in the gendered and sexual politics of vampire lore and legend. As she said, "I wanted to make a vampire film that dealt explicitly with the sexuality implicit in the vampire legend."[7] As a result, Rothman made her vampire a woman, the type of Carrollian reversal of expectation she was fond of. She and Swartz wrote the script with Maurice Jules; Swartz produced while Rothman directed. She approached the genre with an awareness of its conventions and a desire for innovation, making a film that is an example "of a conscious reworking of classic cinema along postclassical lines."[8]

Writing on the figure of the vampire, Kimberly Lau notes that the "vampire finds formal resonance in a tightly formulaic and highly intertextual genre, a genre whose conventions limit its narrative development."[9] Indeed, Rothman recognizes vampiric genre conventions. Her vampire, Diane, is immortal and subsists on human blood. Diane has a human servant, Juan, who caters to her needs and knows her secrets. Diane's surname is Le Fanu, a direct reference to J. Sheridan Le Fanu's *Carmilla*, a nineteenth-century story about a woman vampire and her queer bloodlust. Diane's friend and occasional victim procurer is gallery owner Carl Stoker, named for Bram Stoker. Lastly, like Stoker's Dracula, Diane is a cultured and seemingly refined creature whose appearance and mannered comportment belie her vampiric nature.[10]

Parallel to these conventions are Rothman's innovations. Diane is diurnal, she consumes food and beverages, and she lives in the California desert. Upending the mythic idea that vampires cannot endure daylight, Diane races her dune buggy across the sands of the Mojave in the middle of the day with only long sleeves and a hat for protection. Most importantly, Diane's interest in Lee and Susan Ritter, a couple she meets at an art gallery, is driven first by erotic desire and followed by hunger. Indeed, as Dannis Peary argues, while "it must be classified as a horror film and does in fact contain much in the classic horror tradition, it is basically concerned with an unconventional love triangle in which one of the two women just happens to be a vampire."[11] After their initial meeting, the Ritters join Diane at her desert home for the weekend, where the love triangle blooms.

Alone in her secluded desert home, Diane has ample opportunity to feed on the Ritters, but she sublimates her hunger to her sexual and affective desire for their coupledom. Diane became a vampire in the late 1800s and killed her husband in a fit of hunger. She mourns his loss daily, regularly digging up his grave to prostrate herself on top of his coffin. Diane hates the desert and tells Lee as much. When he asks why she stays, she tells him that a local indigenous community embalmed her husband's body. If she leaves the desert, he will decompose and be lost to her forever. Tied to the desert by grief and guilt, Diane covets the Ritters' intimacy, mobility, and interconnectedness.

Each evening, Diane secretly watches the Ritters from behind a two-way mirror. Observing them in bed, she sees petty arguments, quick sex, mundane conversation, and the easy way that two bodies familiar to one another intertwine in bed. Once asleep, Diane creates a shared dream for the three of them. The Ritters, nude and in bed, are transported to the empty desert, surrounded by an ornate mirror and a seductive Diane. Rothman doesn't adjust for the harsh sun in the outdoor shoot, instead letting the light blow out until the sandy-brown dunes resemble something more akin to a distant planet. She films the scene in soft focus, visualizing the Ritters' hazy confusion and disorientation at their new circumstances. Diane leads a naked Lee from the bed, and they caress while Susan looks on confusedly. The Ritters awake, aware they've just shared the dream. During the day, their confusion lingers, materialized in Rothman's camera movements around Diane's house after the three have returned from a trip to the desert. The house has an unconventional layout; all the rooms seem to connect and dead-end at the same time. Rothman heightens this confusion as her camera follows Susan around the home's interior. Rather than creating a clear sense of space by tracking Susan as she walks, Rothman cuts repeatedly, moving the camera around Susan so the audience is unsure if she is coming or going, turning left or right, next to a room or beyond it. Awake or asleep, nothing is as it seems.

Two nights later, the triad enters their shared dream again. This time, however, Lee is removed from the bed so Diane can stroke Susan as she gently cuts her above her bare breasts, then drinking from the wound. In both cases, Diane has successfully inserted herself into the Ritters' marriage bed, alternating her role between husband and wife. Through the looking glass of the desert mirror, the three exist in a polyamorous dream world. This utopic dynamic cannot last long in waking reality though. Diane and Lee have intercourse, and soon after, she moves onto Susan. Lee, angered at losing his role as the man desired by both women, becomes eager to leave the desert. Although queerness and the vampire are intimately intertwined, that same queerness "disturbs the social in a number of profound (and profoundly anxiety-producing) ways."[12] Lee's satiated lust transforms into eruptive anger and anxiety around Susan's sexual desire for Diane. This erotic transference so disturbs Lee because it exists outside of him, and he confronts Diane. This confrontation will eventually lead to all three of their deaths, but the fulfillment of vampirism's ever-present specter of death is much less interesting to Rothman than the dynamic between Diane and the Ritters. To wit, Diane the desert vampire is killed by a combination of sunlight and crucifixes. It is an antithetical death and the film is indifferent; the real interest lies in sexual politics.

Rothman was an ideological filmmaker who used the trappings and freedoms of second-wave exploitation to explore contemporary social issues and offer her own solutions. Once the pretty if less than serviceable actors were cast and the requisite amount of sex and blood added, she was free to explore larger themes, ideas, and messages as she chose. Rothman leveraged second-wave exploitation narrative in service of larger ideological explorations; it is the hallmark of her filmmaking. In *The Velvet Vampire*, Rothman is concerned with the destruction of relationships due to dishonesty. Diane's honest appraisal of her undead hunger and self-control would have avoided her husband's murder, thereby circumventing her own pain and grief. Lee and Susan's honesty about their mutual attraction to Diane could have spared deeply hurt feelings and the dissolution of their relationship. The three's attraction to each other and Diane's vampiric nature may have coalesced into mutually beneficial polyamory, yet dishonesty prevailed, and everyone died.

Despite this bleak ending, Rothman presents her solution to dishonesty in the film's dreamscape scenes, where the contentment between the three troubles normative relationship constraints. In the shared dreams, which Rothman films without dialogue, the language of constraint is dominated by desire, constructing a blissful, honest triumvirate. Rothman would return to the idea of shared sexual lives as utopic relationship form in *Group Marriage* (1972), the film she made immediately after *The Velvet Vampire*. But unlike Diane and the Ritters, the characters in *Group Marriage* are unfailingly honest about their desire, earning them the happy ending lost to the characters in *The Velvet Vampire*.

Gendered Accreditation

The Velvet Vampire was Rothman's last film with Corman. In 1972, Rothman, Swartz, and New World colleague Lawrence (Larry) Woolner formed the production/distribution company Dimension Pictures, where Rothman served as the vice president in charge of creative development. At the time, she was one of the few female production executives working in Hollywood. At Dimension, she helmed *Group Marriage* and *Terminal Island* (1973) and *The Working Girls* (1974). Rothman and Swartz would leave the company later that year after financial disagreements with Woolner. She attempted to move into mainstream Hollywood filmmaking to no avail. Rothman recalls, "[I received] dire warnings from men who were film executives but not filmmakers, that I would never be allowed to direct, and that even if I were, male crew would never work for me. I have always thought this was a veiled way, or what they mistook for a veiled way, of telling me that they did not want to see me progress."[13] After ten years of trying to break through the gender barrier for directors, Rothman retired from the film industry in 1984.

Despite her productive if abbreviated career, Rothman's films have been historicized primarily through the men she worked with, particularly Corman. Corman, the self-professed "king of the Bs," has a talent for self-mythicization, and assigning creative credit for any film involving him is often difficult. Corman has an overriding tendency to call any movie he has come into contact with "his" movie. As directors often came and went on Corman-related projects, there are cases where screen credits, filmmaking records, and Corman's own narrative tell radically different stories. This type of confusion facilitates Corman's co-optation of others' legacies.

Creative accreditation is weighted in Corman's favor because his career is archived in film histories. The subject of numerous books and documentaries as well as an autobiography, Corman is regularly written into film history by himself and others. Many Corman-related materials feature interviews, comments, or stories from people who worked with him during the "Corman school," as Rothman did. She has yet to be asked to participate in any of these archives: "I think one person wanted to approach me; no one else ever has. I have not been included, and part of the reason for that, I think, is that the people who have been included have become famous and successful. They are the ones who he wants to talk about him."[14]

Examples of improper creative accreditation are embedded in the origin story of *The Student Nurses*, which Rothman developed and directed for Corman. He says of the women in the film, "I insisted each had to work out her problems without relying on a boyfriend."[15] Yet Rothman tells a very different story about Corman's perspective on the characters Rothman created: "When he first saw the rough cut, he told me he didn't think it was 'raunchy' enough. . . . It concerned him that the girls were too intelligent."[16] Woolner, Rothman's colleague at New World and later partner at Dimension, was also given credit for Rothman's work. Take the following statement from 1991: Woolner "suggested to Corman . . . that they coproduce a movie he had dreamed up called *The Student Nurses*. . . . Woolner made his *Student Nurses* film with Stephanie Rothman as director and her husband Charles Swartz, as producer."[17] Woolner had an idea for a film about women training to become nurses. Rothman conceived of the story and the cast for the film and directed and coproduced it, but she is deleted from the narrative. I asked Rothman how she felt about her work regularly attributed to anyone but her. She said, "Do I feel any ownership over them? Well, yes, I made them—with my husband. I mean, we both felt ownership of them in that sense, of course. They wouldn't exist without us; we made what was just an idea—a vague idea—concrete."[18]

Yet film histories do exist without Rothman. Despite her pioneering directorial efforts and the ideological depth of her films, she's been mislaid in cinematic memory. In part, this lack is fostered by the double marginalization as a woman who made second-wave exploitation films. This loss, and others like it, is a terrible deprivation for film history as it constructs a false homogenization of the industry and its artists. This disadvantage applies to most women working in genres stereotyped as masculine like horror or science fiction. Women directors like Coralie Fargeat, the Soska sisters, Rebekah McKendry, Julia Ducournau, and Rachel Talalay are given less historical space than their male counterparts, exoticizing them as rare exceptions to generic rules. Concurrently, the lack of women in film history also demotivates more robust hiring and employment of women in film today, since the historical record offers no successful models to follow. It is a vicious and misogynistic circle.

Feminist film scholars have, however, begun to intervene in this process. This book is an excellent example of this intervention. Reorienting the archive is a process, but it is oftentimes easier than one may think. When I first began researching Stephanie Rothman, I hit a wall early on, as most information I found about her career was conflictual and unverifiable. Stymied and frustrated, I did the only thing I could think to do—I asked her about her career. This is the untold secret of feminist interventions in film histories: many women are waiting to talk about their films and careers, but no one has ever asked. In speaking about the factors that have nurtured her relative obscure position in film history, Rothman said as much: "Nobody ever contacted me—which is interesting actually because unlike most people who live in (and I've worked in) Hollywood, my phone number is in the phone book, and so is my name. So, all they had to do is open up a phone book or call the operator."[19] It is time to start asking.

Notes

1 Images are archived on VHS Collectors at https://vhscollector.com/movie/velvet -vampire# and Horrorpedia at https://horrorpedia.com/wp-content/uploads/2013/ 04/the-waking-hour-velvet-vampire.jpg.

2 Valerie J. Nelson, "Charles Swartz, 67; Took Film to the Digital Age," *Los Angeles Times*, February 14, 2007, http://articles.latimes.com/print/2007/feb/14/local/me -swartz14.

3 For select examples, see Calum Waddell, *Jack Hill: The Exploitation and Blaxploitation Master, Film by Film* (Jefferson, N.C.: McFarland, 2009); Chris Nashawaty, *Crab Monsters, Teenage Cavemen, and Candy Stripe Nurses: Roger Corman, King of the B Movie* (New York: Abrams Books, 2013); Randell Clark, *At a Theater or Drive-In Near You: The History, Culture, and Politics of the American Exploitation Film* (New York: Garland, 1995); Ernest Mathijs and Jamie Sexton, *Cult Cinema: An Introduction* (Oxford: Blackwell, 2011); Thomas Elsaesser, Alexander Horwath, and Noel King, *The Last Great American Picture Show: New Hollywood Cinema in the 1970s* (Amsterdam: Amsterdam University Press, 2004).

4 For work on Wishman, see Moya Luckett, "Sexploitation as Feminine Territory: The Films of Doris Wishman," in *Defining Cult Movies: The Cultural Politics of Oppositional Taste*, ed. Mark Jancovich (Manchester: Manchester University Press, 2003), 142–156; Tania Modleski, "Women's Cinema as Counterphobic Cinema: Doris Wishman as the Last Auteur," in *Sleaze Artists: Cinema at the Margins of Taste, Style, and Politics*, ed. Jeffrey Sconce (Durham, N.C.: Duke University Press, 2007), 47–70; Rebekah McKendry, "Fondling Your Eyeballs: Watching Doris Wishman," in *From the Arthouse to the Grindhouse: Highbrow and Lowbrow Transgression in Cinema's First Century*, ed. John Cline and Robert G. Weiner (Lanham, Md.: Scarecrow, 2010), 57–74; Michael J. Bowen, "Embodiment and Realization: The Many Film-Bodies of Doris Wishman," *Wide Angle* 19, no. 3 (1997): 79–80.

5 Lisa Gitelman, *Always Already New: Media, History, and the Data of Culture* (Cambridge, Mass.: MIT Press, 2006), 2.

6 Martha M. Lauzen, *The Celluloid Ceiling: Behind-the-Scenes Employment of Women on the Top 100, 250, and 500 Films of 2018* (California: San Diego State University, Center for the Study of Women in Television in Film, 2018), https://womenintvfilm .sdsu.edu/wp-content/uploads/2019/01/2018_Celluloid_Ceiling_Report.pdf.

7 Dannis Peary, "Stephanie Rothman: R-Rated Feminist," in *Women and the Cinema*, ed. Karyn Kay and Gerald Peary (New York: E. P. Dutton, 1977), 185.

8 Terry Curtis Fox, "Fully Female," *Film Comment* 12, no. 6 (November/December 1976): 46.

9   Kimberly J. Lau, "The Vampire, the Queer, and the Girl: Reflections on the Politics and Ethics of Immortality's Gendering," *Signs: Journal of Women in Culture and Society* 44, no. 1 (2018): 4.

10   Aysha Bey, "The Vampire: 'I Too Can Love' Enticing Parasite and Social Signifier," *Proteus* 26, no. 2 (Fall 2009): 33.

11   Peary, "Stephanie Rothman," 185.

12   Lau, "Vampire," 7.

13   Quoted in J. Pyros, "Women on Women in Films," *Take One* 3, no. 2 (February 1972): 13.

14   Stephanie Rothman, interview with author, February 5, 2014.

15   Roger Corman and Jim Jerome, *How I Made a Hundred Movies in Hollywood and Never Lost a Dime* (New York: Random House, 1990), 181.

16   Rothman, interview with author.

17   Fred Olen Ray, *The New Poverty Row: Independent Filmmakers as Distributors* (Jefferson, N.C.: McFarland, 1991), 149–150.

18   Rothman, interview with author.

19   "Diskussion im Anschlub an den Virtrag von Stephanie Rothman" [Post-film discussion], *Girls, Gangs, and Guns Festival*, Germany, November 28, 1999, transcript, author's personal archive.

3

Inside Karen Arthur's
The Mafu Cage

ALEXANDRA HELLER-NICHOLAS

Director Karen Arthur made the feature films *Legacy* (1975), *The Mafu Cage* (1978), and *Lady Beware* (1987) before dedicating herself solely to a near half-century-long career in television. Her long list of achievements renders her well-overdue recognition as a pioneering woman filmmaker, and *The Mafu Cage* is a stand-out film that should be familiar to all horror fans and critics. This "should" lies at the heart of this chapter, as it implies a fundamental glitch in the horror canon spawned from the gendered biases of critical, archival, and popular memory. It is in this spirit that this chapter offers a preliminary critical cartography of Arthur's early career with hopes that it sparks further attention not only toward her work in particular but also in the shared sense of reclamation for other overlooked women horror filmmakers.

Arthur refined her craft with *Legacy* first and then *The Mafu Cage*, which (beyond the cult audiences that have rediscovered it in recent years) remains a testament to how original, high-quality horror films that just happen to be directed by a woman can slip through the canonical net. In terms of quality, at least, *The Mafu Cage* arguably equals the originality, potency, and ideological punch of the more recognizable 1970s North American horror classics by David Cronenberg, Wes Craven, Tobe Hooper, John Carpenter, and George A.

Romero. These directors are not selected randomly; their work has famously been championed in foundational writing on American horror cinema by Robin Wood, among others.[1] In fact, the existence of a horror "boys' club" is so broadly assumed as to almost appear to be conventional wisdom; as Alejandra Armendáriz Hernández encapsulates, "The horror genre is often considered to be a male-dominated domain, especially with regard to the overwhelming number of male directors, producers and others in filmmaking roles."[2]

But before a line is drawn between men and women critics, academics, and filmmakers, it is worth underscoring that this question of diversity and visibility has historically not played out across obvious gender biases; it simply isn't the case that male critics have ignored women filmmakers and women critics have championed them. For example, in 1980, Wood highlighted the world of Stephanie Rothman, and two years before that, Calvin Thomas Beck devoted an entire chapter to Rothman's work in his *Scream Queens: Heroines of the Horrors*, which also begins with a chapter on the work of pioneering filmmaker Alice Guy-Blaché and her relevance to the genre.[3] On the flip side, two of the most foundational works of feminist horror film criticism—Barbara Creed's *The Monstrous-Feminine: Film, Feminism, Psychoanalysis* (1993) and Carol J. Clover's *Men, Women, and Chain Saws: Gender in the Modern Horror* (1992)— both arguably share a broad assumption that horror is almost completely made and consumed by men. Clover's book refers on no less than four occasions to her belief that horror is oriented toward a "largely male" audience, and despite her briefly mentioning *Blue Steel* (1989) and *Near Dark* (1987), the director Kathryn Bigelow is not named at all (let alone any possibility her gender might be of interest to Clover's broader arguments).[4] This is also the case with her brief critique of Gabrielle Beaumont's *The Godsend* (1980), and while Clover *does* acknowledge that Amy Holden Jones's 1982 slasher *The Slumber Party Massacre* was both directed and written by women, there is again no consideration how (or even if) the gender of the filmmakers might relate to Clover's central arguments about gender, identification, and the horror film.[5] In fact, the only woman-directed film Clover does discuss at length is Janet Greek's rape-revenge girl-gang drama *The Ladies Club* (1986), which is arguably not even a horror film per se. But once again, there is still no unpacking of how Greek's gender does (or, just as importantly, does not) relate to Clover's argument that horror is a genre largely made by and for men.[6]

Alternatively, while Creed acknowledges that different spectatorial mechanics may be in place for female horror film audiences, she mentions only in passing Rothman's *Blood Bath* (1966, codirected with Jack Hill) and *The Velvet Vampire* (1971) and Jackie Kong's *Blood Diner* (1987), the names of their filmmakers (let alone their genders) are not discussed, and only Rothman appears in the filmography at the end of the book.[7] Like Clover, Creed identifies that *The Slumber Party Massacre* was written and directed by women, but again this is mentioned only very briefly, and once more, the gender of the filmmakers is mentioned as little more than a novelty rather than being a point warranting any serious critical attention.[8] That Creed mentions these films but consciously chooses not to discuss them is somewhat bewildering when positioned in the context of her statement in *The Monstrous-Feminine* that while "most horror films are made by men . . . if women made horror films, the latter area would be explored more fully."[9] In her defense, it is worth highlighting that Creed was writing in Australia in the 1980s and early 1990s, where access to films would have been far more limited than it was at the time to her colleagues in the United States (cable television, for instance, was not introduced to Australia until 1995 and then primarily was used to broadcast sports).[10]

As this brief overview reveals, directors like Arthur were simply not discussed in historical horror criticism to anywhere near the same degree as Romero, Cronenberg, Carpenter, and De Palma. This is, then, no simplistic "boys versus girls" scenario of text-selection bias. While some male critics were attempting to highlight the work of women horror filmmakers during the 1970s and 1980s, some feminist horror film critics in the 1980s and 1990s were choosing to focus their critical attention only on male-directed horror films. Creed's statement that "if women made horror films, the latter would be explored more fully" is therefore an important one. Despite Creed's undeniable impact on gender and horror studies, despite her being demonstrably aware of both the importance of discussing horror films made by women and the existence of at least a handful of key titles, she nevertheless made a conscious decision to not study them.

To be clear, my point is not to attack or dismiss wholesale the legacy of these earlier feminist horror critics, as I recognize in practical terms alone questions of distribution and access were much more of a significant research challenge than they are for contemporary researchers today. Rather, by using Arthur as a case study, I raise these issues as a launchpad to examine precisely *what* women horror filmmakers were doing at this time, despite failing to receive the same signal boost as their male counterparts. The reason we can do this now is, once again, access; films like *The Mafu Cage* have very recently begun to find their audiences through boutique home entertainment companies like Scorpion Releasing and online streaming services and pirate torrenting communities like Cinemageddon. The film has also recently begun to enjoy more public screenings. In 2012, it was included in Fantastic Fest in Austin, Texas, where it featured in the "House of Psychotic Women" program curated by Kier-La Janisse; in 2018, the U.K.-based feminist film collective the Final Girls screened *The Mafu Cage* in Bristol and in London; and in 2019, it screened in the "Female Terror" strand, curated by Alison Peirse, at the /slash Filmfestival in Vienna, Austria. Given that *The Mafu Cage* is finally now more accessible, this chapter is a timely deep dive into the journey of one woman horror film director's career.

Mother(s) of Us All

Making a horror film during the 1970s might at first most immediately align Arthur with fellow women genre directors like Rothman, discussed in chapter 2, but Arthur's career trajectory finds her well outside the "Corman school" model that would also intersect with later monster movie filmmakers like Barbara Peeters and the makers of the *Slumber Party Massacre* slasher franchise (consisting of *The Slumber Party Massacre, Slumber Party Massacre II* [1987], and *Slumber Party Massacre III* [1990], the latter two directed by Deborah Brock and Sally Mattison, respectively). While for horror fans and critics, these might be the first women-directed horror movies that we think of, Arthur comes from an altogether different heritage. As Maya Montañez Smukler has observed, Arthur's earlier work on her debut, self-funded independent art film feature *Legacy* and its impact on the international film festival circuit, made her more comparable with women filmmakers like Barbara Loden and her international festival success with *Wanda* in 1970.[11]

For Stephen Thrower, *The Mafu Cage* is "a claustrophobic, distressing film," while to Kier-La Janisse, it remains "one of the most compelling and uniquely dark films of the psychotic woman subgenre."[12] Arthur has described the plot of *The Mafu Cage* as the "story of two sisters caught in a very symbiotic, abusive, enabling sexual relationship, a very bizarre tale, and at the core of it was an illness, a psychosis, invested in African lore [and] their father."[13] The sisters are Ellen and Cissy, played respectively by Lee Grant and Carol Kane (the latter also plays protagonist Dorine in *Office Killer*, discussed in chapter 7 by Dahlia Schweitzer). Ellen is a mother-sister-carer figure who becomes increasingly aware of Cissy's deteriorating mental health; the latter is marked by an increasingly murderous violence that shifts from her simian research subjects to actual human victims. The "mafu cage" of the title is the jail-like enclosure where Cissy keeps, nurtures, and then tortures to death her victims.

Arthur only made one more feature film after this, *Lady Beware*, the experience of which left her so disillusioned that she gave up feature filmmaking and instead turned toward television. It was here where she continued to further develop her reputation, winning Emmys and becoming the first woman to direct an American miniseries, with *Crossings* (1986).[14] While not as immediately recognizable as later women horror directors like Kathryn Bigelow, Jennifer Kent (*The Babadook*, 2014), or Ana Lily Amirpour (*A Girl Walks Home Alone at Night*, 2014), the scale of Arthur's achievements and her significance (to the history not just of women's genre filmmaking but also of women's work in television and film in general) make her a crucial figure for reappraisal.

Arthur was the third woman to receive the Directors Guild of America (DGA) membership after Dorothy Arzner and Ida Lupino. Indeed, there are striking yet often unacknowledged similarities between Arthur and Lupino, who both began as actors and turned to directing later in their careers. They also both shifted away from independent feature filmmaking to what they felt was the more flexible world of television. Both Lupino's *The Hitch-Hiker* (1953) and Arthur's *The Mafu Cage* demonstrate how women were experimenting with the codes and conventions of horror filmmaking at a time when, as discussed previously, it was broadly assumed to be a predominantly male terrain. Lupino's and Arthur's careers intersect in other ways too. In a 1987 interview, Arthur laid out the challenges of funding independent films and her difficult and unfulfilling attempted transition to feature filmmaking in the studio system after the success of her self-funded features *Legacy* and *The Mafu Cage*. She noted, "You need the money for your movie. We're all like mothers when it comes to that. We will lie, steal, beg and cheat for our kids. For our films."[15] Arthur's metaphor notably rejects the dominance of filmmaking as a fundamentally male role, typified famously in Andrew Sarris's all-male "pantheon" of film directors in his influential book *The American Cinema: Directors and Directions, 1929–1968*.[16]

In light of the curious parallels between their careers, it's difficult to read Arthur's quote and not recall Lupino's iconic director's chair that she had on her film sets, embossed on the back not with her name as is tradition but instead with the title "Mother of Us All." For Lupino, the woman-director-as-mother metaphor allegedly took the edge off the possible gender imbalances that the role might suggest: "I would never shout orders at anyone. I hate women who order men around, professionally or personally. I wouldn't dare do that with my old man . . . and I don't do it with guys on the set. I say, 'Darlings, Mother has a problem. I'd love to do this. Can you do it? It sounds kooky, but I want to do it.' And they do it."[17]

While Lupino today is broadly—and quite rightly—considered a pioneer of women's filmmaking, quotes like this that made her persona non grata in some earlier and influential feminist film criticism. For example, Molly Haskell offers a brutal dismissal of Lupino-the-director in her foundational 1974 book *From Reverence to Rape: The Treatment of Women in the Movies*: "The movies she made (*Hard, Fast, and Beautiful*, *The Bigamist*, *The Hitchhiker* [sic]) are conventional, even sexist; and in her interviews, like so many women who have nothing to complain about, she purrs like a contented kitten, arches her back at the mention of women's lib, and quotes Noël Coward to the effect that woman should be struck regularly like gongs."[18] As I have noted elsewhere, such dismissals ignore Lupino's extraordinary bravery in dealing with complex and often controversial issues of specific relevance to women, such as rape trauma in her unheralded masterpiece *Outrage* (1950).[19] In more recent decades, better access to Lupino's broader filmography has no doubt assisted in the reassessment of her work, and likewise, the very recent release of Arthur's first two groundbreaking features through boutique home entertainment companies and *The Mafu Cage*'s inclusion at international film festivals now offers a timely opportunity to illuminate Arthur's life and work.

Arthur is a curious yet generally ignored figure for contemporary feminist film critics and horror fans looking for evidence of the genre's progressive history. Take, for instance, the following selection of quotes. In 1987, she commented, "Because I'm a woman, every time I turn around, somebody says 'What's it like to be a woman director?' Well, it's like being a director, thank you very much. I just wear pantyhose and you don't."[20] And yet, in 1993, she acknowledged that she felt there were distinct benefits to being a woman director: "As a woman I can get certain things out of actors that if I were a man, I don't think I could. Sometimes the male ego balks with another male ego, or a male ego intimidates a female ego or vice versa. It's not saying one is better than the other, it's just saying that you can get something different."[21]

From a contemporary perspective, what remains most distinctive about Arthur's filmmaking practice is her emphasis on gender parity among her crew, a question that remains highly controversial today and is the focus of a number of research projects into industry equality.[22] In the same 1993 interview, Arthur explained, "When I'm making a film, if I'm producing or have raised the money for it, I always demand as many women as I can get behind the camera. But I try to balance it with men to make it harmonious." She continued, "We live in a collective society. It's a wonderful energy when you're on a set and you've got half women and half men. . . . I'd love to see more of that in Hollywood. This is the place of opportunity."[23] Although disinterested in politics when she first moved to Hollywood, as a filmmaker, she found gender politics a driving fascination in her films.[24] Arthur then found her reputation as a "political" director worked in her favor, explaining that she was "fortunate to be typecast by making films that have to do with issues . . . more serious types of statements, heavy dramatic statements dealing with psychosis or neurosis or what have you." She reveals, "That's great for me, because that's the kind of thing I want to see when I go to the theater. That's the kind of thing I want to read when I'm reading books. So I'm very happy to be typecast in that realm."[25]

The Legacy of *Legacy*

Arthur's artistic career ambitions were with her from childhood.[26] Born in Nebraska, she moved with her single mother to Florida, where at eight years old, she began ballet at Frank Hale's Palm Beach Ballet Company, becoming their featured soloist by the age of fifteen.[27] She moved to New York in 1960 at the age of eighteen to develop her career as a dancer and soon turned to choreography.[28] Arthur has explained that her career as a film director originated from her work as a choreographer; in the commentary track for the 2010 Scorpion Releasing DVD of *The Mafu Cage*, she notes that this expertise gave her "a sense of vision . . . what I wanted to see in the frame," with a particular emphasis on movement.[29] Certainly this background is evident in the small but memorable dance sequences in *The Mafu Cage* and a 1974 *Los Angeles Times* review of *Legacy* that describes it as a "rare and beautiful feature . . . a fluid, rich, well-choreographed film."[30]

Arthur then moved from New York to Hollywood in 1966 to pursue her career as a theater actor, where she could combine her acting and dancing skills. During this period, she began working on television and joined the Melrose Theater, where her interest in directing blossomed.[31] It rapidly became clear to her that in California, it was the screen and not the stage that offered her the greater potential for her myriad talents to flourish.[32] As Smukler observes, while the move from stage to screen made sense in Hollywood, Arthur did not have the necessary screen skills to direct, so she "began to strategize how to build her skill set by tapping into the resources available in Los Angeles's wider film community."[33] In 1971, she spent a tax rebate on a short six-week filmmaking course at University of California, Los Angeles (UCLA), where she learned the basics of writing, editing, directing, and cinematography, making her directorial debut with *Hers*, a fifteen-minute short film.[34] *Hers* was a game-changer for Arthur, leading to a place in the American Film Institute's (AFI) internship program, where she worked on Arthur Penn's *Night Moves* (1975). It was here Arthur met two of her future collaborators on *Legacy* and *The Mafu Cage*, the husband-and-wife team of cameraman John Bailey and editor Carol Littleman.[35]

Arthur received vital support from the AFI across this formative period of her filmmaking career. A $10,000 AFI Independent Filmmakers Grant allowed her to finish *Legacy*, and while sourcing funding for *The Mafu Cage*, she was also granted a place in the pilot program of the AFI's Directing Workshop for Women (DWW), introducing her to one of that film's stars, Lee Grant.[36] Jan Haag, the founder of the AFI's DWW program, also personally invested in *Legacy*.[37] Although not a horror film per se, *Legacy* is regardless an extraordinary—and often deliberately very difficult—viewing experience. After Bessie Hapgood (played by Joan Hotchkis) briefly visits her senile mother at an expensive care facility, *Legacy* is set primarily in Bessie's opulent home, the narrative following her across one day as she prepares for a dinner party that never happens. Barely a moment is left unfilled by Hotchkis's extraordinary monologues (interrupted only by phone conversations, of which we only hear her part of the exchange). She also potters, frets, masturbates, dresses, and constructs an ornately ridiculous dining table centerpiece out of Christmas baubles and her wedding veil, by which time her (initially discrete) mental instability and extreme racism have become visible. Despite reaching out to her psychiatrist, good manners force her to not push her request for help too far, and the film's shocking finale witnesses Bessie's total and venomous meltdown; a torrent of shocking racial insults and graphic foul language spew forth, revealing the inner life of a destroyed, broken woman.

Although Hotchkis was more famous for mainstream fare such as *The Odd Couple* (1970–1975) and Clint Eastwood's *Breezy* (1973), Arthur saw her perform her one-woman show *Legacy* on stage and was struck by its potential for a

screen adaptation, convincing Hotchkis to collaborate and even sourcing investment funding from Hotchkis's own family. Smukler summarized the film as a
"close read of a woman experiencing the unravelling of her sense of self" while
also providing a telling snapshot of the state of play for women filmmakers during this period.[38] In her groundbreaking critical examination of Arthur's career,
Smukler emphasizes how unusual women filmmakers at this time were. In particular, Smukler considers the challenges they faced regarding "the burden of
representation," despite the supposed progress made by the women's liberation
movement in the late 1960s and 1970s in the United States.[39]

It was in this context that *Legacy* failed both commercially and critically in
the United States for committing the ultimate sins in terms of orthodox portrayals of women in Hollywood cinema: Bessie "is sexually explicit without
being sexy, and vulnerable without being sentimentalized; she is critical of her
social strata, while benefiting from her privileged social status; she is unlike-
able because she is not relatable; and she is unique in how the filmmaker took a
familiar image and had her strip down, physically and psychologically."[40] Aside
from both being adapted from stage plays, *Legacy* and *The Mafu Cage* also share
much in terms of many of these features that Smukler identifies. Both films are
built on themes of class, race, and gender; both are narratively framed around
the "madwoman in the attic" trope of the trapped, psychologically delicate
woman; and in both cases, the women are effectively housebound due to their
own inability to face reality. But whereas *Legacy* is a portrait of a psychological breakdown in the context of a domestic drama, *The Mafu Cage* evolves into
something far darker as Arthur's first—and only—horror film.

Toward *The Mafu Cage*

While seeking funding for her second feature film, Arthur worked in a variety
of professional capacities and contexts, including supervising scripts on adult
films and commercials, editing documentaries, and even taking the night shift
at Universal's camera room preparing cameras for the following day's shoot.[41]
She directed an episode of *Rich Man, Poor Man Book II* (the series sequel to the
1976 miniseries of the same name) and worked as a director on popular television
series like *Hart to Hart* (thanks to the support of women directors by the series'
star Stephanie Zimbalist).[42] Reflecting on the contrast between how she thought
things worked when she had made *Hers* and the actual reality of the industry, she
commented, "I made my first little film and took it around thinking of course
that the world would herald a new talent. I was patted on the head a lot by every-
body." She continued, "So I thought, fine, they need to see that I can really make
a film. So I went out and made *Legacy*, which was a feature film. Then I dragged
that around. It was 35mm, the whole thing. Again I was patted on the head."[43]
Head patting wasn't going to fund *The Mafu Cage*; instead, the funds came from
a single investor from Arizona.[44]

The shift to horror with *The Mafu Cage* was a strategic one for Arthur, the filmmaker wanting to move away from the art film terrain of *Legacy* and toward what she called "something commercial" for her follow-up: "Maybe I'll do something like a horror film, it's kinda noirish and still offers a lot of room for expression."[45] In a decade where low-budget horror films had a reputation for being an almost guaranteed moneymaker, *The Mafu Cage* spoke to Arthur as a shrewd business decision as much as a creative one.[46]

While touring *Legacy* at an international film festival in London, Arthur took a trip to Cambridge to see Eric Westphal's 1971 play *You and Your Clouds* (*Toi et tes nuages*), which became the source material for *The Mafu Cage*.[47] Westphal's description of his play indicates a similar narrative and thematic overlap with what Arthur sought to capture in her screen adaptation: "*You and Your Clouds* is, to a certain extent, a type of love story . . . with sordid, morbid and masochistic innuendoes."[48] But where they deviate is in Westphal's explicit interest in philosophical and theological questions; instead, Arthur turns her attention toward the sisters' psychology.[49]

Another significant alteration in the adaption process was Arthur's insistence on changing the careers of her two characters; on *The Mafu Cage*, Adele the civil servant becomes Ellen the astronomer, while Ernestine's writer character becomes Cissy's artist. Arthur was determined to give her characters jobs that revealed deeper aspects of their worlds; she comments, "I try to give the characters occupations that allow them to express visually what they are going through emotionally. The actors are then always doing something that is revealing the character's inner self."[50] In the case of *The Mafu Cage* in particular, she added, "In the original play, the woman was a writer. . . . I made her an artist so we didn't have to say 'OK now she's mad'. You saw she was mad; there was madness in her murals."[51]

Cissy's murals and paintings were crucial to how Arthur visualized the mental state of Carol Kane's character. While not undermining the work of the film's screenplay, adapted by Don Chastain, Arthur extensively researched this role. She checked herself into Bellevue Hospital's renowned psychiatric unit and visited an art exhibition at a psychiatric hospital consisting of works made by its patients.[52] Of the latter, Arthur noted that in their art, the patients were able to express things they were incapable of doing through verbal language.[53]

The film's aesthetic was consciously built around a deliberate tension between the generically "African" artwork and style of much of the sisters' home (shot on location in an empty mansion in the Hollywood Hills) and the more Western, distinctly Victorian style of Ellen's bedroom.[54] *The Mafu Cage* is a rich terrain for further critical analysis of the colonial imagination at work, where the total appropriation of African culture into Cissy's identity is aligned with a kind of madness, an extreme mode of "symbolic" colonization that results in severe damage to both the colonized and colonizer. From this perspective, the absence of the "colonized"—actual African people—from the film is particularly significant. African culture is replaced entirely by a dominant, colonizing white imaginary, represented arguably in Ellen's "Victorian" flip side. For Arthur, these two spaces had to be "hermetic," and for her, the spectacular impact of the "Africanized" space was a deliberate way to defamiliarize the unorthodox lifestyle of these two white American sisters.[55] Emphasizing the conscious decision to only show the main living area of the home at this point, which includes the mafu (monkey) cage, Arthur notes, "It's a world created that is special and unique and different and . . . it feels very natural; the audience has accepted by now that this is how these folks live." For Arthur, the arrival of Ellen's boyfriend David is key. Through David's eyes, "you see how fucking bizarre and over the top it is. . . . He is now the audience, and he is going—oh shit. And he sees the cage. . . . The things we've been asked to take as normal are given voice."[56]

The tight bond between Cissy and Ellen is made explicit through an incestuous relationship, and this kind of incestuous girl-on-girl sexuality might be a titillating spectacle for another horror film from this era (perhaps on the grindhouse circuit). However, while *The Mafu Cage* clearly communicates that their relationship is sexual, there is little shown. Rather, Arthur, Kane, and Grant shrewdly utilize the relationship to symbolize the broader perversities of the sisters' relationship. All three women have since discussed how and why Arthur had to learn to adapt to the tonal and emotional needs of her two leads for them to fully embody their complex, difficult characters. Grant, for instance, called Arthur "the most upbeat lady in the world," which, while unarguably supportive and positive, did not help her and Kane work with the necessary darkness that their roles required.[57] Grant recalls this moment with Arthur on the Scorpion Releasing material: "What we had was permission for us to sit down together and to say, 'That isn't the way it's going to help us. Your enthusiasm is fine for a different picture. But on this one, you really have to back off and damp down that joy because joy is not a part of the lives that Carol and I have to bring to this.' And you did. But that's a kind of really remarkable positive thing, because [we] . . . were able to say, 'This is what we need,' and you were able to say, 'I see, OK.'"[58] Similarly, Kane speaks more explicitly of a "deep regret" that was needed for her and Grant to connect in a way that forbade anyone else entry into their relationship, even the director of the film herself: "As part of our process, we did bond in a way that was exclusive of everything else. . . . As part of what we needed to do to be these characters, we were almost like animals protecting ourselves from the rest of the world."[59] Grant says, "While it is a sick, terribly sick, sick, sick relationship, to us—to Carol and to me in playing those parts—it's normal. . . . I think those feelings that you have as an actor that you have for your fellow actor spilled over into our lives, because in that period, we were . . . contemptuous of everything outside of our relationship. That bonding is why that relationship works on film."[60] Indeed, it is precisely how this relationship works and the way that Arthur captured it with such a unique directorial vision that has rendered the experience of watching *The Mafu Cage* such a powerful experience, even more than four decades since its original release.

Trapped in *The Mafu Cage*

The Mafu Cage is marked by almost somatic rhythms; it is a film that less ebbs and flows in its extreme moods and instead seems to inhale and exhale. The film's tonal peaks and troughs are not just dominated but determined by and through Cissy's body, her gentleness and softness as much as her terrifying outbursts of extreme and chaotic aggression. Her aggression is where the traditional "horror" occurs: Cissy beats her first mafu with a chain and slashes her wrists to emotionally blackmail Ellen into getting her a new mafu to replace the one she has murdered. Yet some of the film's moments disturb in a quieter, more poetic manner. After killing David, Cissy lies in a bath of opaque dark-orange water. She washes off the ceremonial clay she adorned herself with in order to carry out the ritualized murder, and as she washes, she chatters almost mindlessly to herself, enacting an imagined conversation with her sister.

But the film's horror stems not solely from Kane but also through the intense collaboration between Kane and Grant. As a textbook enabler, it is Ellen's willful, conscious refusal to get Cissy the help she desperately needs that makes the film's tragic ending inevitable. As much mother/daughter, carer/patient, and dom/sub as sisters, the horror truly emerges from the interdependency between the two women. The film's climax is where the interplay between Grant and Kane is most heightened, Ellen ceasing to speak when she realizes Cissy has killed David and silently committing herself to the role of Cissy's new human "mafu." Cissy may be dangerously unstable, but she is no fool, and the battle of wills between the sisters as the film moves toward its conclusion hinges primarily on Cissy's determination to not let Ellen die, to not become another mafu. This is because, as has been noted throughout the film both implicitly and explicitly, without Ellen, Cissy will die too. Ellen rejects food, and there are tiny, heart-wrenching, performative gestures, improvised by Kane and Grant, as Ellen slowly drools the food out of her mouth, or when Cissy rubs Ellen's throat to try to force her to swallow. Unlike the previous deaths in the film (human or animal), Ellen has power when she chooses to die, knowing it is the only way that she can stop Cissy. And it is the moments of connection between these two actors and from the world built and directed by Arthur that make it such an effective conclusion.

After *The Mafu Cage*

At first, *The Mafu Cage* held enormous promise for a self-funded, low-budget, wholly independent horror feature. It made an impressive debut on the first night of the Director's Fortnight program at the Cannes Film Festival in 1978, where, after a standing ovation, Arthur was joined on stage by the likes of François Truffaut.[61] But like *Legacy*, while *The Mafu Cage* was distributed in Europe, it was not in the United States. *Legacy*'s attempt at a cinema run had been ended by an early negative review by Vincent Canby in *The New York Times*, while *The Mafu Cage* found a similar lack of critical support.[62] Unlike Roberta Findlay or Doris Wishman, who were connected to the grindhouse circuit, or Stephanie Rothman and Barbara Peeters, who had (for at least some of their career) the distribution channels due to their association with Roger Corman, Arthur did not have a network. After attempting to distribute the film herself, Arthur signed a disastrous four-film development deal with Universal. No films were made as a result of the deal, and Arthur became so completely disheartened by feature filmmaking that she switched her attention to predominantly television, where she then excelled for forty years.[63]

The "predominantly" here is significant though, as Arthur did make one final feature film, the psychological thriller *Lady Beware*, which was eventually released in 1987. Arthur found difficulties working within the studio system. Her desire to make a film about "psychological rape" was ignored; instead, the studio "wanted her to portray the rape with physical violence," and even when it was made at a smaller studio, "she didn't get final cut, and the film turned out different than she had intended."[64] The differences included nude scenes of Ladd added without Arthur's knowledge, and as Smukler notes, while this is not specific to women filmmakers, "women are disproportionately represented among directors who wield less authority and are therefore vulnerable to losing creative control of their work."[65]

Although Karen Arthur's feature filmmaking is limited to three films—as impressive as both *Legacy* and *The Mafu Cage* are—her career can only be fairly understood as excelling when she chose to dedicate herself more fully to television, a medium where her work has garnered a number of high-profile industry awards. But beyond formal accolades, for Arthur, the satisfaction comes simply from getting her work out there: when asked why she likes working on television, she answered, "The fact that I don't have to wait eight years to do it!!! The fact that once it's done, I know it's going to go on the air February 13. The fact that even if it isn't a huge success, twenty-five million people will see it."[66]

Even with the current spike of interest in women's horror filmmaking, it remains unlikely that anywhere near twenty-five million people will ever come even close to watching *The Mafu Cage*. Regardless, it stands as an extraordinary achievement, not only in horror filmmaking but also in the history of women film directors. The film is fearless, clear in its vision, and determined in its refusal to soften its thematic edges in order to adhere to more traditional notions of "feminine" cinema. That Arthur—and for that matter, Lupino—ultimately found more creative autonomy and financial stability working in television speaks volumes of the limitations seemingly built into feature filmmaking for the women who dared to tell the stories they so passionately fought to share.

Notes

The author would like to thank Gillian Horvath, Peter Labuza, Shawn Levy, Kevin Ferguson, and especially Eddie Bowen for their invaluable assistance researching this chapter.

1 Robin Wood and Richard Lippe, eds., *American Nightmare: Essays on the Horror Film* (Toronto: Festival of Festivals, 1979); Robin Wood, "The American Family Comedy: From *Meet Me in St. Louis* to *The Texas Chainsaw Massacre*," *Wide Angle* 3, no. 2 (1979): 5–11.

2 Alejandra Armendáriz Hernández, "Scream Queen Filmfest Tokyo," in *The Encyclopedia of Japanese Horror Films*, ed. Salvador Jimenez Murguía (Lanham, Md.: Rowman & Littlefield, 2016), 278.

3 Robin Wood, "Neglected Nightmares," *Film Comment* 16, no. 2 (March/April 1980), 24–32; Calvin Thomas Beck, *Scream Queens: Heroines of the Horrors* (New York: Macmillan, 1978).

4 Carol J. Clover, *Men, Women, and Chain Saws: Gender in the Modern Horror Film* (Princeton, N.J.: Princeton University Press, 1992), 43, 53, 201, 227, 232.

5 Clover, 75, 81, 37.

6 Clover, 151, 146.

7 Barbara Creed, *The Monstrous-Feminine: Film, Feminism, Psychoanalysis* (London: Routledge, 1993), 9, 60, 62, 155.

8 Creed, 127.

9 Creed, 156.

10 Lisa French, "Patterns of Production and Policy: The Australian Film Industry in the 1990s," in *Australian Cinema in the 1990s*, ed. Ian Craven (London: Frank Cass, 2001), 30.

11 Maya Montañez Smukler, *Liberating Hollywood: Women Directors & the Feminist Reform of 1970s American Cinema* (New Brunswick, N.J.: Rutgers University Press, 2019), 102.

12 Stephen Thrower, *Nightmare USA: The Untold Story of the Exploitation Independents* (Godalming, U.K.: FAB, 2007), 475; Kier-La Janisse, *House of Psychotic Women: An Autobiographical Topography of Female Neurosis in Horror and Exploitation Films* (Godalming, U.K.: FAB, 2012), 281.

13 "Visions of Clouds: An Interview with Karen Arthur," bonus feature on *The Mafu Cage* DVD (Mercer Island, Wash.: Scorpion Releasing, 2010).

14 "Dialogue on Film—Karen Arthur," *American Film*, October 1987, 10.

15 "Dialogue on Film," 12.

16 Andrew Sarris, *The American Cinema Directors and Directions, 1929–1968* (New York: Dutton, 1968).

17 Melissa Anderson, "Ida Lupino, Pioneer. But, Please, Just Call Her 'Mother,'" *Village Voice*, August 25, 2010, https://www.villagevoice.com/2010/08/25/ida-lupino-pioneer-but-please-just-call-her-mother/.

18 Molly Haskell, *From Reverence to Rape: The Treatment of Women in the Movies* (Harmondsworth, U.K.: Penguin, 1974), 201.

19 Alexandra Heller-Nicholas, "*Outrage* (1950): Ida Lupino's Vision of Rape Trauma," *Senses of Cinema*, no. 88 (October 2018), sensesofcinema.com/2018/cteq/outrage-1950-ida-lupinos-vision-of-rape-trauma/#fn-35471-1.

20 "Dialogue on Film," 13.

21 Janis Cole and Holly Dale, *Calling the Shots: Profiles of Women Filmmakers* (Kingston, Ont.: Quarry, 1993), 25.

22 "Mind the Gap: Gender Equality in the Film Industry," *UNESCO Diversity of*

Cultural Expressions, February 25, 2019, https://en.unesco.org/creativity/news/mind
-gap-gender-equality-film-industry.

23 Cole and Dale, *Calling the Shots*, 28.
24 Smukler, *Liberating Hollywood*, 107.
25 Cole and Dale, *Calling the Shots*, 22–23.
26 "Dialogue on Film," 10.
27 Cole and Dale, *Calling the Shots*, 19.
28 Cole and Dale, 19.
29 Smukler, *Liberating Hollywood*, 103; Karen Arthur, commentary track, *The Mafu Cage* DVD (Mercer Island, Wash.: Scorpion Releasing, 2010).
30 "Dialogue on Film," 10.
31 "Dialogue on Film," 10; Smukler, *Liberating Hollywood*, 103.
32 Cole and Dale, *Calling the Shots*, 20.
33 Smukler, *Liberating Hollywood*, 103.
34 Smukler, 105; Cole and Dale, *Calling the Shots*, 19.
35 Smukler, *Liberating Hollywood*, 105.
36 Smukler, 105, 110–111.
37 "Visions of Clouds."
38 Smukler, *Liberating Hollywood*, 105, 107.
39 Smukler, 107.
40 Smukler, 108.
41 Cole and Dale, *Calling the Shots*, 30.
42 "Visions of Clouds."
43 Cole and Dale, *Calling the Shots*, 21.
44 Smukler, *Liberating Hollywood*, 111.
45 Smukler, 109; "Visions of Clouds."
46 Philip R. Cable, *Make Movies That Make Money! The Low-Budget Filmmaker's Guide to Commercial Success* (Jefferson, N.C.: McFarland, 2009), 7.
47 "Visions of Clouds."
48 Bettina L. Knapp, "Interview with Eric Westphal," *Studies in the Twentieth Century*, no. 8 (Fall 1971): 99.
49 Knapp, 100.
50 "Dialogue on Film," 12.
51 "Dialogue on Film," 12.
52 Arthur, commentary track.
53 Arthur, commentary track.
54 "Visions of Clouds."
55 "Visions of Clouds."
56 Arthur, commentary track.
57 "Solar Flare: An Interview with Lee Grant," bonus feature on *The Mafu Cage* DVD (Scorpion Releasing, 2010).
58 "Solar Flare."
59 "Cissy and Her Clouds: An Interview with Carol Kane," bonus feature on *The Mafu Cage* DVD (Scorpion Releasing, 2010).
60 "Solar Flare."
61 "Visions of Clouds."
62 Smukler, *Liberating Hollywood*, 107, 111.
63 Smukler, 112.
64 Cole and Dale, *Calling the Shots*, 19.
65 Smukler, *Liberating Hollywood*, 112.
66 "Dialogue on Film," 13.

4

The Secret
Beyond the Door

Daria Nicolodi and *Suspiria*'s
Multiple Authorship

MARTHA SHEARER

Suspiria (1977) opens with a voice-over describing protagonist Suzy Bannion's flight from New York to Freiburg, followed by a shot of the arrivals board. As the sequence progresses, we see Suzy walking through the airport, just in front of a woman in a red suit. That woman speeds up and passes Suzy; the film then shifts to Suzy's point of view as we see her walk out of the airport door into the rain outside. The woman is not seen again. In the Italian version of *Suspiria*, that opening voice-over is voiced by the film's director, Dario Argento. Writing on the film often describes the woman in the red suit as a cameo appearance by the film's screenwriter, Daria Nicolodi.[1] Yet her appearance in this sequence has been disputed by horror expert Alan Jones.[2] Argento's factual voice-over is thoroughly incongruous with the film's supernatural content and has been read as an "authorial stamp, to cue us in to exactly whose perspective we are seeing this through," consistent with the wealth of scholarship on Argento that reads films he directed as defined by his authorship.[3] Meanwhile, Nicolodi's appearances in analyses of the film and its authorship have been just as elusive as her presence in the film itself.

Argento's status as an auteur has been regularly asserted by fans. Mapping the history of Argento's scholarly and fan reception, Peter Hutchings argues that fan magazines display an "unashamed auteurism, one which is very much concerned to raise the cultural status of Argento's work."[4] Russ Hunter argues that Argento's cultural status relies in particular on preserving the reputation of earlier "good works," especially *Suspiria*, in a context of increasing critical and commercial failure since the early 1980s.[5] Argento's auteur status in fan culture is arguably a product of not only his distinctive visual style but also the lowbrow, cult, transgressive nature of his work. Just as the auteur, in early studies of film authorship, transcended the restrictions and conventions of classical Hollywood, so Argento transcends the lowbrow, trash, and video nasty to become Art. That sort of fan culture has arguably precluded attention to female authorship of Argento's films. But those limitations are an effect of not simply auteurism but also the masculinization of cult fandom and scholarship, which, as Joanne Hollows and Jacinda Read have demonstrated, relies on an opposition to a "mainstream" perceived as feminine, whether that is feminine mass culture or an institutionalized feminist film theory.[6]

But Hutchings also claims that an auteurist approach is limited to popular contexts, whereas scholarship on Argento has "tended to shy away from viewing him as an auteur-director in the traditional sense of that term," instead viewing his work as "symptomatic, as a window on themes and issues that do not pertain to Argento alone."[7] Argento films have indeed been discussed as windows onto issues of gender and spectatorship, for example. And yet they are invariably understood as *Argento* films. Hutchings notes that Maitland McDonagh's unabashedly auteurist book *Broken Mirrors, Broken Minds: The Dark Dreams of Dario Argento* (1991) has been well received in fan circles.[8] Yet other scholars, perhaps even despite themselves, have also tended to rely on an auteurist underpinning. L. Andrew Cooper, for example, notes that given Argento's sustained collaborations, his work could "help to qualify any illusion of the film director as a solitary author," and yet the "works that bear the Dario Argento brand are in some ways profoundly cohesive," proceeding to place "Argento" in quotation marks and conclude that "'Argento's' works contain facets that far exceed the efforts of Dario Argento the man."[9] This, of course, is a fairly standard post-auteur-structuralism fudge, but what I want to draw attention to is how such approaches both raise and then set aside the possibility of other authorial voices shaping the films that Argento directed.

Nicolodi also wrote a treatment for *Inferno* (1980), the second in what would become known as the Three Mothers trilogy, three films directed by Argento based on the mythology established in *Suspiria*. Nicolodi has highlighted the ways that both *Suspiria* and *Inferno* differ from Argento's other films, particularly the *gialli* he made before and after, asking, "Do they look like any other argento's film? Then they should be considered . . . mine."[10] One common trope of Argento scholarship has been to situate *Suspiria* as a shift in Argento's career from the *giallo* toward supernatural horror, presented as a shift in *his* career rather than as her authorial intervention. By contrast, Nicolodi has stated, "everything belongs to me in *Suspiria*," elaborating that the film's title, concept, references, supernatural themes, and sensibility came from her: "I really want to stress that in *Suspiria*, as well as in *Inferno* there is a lot of myself, my cultural background and my experience, even though Dario did have an inner predisposition towards the genre. He had reached a point where, after the thriller period, he didn't know which path to take and I suggested the field of fantasy."[11]

She has repeatedly recounted what has effectively become the film's origin story: that her grandmother had attended an academy to study piano but ran away when she discovered that black magic was taught there. Nicolodi recounts that she and Argento visited the site, which had since burnt down and been rebuilt, where "we were able to see with our own eyes that everything my grandmother had told us was true."[12] Argento has since disputed the veracity of Nicolodi's grandmother's story, but in terms of the source for the film, whether this story is literally true is hardly relevant; the point is that it is Nicolodi's story, that these ideas for the film originated with her.[13]

She also takes responsibility for the film's invocations of the work of Thomas De Quincey, the source for both the film's title and its Three Mothers mythology. She states that while Argento had a "superficial knowledge of De Quincey's literature," she was "reading it intently in that period" and had suggested it to him.[14] Argento meanwhile claims, "*Suspiria* and *Inferno* came from the fact that I loved the Thomas De Quincey essay 'Levana and Our Ladies of Sorrow.'"[15] It would be easy to frame these sorts of discrepancies as "he said, she said" disputes, but as is so often the case, even when Nicolodi's claims are acknowledged, they are often framed as just that, "claims," while Argento is granted authorial authority. While the "he said, she said" formulation so often diminishes the "she" in question, my intention in this essay is to take Nicolodi seriously.

On social media, she often describes herself as "the author" of both *Suspiria* and *Inferno*, responding, for example, to one tweet including a gif of Suzy stabbing Helena Markos at the film's conclusion with, "I imagined and wrote this scene Thx."[16] The emphatic case that Nicolodi makes for herself as *Suspiria*'s sole author needs to be understood in a context whereby her authorship has been repeatedly denied or minimized in more or less overt ways. She had to fight to be credited for the film's screenplay in the first place.[17] Other accounts, including those since made by Argento himself, have minimized Nicolodi's involvement to the point of outright denial. Alan Jones quotes Argento describing his writing process, specifically on *Suspiria*, as solitary, the product of "months of living like a monk in self-imposed exile": "I lock myself away for months on end. . . . Eventually my second soul gives in and I come up with something."[18]

Others have acknowledged Nicolodi's screenwriting credit or contributions to the film while simultaneously minimizing her actual authorship: Jacqueline Reich acknowledges Nicolodi as cowriter and notes the film's contested authorship in a footnote, yet this seems to have no bearing on her thoroughly auteurist reading of the film itself; for James Gracey, she is a "muse"; for Stephen Thrower, her credit provides strategic cover for Argento, "freeing him to take on the more destructive qualities of womanhood, without the defensiveness that would otherwise be required to 'mitigate' his maleness"; for Adam Knee, as a frequent Argento collaborator, Nicolodi "serves as a kind of female double for the male director."[19] Even when her contributions have been acknowledged, there has been a tendency to treat Nicolodi as a muse or origin story rather than taking her seriously as a screenwriter or simply to acknowledge her but all the while focusing on Argento as the source and overriding determinant of meaning.

Nicolodi's screenwriting work is perhaps exemplary of the place of women's creative labor in horror. The scale of her input into the Three Mothers trilogy has been minimized in production: a fight for credit on *Suspiria*, denial of screenwriting credit on *Inferno*, her script for *Mother of Tears* (2007) abandoned entirely. She has been further marginalized in reception/scholarship overwhelmingly attached to an auteurist paradigm. Shelley Cobb has argued that auteurism is thoroughly exclusionary, "a term that, because of its masculine connotations, has neither been readily available for women filmmakers nor wholly accepted by feminist film theorists."[20] Scholarship on women's cinema has also tended to neglect the authorship of women not working as directors. Judith Mayne, for example, explicitly states that women's cinema refers to film made by women directors "as opposed to, say, screenwriters or actresses."[21] Steven Maras argues that screenwriting scholarship has often taken up the cause of screenwriting or the screenplay in order to rectify "the allocation of authorship to director and not writer," taking what he calls a "restorative" approach.[22] Such an approach may be especially vital for women's screenwriting work, which Bridget Conor suggests is "arguably even more prone to invisibility."[23]

Suspiria necessitates a model of multiple and collaborative authorship. Recent scholarship on multiple authorship has sought to foreground not only the collaborative nature of filmmaking but also models for thinking of films as shaped by multiple authors by paying attention to both film texts and production history.[24] Alan Lovell and Gianluca Sergi's study of contemporary Hollywood film production and Aaron Hunter's book on Hal Ashby and his collaborators both foreground the authorial contributions of creative practitioners other than the director: screenwriters, editors, production designers, and cinematographers.[25] This chapter considers what happens if we take Nicolodi's creative labor and claims to authorship seriously, to examine how doing so produces a new understanding of the film itself. What does it mean to read *Suspiria* as having multiple authors, as having a female author?

So Absurd, So Fantastic

One way to read *Suspiria* is as an adaptation of the Bluebeard fairy tale: a woman comes to live in a large mysterious home, suspects those around her of wrong-doing, and then locates a locked space containing threatening secrets. In this light, Nicolodi was one of a number of women writers in the late 1970s and early 1980s reworking Bluebeard. Notable examples include Angela Carter in *The Bloody Chamber* (1979), Margaret Atwood in *Bluebeard's Egg* (1983), and Isabel Allende in *The House of the Spirits* (1982); this trend has persisted in films directed by women, including *The Piano* (Jane Campion, 1993), *Barbe bleue* (Catherine Breillat, 2009), and Anna Biller's forthcoming Bluebeard project.[26] In so doing, *Suspiria* also reworks the specifically cinematic tradition of the paranoid woman's film, the cycle of 1940s Hollywood films following *Rebecca* (1940), with Blue-beardesque narratives driven by the fears of a female protagonist that her husband may be trying to murder her or whose intentions are otherwise obscure. Notably, recent scholarship has situated the paranoid woman's film in a tradition of horror for and about women.[27] *Suspiria*'s debt to that cycle is made explicit in the casting of Joan Bennett, star of *The Secret Beyond the Door* (1948), as Mme Blanc.

Significantly, the paranoid woman's film provides a model of multiple authorship. Tania Modleski argues that *Rebecca* troubles conceptions of the auteur. The film's identification with Du Maurier's source novel was such that Hitchcock "felt that the picture could not be considered his own."[28] As Kaja Silverman points out, in Modleski's account, *Rebecca* is "driven by conflicting authorial systems, in this case one 'male' and the other 'female,'" such that Hitchcock's "authorial system" may "contain a female voice as one of its constituent although generally sub-merged elements."[29] That was not simply an effect of adapting the work of a female writer but also the film's "feminine" concerns, with which there are many parallels with *Suspiria*. Both films are the "story of a woman's maturation," concluding with a house engulfed in flames. That woman's childlike qualities are foregrounded by the use of doorknobs, at shoulder-level in *Rebecca* and oversized in *Suspiria*, and she is contrasted with another powerful, apparently all-seeing woman. Modleski even describes Mrs. Danvers's death in *Rebecca*'s fire as "the usual punishment inflicted on the bad mother/witch."[30] But while Marina Warner argues that the Bluebeard figure has drawn female writers as he "often embodies contradictory feelings about male sexuality," Nicolodi removes the heterosexual dynamic that has historically underpinned the tale.[31]

Suspiria's narrative is instead organized around a series of murders whose killer is unclear. The first murder sequence takes place after Pat has run from the dance academy to take refuge at a friend's apartment. The sequence begins with a series of cuts, alternating between Pat standing next to a window, shots from outside the building looking through that window, and shots from her point of view. She looks out of the window before holding a lamp up to the window, foregrounding her look and curiosity as well as the mystery of who exactly is tormenting her. Disembodied eyes then stare at her from outside the window before apparently disembodied hairy arms grab her and press her face against the window. She is then stabbed repeatedly and, in the course of trying to escape, hanged through stained glass, glass that inadvertently stabs her friend, pinning her to the floor. Adam Knee notes that Argento films tend to withhold both the identity and the gender of the killer until their conclusions and are marked by killers who are ambiguous in their gender identity and sexuality and who often turn out to be "bi-gendered and multiple personed."[32] In *Suspiria*, Knee notes, that mystery is amplified by the film's supernatural nature, whereby the events we see cannot be logically explained. The film specifically foregrounds these challenges of interpretation when Pat tells her friend, "It's useless to try to explain it to you. You wouldn't understand. It all seems so absurd, so fantastic." The problem the film poses in its first murder and those that follow is one of authorship: Who could be responsible for these murders, who could craft them, and how?

In the blind pianist Daniel's death, for example, there are a series of shots from the roof of a building in the square he is walking through, shots of his guide dog frantically barking, and shots of that building from below. The reason for the dog's agitation and attack is not visible to either Daniel, due to his blindness, or the spectator. That tension is amplified by the score, without which the reactions of neither the pianist nor the dog would make sense. The film, then, builds terror through its form, through what Chris Gallant calls "dislocated point-of-view shots," where it is unclear whether we are seeing point-of-view shots or simply unmotivated camera movements, what Knee calls an "assaultive gaze," where "the gaze itself often seems to have omniscience and power—even superhuman power."[33] On one level, Daniel's dog simply attacks him, but the film's style produces the idea of supernatural forces behind that attack, rendering it rationally inexplicable. To generate their terror and mystery, then, the film's irrational deaths require excessive displays of visual style. Alexandra Heller-Nicholas sees the death sequences as key evidence of Argento's authorship, the "perfect loom upon which to weave his elaborate audio-visual tapestry."[34] The film's screenplay both allows for the display of visual style and constructs mysteries of authorship on which its plot hinges. It relies on a tension that Heller-Nicholas identifies: the film always seems "at once carefully crafted and thoroughly out of control."[35]

The authors of those murder scenes, of course, turn out to be women: witches. Furthermore, the witches' project, in their dance-academy-cum-coven, is to use women's bodies for the creation of art, whether through ballet or through murder. Mme Blanc is first interested in Suzy as an aesthetic object, telling her she is "pretty, very pretty indeed." Ms. Tanner, meanwhile, says to Suzy of Pavlos, "He's really ugly. Don't be afraid to say so." The witches' fascination with the "pretty" is replicated in the film's own aesthetic, in that excessive visual style that produces its mysteries of authorship. The film incorporates many of the formal strategies that Rosalind Galt argues characterize the "pretty": images that are "colorful, carefully composed, balanced, richly textured, or ornamental," "deep colors," "detailed mise-en-scène," an "emphasis on cinematographic surface," self-evident design, an image that is "too much" (which is precisely how Kim New-man describes *Suspiria*).[36] Galt traces the etymology of "pretty" to "a trick, a wile or a craft": the pretty is not, like beauty, an image to be coolly admired but trick-ery.[37] The film takes those very terms—trickery, witchcraft, the pretty image—as its explicit subject. In *Suspiria*, witchcraft is the ultimate feminine art. *Suspiria* poses challenges for a masculinist auteurist reading at the level of both content and form in its preoccupation with the feminine in representational terms (very few male characters, ballet, witches, etc.) and its pretty visual style.

Galt argues that the "rhetoric of cinema" has denigrated such "surface dec-oration" as "false, shallow, feminine, or apolitical."[38] That trouble provoked by the pretty is perhaps evident in the preoccupation with auteurism in *Suspiria*'s critical and academic reception. Galt points to authorial control as one of the key features of the pretty: the films of Bernardo Bertolucci, Baz Luhrmann, or Wong Kar-wai may be excessive, but they are also carefully controlled; the pretty is "a style that does not go far enough as much as it describes one that goes too far," excessive but not radically so.[39] *Suspiria*, as lowbrow cult horror, perhaps does offend good taste, but auteurism allows it to be reframed in terms of Argento's mastery of the image, forestalling its feminine prettiness through notions of masculine authority and control. Indeed, a recurrent theme of *Sus-piria*'s critical and academic reception is the assertion that Argento's visual style overwhelms its "weak" script.[40] Rather, the script works hand in hand with visual style. The witches possess a level of control over both narrative events and film form comparable to a cinematic author, but that author needs to be under-stood as encompassing both director and screenwriter.

The film enacts the witches' desire for the pretty in both its depictions of their murders and in its hyperstylized aesthetic. The film frequently uses red, green, and blue filters, bathing its subjects in the light of that color; not only does that produce a highly aestheticized image, but those are also the primary colors of light and of three-strip Technicolor, in which the film was shot. The film, then, calls attention to its own prettiness. The "blood" we see flowing in the opening murders is the same deep pink as the filters that bathed Suzy in light earlier in the film and most of all resembles paint, as does the drugged wine that she pours down her sink later in the film. This would be very easy to read simply as a failure of verisimilitude. But the combination of this paint-like blood with the perfectly painted faces of the glamorous female victim and the stained glass that killed one of them and through which the other girl hanged suggests, most of all, that the murders themselves are acts of artistic creation, that in death, Pat's friend has been converted into an artwork, pinned to a surface. Indeed, Maria Tatar identifies parallels with the production of art in the Bluebeard tale, given that his wives are "often put on display, with their heads on pedestals or with their bodies hanging from the walls, like portraits in a gallery."[41]

Suzy's investigation of the strange events she sees and hears about is in fact an interrogation of the image. Doane argues that the paranoid woman's film frames domestic space, "the paradigmatic woman's space," in terms of a "crisis of vision."[42] *Suspiria* amplifies that crisis. Most obviously, Suzy spends much of the film trying to recall the details of her arrival at the dance and specifically the words she had heard Pat speak into the academy's intercom. Her efforts at recollection are demonstrated through repeated flashbacks of the film's opening sequence. An emphasis on decoding sounds and images runs through the film. When a maggot outbreak forces the students to camp downstairs, Sara identifies Markos, the directress, sleeping behind her due to the distinctive sound of her snoring. She and Suzy later listen to the footsteps of the academy's staff as they are supposedly leaving the building, allowing Suzy to locate the secret passageway to the witches' chambers. Threat, meanwhile, is expressed through light and shadow: the bright light shone in Suzy's face that first causes her to feel weak and to collapse while dancing, the shadows that appear prior to both Daniel's and Sara's murders, the light that Sara sees come on in the room next door after she says the word "witches."

The film frustrates the spectator's investigative capacity, denying us the synchronicity of sound and image. This reinforces the sense that Suzy is investigating the texture of the film itself. At one early stage, a flashback is shown to us without sound, as in voice-over, Suzy recalls the words she has heard Pat say: "secret," "iris." Sara's footstep counting is accompanied by unmotivated camera movement through the academy's corridors but without the actual sound of footsteps, instead accompanied by the film's unsettling, sensorially overwhelming score by Italian prog band Goblin. It is only when Suzy follows the footsteps (which we then both see and hear) that she is able to piece together her memories of Pat. It is then that we are shown the flashback where the words Suzy requires are clearly audible: "The secret! I saw behind the door." The film's opening sequence displays clues that Suzy uses later in the film, although in less detail: we see Pat speak, and the words "behind the door," "iris," and "flower" are audible, while the nondiegetic soundtrack includes the word "witch." The film's sensory overload and investigative structure, however, is such that it is difficult to take in this information without knowing in advance where to look and listen. The film's narrative then follows Suzy's efforts to figure out where to look and listen. Her degree of mastery over the film's sounds and images at any particular stage in the narrative shapes how those sounds and images are presented to the spectator.

Unlike the typical heroines of Bluebeard tales, Suzy's investigation takes place not in an exclusively domestic space but in a dance school, a home of primarily female creative artists. Much work on women's writing and filmmaking has highlighted such representations of female creativity. Cobb, for example, argues that women "authorize" themselves through such proxies: female writers, creative artists, and creators of some variety; her examples range from videographer to quilt maker.[43] This reading strategy has its roots in Sandra Gilbert and Susan Gubar's landmark literary study *The Madwoman in the Attic: The Woman Writer and the Nineteenth-Century Literary Imagination*. They argue that women writers have both identified with and revised "the self-definitions patriarchal culture has imposed on them," particularly angel/monster dichotomies.[44] Those monsters are fundamentally contradictory, embodying both "the author's power to allay 'his' anxieties by calling their source bad names (witch, bitch, fiend, monster) and, simultaneously, the mysterious power of the character who refuses to stay in her textually ordained 'place.'"[45] As such, witches incarnate "male scorn of female creativity."[46] But they also allow female writers to covertly express anger and "come to terms with their own uniquely female feelings of fragmentation, their own keen sense of the discrepancies between what they are and what they are supposed to be."[47] *Suspiria* is itself indebted to that literary corpus, notably the line of Bluebeard-inspired literature of which *Jane Eyre* (1847) is a key example. Nicolodi has positioned the film in such traditions of women's literature: "*Suspiria* and *Inferno* the two 'fantastic' films that I wrote for Argento, who at the time was a *giallo* director, are I think as good as *Frankenstein* by Mary Shelley and could only have been thought up by a woman."[48] Suzy is both a creative artist living among creative artists, and as the narrative progresses, she becomes paralleled with the kinds of figures that Gilbert and Gubar interpret as connected to female creativity. A focus on Nicolodi's authorship brings to the surface the film's themes of female artistic production, otherwise obscured by a focus on one single male auteur.

In Doane's theorization of the paranoid woman's film, the victim/investigator heroine is identified with a mode of vision that is "objectless, free-floating," "a drive without an object," that draws the protagonist toward the abject, in Julia Kristeva's terms, "the place where meaning collapses."[49] The heroine is consistently paralleled with a woman whose fate she seems destined to follow.[50] But that woman is unrepresentable. In the film *Jane Eyre* (1943), the place where meaning collapses is "the space assigned to the madwoman, a point-of-view shot from a room in blackness."[51] That unrepresentability suggests that the heroine is confronting the "nonobject of her own fear": a "representation of herself displaced on to the level of the nonhuman."[52] *Suspiria*'s equivalent of the madwoman in the attic, the ancient witch in the secret chamber, is literally unrepresentable: she is invisible. That invisibility is an effect of and the source of her power. If she cannot be seen, she cannot be destroyed. She exists purely as sound, until lightning reveals her backlit outline, allowing Suzy to stab her, revealing her full image and corporeal form. Just as with Suzy's memories, the sequence builds toward the unity of sound and image. The witches may be preoccupied with prettiness, both in women and in their beautiful art murders, but once Suzy stabs Markos, her invisibility falls away to reveal her ancient, repulsive form. Markos is able to evade Suzy to the extent that she is able to evade representation. Suzy's destruction of her is predicated on her revelation as an image, another image that Suzy must gain control over. Markos is also Suzy's opposite: where Suzy is "very pretty indeed," Markos is decaying and dying, the very embodiment of the abject. But rather than functioning as polar opposites, Suzy and Markos have much in common.

Just as Suzy and Sara observe the sounds and images around them as part of their investigation, so the witches do the same. One way in which the film produces its horror is through the replication of its "assaultive gaze" in nonviolent sequences: a crane shot of girls camping, the aerial shot and zoom into Suzy and Sara in the academy's swimming pool (itself echoing the swimming pool sequence of *Cat People* [1942], another film that relies on supernatural implication for its production of terror). Their surveillance, their control of the image as it is presented to the spectator, and Suzy's investigation of that image reinforce parallels between Suzy and the witches that develop as the film progresses. The film depicts the production of women's decorative bodies as art objects and the attempt of women to gain control of the image, to become authors themselves. While Suzy does hardly any actual ballet at the dance academy, what she does do is murder someone. She is incapacitated early in the film when she collapses during a dance rehearsal, losing control of her body; later she is able to regain that control and produce the beautiful image of a burning building with which the film ends. By confronting and then destroying Helena Markos—not ever identified with the actual instruction of ballet—she is coming to occupy not the position of dancer for which she has been training but Markos's position as author/murderer.

In the contemporary boom of scholarship on women in film history, there has been a notable attention to the historiographical problems such scholarship entails, a discomfort with straightforward restorations of women discovered in "the archive." Jane Gaines warns against the twin pitfalls of feminist narratives of under- and overestimation.[53] The ambiguity surrounding the empirical details of *Suspiria*'s authorship, the conflicting accounts that circulate, renders those pitfalls especially acute. Christine Gledhill and Julia Knight also note "the particular problem that many women have left few historical traces, their roles in production or film culture obscured by more publicly visible or self-promotional male partners or concealed behind collective or collaborative practices."[54] The assumption, explicit or implicit, that Argento is the source of *Suspiria*'s meaning has underpinned the film's scholarship and criticism. An openness to Nicolodi's authorial claims not only allows for a different historical account of the film but also generates new readings of the film, a way of taking account of the film's central conundrums and preoccupation with the feminine.

While much *Suspiria* criticism relies on the idea that order is restored at the film's conclusion, this is an ending where all we see is everything on fire, albeit with Suzy walking free.[55] This seems less like the restoration of the symbolic order and more like a simultaneous collapse of meaning and a cathartic moment of artistic production, which, as, for the witches, is achieved through destruction.

It concludes by expelling the feminine abject, replacing it with a younger, "very pretty" model. Within its own logic, artistic production is achieved through an embrace of the "pretty" image, one that saturates the film itself. Indeed, Suzy's murder weapon is a literal ornament. It may not come to a coherent feminist statement, but it is a text that can be read in terms of questions of female authorship, as narrating the seizure of authorial control by a woman. As Suzy walks away from the burning dance academy, she wipes her hair back, turning her face upward toward the rain, smiling broadly: she now has control, she has solved the film's mystery of authorship, and finally, she too has become an author.

Notes

1 See James Gracey, *Dario Argento* (Harpenden, U.K.: Kamera Books, 2010), 69; Alexandra Heller-Nicholas, *Suspiria* (Leighton Buzzard, U.K.: Auteur, 2015), 30.
2 Alan Jones, audio commentary, *Suspiria* DVD (London: Nouveaux Pictures, 2015).
3 Chris Gallant, "The Phantom's Bride: Hysteria, Abjection and Corporeality: The Gothic Heroine from Page to Screen," in *Art of Darkness: The Cinema of Dario Argento*, ed. Chris Gallant (Guildford, U.K.: FAB, 2000), 52.
4 Peter Hutchings, "The Argento Effect," in *Defining Cult Movies: The Cultural Politics of Oppositional Taste*, ed. Mark Jancovich, Antonio Lázaro Reboli, Julian Stringer, and Andy Willis (Manchester: Manchester University Press, 2003), 134.
5 Russ Hunter, "'Didn't You Used to Be Dario Argento?': The Cult Reception of Dario Argento," in *Italian Film Directors in the New Millennium*, ed. William Hope (Newcastle, U.K.: Cambridge Scholars, 2010), 64.
6 Joanne Hollows, "The Masculinity of Cult," in Jancovich et al., *Defining Cult Movies*, 35–53; Jacinda Read, "The Cult of Masculinity: From Fan-Boys to Academic Bad Boys," in Jancovich et al., *Defining Cult Movies*, 54–70.
7 Hutchings, "Argento Effect," 135–136.
8 Hutchings, 140n5; Maitland McDonagh, *Broken Mirrors / Broken Minds: The Dark Dreams of Dario Argento*, expanded ed. (Minneapolis: University of Minnesota Press, 2010).
9 L. Andrew Cooper, *Dario Argento* (Champaign: University of Illinois Press, 2012), 3.
10 Daria Nicolodi (@NicolodiDaria), "suspiria and inferno..do they look like any other argento's film? Then they should be considered..mine..," Twitter post, March 13, 2014, https://twitter.com/NicolodiDaria/status/444128822989168640.
11 Luca M. Palmerini and Gaetano Mistretta, *Spaghetti Nightmares: Italian Fantasy-Horror as Seen through the Eyes of Their Protagonists* (Key West, Fla.: Fantasma Books, 1996), 114; see also Alan Jones, *Profondo Argento: The Man, the Myths & the Magic* (Godalming, U.K.: FAB, 2004).
12 Palmerini and Mistretta, *Spaghetti Nightmares*, 114.
13 Heller-Nicholas, *Suspiria*, 29.
14 Palmerini and Mistretta, *Spaghetti Nightmares*, 114.
15 McDonagh, *Broken Mirrors / Broken Minds*, 240.
16 Daria Nicolodi (@NicolodiDaria), "I imagined and wrote this scene Thnx," Twitter post, January 26, 2018, https://twitter.com/NicolodiDaria/status/957000058104373248. See also "Sorry Dr., I'm the author of Suspiria and Inferno..," Twitter post, June 7, 2014, https://twitter.com/NicolodiDaria/status/475354463558176769, and "A woman imagined and wrote Suspiria: me," Twitter post, July 14, 2017, https://twitter.com/NicolodiDaria/status/885916710263545856.

17   Jones, *Profondo Argento*, 74.

18   Alan Jones, "Argento," *Cinefantastique* 13, no. 6 / 14, no. 1 (1983): 21.

19   Jacqueline Reich, "The Mother of All Horror: Witches, Gender, and the Films of Dario Argento," in *Monsters in the Italian Literary Imagination*, ed. Keala Jewell (Detroit: Wayne State University Press, 2001), 96, 104; Gracey, *Dario Argento*, 16; Stephen Thrower, "*Suspiria*," in Gallant, *Art of Darkness*, 141; Adam Knee, "Gender, Genre, Argento," in *The Dread of Difference: Gender and the Horror Film*, ed. Barry Keith Grant, 2nd ed. (Austin: University of Texas Press, 2015), 253.

20   Shelley Cobb, *Adaptation, Authorship, and Contemporary Women Filmmakers* (Basingstoke, U.K.: Palgrave Macmillan, 2015), 1.

21   Judith Mayne, *The Woman at the Keyhole: Feminism and Women's Cinema* (Bloomington: Indiana University Press, 1990), 2.

22   Steven Maras, "Some Attitudes and Trajectories in Screenwriting Research," *Journal of Screenwriting* 2, no. 2 (2011): 276.

23   Bridget Conor, *Screenwriting: Creative Labor and Professional Practice* (New York: Routledge, 2014), 9.

24   Efforts to theorize multiple and collaborative authorship include C. Paul Sellors, "Collective Authorship in Film," *Journal of Aesthetics and Art Criticism* 65, no. 3 (Summer 2007): 263–271; Sondra Bacharach and Deborah Tollefsen, "We Did It: From Mere Contributors to Coauthors," *Journal of Aesthetics and Art Criticism* 68, no. 1 (Winter 2010): 23–32.

25   Alan Lovell and Gianluca Sergi, *Making Films in Contemporary Hollywood* (London: Bloomsbury Academic, 2005); Aaron Hunter, *Authoring Hal Ashby: The Myth of the New Hollywood Auteur* (London: Bloomsbury Academic, 2016).

26   John Patterson, "*The Love Witch* Director Anna Biller: 'I'm in Conversation with the Pornography All around Us,'" *Guardian*, March 2, 2017, https://www.theguardian .com/film/2017/mar/02/love-witch-director-anna-biller-conversation-pornography.

27   Tim Snelson, "'From Grade B Thrillers to Deluxe Chillers': Prestige Horror, Female Audiences, and Allegories of Spectatorship in *The Spiral Staircase* (1946)," *New Review of Film and Television Studies* 7, no. 2 (2009): 173–188; Alison Peirse, "The Feminine Appeal of British Horror Cinema," *New Review of Film and Television Studies* 13, no. 4 (2015): 385–402.

28   Tania Modleski, *The Women Who Knew Too Much: Hitchcock and Feminist Theory*, 3rd ed. (New York: Routledge, 2016), 53.

29   Kaja Silverman, *The Acoustic Mirror: The Female Voice in Psychoanalysis and Cinema* (Bloomington: Indiana University Press, 1988), 210–211.

30   Modleski, *Women Who Knew Too Much*, 44–45, 50–51.

31   Marina Warner, *Once Upon a Time: A Short History of Fairy Tale* (Oxford: Oxford University Press, 2014), 92.

32   Knee, "Gender, Genre, Argento," 243.

33   Chris Gallant, "Threatening Glances: Voyeurism, Eye Violation and Camera: From *Peeping Tom* to *Opera*," in Gallant, *Art of Darkness*, 13–15; Knee, "Gender, Genre, Argento," 247; see also Alison Peirse, "Ocularcentrism, Horror and *The Lord of the Rings* Films," *Journal of Adaptation in Film & Performance* 5, no. 1 (2012): 41–50.

34   Heller-Nicholas, *Suspiria*, 7.

35   Heller-Nicholas, 43.

36   Rosalind Galt, *Pretty: Film and the Decorative Image* (New York: Columbia University Press, 2011), 11; Kim Newman, *Nightmare Movies: Horror on Screen since the 1960s* (London: Bloomsbury, 2011), 146.

37   Galt, *Pretty*, 7.

38 Galt, 1–2.

39 Galt, 203.

40 See Gary Arnold, "*Suspiria*: Upstaged Terror Gone Wild," *Washington Post*, August 24, 1977, B7; "*Suspiria*," *Variety*, March 9, 1977, 17; Jones, *Profondo Argento*, 15; Gracey, *Dario Argento*, 75; Lindsay Hallam, "'Why Are There Always Three?': The Gothic Occult in Dario Argento's Three Mothers Trilogy," *Journal of Italian Cinema & Media Studies* 5, no. 2 (2017): 212.

41 Maria Tatar, *Secrets beyond the Door: The Story of Bluebeard and His Wives* (Princeton, N.J.: Princeton University Press, 2004), 65.

42 Tatar, 96; Mary Ann Doane, "The 'Woman's Film': Possession and Address," in *Re-vision: Essays in Feminist Film Criticism*, ed. Mary Ann Doane, Patricia Mellencamp, and Linda Williams (Los Angeles: American Film Institute, 1984), 70.

43 Cobb, *Adaptation*, 52.

44 Sandra M. Gilbert and Susan Gubar, *The Madwoman in the Attic: The Woman Writer and the Nineteenth-Century Literary Imagination*, 2nd ed. (New Haven, Conn.: Yale University Press, 2000), 79.

45 Gilbert and Gubar, 28.

46 Gilbert and Gubar, 29.

47 Gilbert and Gubar, 78.

48 Daria Nicolodi (@NicolodiDaria), "La ringrazio. Suspiria e Inferno i due film 'fantastici' che ho scritto per Argento, all'epoca regista di gialli, penso sian belli come Frankenstein di Mary Shelley e che solo una donna potesse concepirli," Twitter post, September 1, 2018, 6:43 p.m., https://twitter.com/NicolodiDaria/status/1035946327170007041. My thanks to Louis Bayman for his assistance with the translation from Italian.

49 Mary Ann Doane, *The Desire to Desire: The Woman's Film of the 1940s* (Bloomington: Indiana University Press, 1987), 141; Julia Kristeva, *Powers of Horror: An Essay on Abjection*, trans. Leon S. Roudiez (New York: Columbia University Press, 1982), 2.

50 Doane, *Desire to Desire*, 141–142.

51 Doane, 141.

52 Doane, 142.

53 Jane Gaines, *Pink-Slipped: What Happened to Women in the Silent Film Industries?* (Champaign: University of Illinois Press, 2018), 9.

54 Christine Gledhill and Julia Knight, "Introduction," in *Doing Women's Film History: Reframing Cinemas, Past and Future*, ed. Christine Gledhill and Julia Knight (Champaign: University of Illinois Press, 2015), 4.

55 See Reich, "Mother of All Horror."

5

Personal Trauma Cinema and the Experimental Videos of Cecelia Condit and Ellen Cantor

KATIA HOUDE

Experimental cinema was influenced by the shifting social and political cultures of the late twentieth century, including the emergence of identity politics. This position resonated with women experimental filmmakers who began to make films that represented their worldview and embodied experiences.[1] This ideological shift enmeshes "the prerogatives of personal experience—memory, autobiography, direct observation of everyday life—with the constraints of a socially–shared past, recasting radical subjectivity as the interpenetration of public and private spaces."[2] From the 1970s onward, feminist film scholars also began investigating how, in order to impact patriarchal cinematic culture, women filmmakers needed to move away from making "the visible invisible," as Mulvey heralded in 1975 in "Visual Pleasure and Narrative Cinema," and turn toward a cinema that "produces the conditions of visibility for a different social subject," understood by Teresa de Lauretis as "women's cinema."[3]

This chapter explores the artist films of Cecelia Condit and Ellen Cantor, which combine experimental film form with horror film tropes, images, and motifs. While women working in narrative cinema continue to be underrepresented in scholarly works, this lack of recognition is even more pronounced in critical writing on women working in the experimental field. Jean Petrolle and Virginia Wright Wexman suggest this may be because "many critics tend to ignore or undervalue this work in part because women's experimental films frequently revise the very paradigms within which this cinema has traditionally been considered."[4] Yet Condit and Cantor are not alone in exploring the relationship between horror and experimental form. Other women experimental filmmakers, including Aïda Ruilova, Cynthia Maughan, Julie Zando, Hester Scheurwater, and Sue de Beer, also employ grotesque and macabre imagery in their moving image works, images more commonly found in thriller, slasher, rape-revenge, or body horror films.

Exploring Condit's *Possibly in Michigan* (1983) and Cantor's *Within Heaven and Hell* (1996), this chapter argues that their combination of experimental form with horror film tropes creates a model of personal trauma cinema. I define personal trauma cinema as films that use the experimental form to represent the internal workings of the trauma psyche while invoking tropes and motifs from conventional narrative cinema to provide a familiar and, by extension, a safe path to processing repressed and intrusive memories. My framing draws on Janet Walker's seminal research on trauma cinema, which she defines as "a group of films that deal with a world-shattering event or events, whether public or personal."[5] Walker's *Trauma Cinema: Documenting Incest and the Holocaust* (2005) has engendered numerous responses from academics who frame her work in the context of historical, cultural, and public traumas and its impact on cinematic representations of collective memory.[6] Walker's definition and positioning of trauma cinema have advanced thinking on the representation of historical and cultural trauma on film and provide an important framing for how experimental filmmakers use the documentary form to explore personal traumas. However, there remain important experimental works that do not fall under this category but can also be understood as trauma cinema. Walker's definition of personal trauma cinema (which she examines in terms of the representation of incest in feminist autobiographical experimental documentaries) invites further opportunities for research, and as such, this chapter offers a new interpretation of personal trauma cinema, where experimental form represents the internal trauma psyche and the conventional narrative tropes of horror film externalize the inner demons of trauma survivors.

Experimental Form and Trauma

Experimental cinema is a genre of filmmaking that challenges notions of content and form in ways that do not conform to mainstream cinema. This is due in part to experimental cinema's independent mode of production, microbudgets, operation outside studio systems, and independent or self-distribution.[7] These factors allow for freedoms of expression and idiosyncratic aesthetics that are unhindered by pressures of box-office revenue or a need to conform to marketable subjects. Further, experimental cinema is unconstrained by narrative film lengths. As a result, experimental cinema is one where "visual poetry and the individual concerns of the artist" are driving creative elements, engendering raw self-expression, and explorations of nonconventional and often taboo subjects.[8]

From Alice Guy-Blaché in the late 1800s to Maya Deren in the 1940s, of whom the latter "became the first independent filmmaker to successfully exhibit her work," female filmmakers have a long tradition of using experimental cinema to express their embodied subjectivity on-screen.[9] Laura Mulvey has famously suggested that experimental cinema is the only form that permits women to accurately represent their subjectivity: "What recurs overall is a constant return to woman, not indeed as a visual image, but as a subject of inquiry, a content which cannot be considered within aesthetic lines laid down by traditional cinematic practice."[10] Petrolle and Wright Wexman argue that films made by women are always political acts as they, by definition, stand in opposition to men's cultural space.[11]

In addition to subversion, experimental cinema is particularly well suited for the exploration of personal emotional experiences and viewpoints. Walker recognizes that experimental form is ideal for expressing trauma through non-linearity and metaphorical language: "The stylistic and narrative modality of trauma cinema is nonrealist. Like traumatic memories that feature vivid bodily and visual sensation over 'verbal narrative and context,' these films are characterized by non-linearity, fragmentation, nonsynchronous sound, repetition, rapid editing and strange angles. And they approach the past through an unusual admixture of emotional affect, metonymic symbolism and cinematic flashbacks."[12] Some psychological wounds caused by traumatic events can be so great that the memories of these cannot be assimilated and integrated into accessible memory. They remain hidden from, disremembered by, repressed by, and even at times unknowable to the person who has suffered the trauma.

As Cathy Caruth explains, it is not just past events that plague trauma survivors but also "the reality of the way that its violence has not yet been fully known."[13] As a result, trauma memories cannot be retrieved or recalled in the same way that other processed and integrated life memories can, as they remain unintegrated and unattached, unlike narrativized memories.[14] As psychiatrist and trauma scholar Bessel van der Kolk explains, because trauma memories remain unintegrated and unprocessed, they haunt the mind and return as violent flashbacks and disturbing intrusive memories: "Trauma is not stored as a narrative with an orderly beginning, middle, and end. . . . Memories return . . . as flashbacks that contain fragments of the experience, isolated images, sounds, and body sensations that initially have no context other than fear and panic."[15] These uncontrollable, horrifying repetitions of trauma cycles rewind and retraumatize the person who experiences them. John Orr explains that this "compulsion to repeat" has harmful effects in that "the original trauma is intensified, not diminished, and with it is enlarged the feeling of pain."[16]

Trauma survivors often experience a loss of linearity, as experienced through the impossibility of stitching together fragments of trauma memories into a cohesive narrative. They remain at the mercy of uncontrollable and intrusive visceral memories and violent flashbacks that lack context of time and place and throw the body and all its senses into the horrifying and unfathomable shock.[17] In psychology, post-traumatic stress disorder (PTSD), which often affects those who have suffered catastrophic events, results in memory disturbances that range "from complete amnesia to impairments in organizing the memory, which subsequently lead to both disorganized, disintegrated intentional narrative recall and frequent, automatic memory intrusions."[18] The language of experimental film is ideally suited to capture the essence of the trauma psyche through its aesthetics of fragmentation, repetition, ellipsis, and fluid time-based movement and shifting temporalities, which embody the sensory distortions experienced by those who have suffered trauma. Further, as experimental cinema is not typically concerned with the narrative form of causal connections, it offers new ways of seeing and experiencing the world, often evoking a sensuous cinema that is more metaphorical than literal.

One way to avoid retraumatizing is to work through trauma memories under predictable and controlled circumstances. This chapter argues that horror tropes can provide such a contained surrogate, as the genre provides the ritualistic rites to work through vestiges of unresolved trauma. By externalizing internal demons through the vehicle of horror, trauma memories are rendered visible and therefore knowable and destructible. As such, I will now argue that experimental form combined with horror films tropes enables personal expressions of trauma that are not possible in conventional narrative cinema.

Possibly in Michigan (1983)

Condit wrote and directed the twelve-minute color-and-sound video *Possibly in Michigan* with funding from two American art grants. The video focuses on the female experience of obsessive and unwanted love, gendered violence, revenge, murder, and cannibalism. She approaches these themes by combining humor with the macabre, creating a tension between innocence and violence. Condit draws viewers in with seemingly beautiful and often alluring images only to twist them into grotesque worlds that reveal the violence that exists in many women's daily lives. As Robin Blaetz notes, this is not an uncommon strategy in female experimental works: "With notable frequency, many of the films evoke and comment upon the sometimes humorous often surreal dissociations between patriarchal culture and women's lives within it. If there is a thematic link . . . it would be that of looking beneath and uncovering. What is revealed below the literal and metaphorical layers in the films take many forms but in almost every case involves emotion."[19] This is certainly the case in *Possibly in Michigan*, which explores the dark undercurrents beneath a seemingly idyllic, suburban setting of domesticity.

Condit incorporates conventions from the stalker horror subgenre to give narrative shape to her experimental video. Horror enthusiasts will easily recognize tropes and motifs from *Halloween* (1978), as Condit most closely mirrors imagery from this seminal film. Condit includes several ubiquitous horror tropes and motifs, like those listed in Carol J. Clover's 1992 study of the slasher film *Men, Women, and Chain Saws*: the house in the suburbs, the phone call for help, the stalker breaking his way in, the physical violence, the knife attack, the protagonist's unsuccessful attempts to run and fight back, the stalker being unmasked as someone familiar (here a jilted lover), and the rescue by a friend armed with a gun. Formally, Condit makes use of canted and low angles, jittery camera shots, and rapid zoom-ins to terrified eyes and objects of vital importance: the ringing telephone, the protagonist's lifeline. She also uses these formal and narrative elements to build up the Final Girl character. Clover first defined the Final Girl as the one who does not die in horror films. The price for her survival is seeing her friends die savagely one by one, knowing she is next on the killer's list: "She alone looks death in the face, but she alone also finds the strength either to stay the killer long enough to be rescued . . . or to kill him herself."[20] The Final Girl is the "tortured survivor," her trauma scars raw and everlasting.[21] Clover's positioning of the Final Girl is useful in understanding how this horror trope works in personal trauma cinema, arming the protagonist with the foreknowledge that she will ultimately be safe, even when experiencing abject terror. By externalizing her repressed traumatic memories into a physically real monster, Condit renders her protagonist's internal demons visible and by extension conquerable. By calling on conventional horror tropes and motifs, Condit thus exposes the triggers and traps that normally remain hidden in the traumatized psyche, allowing her protagonist the ability to safely shine a light in the dark recesses of her traumatic memories and face the inner demons that haunt her.

As with conventional horror film narratives, warnings signs are presented for the protagonist and the viewers: the stalker picks up a rock in the garden, and the skull beneath suggests he has killed others; the protagonist devours a bloody piece of raw meat, hinting at the cannibalistic ritual she is about to engage in; worms are superimposed onto the protagonist's photograph, suggesting death and decay are imminent. In *Possibly in Michigan*, these moments are disjointed and fragmented, lacking context and without a linear narrative or timeline. They are represented through jumps cuts and ellipses and are often looped and repeated. This echoes the inner workings of the trauma psyche that constantly monitors for hidden dangers, as the traumatized victim cannot differentiate between triggered flashback memories and the present, which is now safe.[22]

Aesthetically, Condit also mediates her protagonist's experience by depicting the abuse through monitor–like screens. This mediation has two distinct effects: first, as these suggest CCTV footage, it creates a spatial distancing for the viewer from the violent images shown; second, because of the apparent temporal distancing, the mediated screens suggest to viewers that they are watching documentation of a past event, even as the attacks are also happening in real diegetic time. Through her conflation of past and present timelines, Condit implies that viewers are witnessing a cycle of repeated abuse. Furthermore, Condit incorporates still photographs of the protagonist. These are not images from her past, they are representations of on-screen moments viewers have just witnessed. By integrating stills, Condit freezes time, suggesting that Sharon is in fact trapped in a psychological trauma loop. Her liminal, trapped state between repression and awareness is captured through the superimposition of a rotting mummy's face onto Sharon's. Once the protagonist recognizes her lover for the monster he is, the cycle of abuse is broken, and she is freed both narratively and cinematically from the entrapment of mediation.

Within Heaven and Hell (1996)

Within Heaven and Hell is a sixteen-minute color-and-sound video, composed of appropriated and reedited images from *The Texas Chain Saw Massacre* (1974) and *The Sound of Music* (1965). Cantor ties these seemingly disparate films together using voice-over narration to tell a raw and visceral story of sexual abuse, love, and taboo female desire. Juxtaposing gruesome and violent images from the slasher film with the pastoral and idyllic beauty of the musical, Cantor proposes a new text that exposes the subject of abuse, all too often hidden in patriarchal narratives. As Alison Butler argues in *Women's Cinema: The Contested Screen*, all women's art-making practice inherits a history of patriarchal codification and conventions, and in order to subvert this, women need to rework and contest these established traditions.[23] The reworked footage, specifically *The Texas Chain Saw Massacre*, is well suited to this project, as it contains recognizable visual and narrative tropes, rendering it "particularly liable to subversion."[24] Further, the intertextuality Cantor brings to it in *Within Heaven and Hell* allows an avenue for "the male dominant point of view [to be] displaced by the female."[25]

In one particular sequence, Cantor takes the Final Girl trope and allows her protagonist to live in order to tell her tale of trauma and abuse. Here, Cantor only incorporates scenes from *The Texas Chain Saw Massacre*, none from *The Sound of Music*. Using particularly graphic images from the film, Cantor represents affectively the embodied experience of sexual violence and abuse. In her reediting, Cantor removes cause and effect from the original film's narrative, thereby rendering the out-of-context images even more violent, and overlays her diary-like confession of assault onto these horrific images. The sequence begins with a voice-over message sampled from *The Texas Chain Saw Massacre* that encourages viewers to believe in the magic of the moment: "There are moments when we cannot believe that what is happening is really true. Pinch yourself and you may find out that it really is." However, those familiar with *The Texas Chain Saw Massacre* know that this is in reality a warning of the unimaginable horror that is about to take place. Cantor uses this quote to frame her experience of abuse: "He was really causing me a lot of pain, and I was struggling to get away, and he was holding me down, and I was crying that he was really hurting me." The accompanying visuals are of Leatherface, who hangs Pam, the female protagonist, up on a meat hook, by her back. She screams as he approaches her with a chainsaw. While the narration describes abuse, both physical and psychological, it is the images that Cantor selects that truly bring out the horror and violence of the sexual assault she recounts.

Cantor then cuts to another scene in *The Texas Chain Saw Massacre* when Leatherface prepares to put Pam into a large freezer. She screams in terror, and Cantor continues her narration: "He was screaming in my face that I was crazy, that I was mad. He was yelling in my eyes, 'You don't respect me, you must respect me. You don't realize that I'm ill.' Later I thought about it, and I thought maybe he's right." By merging the horror film's gruesome images with her confession of abuse, Cantor makes the pain of her lived experience undeniable. And yet, her own words seem to discount her interpretation of the situation. She begins to doubt her own experience, conceding that maybe he was right, maybe she was the one who was insane after all. Cantor's doubts result from systemic abuse and shame, combined with the all-too-often accusation that women are crazy, exaggerating, or made to feel their experiences of events are untrue and devalued. At this point, Leatherface stuffs Pam into the freezer, leaving her to die and, in effect, silencing her.

The sequence closes with Cantor shifting the temporal position of her narrative, jumping to the night before: "We were so happy. We were drinking champagne, and we were fucking our brains out." The sharp shift in tone and time echo the lack of linearity and fragmentation of trauma memories as well as a marked desire to repress the horror of her experience. Flashes of gruesome mummified body parts appear with no context or causal links. Maureen Turim argues that "montage offers a means of representing the interiority of the female protagonists, as we see psyches slashed by blows of antagonistic and cruel worlds responding to that psychic hurt with violent desires."[26] Here, Cantor's disjointed editing represents on-screen the experience of intrusive memories and flashbacks. The closing image of the sequence is of Sally, the Final Girl covered in blood, screaming. She serves as a reminder that—while viewers know her horrific journey has come to an end—the trauma she has incurred will continue to manifest through intrusive memories, a fragmented and disjointed internal psyche, and violent flashbacks.

Conclusion

This analysis reveals that not only is there an innate connection between women and experimental video and film, but there is also a strong link between the experimental form and horror through the depiction of violence. As Turim notes, "Women's art clearly grows richer by its willingness to represent violence rather than avoid it. Women bring the avant-garde's preoccupation with violence the unique metaphors of their bodies. They write on their filmic, performative, or tableau bodies by cutting through to a specific anger and a corollary need to heal."[27] This impulse is galvanized in Cantor's *Within Heaven and Hell*, where her use of footage from *The Texas Chain Saw Massacre* narrativizes traumatic memories, giving them voice and bearing witness.

In writing this chapter, I attempt to address the underrepresentation of women filmmakers and creators in academic writing in general and the lack of critical address of trauma suffered by women more specifically. This lacuna is due in part to the complexity of personal trauma. One way to address this challenge is to develop a framework for analyzing personal trauma that focuses on formal elements as an entry for critical discourse on its representation. I have argued here that experimental cinema's form is ideal for representing the inner psyche of the trauma mind through its aesthetics of fragmentation, repetition, and ellipsis, while conventional horror film tropes and motifs, through their predictability and familiarity, allow for a safe processing of repressed trauma memories. This analysis has documented how Condit and Cantor turn to horror tropes and motifs to externalize and narrativize haunting trauma memories of gendered abuse and sexual violence while at the same time use experimental form to capture their protagonists' embodied experience of trauma. And in so doing, this chapter has proposed a new formulation of personal trauma cinema, one that echoes the sequelae of catastrophic events while using conventional horror tropes to work through its vestiges.

Notes

1 Wheeler Winston Dixon and Gwendolyn Audrey Foster, "Introduction: Toward a New History of the Experimental Cinema," in *Experimental Cinema: The Film Reader*, ed. Wheeler Winston Dixon and Gwendolyn Audrey Foster (New York: Routledge, 2002), 281.
2 William C. Wees, "Carrying On: Leslie Thornton, Su Friedrich, Abigail Child and

American Avant-Garde Film of the Eighties," *Canadian Journal of Film Studies* 10, no. 1 (Spring 2001): 73.

3 Teresa de Lauretis, *Alice Doesn't: Feminism, Semiotics, Cinema* (Bloomington: Indiana University Press, 1984), 8–9.

4 Jean Petrolle and Virginia Wright Wexman, "Introduction: Experimental Filmmaking and Women's Subjectivity," in *Women and Experimental Filmmaking*, ed. Jean Petrolle and Virginia Wright Wexman (Champaign: University of Illinois Press, 2005), 1.

5 Janet Walker, "Trauma Cinema: False Memories and True Experience," *Screen* 42, no. 2 (2001): 214.

6 Janet Walker, *Trauma Cinema: Documenting Incest and the Holocaust* (Berkeley: University of California Press, 2005).

7 Winston Dixon and Foster, "Introduction," 2.

8 Winston Dixon and Foster, 3.

9 Winston Dixon and Foster, 1, 4.

10 Laura Mulvey, *Visual and Other Pleasures*, 2nd ed. (New York: Palgrave Macmillan, 2009), 130.

11 Petrolle and Wexman, "Introduction," 5.

12 Walker, "Trauma Cinema," 214.

13 Cathy Caruth, *Unclaimed Experience* (Baltimore: Johns Hopkins University Press, 2016), 6.

14 Cathy Caruth, *Trauma: Explorations in Memory* (Baltimore: Johns Hopkins University Press, 1995), 153; Janina Fisher, *Healing the Fragmented Selves of Trauma Survivors: Overcoming Internal Self-Alienation* (New York: Routledge, 2017), 36.

15 Bessel van der Kolk, *The Body Keeps the Score: Brain, Mind, and Body in the Healing of Trauma* (New York: Penguin Books, 2014), 137.

16 John Orr, "The Trauma Film and British Romantic Cinema 1940–1960," *Senses of Cinema* 51 (July 2009), http://sensesofcinema.com/2009/feature-articles/trauma -film-british-romantic-cinema/.

17 Lyn Nadel and W. Jake Jacobs, "Traumatic Memory Is Special," *Current Directions in Psychological Science* 7, no. 5 (October 1998): 156.

18 Michele Bedard-Gilligan and Lori A. Zoellner, "Dissociation and Memory Fragmentation in Post-traumatic Stress Disorder: An Evaluation of the Dissociative Encoding Hypothesis," *Memory* 20, no. 3 (2012): 278.

19 Robin Blaetz, "Introduction: Women's Experimental Cinema. Critical Frameworks," in *Women's Experimental Cinema: Critical Frameworks*, ed. Robin Blaetz (Durham, N.C.: Duke University Press), 14.

20 Carol J. Clover, *Men, Women, and Chain Saws: Gender in the Modern Horror Film*, updated ed. (Princeton, N.J.: Princeton University Press, 2015), 35.

21 Clover, x.

22 Fisher, *Healing*, 135.

23 Alison Butler, *Women's Cinema: The Contested Screen* (London: Wallflower, 2002), 60, 22.

24 Butler, 10–12.

25 Butler, 10–12.

26 Maureen Turim, "The Violence of Desire," in Petrolle and Wexman, *Women and Experimental Filmmaking*, 75.

27 Turim, 90.

6

Self-Reflexivity and Feminist Camp in *Freddy's Dead: The Final Nightmare*

TOSHA R. TAYLOR

In her seminal essay "Notes on Camp," Susan Sontag writes that "the essence of Camp is its love of the unnatural: of artifice and exaggeration."[1] The *Nightmare on Elm Street* franchise has never shied away from camp, and the franchise's sixth installment, *Freddy's Dead: The Final Nightmare* (1991), expresses camp sensibilities to perhaps the greatest extent. The film undoubtedly owes its camp, at least in part, to the influence of its story creator and director, Rachel Talalay. As a production assistant on John Waters's *Polyester* (1981) and producer on his *Hairspray* (1988) and *Cry-Baby* (1990), Talalay brings significant experience in camp filmmaking to her directorial debut. In addition, her work as a production manager on *A Nightmare on Elm Street* (1984) and *A Nightmare on Elm Street 2: Freddy's Revenge* (1985) and as a producer on *A Nightmare on Elm Street 3: Dream Warriors* (1987) and *A Nightmare on Elm Street 4: The Dream Master* (1988) also provides an aesthetic and stylistic foundation for her work on the sixth film. This style offers a conspicuous self-reflexivity, by which the film's own narrative devices (particularly those based in humor) suggest a metatextual awareness of the film franchise. Camp and self-reflexivity, then, merge in the film *Freddy's Dead*, which finally, albeit temporarily, kills Freddy Krueger.

The late addition to the *A Nightmare on Elm Street* series may challenge the identification of to whom the film belongs, especially as Talalay has not directed other films within the franchise. While, as Annette Kuhn notes, literal ownership of a film frequently seems to belong to corporate entities, the history of the auteur demonstrates a cultural and critical tendency to treat films as belonging to their directors.[2] The opening credits of *Freddy's Dead* establish an element of ownership for Talalay. The fourth title card identifies "A Rachel Talalay Film," and Talalay receives further visual credits as director and creator of the story on which the film is based. *Freddy's Dead* arguably presents a complex case for evaluating Talalay's role as a distinctly feminist director or even an auteur. Yet while the primacy of the auteur has long positioned the director as the author of a film, filmmaking remains a collaborative art form.[3] Talalay created the story outline but has openly credited the film's screenwriter, Michael De Luca, with transforming a previous screenwriter's initial unsatisfactory script.[4] Her acknowledgment of the screenplay's multiple authors confounds our urge to recognize the hand of a female auteur in this film while demonstrating a greater appreciation for the collaborative process.

Talalay was not the only woman directing horror in the 1980s and early 1990s, but she is the only woman to direct an *Elm Street* film. Given that the franchise deploys the Final Girl trope so consistently, the presence of a female filmmaker adds another layer of meaning for feminist examinations of the film. Talalay's formative experiences on camp films further encourage us to ask questions about the relationship between gender, filmmaking, and camp.[5] This chapter thus explores camp in *Freddy's Dead* to investigate how the franchise's singular woman director negotiates discourses of women's agency, trauma, and spectatorial engagement within a preexisting horror mythos. I argue here that Talalay employs camp humor and self-reflexivity to wield power over the franchise itself.

Camp has undergone several—sometimes contradictory—critical treatments in efforts to definitively qualify it. For my purposes, I undertake Sontag's initial characterizations of camp as a starting point, with a concession that Sontag, as others have pointed out, errs in dismissing camp's politics.[6] Working, too, from Sontag's distinguishing of camp from kitsch on the grounds that kitsch lacks the "love" of exaggeration integral to camp, this chapter is also informed by David MacGregor Johnston's argument that while camp is capable of making fun of itself, kitsch can only be made fun of.[7]

Freddy most conspicuously invites the "camp" label. His crude humor invites the viewer to laugh at his victims' terror, to cringe without empathy at their bodily destruction, and to enjoy horror narratives that seem increasingly less designed to frighten. Freddy himself is an exaggeration: his burn scars are clearly prosthetic, and his hand is augmented by a home-modified glove with blades for fingers. As he attacks his victims, he transforms his own body to the point of inhuman deformation. In the first film, his mouth becomes the mouthpiece of a phone in Nancy's dreams, and in the third film, he transforms into a giant snake to devour Kristen. Casey Ryan Kelly characterizes camp horror as having "low production values, exaggerated depictions of the grotesque, preposterous death and dismemberments, detached humor, and conscious deployment of generic tropes."[8] While the majority of the franchise revels in such elements, Talalay's addition offers the most camp self-reflexivity (up until the seventh installment). Dreams blend seamlessly with reality in all the films, but this one rarely ventures into reality, instead offering up dreams within dreams within dreams. Rather than being tangential to the main plot—as, for instance, Joey's death in the third film—these nested dreams drive some of the narrative action.

Johnston writes that kitsch horror films—and he includes the *Elm Street* sequels here—"are frightening, but generally they are frightening in ways that do not challenge us to question these films, our responses to them, or the worlds they represent."[9] While *Freddy's Dead* is less conventionally frightening, it does invite the viewer to question all previous thoughts and assumptions about the franchise. Its value as a horror film, as a horror *sequel*, and as an example of camp lies less in visual realizations and more in Talalay's amendments to the mythology of the franchise. Perhaps the boldest of Talalay's decisions is a retcon of Freddy's origin story. The franchise had established Freddy as a child killer who was, in turn, killed by the parents of his victims when the justice system failed them. Talalay's retcon imagines him as a perversion of the quintessential family man, living comfortably in a middle-class house with a wife and young daughter. The terrifying boiler room established in previous films as the location of Freddy's crimes is now reworked as a hidden room within the Krueger family cellar. Human Freddy plays in his garden with his daughter, and suggestions of his evil intentions come only from the spectator's awareness of his crimes.

The retcon also removes some of Freddy's own power over his supernatural existence. Rather than leaving the audience to assume that Freddy's dream world resurrection occurs as a result of his own evil, the film establishes that he drew the attention of three demons. Called the "dream people" by Freddy and the "snake demons" in the film's ending credits, these demons appear to human Freddy and promise that if Freddy allows them to enter him, he "shall be forever." It is their will, not Freddy's, that allows his soul to live on after he is burned to death, and when he dies at the end of the film, they unceremoniously depart. Freddy's reliance on the "dream people" arguably transports him (and the franchise) to a new level of camp exaggeration: it goes from being a narrative about a dead murderer who manifests in teenagers' dreams to kill them in real life to becoming, retroactively, a narrative about a dead murderer who manages to do so because he is possessed by three crudely animated demons. However, *Freddy's*

Dead cannot be labeled as *pure* camp, which, according to Sontag, "is always naïve" rather than intentional.[10] Such camp emerges from a "seriousness that fails" rather than a deliberate construction of camp, which Sontag does not find to be the most truly camp form.[11] Yet just as Sontag concedes that failed seriousness is not always camp, not all camp can be held to this standard; indeed, many, if not most, modern horror films described as camp would not deserve the label under such strict criteria. Nonetheless, by Sontag's and Johnston's respective definitions, the film's deliberate camp risks banishing it to kitsch.

One element that preserves *Freddy's Dead*'s camp status is its deployment of artifice and representation. Indeed, representation is a crucial element of camp in the franchise as a whole. Sontag writes that "Camp sees everything in quotation marks. It's not a lamp, but a 'lamp'; not a woman but a 'woman.' To perceive Camp in objects and persons is to understand Being-as-Playing-a-Role."[12] Throughout the franchise, Freddy takes the form of a multitude of people and objects as he torments his victims; that he does so in their dreams allows such transformations to become truly outlandish.[13] Talalay's film privileges such artificial representations. In Carlos's dream, for instance, the device attached to his ear is not a hearing aid but a painful, moving flesh augmentation in the guise of a hearing aid. The woman he sees as his mother is actually Freddy taking on the form of his mother. As will be discussed in more detail later, actor Roseanne Barr is not truly a character called Ethel but is, rather, Roseanne-Barr-as-Ethel, just as musician Alice Cooper is not playing Freddy's foster father so much as he is Alice-Cooper-as-Freddy's-foster-father.

The film owes some of its focus on artifice to its self-reflexivity. Carol Clover finds self-reflexivity particularly evident in the horror genre, and Jeffrey Sconce argues for its conspicuousness in *Freddy's Dead*.[14] At all times, unlike its predecessors, *Freddy's Dead* is conspicuously aware of itself. While Talalay's film is not unique in its engagement with self-aware camp, it is perhaps the *most* self-aware at this point in the franchise.

Sontag places a camp value on lists of allegedly "bad" films due to an abundance of fans who can be counted on to see such films "in a high-spirited and unpretentious way."[15] Such viewers have expectations around the typical quality and narrative conventions of these films and bring these expectations to the viewing experience. *Freddy's Dead* assumes the spectator is already familiar with the previous franchise installments. Even as it partly reconfigures Freddy's origin, a feat that allows for wholly new viewers to better follow his demise, it invites the franchise fan to notice its idiosyncrasies and to be surprised by the revelation of Freddy's daughter and by the insertion of literal demonic forces as the source of Freddy's power. Thus they are made to reexamine the character they have believed they understood since his initial appearance.

The film welcomes the viewer to share in its self-mockery. In one particular scene, gamer Spencer awakens in the dream world of a game and proceeds to travel through its two-dimensional plane. He eventually comes to a boss fight with an avatar of his abusive father and then, once having defeated him, to the game's avatar of Freddy. Outside the game and beyond Spencer's awareness but still within the dream world, Freddy himself controls the game. To Talalay's expressed consternation, 3D sequences were meant to be one of the film's selling points, but the film makes a clear effort to reproduce eight-bit graphics and to insert a live-action Spencer into them.[16] The cheesy sounds of the game and Spencer's exaggerated movements occur on two screens: Freddy's television as dream-Spencer progresses through the game and the screen on which the audience watches the film as the sleeping Spencer sleepwalks and jumps through the house. To a contemporary audience, the graphics of Spencer's dream are unquestionably of low quality, yet we cannot dismiss them as simply a product of their time. Freddy's assessment of "great graphics," spoken only to the spectator, fully reveals the camp self-mockery of the scene. Robert Englund's makeup and prostheses create a far better embodiment of special effects and elevate the joke's self-awareness further.

In contrast to both the ridiculous visual of Spencer superimposed over cheap video game graphics and gory disfigurements, the camp with which Sontag is concerned exaggerates beautiful features; "the hallmark of Camp is the spirit of extravagance."[17] Yet this may be translated into an exaggeration of the conventions of horror in discussions of the genre. We can locate such a translation in the doubling of persons and embedding of dreams within dreams in *Freddy's Dead*. As with many of the film elements discussed in this chapter, *Freddy's Dead* is not the only film in the franchise to embed dreams; indeed, the disorienting transgressions of the boundaries between the waking and the dreaming worlds are integral to each film's tension. Talalay's installment, however, deploys this element to the point of self-aware ridiculousness. John experiences recurring dreams of a house that is lifted into the air; early in the film, the dream references *The Wizard of Oz* (1939)—an accidental camp classic—as Freddy appears as the Wicked Witch. Later, instead of hovering over the town of Springwood, the house flies all the way into outer space. John wakes from one dream to the next so many times that he ceases to be frightened by the experience. In one such dream sequence, knowing from previous dreams that it is only when he rises from his bed that Freddy will attack, John proclaims that nothing can make him leave the bed, at which point the bed unceremoniously catches fire. John reacts with exasperation rather than fear. Here, the film nods to the audience, whom it knows is equally familiar with such tropes and perhaps is equally bored of them.

Celebrity cameos are also employed in a self-reflexive and camp manner. Just as Talalay credits John Waters as an influence on her filmmaking approach, she suggests her work on *Cry-Baby* guided her decision to include multiple celebrity cameos in *Freddy's Dead*.[18] When Maggie and the teens arrive at the Springwood Town Fair, Tracy, Carlos, and Spencer are soon accosted by a couple, portrayed by Roseanne Barr and Tom Arnold. *Cry-Baby* star and *Elm Street* veteran

Johnny Depp cameos in an antidrug commercial. Rock star Alice Cooper appears in a flashback as Freddy's abusive foster father. Finally, Iggy Pop sings over the film's ending credits, explicitly referencing Freddy in the song's lyrics. While a cameo is not inherently camp, those appearing in *Freddy's Dead* boast an undeniable camp value.

Roseanne Barr provides the only female and arguably most camp cameo. While she has marred her contemporary reputation with problematic political remarks, at the time of Talalay's film, Barr was known as a comedian and actor, often in roles that evoked camp sensibilities. Popularly considered "authentic" in her portrayal of a working-class wife and mother on her sitcom, Barr embodied the "fat female who is not embarrassed by being what social propaganda describes as physically unacceptable and, even more disconcerting, who flaunts her sexuality."[19] Furthermore, she was at the time considered a "disruptive" figure who stood "in opposition to bourgeois and feminine standards of decorum."[20] Her brashness, irreverence, and "refusal to apologize" for her antihegemonic appearance made her prone to media criticism but also imbued her with great potential for camp value, and she had indeed already engaged in self-aware camp performance prior to her *Freddy's Dead* cameo.[21] Although parenthood is already the main theme of *Freddy's Dead*, Barr's performance as deranged mother Ethel lies at an extreme in Barr's preexisting performance trajectory.[22]

Barr's cameo is a camp embodiment of a doting mother. She speaks to the three teenagers as if they are small children, touching their faces and promising that if they go home with her, she will protect them from an unnamed male figure. Just before she is interrupted by her husband, she "gets" the teens' noses, continuing in a parodic display of motherhood. Together, the two appear more as buffoons than grieving parents, yet their antics receive a grotesque gloss that discourages outright comedy. The teens do not yet know the legend of Freddy Krueger, but the audience realizes he is the nameless evil the couple fears, the cause of their children's deaths, and the reason for the town's trauma. The appearance of two celebrity comedians as the only grieving parents imbues the scene with the security of camp while the film navigates a plot more explicitly centered on child abuse than its predecessors.

Depp's cameo also occurs within a camp context. While, like Barr's, Depp's current reputation is far less positive than it once was, he also brings a camp gloss to the film. He had already suffered a dramatic death in the franchise's first installment and had, at the time of filming, recently performed in *Cry-Baby* and *Edward Scissorhands* (1990). Depp's cameo is limited to an appearance in Spencer's dream, in which he re-creates a low-quality antidrug advertisement. Once the audience has had time to recognize him and hear the obligatory line, Freddy disposes of him by hitting him in the head with the frying pan. Where Barr's and Arnold's cameos provide some advancement to the plot, Depp's simply functions as a proverbial wink to the viewer and, in the case of fans of the franchise, an in-group communique. Indeed, humorous self-awareness and cameos provide an appreciable, if at times kitschy, horror-comedy foundation for the film.

Through such casting decisions, *Freddy's Dead* celebrates its own engagement with low culture. It reminds us of what it is and continuously reveals that it *knows* what it is. Where consideration of camp must become more nuanced, however, is in the film's treatment of its more disturbing subject matter. Sexual abuse is an underlying narrative of much of the franchise, and critics have explored readings of Freddy as a substitute villain for actual incest being committed against teen protagonists. David Kingsley, for instance, argues that Freddy is a doppelgänger for Nancy's father.[23] However, unlike its first film's eventual remake in 2010, the original franchise largely maintained the theme of child molestation as an undercurrent. Characters' consistent failure to say what, specifically, Freddy did to the children of Elm Street allows for the continued oppression of the community's youths, unaware of the forces that threaten them.[24]

Freddy's Dead, however, explicitly acknowledges childhood sexual assault and incest in the waking world. Rather than preventing the film from engaging with such dark themes, its camp sensibilities fulfill the metaphorical contract of Freddy Krueger films while challenging fans' enjoyment of the character.[25] Sontag reminds us that despite its humor, camp may concern "grave matters."[26] Freddy's puns, one-liners, and sight gags turn the franchise's films into comedy horror at times, and his humor is so intrinsic to his violence that, Sconce argues, he may be the "real hero" whose victory the audience wishes to see.[27] Because the franchise avoids explicitly identifying Freddy as a pedophile, fans may enjoy his jokes and over-the-top violence without seeming to delight in fictional sexual abuse.

Talalay's film compromises this comfort, emphasizing both camp humor and exaggeration *and* the truth of Freddy's sexual crimes. His pithy remarks are then placed in juxtaposition with the audience's increasing knowledge. In a bright, colorful flashback, humor is transformed into fear when Maggie plays with Freddy in the garden. While he does not threaten her, danger is present when he crouches to extend his hands to her; Loretta's scream and subsequent emergence from the cellar simply redirect that growing dread from daughter to mother. As we hear Freddy's grunts as he kills Loretta aboveground, Maggie wanders into the dark space where her father abuses children. Her tearful childhood promise, "I won't tell," echoes her mother's plea and conspicuously mirrors common experiences of childhood sexual assault victims. A similar challenge to the usual fan enjoyment of Freddy occurs when he impersonates Tracy's father in her dream and tries to molest her. It is clear from Tracy's reactions that Freddy's interpretation of her father as a sexually abusive man is an accurate one; thus we realize that Freddy is revisiting trauma upon a teenage victim of incest. Tracy's memory of her own father adds a discomforting potential for sexual threat in Maggie's connection to Freddy, one that was missing from Freddy's interactions with John.

This is not to say, of course, that the seriousness of childhood sexual assault is to be expected in the work of a female filmmaker taking control of the *Elm Street* narrative. However, we would be remiss to overlook the fact that the only film in the franchise that explicitly incorporates sexual abuse into its narrative is the only one with a woman director. In doing so, we naturally come to consider the possibility of a feminist approach to the film's treatment of its subject matter. Does Talalay's invocation of camp and deployment of two Final Girls necessarily make her film feminist? This is an expected question, one often posed in regard to women's filmmaking as a whole.[28] The mere presence of a female director does not necessarily equate a feminist approach to filmmaking, and critics have sought to unpack how, precisely, we may locate the film director within larger historical and theoretical contexts.[29] Certainly, too, might we typically expect the franchise's only female director to place a feminist gloss on her installment, especially when the series itself has been so concerned with the victimization of women and vulnerable youth. Talalay has linked horror to the feminist movement of the time: "I'm going to be part of this revolution, where I do whatever I think is right, and I'm not going to be stopped. So when horror came along and horror was cool, I did horror."[30] Her decision does not satisfy desires to see women working in the genre out of sheer love for it, but it does point toward a deliberate feminist context for her tenure on the franchise and especially her story and direction. We can, therefore, seek a feminist reading of the film, especially within the context of a male-dominated genre.

An initial feminist subversion occurs in the film's negotiation of Maggie's place within the youth shelter. When she and Tracy return from Springwood, they find that Freddy has somehow "erased" the memories of other characters so that they forget their dead friends. Maggie's boss interprets her insistence on the boys' existence as a sign of fatigue, mirroring the frequent dismissal of women's concerns both within the medical industry and in their own professional spheres. Tracy's traumatized responses are at times dismissed or overlooked. Both women's cases parallel the circumstances in which previous women of Elm Street have been written off as tired, mentally unstable, or paranoid. Jonathan Markovitz acknowledges that horror may challenge presumptions of "female paranoia" by establishing it "as a reasonable response to a world that is hostile to women" but also finds such "critiques" of this implicit societal misogyny to be "blunted . . . when the Final Girl's paranoia is revealed as delusional after all."[31] Other films within the franchise do, at times, fail to challenge such presumptions. Freddy is, after all, primarily limited to the dream world. *Freddy's Dead*, however, centers on the realistic traumas of child abuse that occur prior to Freddy's arrival in characters' dreams. With the exception of John, whose amnesia remains until his death, all the principal characters in the film have been tormented by flesh-and-blood people close to them before they encounter Freddy in the dreamscape.

Yet the film does not go as far as we might perhaps like. Freddy is not made to reckon with his crimes; rather, he dies with a joke, addressing the spectator directly as he mutters, "Kids . . . ," inviting the viewer to once more share in his humor. The film ends with Maggie happily saying, "Freddy's dead," but we are left to imagine what that means for her. So too are we left to imagine what, if any, effect these events will have on Tracy's trauma. That Freddy also suffered in life is made clear. When Maggie pulls Freddy out into the waking world, he pleads with her, "It wasn't my fault. It wasn't. You saw what they did to me." Yet while this literally rehumanized Freddy calls for sympathy and tells the truth about his own murder, he remains nightmarish. He still wears his signature glove, his hand hidden behind his back, thus revealing the threat he still poses to Maggie. As camp "doesn't reverse things" or "argue that the good is bad, or the bad is good," she cannot accept Freddy's trauma as justification for his crimes.[32] It is then satisfying to see her use the glove to kill him, particularly due to camp appropriation of the franchise's iconic fetish object. In this way, too, Maggie challenges the patriarchal order that Freddy represents.[33]

Freddy is *not* a serious character, although his actions have serious ramifications. Sontag ultimately finds that the "whole point of Camp is to dethrone the serious," often through the "frivolous."[34] As his daughter, Maggie is the ideal agent to depose Freddy, and her adoption of his glove as a weapon against him establishes her as an heir to his proverbial throne, a role she shirks once he is dead. She lives out the Final Girl revenge fantasy by briefly tormenting her tormentor, her father, who may (or may not) have abused her—but about whom she has certainly repressed dark memories. Then, however, she simply walks away from the scene, rendering Freddy's dethronement a frivolous act that at the same time successfully defeats a serious monster.

It is likely that some of the film's visually camp qualities were the result of financial limitations rather than directorial choice. Talalay has openly expressed disappointment in some areas of the film, such as its more lackluster special effects, and has also wondered "if it was a mistake to go the humorous, tongue-in-cheek route with Freddy" instead of "full-on horror."[35] Yet she has followed such questions with an assurance that the film was, for all its flaws, a response to how "predictable" horror had become. The film then requires the franchise and its viewers to engage in new ways with familiar content. That this is largely achieved through camp imbues the film with a critically overlooked value that warrants further consideration of its place in feminist filmmaking.

Analysis of the film with regard to its maker causes us to consider how, precisely, we locate Talalay within this work. Considering women film directors within a feminist framework requires additional efforts not to simply add them to discussions of a male-dominated medium.[36] When women are recognized as makers within the horror genre, they are frequently regarded with contradictory tendencies that regard them as valuable feminist voices while lambasting them for engaging in the tropes and imagery of a genre frequently accused of being misogynistic.[37] Women directors making horror films thus come to the genre already burdened with the pressures of conflicting and extensive expectations. Talalay's acknowledgment of the collaborative nature of filmmaking may challenge attempts to credit her as a creator or even auteur in this case. However, while her story was not the only one considered for the film's narrative, her outline was chosen, an outline that replaced the male hero with a female one. Women viewers might especially take pleasure in Talalay's bait-and-switch replacement of John with Katherine as Freddy's true heir and the film's hero. In this way, Talalay participates in the rewriting of the male-dominated cultural script that is so historically significant to women's filmmaking.[38] This does not in itself necessarily impose a feminist value on the film, but it does offer such possibilities for the viewer to do so; indeed, Jane Gaines cautions us not to overlook the audience as another contributor to a film's meaning.[39]

One of the richest areas in which we may find feminist value lies in Talalay's own irreverence toward the film. As discussed earlier, she has openly addressed the film's flaws and has expressed ambivalence about her and her collaborators' approach to the film as a whole. She has also expressed a lack of decision-making power in the film's editing for television and DVD releases, and her similar candor in these admissions further reminds us of a director's limitations.[40] We may thus retrospectively see the frank self-awareness of the film as a reflection of her directing philosophy. Perhaps the greatest instance to enable such a reading occurs in the inclusion of Iggy Pop's "Why Was I Born (Freddy's Dead)" over the end credits. The final lyrics pose the cynical question "You think Freddy's dead? You really think Freddy's dead?" Talalay reveals that this was not initially a planned challenge to the film but says, "It's so ballsy that we kept that. It's like our own fuck you to ourselves, I think."[41]

Tasked with the film that would kill Freddy Krueger, Talalay had the opportunity to create a definitive conclusion to a franchise, albeit within the parameters imposed by the studio. Iggy Pop's song contradicts Talalay's own conclusion, but her allowance of it as the final word on the film demonstrates a bold, antiauteur choice that may even increase the film's self-reflexive camp. Ultimately, while Talalay is not the mythological ideal of the feminist horror director simultaneously sought after and condemned by critics, she nonetheless positions herself in an appropriate place of refreshing authenticity.

Notes

1   Susan Sontag, "Notes on Camp," in *A Susan Sontag Reader*, ed. Elizabeth Hardwick (New York: Farrar, Straus and Giroux, 1982), 105.
2   Annette Kuhn, *Women's Pictures: Feminism and Cinema* (London: Verso, 1994), 24.
3   Peter Bloore, *The Screenplay Business: Managing Creativity and Script Development in the Film Industry* (London: Routledge, 2013), 11.

4   "Exclusive Interview: Rachel Talalay," Nightmare on Elm Street Companion, March 22, 2005, http://nightmareonelmstreetfilms.com/site/exclusive-interview -rachel-talalay.

5   Pamela Robertson, "What Makes the Feminist Camp?," in *Camp: Queer Aesthetics and the Performing Subject: A Reader*, ed. Fabio Cleto (Ann Arbor: University of Michigan Press, 1999), 266–283.

6   Andrew Britton, "For Interpretation: Notes against Camp," in Cleto, *Camp*, 136–142.

7   Sontag, "Notes," 105; David MacGregor Johnston, "Kitsch and Camp and Things That Go Bump in the Night; or, Sontag and Adorno at the (Horror) Movies," in *The Philosophy of Horror*, ed. Thomas Fahy (Lexington: University Press of Kentucky, 2010), 238.

8   Casey Ryan Kelly, "Camp Horror and the Gendered Politics of Screen Violence: Subverting the Monstrous-Feminine in *Teeth* (2007)," *Women's Studies in Communication* 39, no. 1 (2016): 93.

9   Johnston, "Kitsch," 233–235.

10 Sontag, "Notes," 110.

11 Sontag, 112.

12 Sontag, 109.

13 See James Kendrick, "Razors in the Dreamscape: Revisiting *A Nightmare on Elm Street* and the Slasher Film," *Film Criticism* 3, no. 3 (2009): 17–33.

14 Carol J. Clover, *Men, Women, and Chain Saws: Gender in the Modern Horror Film* (Princeton, N.J.: Princeton University Press, 1992), 168; Jeffrey Sconce, "Spectacles of Death: Identification, Reflexivity, and Contemporary Horror," in *Film Theory Goes to the Movies*, ed. Jim Collins, Hilary Radner, and Ava Preacher Collins (New York: Routledge, 1993), 111.

15 Sontag, "Notes," 108.

16 "Exclusive Interview."

17 Sontag, "Notes," 112.

18 Aaron Williams, "*Freddy's Dead* (for Now, Anyways . . .): Director Rachel Talalay!," Bloody Disgusting, November 14, 2011, http://bloody-disgusting.com/interviews/ 27226/interview-freddys-dead-for-now-anyways-director-rachel-talalay.

19 Zita Z. Dresner, "Roseanne Barr: Goddess or She-Devil," *Journal of American Culture* 16, no. 2 (1993): 37–38.

20 Kathleen K, Rowe, "Roseanne: Unruly Woman as Domestic Goddess," *Screen* 31, no. 4 (1990): 411.

21 Dresner, "Roseanne Barr," 40.

22 Janet Lee, "Subversive Sitcoms: *Roseanne* as Inspiration for Feminist Resistance," *Women's Studies* 21, no. 1 (1992): 94–95.

23 David Kingsley, "Elm Street's Gothic Roots: Unearthing Incest in Wes Craven's 1984 Nightmare," *Journal of Popular Film and Television* 41, no. 3 (2012): 145–153.

24 Sarah Trencansky, "Final Girls and Terrible Youth: Transgression in 1980s Slasher Horror," *Journal of Popular Film and Television* 29, no. 1 (2001): 68–69.

25 Sconce, "Spectacles," 104–105.

26 Sontag, "Notes," 106.

27 Sconce, "Spectacles," 104.

28 Kuhn, *Women's Pictures*, 219.

29 Kuhn, 10.

30 S. E. Smith, "'Now More Than Ever, We Need to Keep up the Battle': A Conversation with Feminist Director Rachel Talalay," *Bitch Media*, January 3, 2017, https://www .bitchmedia.org/article/q-rachel-talalay-sherlock-dr-who-feminist-director.

31 Jonathan Markovitz, "Female Paranoia as Survival Skill: Reason or Pathology in *A Nightmare on Elm Street*?," *Quarterly Review of Film and Video* 17, no. 3 (2000): 219.

32 Sontag, "Notes," 114.

33 Trencansky, "Final Girls," 68–72; Markovitz, "Female Paranoia," 211–219.

34 Sontag, "Notes," 116.

35 "Exclusive Interview."

36 Claire Johnston, "Dorothy Arzner: Critical Strategies," in *The Work of Dorothy Arzner: Towards a Feminist Cinema*, ed. Claire Johnston (London: BFI, 1975), 2.

37 Katarzyna Paszkiewicz, "When the Woman Directs (a Horror Film)," in *Women Do Genre in Film and Television*, ed. Mary Harrod and Katarzyna Paszkiewicz (New York: Routledge, 2018), 45–48.

38 Johnston, "Dorothy Arzner," 4–6.

39 Jane M. Gaines, "The Genius of Genre and the Ingenuity of Women," in *Gender Meets Genre in Postwar Cinemas*, ed. Christine Gledhill (Champaign: University of Illinois Press, 2012), 15.

40 "Exclusive Interview."

41 Williams, "*Freddy's Dead*."

Why *Office Killer* Matters

DAHLIA SCHWEITZER

Office Killer (1997) is the story of lowly and awkward Dorine Douglas, copyeditor for *Constant Consumer* magazine. After accidentally electrocuting the office sleaze, Dorine realizes she can circumvent the isolation brought on by corporate downsizing by simply moving the office home with her. One by one, she murders her former colleagues. The over-the-top and slightly "off" camp horror emerges as Dorine tends to her dead colleagues in her basement at home. She tapes over the gaping holes in their bodies, sprays glass cleaner as a general disinfectant, and neatly arranges the bodies so they can all watch television together. Only when her work is done, when she has re-created the office at home with her victims' corpses, does Dorine drive off into the sunset, ready to find other work and other friends in a new city.

One of the most striking aspects of *Office Killer* is that it is the only film made by Cindy Sherman, an artist known internationally for her photographs dealing with identity, gender, and media. Born in New Jersey in 1954, Sherman spent her childhood on Long Island, immersed in the television and culture of the era. The 1950s combined worries of nuclear war with dreams of a better life and conformity with capitalism, all amid a growing blitzkrieg of images selling everything from washing machines to cigarettes, bras to Cadillacs. What better time to be watching (and absorbing) television? What better time to be introduced to the constant consuming at the heart of American life? The climate of her early years, which explored what it meant to be a woman through the cultural vernacular of the 1950s, influenced not only Sherman's first major series, "Untitled Film Stills," but also all of Sherman's later photographs and *Office Killer*.

The original concept for *Office Killer* came from executive producers James Schamus and Ted Hope's desire to make a smart horror film, an experiment to see if people with more independent orientations could contribute to the genre. Between them, they were producers / executive producers on many independent films, including *Eat Drink Man Woman* (1994), *Safe* (1995), *The Ice Storm* (1997), and *Happiness* (1998). Schamus and Hope were intrigued by the possibility of making hybrid films that could work as both genre films and art-house films. As Schamus explains, these films are known as "tweeners," as in films that fall between genres and specific audiences. The problem with these films is that, by their very nature, they do not "address or satisfy the received and perceived cultural needs and desires of any specific intended audience," which means that in order for an "in-between" film to succeed, it must have either "extraordinary good fortune" or be an extremely powerful text.[1]

Schamus and Hope approached Christine Vachon, producer / executive producer on *Poison* (1991), *Swoon* (1992), *Go Fish* (1994), *Kids* (1995), and *Safe*. In turn, Vachon approached Sherman, who was represented by the same gallery as Vachon's girlfriend. Sherman, amazingly for someone who always prefers to work alone, agreed to do the project. She was reassured by Vachon that she would have full creative freedom, despite being a first-time director who had never worked in film before. Once she had signed on, *Office Killer* costume designer Todd Thomas confirmed, "There was a collective reverence, on behalf of the entire crew, to participate in making a film that was something truly Shermanesque. I mean *everyone* was on board. We were all so excited to be involved in this project."[2]

The excitement was understandable. After all, *Office Killer* is also one of the most important horror films you have never seen. Here's why:

It Reinvents Horror

At first glance, *Office Killer* seems clear, simple, and comfortable in its clichés. It is a horror film. There are dead bodies. There is murder, a killer, and a self-styled detective. There is some fear, some camp, some screaming. In fact, when *Office Killer* was first released, it seemed so basic that many film critics, art critics, and academics ignored it altogether. That was a mistake. First of all, there is nothing basic about *Office Killer*. The fact that it is the only film directed by Cindy Sherman is just the beginning. As a "tweener," the film lurks between genres; it is more of a dark "chick flick" combined with elements of neonoir, black comedy, and horror. All the main characters are female, and their relationships echo a Joan Crawford–led women's picture from an earlier era, where films like *The Women* (1939) and *Mildred Pierce* (1945) explored the complicated interpersonal dynamics between women and their struggles for men, power, and independence. There are also numerous thematic and atmospheric parallels between *Office Killer* and *Whatever Happened to Baby Jane?* (1962), another mix of horror and melodrama from three decades earlier. Nothing about this movie follows the rules (of genre).

Carol Clover + Christine Vachon + Cindy Sherman + Tea = *Office Killer*

When James Schamus was working on his PhD at the University of California, Berkeley, his dissertation advisor was Carol Clover, the renowned writer of the canonical book *Men, Women, and Chain Saws: Gender in the Modern Horror Film* (1992). When Clover was in New York during the mid-1990s, Schamus decided it would be fascinating to bring the writer of "the greatest book of analysis on slasher films ever written" together with "the woman who's completely re-envisioned how you look and feel about the entire heritage of movies." So Schamus invited Vachon and Sherman to join him and Clover at his home for tea. While the exact content of the evening remains confidential—although Sherman does confirm that Clover's book *Men, Women, and Chainsaws* was very inspirational—the result of the evening is clear: *Office Killer*.[3]

It Is an Integral Part of Cindy Sherman's Body of Work

This is Sherman's only work with sound, motion, and a title and that involves collaboration with other people. So why there is so little discussion of *Office Killer* as a film? It is almost completely ignored in critical discussions of Sherman's work post-1997, and when it appears, it is merely as a means to turn the conversation to her photos. This creates a limited, one-dimensional perspective that prohibits any real complex understanding of her work.[4] If we examine the film and the way that, like her photos, it twists and parodies horror, fashion, and melodrama, we gain not only insight into the work of one of American's greatest living photographers but also a richer understanding of social and cultural complexities during the late 1990s. *Office Killer* constantly references the circulation of materials, as articles move from one desk to another, emails from one computer to another, all mimicking the path of "Gary's cold," much as AIDS spread in New York City in the 1980s. Visually and metaphorically, the film also represents a culture that began in the 1990s but continues to this day: of being homebound at an inappropriate age, fighting to slow down body decomposition, and struggling with an increasing awareness of the contagions that must be kept at bay. Gary Michaels, it is made clear from the beginning of the film, is the staff slut, the lothario who is also the magazine's head writer. He spreads words at the same time as germs. We can trace the route of "Gary's cold" by its remnants, which are everywhere: the pills on Gary's desk, the echinacea on Virginia's desk, and Norah's stuffy nose. Norah, the magazine's manager, passes out the downsizing pink slips with a dirty tissue clenched in her hand. Her pink slips are little notices of doom indicating the metaphorical equivalent of a positive or negative test result. She spreads contagion with every slip she gives out. The office has been infected with more than just a cold.[5] This movie helps us understand the impact AIDS had on intimacy and our awareness of our own susceptibility to death and of the increased attention to the maintenance required in order to stay alive.

It Acts as a Time Capsule

While some movies are timeless, featuring plots and/or characters that can easily be adapted for any decade, *Office Killer* is a film uniquely of its moment. As Tom Kalin, who worked on the script for *Office Killer*, explains, the film specifically examines the role of women in the workplace as well as what is valued in that space. In particular, Kalin was drawn to the idea of a culture moving past someone who had once been qualified: "People have forgotten what happened post-eighties and the crash into the early nineties, but this feeling of downsizing, the feeling of reduced expectations, which we're now quite familiar with in America, there was a kind of freshness to that in the midnineties at the time."[6] If you want to understand America in the 1990s and the impact that technology had on the workplace during the early days of email, you need to watch this movie.

The Monster Is a Woman; the Monster Is Also Capitalism

Norah is responsible for shifting the status quo and for altering the equilibrium in the narrative. As such, she is the film's vampire: a monster and Dorine's antagonist. Responsible for downsizing the staff, changing working patterns from full time to part time, and setting up employees to work from home, Norah is the capitalistic force destroying the status quo at *Constant Consumer* magazine. Not only does Norah represent our fears of being downsized as well as our fears of powerful and manipulative women (a reference to both noir films and changing gender roles in the workplace), but she also reflects the aspect of capitalism in which the bottom line is valued over everything else, where quality of life is sacrificed for ambition and success. About halfway through the film, Kim turns to Daniel and asks, "What do you think, Danny boy? Is your girlfriend a corporate monster yet or what?" The question here is not whether she *is* a corporate monster but if she is one *yet*. Tellingly, Norah is the first character to have blood on her hands. Dorine only gets blood on her hands *after* tangling with Norah.

Norah is responsible for sucking the lifeblood out of the company to illegally feed her own bank account; she causes the disequilibrium that precipitates her downfall.

The Serial Killer Is the "Final Girl"

Clover's concept of the Final Girl (discussed in chapter 5 by Katia Houde) can be applied to Dorine, albeit with a twist. She is the only character to be developed in any psychological detail, and hers is the main storyline. She is intelligent and watchful, the first character to respond to the changes happening in the workplace, the first to determine Norah's role in the downsizing, and the first to ascertain the "pattern and extent of the threat." During the film's closing sequence, our attachment to her becomes absolute as we drive off into the sunset together. Having said this, the most unconventional part of Dorine's personality—which does not fit with the model for the classic Final Girl—is her habit of killing her coworkers (not to mention two young Girl Scouts) and accumulating their bodies. If, however, we reframe Dorine's killing as a rescuing of her coworkers from Norah's vampiric clutches and the final basement scene as Dorine versus the monster, the Final Girl template remains the perfect fit.

It Is a Feminist Manifesto

Office Killer is one of the few horror movies with an (almost) all-female cast, featuring Carol Kane, Jeanne Tripplehorn, Molly Ringwald, and Barbara Sukova in lead roles. Many of the people involved in making the film are also female: it is not only directed by Sherman but also cowritten with Elise MacAdam and produced by Christine Vachon and Pamela Koffler. The film itself also interrogates gender expectations within the horror genre. One of the popular criticisms of horror is misogyny, that the genre punishes female sexuality. As Clover explains, "The relation between the sexes in slasher films could hardly be clearer. The killer is with few exceptions recognizably human and distinct male . . . [while] his victims are mostly women, often sexually free and always young and beautiful."[7] However, here, *Office Killer* further contradicts expectations by giving us not only a female monster but also a Final Girl.

By positioning the Final Girl as a figure of strength in the horror picture, John Berger's original dynamic of "men act, women appear" (or "men stab, women die" when it comes to horror) becomes complicated. After all, it is the Final Girl who is tasked with the responsibility of bringing down the evil beast, and in her final battle with Norah in her basement, Dorine stabs Norah with a very long knife. Dorine is not our heroine, because if she were the heroine, then by necessity, she would have been "saved by someone else." Dorine is a *hero* by virtue of the fact that she "rises to the occasion and defeats the adversary with his [or, in this case, *her*] own wit and hands," standing "in the light of day with the knife in her hand," an adult at last.[8] This position fuses archetypes and gender expectations, because as Sherman herself explains, Dorine is very unassuming and then finds empowerment and confidence from killing.[9]

After she has killed Norah, Dorine languorously fluffs her hair off her shoulders, a gesture strangely out of place considering that (1) Dorine is not the beautiful woman we normally associate with this move and (2) she is covered in blood. It is clear, however, that she is now someone new. There is a primal, scorched-earth quality to the eradication of her former self: she sets her house on fire, destroying any traces of her victims or former self in the tradition of a funeral rite. In burning down the house, she also destroys the difficult memories of her sexually abusive father and her disbelieving mother, fully integrating the trauma they caused her into the text of her symbolic tradition. With her mission accomplished and her reinvention complete, Dorine puts on a blond wig, clamps a cigarette between her lips, and drives into the distance, in search of the American dream.[10]

Blonde Ambition

Hair, as every woman knows, is crucial to identity. A redhead will often be defined by her hair, much as a blonde is remembered by hers. Long, shaggy, hippy hair says one thing about you. A neat Louise Brooks style says the exact opposite. When *Office Killer* begins, Dorine's hair is brown, scraggly, uneven, reflecting the type of girl who is considered mousy, awkward, and unattractive. This is why it is important when, in the last scene, as Dorine strikes out on the road, that her hair is smooth, shiny, trim, and *blonde*, a color that represents eroticism, power, and, as Camille Paglia has observed, deception.[11] The idea of "going blonde" is more than just switching hair colors. It is a statement and a state of mind. Blonde has deep cultural significance, and each shade of blonde has its own narrative. There is the Hitchcock icy blonde, personified by Grace Kelly and Kim Novak, and the sunny warm blonde of Farrah Fawcett, Goldie Hawn, and Blake Lively. It represents icons and fairy-tale princesses, Playboy centerfolds, and California girls.[12] With her blond wig, Dorine channels the ultimate ice-queen femme fatale of 1990s cinema, Catherine Tramell, played by Sharon Stone, in neonoir *Basic Instinct* (1992).

Office Killer Is the Unacknowledged Sequel to *Basic Instinct*

Dorine has similarities to Catherine that run deeper than the shade of her hair. Catherine and Dorine threaten the men and the status quo because of their defiance of traditional feminine roles, not merely because they reject their biological responsibility to bear children, but also because of their general defiance of expectations for feminine behavior. Rejecting submissive and obedient roles, they represent the fundamental aspect of the femme fatale: male fear of women. After all, the femme fatale is "defined by her dangerous, yet desirable, sexual presence."[13] Even if Dorine does not look like the conventional femme fatale—she is not beautiful, her figure is not lean and enticing, her outfits are awkward and frumpy—she is just as much a threat, if not more so, than the femme fatale of any classic noir.

The most obvious parallel between the two films is actress Jeanne Tripplehorn, who plays Beth in *Basic Instinct* and Norah in *Office Killer*. If, as Godard famously said, every film is a documentary of its actors, then every film is also a repository of roles previously played by those actors. We cannot separate Molly Ringwald, who plays Kim, from her on-screen persona in *The Breakfast Club* (1985) or *Sixteen Candles* (1984), just as we cannot separate Jeanne Tripplehorn from Beth, the role she played in her feature film debut. Despite the fact that Beth seems less experienced and poised than Norah, both characters are conniving. In *Office Killer* and *Basic Instinct*, Tripplehorn plays characters responsible for disrupting the status quo of the office, for not doing what they are supposed to do, for not performing their jobs from a structural point of view. In *Office Killer*, Norah is the manager who illegally embezzles the magazine's funds; in *Basic Instinct*, Beth is the psychologist who betrays, enables, and sleeps with her patient. Beth and Norah are not the only ones breaking the rules, but they are the central instigators.

One of the biggest mysteries left unanswered in *Basic Instinct* is what happens to Beth. Even though the film implies that the character of Beth Garner is shot to death by Nick, this is never confirmed; we do not see a dead body, and the stretcher leaves the scene empty. For whatever reason, Beth's fate is left unclear, which leads to an unconventional but intriguing possibility. If Beth had lived on, would she have changed her name a second time? Could she have changed her career from psychologist to office manager? Could she have moved from San Francisco to New York? And if she had switched careers and changed her name, would she be embezzling funds and downsizing employees at *Constant Consumer* magazine? Vague, unspoken, sequel-type relationships between films with the same actor and/or by the same director are common in Italian neorealism, including Luchino Visconti's *Ossessione* (1943), *La Terra Trema* (1948), and *Rocco and His Brothers* (1960) or Michelangelo Antonioni's *Story of a Love Affair* (1950). So why not in *Basic Instinct* and *Office Killer*?

The Antitechnology Message Is Even More Relevant Today

Dorine's actions are in retaliation to the late twentieth- and early twenty-first-century reality of corporate downsizing and outsourcing, aided by new technologies and fueled by corporate vampirism. Technology makes the corporeal disappear, replaced by virtual humans separated from each other by physical miles but with the illusion of instant shared community. *Office Killer* saw this coming. Watching the bodies of Dorine's coworkers disintegrate, we are reminded of the oozing organs at the other end of email accounts and twitter feeds. Dorine maintains her coworker's dead bodies, refusing to acknowledge their deterioration. She pulls Virginia's fingernails off, telling her that she will be more comfortable without them. She sprays Gary down with Windex and pulls him back together with tape. "It's so much harder to be on your toes when you're not feeling fresh as a daisy," she tells her former coworkers as she primps and adjusts them. Sherman confesses that the scenes in which Dorine tidies the bodies are her favorite.[14]

Dorine makes bodies real again, a retaliation to the shallow emptiness of contemporary life. As the offices of *Constant Consumer* magazine grow more computer reliant and more sterile, the messiness of person-to-person contact eradicated by the prophylactic of the keyboard, Dorine wages a one-woman campaign to remind us of the superficiality of that pursuit.

It Is the Most Unusual Coming-of-Age Movie You Have Ever Seen

Office Killer, at its most fundamental, is the story of Dorine's journey of self-discovery, her journey to independence. The narrative of the child struggling to "break away from the mother" (especially when the father is absent and the maternal figure is constructed as the monstrous feminine) is a common one in horror film; *Psycho* (1960), *Carrie* (1976), and *The Birds* (1963) revolve around this conflict.[15] The close hold the mother has on the child defines the mother's existence but also prevents the child from having an existence of his or her own. The problem comes down to borders and where to draw them, since the mother's power over the child is one that defies borders. After all, the child was once *in* the mother, and now here she is outside of her but still not free.

At the beginning of *Office Killer*, we see Dorine alternating working and caring for her mother, awkward and uncomfortable in her own skin. The bulk of the film shows Dorine discovering how to talk while defining herself apart from her mother, but it takes the mother's (natural) death for Dorine to be finally separated from her. Dorine's first significant disturbance is the downsizing at work, but her mother's death is the major trauma, a pivotal moment of change in Dorine's existence, one that allows for the ultimate release of her *self* into the world.

After burning down the family home and destroying all ties to her past life, Dorine drives away. As she does so, she looks at herself in the rearview mirror, the first time she truly sees herself. At first, she glances in the mirror, but then she removes her sunglasses and looks again. Even though she is driving, she stares into the mirror at her reflected eyes. Satisfied, she puts the sunglasses back on, and in voice-over, she comments, "If there is one thing I have learned, it is accepting my limitations while accentuating my strengths." In other words, she has now learned who she is and has, finally, come of age.

Conclusion

When asked about the lack of academic and artistic attention paid to *Office Killer*, Schamus points out that part of the "problem" is that the film is "technically an embarrassment." But it is not an embarrassment in the usual sense. Rather, as Schamus explains, it is an embarrassment to "dominant modes of discourse" that traditionally "validate artistic film and video precisely because it's not lending itself to the logic of showing up at a gallery and being editioned as three signed DVDs for a billion dollars each." As Sherman has confirmed, this difficulty of placement made Miramax nervous about "what to do" or "how to market" the film.[16] The "problem" with *Office Killer* then is precisely what makes it interesting; as Schamus argues, "Its mode of address is quite different."

Office Killer, much like Sherman herself, lives in the in-between spaces, defying categorization. Sherman's work is just as likely to appear in an ad for Marc Jacobs as it is a retrospective at the National Portrait Gallery. The film is occasionally screened as part of a Sherman retrospective, but even then, it feels out of place. At the retrospective "Cindy Sherman: Imitation of Life," held in Los Angeles in 2016, the Broad Museum played *Office Killer* on loop in its entirety. Exhibited in a darkened room just off from the main exhibition area, visitors would step inside, perplexed for a minute or two before reemerging, blinking, as they readjusted to the bright lights on the photographs. I doubt anyone sat in that room for the film's full eighty-seven-minute runtime. And that was their loss. Because despite the fact that it eludes categorization—or perhaps precisely *because* it eludes categorization—*Office Killer* is a horror film that redefines not only gender representation but genre expectation. It is not simply a horror film or a comedy film or an art film, and this makes it difficult to market and to pigeonhole. Shortly after its release, film critic Edward Guthmann condemned the film for not being able to decide what it wants to be, a "slasher film, social satire, or revenge comedy."[17] Why not all of the above?

Notes

1   James Schamus, interview with author, January 5, 2012.
2   Todd Thomas, interview with author, January 13, 2012.
3   Cindy Sherman, interview with author, June 5, 2019.
4   Dahlia Schweitzer, *Cindy Sherman's Office Killer: Another Kind of Monster* (Bristol: Intellect, 2014), 6.
5   Schweitzer, 142.
6   Tom Kalin, interview with author, January 19, 2012.
7   Carol J. Clover, *Men, Women and Chain Saws: Gender in the Modern Horror Film* (Princeton, N.J.: Princeton University Press, 1992), 42.
8   Clover, 49, 59.
9   Cindy Sherman, interview with author, May 29, 2019.
10 Schweitzer, *Cindy Sherman's Office Killer*, 101–102.

11 "Commentary with Camille Paglia," bonus feature on *Basic Instinct* DVD (Santa Monica, Calif.: Artisan Entertainment, 2001).

12 Schweitzer, *Cindy Sherman's Office Killer*, 162.

13 Karen Hollinger, "Film Noir, Voice-Over and the Femme Fatale," in *Film Noir Reader*, ed. Alain Silver and James Ursini (New York: Limelight Editions, 2000), 246.

14 Sherman, interview with author.

15 Barbara Creed, "Horror and the Monstrous-Feminine," *Screen* 27, no. 1 (1986): 50.

16 Noriko Fuko, "A Woman of Parts: Interview with Cindy Sherman," *Art in America* 85 (June 1997), https://alanandgretchen.wordpress.com/2011/04/05/american-suburb-x-interview-with-artist-cindy-sherman-a-woman-of-parts/.

17 Edward Guthmann, "Messy *Office Killer* Needs Some Work," SFGate, December 12, 1997, https://www.sfgate.com/movies/article/Messy-Office-Killer-Needs-Some-Work-Mishmash-2790616.php.

8

Murders and Adaptations

Gender in *American Psycho*

LAURA MEE

American Psycho (2000) is an adaptation of Bret Easton Ellis's controversial novel about Manhattanite serial killer Patrick Bateman.[1] On the surface, he leads a life that is simultaneously exceptional and unremarkable. A wealthy and privileged investment banker at a company his father "practically owns," he is interchangeable with his facsimiled Wall Street acquaintances. Impeccably groomed, handsome, and charming, Bateman dresses in the right designer clothes and eats the best dishes in the coolest new restaurants, meticulously researched in an obsessive effort to assimilate with people who share his lifestyle. He is the epitome of the 1980s yuppie, rich and self-centered, an ironic figure of American individualism.

He is also a psychopath. Bateman's murderous tendencies are laid out in lurid detail throughout Ellis's book, and he does not discriminate in selecting victims. While he employs violence as a display of superiority, he inflicts it against men, women, children, animals, colleagues and strangers, partners and sex workers, the wealthy and the destitute. But he especially revels in the torture and mutilation of women. This sadism features in long chapters in Ellis's novel, where graphic accounts of sexual trysts suddenly switch to gruesome sequences of explicit violence, continually narrated in first person in the same detached detail Bateman reserves for describing a designer suit or his favorite Whitney Houston record. The book's sexualized violence ensured a backlash from critics, feminist activist groups, and even its intended publisher, who dropped the novel after a leaked chapter published in *Time* magazine invoked ire. Reviewers dubbed it "obscene" and accused Ellis of "crimes against women," and Tammy Bruce of the National Organization of Women called it "a how-to novel on the torture and dismemberment of women."[2]

The controversy inevitably encouraged interest in adapting the book to screen. Producer Edward R. Pressman purchased the rights soon after publication, and various writers and directors, including Stuart Gordon and David Cronenberg, were attached to the project throughout the early 1990s; Ellis wrote a script for Cronenberg that ended with a musical number atop the World Trade Center, a result of his boredom with the material.[3] Persuaded by her debut feature *I Shot Andy Warhol* (1996), Pressman suggested the adaptation to Mary Harron, who drafted a screenplay with Guinevere Turner and cast Christian Bale as Bateman in a good-faith deal.[4] Distributor Lionsgate, concerned over Bale's then-minimal star appeal, halted progress for talks with other key figures, including Oliver Stone and Leonardo DiCaprio. Harron came back on board when DiCaprio left, and *American Psycho* entered production in 1999.

During filming, protests by the National Organization of Women and the Feminist Majority Foundation (FMF) recalled responses to Ellis's book, with the FMF insisting there were "no redeeming qualities to a misogynist product like this."[5] This reaction was to "an idea" of what the film would be, shaped by the reception of the novel alone.[6] In response to the backlash, as David Eldridge has argued, "the discourse surrounding and justifying the film was deliberately shaped to retrieve the novel from its 'trash' reputation," at once distancing the adaptation from the perceived misogyny of its source while also contributing to the growing reevaluation of Ellis's book as a misunderstood satire of 1980s consumption culture.[7] The involvement of female filmmakers was further promoted as a corrective measure. Harron noted that, as women, they "removed some danger of offense," while Turner suggested it was a "strategic move to get a woman at the helm" and, furthermore, that the controversy, although "painful in spots," could only be good for promotion.[8]

Ultimately, Harron's film is a slick, darkly comic adaptation that quells the shocking violence of Ellis's novel, excluding or reframing a number of its more provocative sequences to ensure it was generally well received by broad audiences. Yet the tension between its origins and its final form meant that it was also not an easy fit within the horror genre. While the critical reception of the novel's perceived misogyny has been explored and Harron and Turner's approaches to tempering the book's violent excesses considered elsewhere, the primary concern of studies of *American Psycho* have been to examine its neoliberal, consumerist satire, often alongside considerations of male identity and masculinity in crisis.[9] This is of course central to the world that Bateman occupies in 1980s Wall Street, and he often conflates his professional work and his dark pursuits. For example, he replies "murders and executions" to a potential victim who asks him what he does. "Do you like it?" she asks, mishearing him, continuing, "Most guys I know, who work in mergers and acquisitions, really don't like it."

Bateman's identity and behavior are intrinsically linked to *American Psycho*'s female characters. The film's representation of gender—especially women—warrants further investigation then, particularly in light of the female creators. This chapter explores Harron and Turner's adaptive approach to gender and misogyny, considering the perspectives of female characters, and develops an understanding of how these choices impact the film's position within the horror genre.

Hip to Be Square: Patrick Bateman

Harron and Turner adapted Patrick Bateman for the screen by emphasizing his ridiculousness. This highlights the contrast between the antagonist and the more sympathetic characters he kills. Harron fought to keep Bale in the role, despite the studio insistence on DiCaprio. During the development backlash, Gloria Steinem warned DiCaprio not to play Bateman in case of any influence on his newfound teen fans of *Titanic* (1997).[10] Other actors including Johnny Depp, Billy Crudup, and Tom Cruise were considered. Cruise ultimately inspired Bale with a particular "energy," a "very intense friendliness with nothing behind the eyes," a fitting muse given Ellis's Bateman is starstruck by the actor, fluffing a chance meeting in an elevator.[11] Harron's insistence on Bale makes sense. His performance, by turns comically manic and emotionally blank, emphasizes the black comedy and horror of the character while embodying his facade, the performative construction of the personality he presents himself as, the "idea of a Patrick Bateman, some kind of abstraction . . . an entity . . . something illusory." In her study of Harron's biopics about controversial female figures including Bettie Page and Valarie Solanas, Linda Badley argues that the director deconstructs this "Great Man genre" through a sociocultural perspective: "[She] rejects the popular psychology associated with therapy culture; [and] instead sustains a postmodern understanding of the self as a social construct and a Foucauldian view of mores and sexuality as culturally scripted, while emphasizing performativity."[12] The same is true of her interpretation of Bateman, and she explains her casting decision. Other actors were too concerned with the character's history, wanting to develop psychological motivation. Bale instead saw Bateman as the construct, the "abstraction" that Ellis had intended and that Harron and Turner wanted to emphasize.[13]

Bale imagined him as "pathetic" and certainly "not a cool guy." His performance has been described as "hammy," but Bateman is not vastly different in the book, where he frequently embarrasses himself in awkward social interactions with his clumsy attempts at smoothness.[14] Bale's performance allows the character to be more readily mocked as he emphasizes Bateman's "loser" nature. Turner noted how men had approached her since the film's release claiming, "Wow, I am Patrick Bateman." "Are you saying you're a dork or a serial killer?" became her standard response.[15] Bale's sculpted, muscular physicality may at first seem counterintuitive to this by emphasizing his attractiveness. In a long sequence early in the film, Bateman addresses the audience, introducing himself and his extensive daily exercise and grooming regimen while shots focus on his body and face. As Kooijman and Laine argue of this scene, "The way Bateman is portrayed as an 'object-to-be-looked-at.' . . . His perfectly sculpted body seems to invite female (and gay) spectators to look in an erotic, active way."[16] "It's straight up objectification," Turner has confirmed, further suggesting that the focus on the masculine form is a response to the misogyny of the text.[17] The novel's sexual focus on women (or rather, on parts of women) is here removed and reframed as a focus on male sexuality. It is not surprising that Bateman's monstrosity is not physically evident. As Steffen Hantke has argued, "The body of the serial killer is not a site of abjection, despite what one might expect from the way its appearance is so often staged. Indeed, the vast majority of serial killers lack that one crucial feature which . . . effectively defines the monstrous: their evil is not written on their bodies."[18] Bateman's good looks play part in a privileged lifestyle that allows him to repeatedly get away with murder. Yet Harron directs Bale in a way that often mocks Bateman's self-obsession and ridicules his sex appeal. A scene in which he films himself having a threesome with two sex workers was directed to be deliberately awkward and ungainly, but he watches himself in the mirror throughout, posing, flexing his muscles, and pointing at his reflection, living his fantasy while totally oblivious to the absurdity of the scenario.[19]

For Harron and Turner, the book's focus on the crisis of masculinity and its response to the rise of feminism was a key consideration in adaptation.[20] Bateman's contempt for women spirals from this crisis, but his status singles him out from other groups on which he also invokes his rage. He murders Al, a homeless man, but not before humiliating and goading him. His homophobia is apparent in the novel, where he makes no effort to hide his disgust toward Luis Carruthers, a closeted gay man in love with Bateman. He also encounters a pride parade, which, he states, "made [his] stomach turn."[21] When Luis shows interest in Bateman in the film, his immediate response, rather than disgust, appears to be panic. He washes his gloved hands and, breaking out in a pale sweat, makes his excuse to leave: "I've got to return some videotapes." Luis and his sexuality cannot fit into Bateman's constructed perfect world. Part of his illusion is the contradiction between his actions and his performative social consciousness: "We have to provide food and shelter for the homeless, and oppose racial discrimination, and promote civil rights, while also promoting equal rights for women," he tells dinner companions in an early scene and warns a friend, "Cool it with the anti-Semitic remarks." But we know this is just a further addendum to his "abstraction" and that for all his construction, Bateman simply is "not there."

Dissecting Girls: *American Psycho*'s Women

The shift from first-person narration is one of the adaptation's major changes. Removing Bateman's voice from the majority of the narrative allows space for him to be more clearly critiqued. While Ellis frequently allows his readers glimpses of other people's reactions to him, this is always through Bateman's perspective. Although his more psychotic episodes sometimes centralize his self-hatred, as Sarah Cardwell has argued, the book "provides for its readers no moral 'safe place', no moral vantage point within the narrative."[22] Eldridge similarly suggests that the novel's narrative style denies condemnation, but conversely in Harron's film, "the camera is outside of Bateman, and so provides an alternative gaze that serves to convict him."[23] This is evident in his interactions with male characters—for example, his friends' puzzled reactions when he mentions Ted Bundy and his discussions with Detective Kimball, which Bateman sweats and bluffs through in an effort to cover up Paul Allen's murder. But it is especially clear in the two scenes with "Christie," a sex worker he employs twice for threesomes, once with "Sabrina," another sex worker, and once with a friend, Elizabeth. Christie and Sabrina exchange bemused glances and subtle eye rolls as Bateman strives to impress them, emphasizing his wealth and status by talking about his job and plying them with expensive wine. After sex, he tortures the women off-screen. When he hires Christie for a second time, promising her safety and extra money, she eyes him cautiously as they negotiate in his limousine, and later as he presses Elizabeth for sex, she initially resists, telling Bateman, "I'm not a *lesbian*." Turner, an out gay woman, plays Elizabeth and notes that this was a joke "for those in the know."[24]

Bateman's relationships with women are, like everything in his life, surface construction. He is engaged to Evelyn, a wealthy socialite, and having an indiscreet affair with Courtney, Luis's fiancée. Publicly, Bateman plays the part of the attentive and caring partner. Yet he practically ignores the women when they are alone. He listens to a Walkman while Evelyn details potential plans for their wedding, for which he says he simply cannot spare the time. He dismisses Courtney when she attempts a conversation after sex, telling her, "You look . . . marvelous. There's nothing to say. You're going to marry Luis." Deleted scenes with Evelyn and Courtney, taken from chapters of Ellis's book, would further demonstrate Bateman's inability to communicate with these women as well as their frustrations with him. A sequence in which Bateman and Courtney miscommunicate during sex, leading to him becoming aggressive, was excluded on account of balance, Harron claims, noting that it is unusual behavior in comparison to his other scenes with the "upper-class girls" in his life (namely, Courtney, Evelyn, and his secretary Jean).[25] In another cut scene, Evelyn refuses sex, looks wearily at his penis, and asks, "What do you want me to do, floss with it?"

Harron notes that Bateman would never kill Evelyn, as she is the only person who stands up to him. Instead, he demonstrates his contempt by humiliating her, pursuing a sexual relationship with Courtney, and ultimately dumping her in a busy restaurant. Evelyn and Courtney are unwilling or unable to hear him even in confession: "My need to engage in homicidal behavior on a massive scale cannot be corrected," he tells Evelyn while she ignores him, complimenting a friend across the room on her jewelry. In turn, his lack of interest in their personal concerns (Evelyn's obsessive social one-upmanship, Courtney's sedated malaise over Luis and her desire for children) clearly contributes to relationships built on neglect and emotional rather than physical abuse.

By contrast, the sex workers he hires or strangers he seduces offer a blank canvas, not just for his sexual frustration and projected violence but also for the opportunity to play out idealized fantasies that his relationships with Evelyn and Courtney cannot sustain. His sexual desires are not only expressed but insisted upon in these scenes. He arbitrarily assigns the women their names, sets the mood by providing a soliloquy on Genesis, and orders them to arrange their bodies in increasingly filthy tableaus:

> Christie, take off the robe. Listen to the brilliant ensemble playing of Banks, Collins, and Rutherford. You can practically hear every nuance of every instrument. Sabrina, remove your dress. In terms of lyrical craftsmanship, sheer song writing, this album hits a new peak of professionalism. Sabrina, why don't you dance a little? Take the lyrics to "Land of Confusion." In this song, Phil Collins addresses the problems of abusive political authority. "In Too Deep" is the most moving pop song of the 1980s, about monogamy and commitment. The song is extremely uplifting; their lyrics are as positive, affirmative as anything I've heard in rock. Christy, get down on your knees so Sabrina can see your asshole. Phil Collins's solo career seems to be more commercial and therefore more satisfying in a narrower way. Especially songs like "In the Air Tonight" and "Against All Odds." Sabrina, don't just stare at it, eat it.

His first sexual demand is lewd enough to take Sabrina by surprise, but his actions leading up to it are, as always, performative. Bateman plays a romantic, an expert in the art of seduction. Dressed in a tuxedo and listening to Simply Red, he runs a bath for Christie and playfully splashes her, fills her glass with "very fine" chardonnay, and offers expensive Varda truffles. He prompts the women to move, pose, and speak as he desires, ordering Christie to wash her vagina from behind so he can watch and asking them, "Don't you want to know what I do for a living?" He is barely able to conceal his disappointment when they tell him no. Just as Bateman's clothes, apartment, and work and social life are shaped by consumerist ideals, a lifestyle packaged and sold, so too are his romantic inclinations. His monologue on Collins, his attempt at conversation, the music, the wine and chocolates, all reminiscent of a potentially perfect date night he might have with Evelyn or Courtney, but here with the bonus of sexual compliance. However, as David Robinson observes, the experience fails to play out as planned, leaving him feeling "vacuous, his appetite unsated."[26] Waking later that night, he tells the women, "We're not through yet," as he opens a drawer full of tools. They leave his apartment bloodied, shaken, and silent.

Jean comes the closest to a real connection with Bateman. In Ellis's novel, the two end up together. She cares for him deeply, while he views their relationship with resignation, a necessity and a preferable outcome to marrying Evelyn. Harron did not want the same conclusion, believing Jean "deserved better."[27] Jean's devotion to him is evident in her servitude, which pleases him; she acquiesces to his insistence that she wear a different outfit and flatters him, his home, and his taste, pandering to his ego. Two key sequences with Jean demonstrate her significance to the addition of female perspectives in the adaptation. At his apartment before a dinner date, Jean talks about "possibilities"— wanting to travel, go back to school, change and grow—while Bateman runs through his own possibilities surreptitiously in the kitchen. He runs his hands over knife edges, duct tape, and power tools before settling on a nail gun only after Jean enrages him by placing her used sorbet spoon on the table. Unbeknown to her, he holds it to the back of her head while she asks him what he is looking for. "A meaningful relationship with someone special," he replies, as if explaining this potential act of self-sabotage. Evelyn calls, distracting him, and he cautions Jean to leave: "I think if you stay, I might hurt you." She interprets this as a warning of a broken heart, but near the end of the film, she discovers Bateman's date diary after he calls her for help following a telephoned confession to his lawyer. This is the film's only full concession to another character's perspective (although the sequence is intercut with his final scenes; Bateman meets his lawyer, who believes he is someone else and his confession was a joke). Jean is horrified to find his doodles of butchered women. Decapitated heads and bloody limbs are drawn next to women's names. From one week with dates with "Laura" and "Daisy," it becomes clear on the next page that this is a murder diary, as the names are replaced with "girl in door stoop" and "GIRL OUTSIDE ATM." Jean cries as the imagery becomes more explicit: mutilated vaginas, knives buried in anuses or piercing eyeballs, a severed head used for fellatio, and alongside in angry scribble, "you deserved it you wanted it you begged me for it," "bitches shut up all of you," "they all fucking ask for it." Jean is the only person who hears his warnings, despite misinterpreting them, and the only living person aware of his actions. In her discovery, the focus is taken away from Bateman, and the moment becomes about her horror and her empathy for these women.

A number of formal and stylistic choices help emphasize the adaptation's shift in perspective. The early chapters of Ellis's book slowly outline a picture of Bateman and his lifestyle. The opening sequence, a dinner at Evelyn's home with his friends, becomes a later scene in Harron's film. Instead, the film begins with just the men at dinner (after clever titles that combine the two sides of Bateman's life, appearing at first to be close-ups of dripping blood and knives slashing at meat, only to turn into haute cuisine plates), complaining that the bathroom in this "chick's restaurant" is not fit for snorting cocaine. Bateman's first encounter with a woman is in the second scene, where he tells a barmaid in a noisy club (played by Harron's sister), "You're a fucking ugly bitch. I want to stab you to death, then play around with your blood." By excluding women in the opening scene and then making his feelings about them clear, we have a measure of him within minutes. His first interactions with female characters are all instructive or dismissive. He rejects Evelyn's wedding plans, chides Jean for her outfit, orders a dish of his choice for Courtney, and asks his neighbor Victoria to deal with the dry cleaner struggling to remove bloodstains from his expensive sheets. This latter exchange immediately follows Bateman meeting (who we presume is) his first victim. He waits to cross a road, looking at the woman next to him, greeting her. Intrigued, she says "Hello" back, and a long shot shows the two walking slowly together. This scene is scored by samples of ghostly female voices, which Harron and composer John Kale included to suggest that other female victims had come before her.[28]

By largely removing Bateman's narration and by including the perspectives of women, Harron and Turner encourage deeper sympathy for his victims than Ellis's book allows, as well as showing the momentary empathy his victims have for each other. This is not to say, of course, that Ellis intended his readers to feel nothing for these women. But the effect of using the exhaustingly detailed first-person narration is the emphasis on the purposelessness of his actions as well as a reflective challenge to the reader: How much of this dispassionate detail can you take in before it begins to anesthetize you to its horrors? Harron and Turner allow us to observe rather than experience "being" Bateman so that we can connect with his victims. This not only makes space for the women within *American Psycho* but is a necessity to the construction of tension and fear: "one cannot understand evil unless one empathized with those who are being victimized, and it is this structure of empathy that is essential to horror (dis)pleasure."[29]

Men, Women, Chain Saws, and Sneakers: Horror, Black Comedy, or Satire?

Ellis's novel and Harron's film have both proved slippery in terms of genre classification. The critical furor surrounding the book's release was often framed within frustrations over how to label it. David Eldridge argues that it was often compared to 1980s Splatterpunk novels as well as slasher films, neither providing satisfactory parameters, in turn providing an opportunity to "suspend normal critical engagement" with the text.[30] Its reframing as social satire has ultimately stuck, despite continued interest in its violence and what some have seen as Ellis's embodiment of Gothic conventions.[31] The expectation of the film was compounded by the book's notoriety and promotional material that emphasized its serial killer antagonist. Harron and Turner worked to dispel this, promoting their enhancement of the story's black comedy and clarifying that "the last thing we wanted" was to "translate [the novel] into an exploitative slasher film." Lionsgate, meanwhile, assumed a guaranteed horror audience and instead targeted a wider, "more discerning" viewership, while the filmmakers connected their take to those of horror auteurs like Polanski, Kubrick, and Hitchcock.[32] Harron emphasizes that she saw the book's potential as a period film and, in her DVD commentary, often makes reference to how the film's genre changes between a social satire and a horror movie. These various strategies ensured that "neither version of *American Psycho* was a tidy fit for any genre," resulting in confusion from critics unsure of how to label it as well as a celebration of its ability to transgress expectations as a generic slasher film.[33]

As I have argued elsewhere, horror, satire, and comedy are not mutually exclusive forms. The satirical or sociopolitical potential of horror is one of its many pleasures, and the variety of subgenres, cycles, and styles within the genre are evidence of its range.[34] The implications of Bateman's violence are horrific, and the adaptation cannot be excluded from the genre purely on account of moving many of these events off-screen. Despite the emphasis on black comedy, it is worth noting that the only violent scene in *American Psycho* played for laughs is Paul Allen's murder. Allen, a man the screenwriters intended to be detestable enough that you would hope for his death, is not just Bateman's peer; he is interchangeable with him. Arrogant, aggressive, obscenely rich, he is a figure to be hated so much that his death is comical. Similarly, we are encouraged to laugh at Bateman during his pathetic confessions and his breakdown, before he returns to his abstract facade in the film's final moments. By contrast, humor is stripped from the other murder scenes. Turner notes there is "nothing funny" about Bateman humiliating and killing Al; the act is the "lowest of the darkest."[35] The film's one planned violent set piece, Christie's death at the end of the evening with Elizabeth, was constructed for emotional effect. As Harron described, "For all the stylization and comedy of the film, I didn't want all the deaths to mean nothing. . . . I wanted, in the end, for the violence to mean something. I wanted you to remember Christie, and I wanted you to feel her death."[36]

Bateman's serial killer status connects *American Psycho* to some obvious genre inspirations, *Psycho* (1960) included, but there is an overemphasis in some readings of the links to more immediate contemporary horror texts, including *The Texas Chain Saw Massacre* (1974). The influence of the film on Bateman is obvious, as are Harron's intertextual references; he watches it as he exercises and later chases and murders Christie with a chainsaw. He also demonstrates his cannibalistic desires, gnawing on Christie's leg, ripping into Elizabeth's genitals with his teeth after cunnilingus, and telling his lawyer that he "ate some of their brains . . . I even tried to cook a little." He is embarrassed by this revelation, and the line is played for humor as part of Bateman's paranoid, pitiful confession. In Ellis's novel, Bateman makes one victim watch a video of him eating mustard-covered pieces of another woman's brain, and in the chapter "Tries to Cook and Eat Girl," he gnaws at intestines and tries to make meatloaf and sausage from human remains. Ellis outlines so much grisly detail here that the humor of the pathetic admission that follows ("I can't tell if I'm cooking any of this correctly, because I'm crying too hard and I have never really cooked anything before") is deadened.[37]

Comparisons between the banking and meatpacking "dynasties" of *American Psycho* and *Chain Saw* and between the boardroom and the slaughterhouse seem misjudged though, particularly given the consensus that the cannibals of Hooper's film are driven by economic necessity, unlike the wealthy yuppie consuming for greed, power, and psychopathic experimentation.[38] Christie is also no Final Girl, despite her best intentions. She watches Bateman lace her and Elizabeth's wine with ecstasy, fakes drinking it, feigns sexual interest in the pair, quietly untangles herself from the bedsheets while Bateman is distracted, kicks him in his bloody face to escape when he chases her, and flees the apartment with a solid head start. With Bateman, bloodied, snarling, and completely naked aside from a pair of white sneakers, following with his chainsaw, Christie screams as she runs down the hallways, hammering on doors that are not answered. Bateman dangles his chainsaw over the stairwell as she races down it and drops it as she reaches the bottom, sawing straight through her back and killing her as he watches from above.

The agency given to Christie in this sequence—our expectation of (or hope for) her escape—is intensified by the shift to her perspective. Ellis's Christie is given no such opportunity. She is tied up and tortured during sex, has her breasts burnt with jumper cables, and then is killed by "mashing" her chest with pliers: "I laugh when she dies," Bateman reflects before fretting about whether to cancel a lunch appointment as he will be tired the following day.[39] The callousness of Bateman's interactions and his disregard for these women's lives is clear. By contrast, Harron keeps Bateman's cruelness apparent while moving the perspective away from him, allowing empathetic connection with Christie as she tries to leave quietly in an act of self-preservation before freezing in fear as she listens to Elizabeth's screams and sees blood soaking through the bedsheets. The camera stays with Christie and her perspective for much of the chase as she opens a closet door in her panic and sees two other corpses, finds Elizabeth's blood-soaked body in the bathroom, and screams in desperation and terror as she runs away. Ultimately, however, her death is inevitable, and the freak improbability of the chainsaw hitting her only serves to underline the futility of her efforts to escape.

Much like Bateman tells us of his confessions in the film's final lines, they have "meant nothing." In Bateman's world, men like him have the upper hand and can get away with murder. Women like Christie are expendable.

Harron and Turner's film is a unique example of female creativity in horror at the turn of the millennium. As the chapters in this collection argue, women have shaped horror cinema throughout its history. Both at its margins and in the mainstream, female writers, directors, producers, and others globally contribute to a genre that in turn regularly engages with stories about women. But no other English-language horror film made by a woman achieved the level of critical or commercial success that *American Psycho* found around the time of its release. Harron and Turner's approach to adaptation and their insistence on creative and casting decisions ensured that the positive responses continued long after the initial excitement over the book's infamy and the involvement of women had quelled.

Katarzyna Paszkiewicz argues that "the critical discourses that circulate around women who direct big-budget horror films tend to emphasize the exceptional—and often 'morbid'—nature of both their tastes and their film practice."[40] Harron, often with Turner, works within "low, ostensibly 'male' exploitation genres," including horror, because as Linda Badley notes, they are "consistently marketable, which is crucial for a female filmmaker who tells stories about women," and furthermore, Harron is "attracted to things that have stigmas" and "the forms that people look down on."[41] Adapting *American Psycho* provided opportunities in both areas: taking a polemic, problematic text and addressing a major concern by developing its female characters. The confusion evident in some critical reactions can be explained in part by this strategy, itself in line with Harron's filmmaking practice: "I don't approach movies with an ideology, with a message. I think I approach them with a perspective. I want to tell stories from a female point of view. That doesn't mean I'm trying to teach a lesson, or that I have a line that I am trying to push, because I'm interested in contradiction, I'm interested in questions I can't answer, that are hard to answer."[42]

Paszkiewicz argues that this centralizing of female perspectives is a common feature of women horror directors flipping conventions in order to address issues of identification with female victims.[43] While we should question the implications of gendered identification for both audiences and on-screen representation and the assumptions this makes about the genre, it is clear that Harron and Turner's *American Psycho* does indeed bring these perspectives to the fore and that this results in a more sympathetic portrayal of female victims than Ellis's novel. It is not my intention to claim that Harron and Turner redeemed the novel in some way. Indeed, the filmmakers have defended Ellis and his book against misconceptions that it is inherently misogynistic and argue for recognition that showing—or writing—despicable acts is not the same as endorsing them.[44] Rather, I suggest that the filmmakers made palatable that which had been unpalatable for many, certainly for a mainstream audience and possibly for some female viewers. The novel and the film offer similar critiques of the misogynistic fallout of a masculinity in crisis and the banal self-involved greed of 1980s yuppie culture. But they take different approaches in their commentaries and especially in their interest in the story's women.

Notes

1 Bret Easton Ellis, *American Psycho* (1991; repr., London: Picador, 2000).
2 Thomas Heise, "*American Psycho*: Neoliberal Fantasies and the Death of Downtown," *Arizona Quarterly* 67, no. 1 (Spring 2011): 139. See also Justine Ettler, "'Sex Sells, Dude': A Re-examination of the Mass Media Feminist Critique of *American Psycho*," *Outskirts* 31 (November 2014), http://www.outskirts.arts.uwa.edu.au/volumes/volume-31/justine-ettler; C. Namwali Serpell, "Repetition and the Ethics of Suspended Reading in *American Psycho*," *Critique* 5, no. 1 (2010): 47–73; Elizabeth Young, "The Beast in the Jungle, the Figure in the Carpet: Bret Easton Ellis's *American Psycho*," in *Shopping in Space: Essays on American Blank-Generation Fiction*, ed. Elizabeth Young and Graham Caveney (London: Serpent's Tail, 1992), 85–122.
3 "Bret Easton Ellis on *American Psycho*, Christian Bale, and His Problem with Women Directors," *Movieline*, May 18, 2010, http://movieline.com/2010/05/18/bret-easton-ellis-on-american-psycho-christian-bale-and-his-problem-with-women-directors/.
4 Mary Harron, "*American Psycho*: From Book to Screen," featurette on *American Psycho*, 15th anniversary ed., Blu-ray Disc (Santa Monica, Calif.: Lionsgate, 2015).
5 David Eldridge, "The Generic *American Psycho*," *Journal of American Studies* 42, no. 1 (April 2008): 22.
6 Harron, "*American Psycho*."
7 Eldridge, "Generic," 22.
8 Harron, "*American Psycho*."
9 For example, see Peter Deakin, "I Simply Am Not There: *American Psycho*, the Turn of the Millennium and the Yuppie as a Killer of the Real," *Film International* 77/78 (2016): 85–101; Amy Bride, "Byronic Bateman: The Commodity Vampire, Surplus Value and the Hyper-Gothic in *American Psycho*," *Irish Journal of Gothic and Horror Studies* 14 (Summer 2015), 3–18; David Robinson, "Identity, Consumerism and the Slasher Film in Mary Harron's *American Psycho*," *Cineaction* 68 (2006): 26–35; Leigh Claire La Berge, "The Men Who Make the Killings: *American Psycho*, Financial Masculinity, and 1980s Financial Print Culture," *Studies in American Fiction* 37, no. 2 (2010): 273–296.
10 Harron, "*American Psycho*."
11 Hillary Weston, "Christian Bale's Inspiration for *American Psycho*: Tom Cruise," *BlackBook*, October 18, 2009, https://bbook.com/film/mary-harron-reveals-inspiration-behind-patrick-bateman/11810/.
12 Linda Badley, "Performance and Gender Politics in Mary Harron's Female Celebrity Anti-biopics," in *Women Do Genre in Film and Television*, ed. Mary Harrod and Katarzyna Paszkiewicz (London: Routledge, 2018), 24.
13 Harron, "*American Psycho*."
14 Serpell, "Repetition."
15 Harron, "*American Psycho*."
16 Jaap Kooijman and Tarja Laine, "*American Psycho*: A Double Portrait of Serial Yuppie Patrick Bateman," *Post Script: Essays in Film and the Humanities* 22, no. 3 (Summer 2003): 53.

17 Guinevere Turner, "Commentary," *American Psycho*, 15th anniversary ed., Blu-ray Disc (Santa Monica, Calif.: Lionsgate, 2015).

18 Steffen Hantke, "Monstrosity without a Body: Representational Strategies in the Popular Serial Killer Film," *Post Script: Essays in Film and the Humanities* 22, no. 2 (Winter 2002): 36.

19 Mary Harron, "Commentary," *American Psycho*, 15th anniversary ed., Blu-ray Disc, directed by Mary Harron, 2000 (Lionsgate, 2015).

20 Harron, *"American Psycho."*

21 Ellis, *American Psycho*, 139.

22 Sarah Cardwell, *"American Psycho*: Serial Killer Film?," *Film Studies* 3 (Spring 2002): 76.

23 Eldridge, "Generic," 14.

24 Turner, "Commentary."

25 Harron, "Commentary."

26 Robinson, "Narrative," 35.

27 Harron, "Commentary."

28 Harron.

29 Kooijman and Laine "Portrait," 53.

30 Eldridge, "Generic," 21.

31 Bride, "Byronic"; Charles Jason Lee, "Wall Street Jekyll: Identity and Meaningless Pleasure in *American Psycho*," *Film International* 3, no. 5 (2005): 22–27.

32 Eldridge, "Generic," 26.

33 Eldridge, 33.

34 Laura Mee, *Devil's Advocates: The Shining* (Leighton Buzzard, U.K.: Auteur, 2017).

35 Turner, "Commentary."

36 Harron, "Commentary."

37 Ellis, *American Psycho*, 328, 346.

38 Robinson, "Narrative," 28.

39 Ellis, *American Psycho*, 290.

40 Katarzyna Paszkiewicz, "When the Woman Directs (a Horror Film)," in *Women Do Genre in Film and Television*, ed. Mary Harrod and Katarzyna Paszkiewicz (London: Routledge, 2018), 43.

41 Badley, "Performance," 23.

42 Jameson Kowalczyk, "Interview: Mary Harron," I on Cinema, April 13, 2016, https://www.ioncinema.com/news/uncategorized/interview-mary-harron.

43 Paszkiewicz, "When a Woman Directs."

44 Harron, *"American Psycho."*

9

Gender, Genre, and Authorship in *Ginger Snaps*

KATARZYNA PASZKIEWICZ

As Jane Gaines reminds us in her essay "The Genius of Genre and the Ingenuity of Women," every reference to film authors "carries the weight of several centuries of literary and art historical criticism." Yet, she contends, "authorship has been taken up too uncritically."[1] In her earlier piece on female authorship in the silent era, she argues that despite wide-ranging critiques in the 1960s that pronounced the "death" of authors, auteurism does matter today as much as ever:

> For the time being, the most sophisticated contemporary film criticism, in order to sidestep the politics of romantic individualism, is quite comfortable with authorship as a critical construct, asserting that if we treat authorship as nothing more than an abstract structure we avoid the political pitfalls of dealing with real historical authors, impossible-to-determine intentions, and the unchecked authority of the dead author over the live text. This widespread critical use of authorship-as-structure, however, has meant that the concept of authorship is still available for every new wave of undergraduates to rediscover it and to reclaim not the structuralist construct but the old individualist and authoritarian notion. Although we

might be teaching Howard Hawks as a structure, our students are understanding the film director as an author.[2]

Perhaps somewhat paradoxically, Gaines—"a confirmed anti-auteurist," as she has called herself on many occasions—is involved in what appears to be a "classical authorship project."[3] As a film historian and the founder of the Women Film Pioneers Project, she has played a pivotal role in restoring to critical importance the work of many "lost" pioneers, not only of such well-known silent-film directors as Alice Guy-Blaché and Germaine Dulac and sound-era filmmakers as Ida Lupino and Dorothy Arzner but also a plethora of other practitioners who worked behind the scenes: producers, editors, camera operators, title writers, costume designers, and more. Importantly, while she does not abandon the feminist commitment to champion innovative women in film history, Gaines does not advocate a return to the romantic notion of individual authorship; instead, she urges us to "turn back the clock": "What if we were to imagine the cinema as more the industrial mass-produced object and less the individually produced work, the product of an analyzable subject?"[4] This move is necessary, she argues, because auteur criticism has historically eclipsed the audience and other texts as sources of meaning—"here 'other texts' reference genre, the repetition with difference of popular forms."[5] And I would add, as many other feminist scholars have already done, that the 1950s and 1960s auteurism in France and the United States—according to which a film director is an individual agent who controls the entire creation process of the film—especially erased the contributions of the women who, due to a number of historical, economic, and cultural circumstances, have had greater access to the positions of screenwriter, editor, actress, and costume designer than to that of director.

These considerations are crucial to thinking about the questions of authorship, genre, and women filmmakers, especially if we turn to horror cinema, a genre from which women have been historically excluded, both industrially and through film criticism. Although women filmmakers' presence can be traced back to the genre's inception in the 1930s, if not even earlier, it is true that horror cinema has discursively been considered to be created by men for presumed male audiences and canonized as such by male scholars and critics.

Interestingly, while the genre has become vital for feminist scholarship on film identification, which significantly questioned the totalizing view of the spectator that had long haunted film studies and reflected upon the potential pleasures of horror for female audiences, horror films *authored* by women have received little critical attention.[6] The reasons behind this oversight are multiple, and although they cannot be analyzed in detail here, we could mention, on the one hand, the difficult relation between feminism and genre (in particular those genres culturally codified as male and thus deemed "not suitable" for women) and industrially produced cinema as a whole (supposedly opposed to feminist film practice) and, on the other hand, recurrent representations of violence against women, which stamped horror cinema as an inherently misogynist genre—as with pornography, horror film was traditionally the object of substantial aesthetic criticism and the target of moral concern and calls for censorship.

This chapter offers an examination of *Ginger Snaps* (2000), Canada's internationally renowned horror film directed by John Fawcett and written by Karen Walton, which draws a playful connection between werewolf monstrosity and the experience of female adolescence and was defined by the filmmakers as a feminist revision of the horror genre. The aim of this study is twofold. First, it engages with questions of how the film might be productively read through a lens that recognizes filmmaking as a collective art form. And second, it seeks to register the significance of women's film authorship within the horror genre histories in which they have been traditionally overlooked, thus responding to Jane Gaines's observation on the historically revisionist value of championing women as generic innovators.[7] I begin by discussing the discursive circulation of the film—in particular in reference to the Fawcett-Walton collaboration—to address the complex relationship between female authorship, the conventions of the horror genre, and feminist reauthoring. Although horror was initially valued unfavorably by feminist criticism, given the association of generic reiteration with the reinforcement of gender clichés as well as high doses of sexualized violence against women, it can also be considered a productive site of reimagining. This approach raises the question of the potential feminist implications of horror films authored by women, linked with the problematic search for female/feminist/authorial "subversion" of genre cinema. Drawing on Alison Peirse, who in her invitation to this volume paraphrased Annette Kuhn's *Women's Pictures* (1982), I also believe that "a horror film made by a woman may not be feminist, and men may make feminist horror films. So, what makes a horror film either a) a woman's film or b) feminist? Is it the attributes of the author, attitudes inherent in the work, or because of the way the film can be read?"[8] And we might further ask how to think about women making horror without reproducing a prestructuralist, romantic discourse of authorship, according to which the auteur is a purely empirical being able to transcend industrial, commercial, or even collective limitations in order to individually "author" her or (much more usually) his films in subversive ways.

While I concur with Gaines's critique of authorial paradigm, I do think that authorship can still be a viable method for thinking about the cinematic practices of women—especially bearing in mind that even today, horror film seems to be the domain of the male auteur. As Judith Mayne argued almost three decades ago, "The notion of female authorship is not simply a useful political strategy; it is crucial to the reinvention of the cinema that has been undertaken by women filmmakers and feminist spectators."[9] Instead of the theory of the death of the author—which, as many feminist scholars have lamented, coincided with the discovery of new works by women—what we need is a new approach to authorship: one that does not rely on a somewhat naive concept of the female auteur as an individual genius who creates masterpieces outside of history and one that does not trivialize the significance of the different forms of cultural agency and agenthood in women's responses to historical developments, as Catherine Grant has argued. Drawing on Judith Butler's positing of gender as a "reiterative or re-articulatory practice, immanent to power, and not a relation of external opposition to power," Grant considers that women filmmakers "have direct and reflexive, if obviously not completely 'intentional' or determining relationships to the cultural products they help to produce, as well as to their reception."[10]

This way of thinking about women's film authorship can be traced back to Janet Staiger's context-activated reception theory, which the scholar has turned into "reconceptualizing individual authorship within a production process and social formation."[11] Drawing on Butler and Foucault (in particular his ideas on how discourses act as "recipes, specific forms of [self-]examination, and codified exercises" that habituate one's behavior to achieve one's goals), Staiger argues that "we might see authoring as one sort of technique of the self, like gender: a performative act that works when an individual, first, is positioned in a social formation in a location in which authoring is expected and, second, behaves as an author (produces objects the social formation views as texts)."[12] As Staiger puts it, authoring becomes "a repetitive assertion of 'self-as-expresser' through culturally and socially laden discourses of authoring. Individuals author by duplicating recipes and exercises of authorship."[13]

The "authorship as techniques of the self" approach, which emphasizes how individuals self-fashion as authors, is extremely useful when thinking about authorship that is not easily spotted, as it allows for the foregrounding of minority expressions: "The implications of this theorizing for authorship theory and feminist historiography include thinking about what and where to look for, and how to analyze, these textual traces of identity and agency, especially in cases in which, for multiple reasons, these traces are submerged, suppressed, and, consequently, missing."[14] However, Staiger is careful not to read the filmmakers' expressive methods as inherently "transcending," "defamiliarizing," "subverting," or "resisting" the system. She suggests that we understand "rebellious or resistant authorship" as "a particular kind of citation with the performative outcome of asserting agency against the normative" and even urges us to consider "whether, in fact, it is primarily individuals with minority selves who make such citational practices . . . or whether the methods of critical analysis have led scholars to seek such deviations."[15]

Building on Grant's and Staiger's methodologies, this chapter raises questions about what is at stake when women make horror films, especially in such instances in which authorship is not easily located or it is distinctly dispersed in the discursive circulation of a film, as was the case with *Ginger Snaps*. It is not my intention to offer a lengthy analysis of the film or its reception, as such an analysis lies beyond the scope of this chapter and has already been provided in several works (see, for example, *John Fawcett's Ginger Snaps*, written by Ernest Mathijs, a book-length study of the film that traces its inception, production, and reception and that, given the scholar's privileged access to most of its cast and crew, has proven to be extremely useful for the present study).[16] Instead, I will focus on several tensions in the discursive circulation of the film and in Karen Walton's mediated authorship—one of the few horror screenwriters who have gained a certain amount of visibility. I wish to look at two sites of significance in exploring Walton's authorship: her authorial (self-)fashioning in interviews and promotional materials and a short fragment of the film: its critically acclaimed opening. By situating Walton along an extratextual path, I will focus on the conditions and limitations of her visibility as a "rebellious" or "resistant" author, in Staiger's terms.

The Malcontented Suburbanite: Karen Walton's Biographical Legend

Toronto-based screenwriter and executive producer Karen Walton was born in Halifax, Nova Scotia, but spent a significant portion of her life in Edmonton, Alberta. She studied at the Canadian Film Centre (CFC) in Toronto, and this is where she wrote the screenplay for *Ginger Snaps*. Over her twenty-year career, Walton has been commissioned to write original and adapted film and television scripts by producers in Canada, Quebec, the United Kingdom, and the United States. Her extensive credits as a writer or writer-producer include episodes of *Orphan Black* (2013–2017), *Queer as Folk* (2000–2005, where she also served as executive story consultant), *Flashpoint* (2008–2012), *The Listener* (2009–2014), *Heart: The Marilyn Bell Story* (2001), and *The Many Trials of One Jane Doe* (2002). She is the winner of the 2002 Best Film Writing Canadian Comedy Award (for *Ginger Snaps*), Canadian Screen Academy's 2016 Margaret Collier Award for Screenwriting, Women in Film and Television's Crystal Award for Mentorship (2017), and the Writers Guild of Canada's prestigious Writers Block Award (2009) for outstanding service to the Canadian screenwriting community at large. While Walton's contributions to film and TV industry are numerous and varied, *Ginger Snaps* is still quoted as her greatest achievement.[17]

In his detailed account of the *Ginger Snaps'* writing process, Ernest Mathijs comments that the genesis of the film "points to a cluster of interwoven relations, skills, and interests that brings into focus the fact that *Ginger Snaps* was very much a collaborative effort."[18] Walton wrote the script in close collaboration with director John Fawcett—it is worth mentioning that both later worked together on other writing projects including *Orphan Black*. Along with Fawcett, a number of other practitioners are frequently quoted in promotional materials and subsequent interviews as having had a profound impact on *Ginger Snaps*, most of whom were gathered around the CFC during the late 1990s: editor

Brett Sullivan; director and screenwriter Vincenzo Natali, who was at that time preparing his script for his 1997 film *Cube* (Natali sketched the storyboards for *Ginger Snaps*); and producer Steven Hoban, who worked on Fawcett's first short film, *Half Nelson* (1992), and the vampire film *Blood & Donuts* (Holly Dale, 1995), in which Natali was in charge of the storyboards. When Walton was working on the script, she was a student at the CFC, and in the same class were Natali and Graeme Manson, the cocreator of *Orphan Black*. As Mathijs observes, "These ties and relations stress the webbed origin of *Ginger Snaps* and paint the climate in which *Ginger Snaps* was written: part of a 'scene' of like-minded efforts with a great generosity towards the horror genre. It is the aggregate of specific close relations and the collaborative momentum that these relations triggered that best explains the creative intentions (and tensions) that brought *Ginger Snaps* into existence."[19]

Perhaps the most revealing in the "story of origin" of *Ginger Snaps* are the ways in which Walton's authorship is discursively devised and positioned within this web of creative intentions. In a number of interviews, Walton—for whom *Ginger Snaps* was her first feature-length screenplay—recalls that she was approached by John Fawcett, who wanted "to do a teen girl werewolf movie" and asked her to write the script. Initially, Walton vigorously resisted the idea, as unlike Fawcett, she did not consider herself a fan of the horror film. She recalls, "I laughed and said no with a long tirade about women being horror's cliché victims, issues of depiction, etc. And then John said, 'that's exactly why you should write one.'"[20] Fawcett convinced Walton this film would reinterpret the genre; as Mathijs reports, even though she was reluctant to write the script for "all the feminist reasons that the genre is formulaic and misogynist," in the end, she agreed under the condition that she would be allowed "to break all the rules."[21] During the process of drafting the script, under working title *Wolfer Grrrls*—which in itself points to her "authorial intention" to push the werewolf tropes in new directions—Walton has been credited as having had considerable creative leeway, particularly in how she reworked horror genre conventions under an alternative feminist lens.

This narrative, also underscored in *Ginger Snaps*' press kit, is crucial in framing understandings of Walton's genre authorship (and of female authorship in the horror genre more broadly); first and foremost, it implies that Walton's gender matters greatly, as her being *female* might somewhat help subvert the horror genre, conceived here as inherently formulaic and patriarchal.[22] A similar gendered discourse circulated around Mary Harron, who was chosen to direct *American Psycho* under an assumption that her "female perspective" would attenuate the protests over representations of violence against women in Bret Easton Ellis's source novel; Diablo Cody, hired to write the script for *Jennifer's Body* (2009, Karyn Kusama) so that the film would take horror in a "new" direction, given that it would be "told from a female point of view, starring women, and written and directed by women"; and Kimberly Peirce, the director of the

2013 adaptation of *Carrie*, whose task was also to infuse the source text with her "female perspective."[23]

All of these films have sparked heated debates over their feminism. There are interesting similarities between *Ginger Snaps'* and *Jennifer's Body*'s critical reception (the latter, nota bene, was accused of imitating *Ginger Snaps* to the point of plagiarizing it): both attracted interpretations of the female monster in the "girl-power" style. Walton has offered an interesting reflection on this issue, saying,

> Ginger's is a story of self-destruction. Which is the antithesis of a feminist story. Of buying into that idea that, "I am getting sexy now, the boys all want to look at me. Because it is all about my gratification." That part of Ginger's transformation is like mimicking a gluttonous, cartoon-like existence that at least in my own writing I associate with the tradition of the white male. The idea that, hey if I am powerful I get to do what I want. This is the opposite to Brigitte who wants to talk to Ginger, see what is wrong and try to fix it. Brigitte sees that she is making herself vulnerable and putting other people in danger.[24]

While enthusiastically embraced by *Ginger Snaps'* fans, the feminist message of the film was fiercely contested by some of the critics.[25] In fact, the film—and Walton in particular—met with a flurry of complaints and outrage in the media during the preproduction; as was the case with other women filmmakers (including Jennifer Lynch, Mary Harron, Diablo Cody, and Karyn Kusama), Walton's contribution to the horror genre was overlaid with moral panic about fictionalization of violence. When it was announced that Telefilm (one of the Canadian government's principal instruments for supporting national audio-visual industry) was funding a horror movie involving two adolescent girls, six prominent Toronto casting directors, who preferred to remain anonymous, announced that they were going to boycott *Ginger Snaps* for its violent subject matter and horror gore along with its particularly vivid language: they decided that "it was not Canadian for ladies to say 'fuck' and talk about their periods. And thought [the] Telefilm money should be taken back."[26] The heated controversy over casting was intermingled with a dispute over the film's cultural value; the werewolf "teen horror flick" was set against more worthy art films, the former being conceived as antagonistic to Canadian culture.

Yet as we can read in the press kit, "the reaction from the casting community was only the tip of the iceberg."[27] When casting director Robin D. Cook agreed to pick up the film, the Columbine shooting, as well as the shootings in Taber, Alberta, suddenly threw the public spotlight on violent teens and the movies they watched: "Word of the toxic combination of violence and teens in *Ginger Snaps* was leaked to the media. A front-page article in the *Toronto Star* made inaccurate claims that *Ginger Snaps* was a teen slasher film while alluding to the recent tragedies in Columbine and Taber. That article launched an intense frenzy in the Canadian media—one that involved call-in radio shows, print articles and ultimately Telefilm Canada having to publicly defend its funding choices."²⁸

The hostile responses to *Ginger Snaps* were acutely gendered in nature. During the media outcry over the film, it was Walton, not Fawcett or any of his male colleagues, who was criticized for contributing to a culture of teenage violence. As Mathijs relates, "Walton was described as 'a self-assured ingénue' and 'nocturnal vamp' with 'red hair and big teeth' (a quote attributed to Walton) whose stories are fuelled by 'fantastic and shocking events.' None of the male crew, by the way, received such commentary. Fawcett, for instance, who stayed largely invisible during the controversy, was prefaced only as 'talented' and 'impressive,' and press reports kept him out of shot."²⁹

Mathijs's compilation of statements from key crew members—which, needless to say, are part of distribution and promotion strategies for *Ginger Snaps*—is particularly revealing, as it shows how Walton's gender and her *unique* take on genre were utilized to distinguish the film from "run-of-the-mill horror films of the time": "Bill House, director of operations at Telefilm, offered that *Ginger Snaps* was 'a parody of violence, cartoon-like. This is about young angst-ridden suburban teens. It's a feminist coming-of-age film . . . and not by any stretch of the imagination exploitative.' . . . Walton identified *Ginger Snaps* as 'a hybrid horror/coming-of-age movie about an unattractive teenager who is turning into a seductive werewolf, and enjoys the attention it brings her.'"³⁰ Given the maligned status of horror film in so many circles—and the controversies around *Ginger Snaps* in particular—it is not surprising that filmmakers and financers would want to distinguish their product from others by enriching it with "feminist meaning," as if to say, "It is not cheap entertainment."³¹ What is significant here is that in promoting *Ginger Snaps* as "a feminist coming-of-age film," Walton's public persona—and in particular her gender—played first fiddle. In this process of meaning making, Walton was quite reflective about her authoring behavior, including creating her "biographical legend," in David Bordwell's terms (1981): a set of discursive motifs and narratives about her life and persona through which her work was interpreted.³²

According to Walton herself, there were three key factors that shaped her screenplay: "the explicit wish to 'break the rules' of the genre without utterly confusing audiences," her own experiences of growing up in the 'burbs, and the process of sharpening the language in collaboration with story editor Ken Chubb.³³ These comments encapsulate a number of overlapping discourses that circulate around Walton and that contribute to the construction of her authorial identity. The focus on language—an obvious strategy in framing a screenwriter's style—might be inscribed within the traditional authorship paradigms, seeking to detect the author's dexterity and individual personality that can be traced in his or her thematic and/or stylistic consistency. In reference to *Ginger Snaps*, Walton has been frequently praised for her witticism and intertextuality while maintaining pace and rhythm. Her screenplay is indeed "snappy," to borrow

112 • Katarzyna Paszkiewicz

Mathijs's pun.[34] The other two factors reveal further narratives that underlie the shaping of Walton's authorial persona but that also raise questions about how to conceptualize women's film authorship in popular genres in a wider sense. On the one hand, they are indicative of her biographical legend, which remains closely intertwined with the representation of teenage girls in *Ginger Snaps*, and on the other, they evidence the logic of genre bending. Thinking back to the problematic issue of subversion of horror formula—going with versus going against genre, to use Jane Gaines's evocative terms—it could be argued that in the discursive circulation of *Ginger Snaps*, Fawcett was *going with* and Walton *against* the horror genre conventions. Mathijs explains that the idea behind the film was "to make the story self-reflexive and thus expose the 'rules of the genre' as conventions open to criticism. . . . As a fan of the genre, Fawcett was ideally placed to help insert allusions to other horror films. . . . Walton injected into the story some fierce feminist commentary on the genre. . . . This is most apparent in how the story constructs the Fitzgerald sisters as outsiders to normality, and how, especially in their dialogue and one-liners, they apply a high dose of film theory to their own positions as outcasts and females."[35] In Fawcett-Walton tandem, then, the former was in charge of the genre—he "very much wanted *Ginger Snaps* to look like a full-fledged horror movie"—and the latter of creating "a unique space for the dramatic center of the story, namely, the tragedy of the dissolution of loyalty in the sisters' bond."[36] Walton herself explains, "*Ginger Snaps* presented an opportunity to make something sophisticated—to create real characters with real problems, characters that are human beings whose struggles are based on relationships."[37] The cultural gendering of genres is very much at stake here. According to Mathijs, in order to separate these two units (the story of the teenage girls from the horror plot), Fawcett "created two stylistic streams, one with the aim of producing ingenious horror, and the other designed to highlight the melodrama of the sisters' suffering."[38] While Fawcett's contribution is more frequently alluded to in reference to the horror genre, Walton's discursive visibility seems to be associated with melodrama, a mode of expression culturally considered more "appropriate" for women, whether as viewers or as filmmakers, and with injecting into the horror formula "some fierce feminist commentary on the genre." And although the feminist take on the story of the sisters was underscored by different members of the filming crew, it is Walton's role that comes to the foreground in the film's perceived criticism of patriarchy and normativity—a discourse that contributes to her positioning as resistant or rebellious auteur. In fact, Walton's subversion of stereotypical representations is often mentioned as a recurrent feature throughout much of her work in film and television. As an article on the Alliance of Canadian Cinema, Television and Radio Artists official website puts it, her "body of work champions society's underdogs and outliers and her dedication to fair representations of gender, gender equity, racial and cultural diversity in entertainment continues, onscreen and off."[39]

In the context of *Ginger Snaps*, it is worth paying attention to how Walton's status as a *female* screenwriter and her biographical details intersect in the shaping of her authorial persona. When explaining why he approached Walton in the first place, Fawcett comments, "I realized that [the project] needed a female voice. . . . I wanted the experience of someone who lived through all the hormonal ups and downs of puberty and adolescence."[40] Putting aside the potentially essentialist implications of his rationale, it is significant how Walton's experience as an adolescent girl in Canadian suburbs has been paralleled with Ginger's and Brigitte's status as "other"—the protagonists cannot fit into a typical high school group. For example, we are told that when Walton moved to Alberta, she suffered from "a profound culture shock, as any drastic uprooting would be for someone at an age when 'struggling to fit in' is the main item on one's personal agenda. But to Walton, the entire experience of suburban alienation felt like a 'malaise,' with its 'unrelenting homogeny, the ubiquitous sameness, the tyranny of the uninspired white picket fence dream leading to an uninspired sameness or brain death.'"[41] Her status as a misfit has been read as pivotal to the final shaping of the script. As Walton herself explained, "I could not find my house for the first week or two. We had to leave a colored rock on the steps. I wasn't stupid or anything, I just had never seen a street where the houses were all the same, like in a horror movie."[42]

The sameness of the residential buildings often seen in Western Canadian suburbs—the "desolate look-alike streets with dead ends," in Walton's words—inspired much of the fictional setting for *Ginger Snaps*.[43] Nowhere is it more evident than in the first scene of *Ginger Snaps*, which opens with the images of the tedious, dormant suburb. The first seven minutes of the film, consisting of the prologue and the credit sequence, in which the sisters are staging various suicide, homicide, and deadly accident tableaux as a part of a school assignment, deserves closer attention, as it is arguably the most significant segment of *Ginger Snaps*. It introduces the main themes and characters, establishes the visual tone of the film, and, as I will try to demonstrate, speaks volumes about Karen Walton's film authorship.

"They'll Be in Awe": Authorial Self-Fashioning

The prologue opens with aerial shots of a suburban landscape: identical houses, endless rooftops, and a fleet of electrical towers stretch in a residential area under somber, ominous skies. October colors—gray, brown, and yellowish—envelop a sprawling suburb. There is an absolute immobility in these opening shots: no people are shown, and there is no music, only the diegetic sound of the dog barking far away. The next image is of a field with wind blowing through it, with a sign in the left corner that reads "Bailey Downs." A tracking shot, that usually codifies the point of view of an evil force or a monster in the horror genre, gets us closer to the town. We then cut to a traveling shot, from right to left, revealing a wooden picket fence, a trope so characteristic of suburbia. A woman rakes leaves on her lawn while her toddler plays in a sandbox. The child is filling a pail with sand, but then he drops the spade in favor of using his hands. The eerie horror music begins to play. The mother smiles lovingly and approaches the kid from behind, asking, "What have you got there?" Petrified, she picks up a bloodied, severed paw. She calls, "Baxter!" and then creeps to the dog house where she suddenly discovers the gutted and half-devoured remains of her beloved pet, who, as we later find out, was torn to shreds by "the beast of Bailey Downs," a large wolf believed to be scavenging in the neighborhood. The woman screams while the camera movement pulls us into the darkness of the dog house. Then the shot fades to black, and the production company credits and the title of the film appear against the blood-red screen.

Next, we see a garage door open, and Brigitte Fitzgerald, a gloomy-looking teenage girl, peers out. She's dressed in ragged and dark attire, and she's carrying a gas can, a torch, a chainsaw, and an extension cord over her shoulder. She frowns at the wailing mother, who is now running with her child toward the front yard. The neighbor kids who were playing street hockey stop to stare at her but quickly resume their game, unaffected. We see another neighbor's dog barking. "Shut up, Norman," reprimands Brigitte. We then cut to a TV screen showing two women dancing together while the narrator and the superimposed text warn us alarmingly, "Can this happen to a normal woman?" In front of the TV, in the foreground, there emerges a knife, gently tested against the wrist of Ginger Fitzgerald, Brigitte's sister. Brigitte enters what looks like a half-finished basement, decorated with candles and macabre adornments, something between a home-improvement project long abandoned, a hidden sanctuary, and an underground bomb shelter that protects the girls from the outside world. In their first interaction in the film, the Fitzgerald sisters discuss suicide:

BRIGITTE: Baxter's fertilizer . . . and everyone is just standing there like . . . staring. Why can't they just catch that thing? How hard can it be in a place full of dead ends?
GINGER: Fuck, wrists are for girls.

Ginger sighs and throws herself on a bed.

I'm slitting my throat. You should definitely hang.

Brigitte surveys the collection of potentially lethal household items.

BRIGITTE: Maybe even your final moment's a cliché around here.
GINGER: Not ours, Bee. Ours'll rock.
BRIGITTE: You don't think our deaths should be a little more than cheap entertainment?
GINGER: You jazzed me on this. Don't wuss now.

BRIGITTE: It's the idea of everyone staring at me, just lying there. I mean, what if they just—laugh?

GINGER: They'll be in awe. Bee, suicide's the ultimate "fuck you." C'mon, it's so us. It's the pact.

Moments later, we get to know what the pact is. While Ginger sticks a badly scarred palm in Brigitte's face, she pronounces, "Out by sixteen or dead in this scene but together forever." Brigitte presses her own scarred palm to Ginger's and recites: "United against life as we know it."

The next scene takes place in a backyard. It starts with a slow traveling shot from left to right that follows a white picket fence and therefore mirrors the traveling movement from the previous sequence. The traveling stops when it reaches Ginger, apparently dead, impaled on the fence. "Too much blood. And I can see your gaunch," Brigitte says, annoyed, pondering her sister's corpse with a camera in hand. Ginger, her body speared on a fence and sticky red blood sprayed across her middle, gives Brigitte the finger and urges, "Just do it." Brigitte brings her camera to her eye and snaps a photo.

Then the second part of the credits follows. Artful-looking handheld camera shots are intertwined with a series of grainy, often unfocused Polaroid stills that compose the "death montage"—a play on a class project title set for the main characters ("Life in Bailey Downs")—that the girls prepare using photos of themselves committing suicide or homicide: Ginger after bleeding to death in her own bed, with a dazed Brigitte in front of her; Brigitte tastefully laid out in a deep freezer, amid frozen food and with arms crossed on her chest; Ginger's entrails tangled in a lawn mower; Brigitte on the bathroom floor, her eyes covered with pennies; Ginger and Brigitte at a poisoned garden tea party; Brigitte hanging from the ceiling with a suicide note on her chest reading, "Alone in the dark, the snow will cover my footsteps" (a real suicide note written in 1801 by a Siberian exile, Pavel T. Shvetsov).[44] Suddenly, the solemn cello and violin music, composed by Mike Shields, stops, and the screen flashes white. We are cut to a classroom: the boys hoot and applaud; Ginger smirks, while Brigitte seems upset. The school teacher looks back at them, first confused and then disgusted: "Wait a minute. Well . . . well, that was completely disturbing, wasn't it? I mean, the Fitzgerald sisters clearly worked . . . God . . . I mean, I am . . . I am completely sickened. Sickened by that." One of the boys asks, "Can we see the ones of Ginger again?"

The credit sentence, especially when considered in tandem with the prologue, allows for addressing a number of discourses that intersect in and shape female authorship and, more particularly, for thinking about what happens when women make horror: the collaborative nature of film production and the question of women's film authorship in the genre (as embodied by the two girls in the film); the importance of the filmmaker's biographical legend (e.g., Walton's experience in suburbs and her female position as potentially alienating);

calls for censorship (the scene with the high school teacher mirrors the moral outrage around the film in real life); and, finally, the fans' response (in the segment, the stereotypical appeal to a male audience is foregrounded, although as a matter of fact, *Ginger Snaps* has earned a predominantly female cult following). In addition to fleshing out these issues, I contend that the credit sequence can also be treated as a particularly fruitful point of entry to thinking about Walton's authorship.

The mixed media—a combination of a making-of with still photos for the slideshow and the mournful music with sound bites of the girls laughing—helps create a conspicuous game of imitation, which underscores the performative and even metareflexive nature of the sequence. Indeed, one might argue that the sisters' school project wouldn't be so successful among their peers if it weren't for their acting skills, the carefully elaborated mise-en-scène, proper lighting, the right shot angle, and above all, their brilliant ideas and collaborative execution. In his insightful analysis of the credit sequence, Mathijs also points to its fundamentally performative nature: "The sequence strikes a peculiar balance between a straightforward comment, grave and grisly, on the world and a playful *performance* of such a comment."[45] The fact that the sequence starts with Ginger lying in bed (presumably after slitting her throat) and finishes with Brigitte hanging from the ceiling—just the way Ginger suggested in her previous dialogue with Brigitte—seems to imply that they did not want real suicide; they wanted to fake it and display it for an audience. The sequence (and the film as a whole) is performative not only due to its smart, savvy attitude but also, as many scholars have argued, because it queers stable interpretations of gender.[46] While I fully agree with this interpretation, I want to push this observation even further and consider the sequence's performativity in reference to Walton's performance as an auteur and thus responding to Staiger's and Grant's calls to rethink authorship methodologies through Butler's positioning of agency. This approach echoes in many ways Timothy Corrigan's concept of the auteur as a "commercial dramatization of self [and] as the motivating agent of textuality," which makes reference to the filmmaker and her public image that is formed "in negotiation with the repertoire of cultural narratives, and who can also regulate the readings, fantasies and pleasures of spectators."[47]

Interestingly, when Mathijs discusses the credit sentence, calling it "a masterpiece," he does not focus specifically on Walton. He writes, "This is probably the best scene of the film, one that awes as a demonstration of brilliance in production design (Cherniawsky), art direction (Wilkinson), and editing (Sullivan)."[48] These components are obviously inseparable in the collaborative mode of film production; nevertheless, I would like to argue that the film's opening might be treated as Walton's declaration of authorial agency. While how exactly Walton participated in crafting the final version of the title sequence is not obvious, her general influence is evident and reinforced by her authorial self-fashioning. This is immediately clear in Walton and Fawcett's interview for *Art of the Title*, an online publication dedicated to creators and innovators who contribute to the field of title-sequence design. When asked by Lola Landekic what Walton pictured when she initially envisioned the opening of *Ginger Snaps*, the screenwriter answered without hesitation, "What you're seeing on the screen is exactly the screenplay. It's exactly what I envisioned."[49] This strong statement, which could be considered a self-authorizing technique, in Staiger's terms, is confirmed by the comparison of the final film with the original shooting script written by Walton, which details the opening title sequence.[50] Walton herself argues that "the credits are part of the story. That's an opportunity while the audience settles, if they're right off the top. . . . It's another opportunity to do something unique with the information, and to this day, I still write in my title sequences."[51]

Of course, this is not to say that she is the *only* author of the sequence. In fact, these statements are later attenuated in the same interview—for example, when she mentions that Fawcett was "very fond of using Polaroids and slideshow-style art and montages," which is how they came up with the idea of "creating a slideshow, which was essentially going to emerge into the girls' class project, at school."[52] However, it is Walton who elaborates on the "creative approach" when she explains that they were "deliberately using all of the paraphernalia of suburban life": "It was about taking that picture postcard suburban environment and messing it up completely. The lawns are cut, the house is set up, everything's lovely."[53] The combination of gory suicide scenes with a range of objects associated with suburban life—meant to parallel the suburban life with a hell of sorts—was already present in the script and might be considered Walton's creative input. She then goes on to detail the differences in Brigitte's deaths versus Ginger's deaths ("They're all down to character attributes, all down to traits that I knew each character would begin their story with"), to which Fawcett adds, "Ginger's pictures are very over-the-top and hilarious, and Brigitte's are more poetic and dark."[54] Significantly, Walton conceptualizes Ginger as "the art director": "I took the creative stance that this project was definitely Ginger's idea. And it's Brigitte's resourcefulness and role as a willing supporter, a willing co-dependent, that would've made sure she had everything she needed to do it. So, it's definitely a Ginger vision, Brigitte execution kind of situation."[55] In this sense, one could draw parallelisms between Ginger and Walton, both coming up with the idea and, between Brigitte and the team, "executing" it (in the same interview, Fawcett assumes precisely this role, as he explains how they "set up the vignettes," "shot the scenes," etc.).

The discursive positioning of the title sequence, emblematic of the conventional separation of conception and execution, is complicated by practices of team writing and rewriting, which were very much at stake in the case of *Ginger Snaps*. Steven Maras argues in his reflections on screenwriting and auteur theory that such separation radically restricts the way in which it is possible to think about authorship and meaning making in film: "Production occurs through a careful process of crystallization that involves negotiating uncertainty and ambiguity, and building consensus between collaborators about the shape, character and resonance of the project."[56]

Walton's statements might certainly be used as a way of conflating the screenwriter and the auteur, a critical move that is plagued with several methodological difficulties discussed by Maras: on the one hand, the difficulty in determining "the qualities and traces that amount to a supposed 'signature'" of a screenwriter; on the other, the dangers of dethroning the director in favor of the screenwriter—that is, "just reversing the dominant bias."[57] Instead of reading Walton's comments as instances of traditional authorship, however, I prefer to see them as self-authorizing citational practices, which are not irrelevant in the context of horror genre histories and criticism that have systematically overlooked women's impactful contributions to horror film, either as writers or directors. And although, in Staiger's words, "the message produced [by Walton] should not be considered a direct expression of a wholly constituted origin with presence or personality or preoccupations, . . . the message is produced from circumstances in which the individual conceives a self as able to act."[58]

Therefore, rather than reinstating the idea of the author as the origin of meaning, I believe it is more productive to locate Walton's authorship in the context of coordinated talents and genre-orientated filmmaking. Much has been written about *Ginger Snaps'* playful self-reflexivity as well as its critical treatment of the menstrual monster and dramatization of antiheteronormative rebellion against the hormonal hell of high school. However, what we might consider "new" and "unique" (or a product of *individual* intention) constitutes yet another citational practice and is present in other genre films—Brian De Palma's *Carrie*, quoted by Fawcett and Walton as one of their sources of inspiration, is a perfect example of this. If we follow Gaines's suggestion "that we start with the social over the individual and conceive innovation as anticipated and 'contained within' the generic, that is, in the sense of already there, already-in-form," then Walton's contribution to the horror film history implies going with genre and not (only) against it.[59] Accepting this means moving beyond the scholarly tendency to simply disregard any form of mass-address forms as hopelessly compromised for feminist purposes by past patriarchal co-optations or to celebrate texts as "subversive" or "progressive" on the grounds of gender or authorship alone. Without diminishing Walton's creativity and artistic achievement (and I do praise her ingenuity as a *horror* filmmaker), I believe that understanding women's embrace of genre not as a subversion but as activating its productive force has the potential to reposition women's film authorship on several levels. It urges us to shift from romantic fictions of "autonomous" being to the sociality of "genre's generative powers," from desperately seeking a female auteur to "accepting that you are in the realm of the already said."[60] Finally, it opens up space for rethinking women's film practice and creativity in genres historically deemed suitable only to the masculine imagination.

Notes

1 Jane M. Gaines, "The Genius of Genre and the Ingenuity of Women," in *Gender Meets Genre in Postwar Cinemas*, ed. Christine Gledhill (Champaign: University of Illinois Press, 2012), 15.

2 Jane M. Gaines, "Of Cabbages and Authorship," in *A Feminist Reader in Early Cinema*, ed. Jennifer M. Bean and Diane Negra (Durham, N.C.: Duke University Press, 2002), Kindle.

3 Gaines.

4 Gaines.

5 Gaines, "Genius of Genre," 15.

6 See Carol J. Clover, *Men, Women, and Chain Saws: Gender in the Modern Horror Film* (Princeton, N.J.: Princeton University Press, 1992); Linda Williams, "When Women Look: A Sequel," *Senses of Cinema* (July 2001), http://sensesofcinema .com/2001/freuds-worst-nightmares-psychoanalysis-and-the-horror-film/horror _women/; Brigid Cherry, "Refusing to Refuse to Look: Female Viewers of the Horror Film," in *Horror, the Film Reader*, ed. Mark Jancovich (London: Routledge, 2002), 169–178.

7 Gaines, "Genius of Genre," 17.

8 See the original *Women Make Horror* call for papers: https://gothicfeminism.files .wordpress.com/2017/10/women-make-horror-edited-collection-overview.pdf.

9 Judith Mayne, *The Woman at the Keyhole: Feminism and Women's Cinema* (Bloomington: Indiana University Press, 1990), 97.

10 Judith Butler, *Bodies That Matter: On the Discursive Limits of "Sex"* (New York: Routledge, 1993), 15; Catherine Grant, "Secret Agents: Feminist Theories of Women's Film Authorship," *Feminist Theory* 2, no. 1 (April 2001): 124.

11 Janet Staiger, "'Because I Am a Woman': Thinking Identity and Agency for Historiography," *Film History* 25, nos. 1–2 (2013): 206.

12 Staiger, 206.

13 Janet Staiger, "Authorship Approaches," in *Authorship and Film*, ed. David A. Gerstner and Janet Staiger (New York: Routledge, 2003), 50.

14 Staiger, "'Because I Am a Woman,'" 207.

15 Staiger, "Authorship Approaches," 51–52.

16 Ernest Mathijs, *John Fawcett's Ginger Snaps* (Toronto: University of Toronto Press, 2013), Kindle.

17 See ACTRA Toronto, "Karen Walton Receives the 2018 Nell Shipman Award," May 25, 2018, https://www.actratoronto.com/karen-walton-receives-the-2018-nell -shipman-award/.

18 Mathijs, *Ginger Snaps*, chap. 1.

19 Mathijs.

20 Lola Landekic, "Ginger Snaps," *Art of the Title*, October 28, 2015, http://www .artofthetitle.com/title/ginger-snaps/; Kerensa Cadenas, "'Fear Teaches Us a Lot about Ourselves'—an Interview with *Ginger Snaps* Writer Karen Walton," *IndieWire*, October 31, 2013, https://www.indiewire.com/2013/10/fear-teaches-us-a-lot-about -ourselves-an-interview-with-ginger-snaps-writer-karen-walton-207971/.

21 Walton quoted in Mathijs, *Ginger Snaps*, chap. 1.

22 See "*Ginger Snaps* Press Kit Final Revised," July 17, 2000, http://www.ginger-snaps .com/presskit.htm.

23 Kevin Misher quoted in Adam Chitwood, "Producer Kevin Misher Talks Finding the Right Cast, Keeping a Well-Known Story Suspenseful, Committing to an R Rating, and More on the Set of *Carrie*," Collider, July 16, 2013, http://collider.com/kevin -misher-carrie-interview/; see also Kate Bussmann, "Cutting Edge: Mary Harron," *Guardian*, March 6, 2009, http://www.theguardian.com/lifeandstyle/2009/mar/ 06/mary-harron-film; Katarzyna Paszkiewicz, *Genre, Authorship and Contemporary Women Filmmakers* (Edinburgh: Edinburgh University Press, 2018), 63.

24 Donato Totaro, "Karen Walton in Montreal: Chatting about *Ginger Snaps*," *Off-screen* 21, nos. 4–5 (2017), https://offscreen.com/view/karen-walton-in-montreal -chatting-about-ginger-snaps.

25 See Mathijs, *Ginger Snaps*, chap. 4.

26 Totaro, "Karen Walton."

27 "*Ginger Snaps* Press Kit."

28 "*Ginger Snaps* Press Kit."

29 Mathijs, *Ginger Snaps*, chap. 1.

30 Mathijs.

31 This is somewhat contradicted by Walton's own statements. "Right from the start we wanted to make a movie that would entertain," she comments; "*Ginger Snaps* Press Kit."

32 David Bordwell, *The Films of Carl-Theodor Dreyer* (Berkeley: University of California Press, 1981).

33 Mathijs, *Ginger Snaps*, chap. 1.

34 Mathijs, chap. 1.

35 Mathijs, chap. 1.

36 Mathijs, chap. 2.

37 "*Ginger Snaps* Press Kit."

38 Mathijs, *Ginger Snaps*, chap. 2.

39 ACTRA Toronto, "Karen Walton."

40 Landekic, "Ginger Snaps."

41 Mathijs, *Ginger Snaps*, chap. 1.

42 Totaro, "Karen Walton."

43 Totaro.

44 These are only some of the snapshots that appear on the screen. For an extensive account of the title sequence, see Mathijs, *Ginger Snaps*, chap. 3.

45 Mathijs, chap. 3.

46 See Aviva Briefel, "Monster Pains: Masochism, Menstruation, and Identification in the Horror Film," *Film Quarterly* 58, no. 3 (2005): 16–27; Pamela Craig and Martin Fradley, "Teenage Traumata: Youth, Affective Politics and the Contemporary American Horror Film," in *American Horror Film: The Genre at the Turn of the Millennium*, ed. Steffen Hantke (Jackson: University Press of Mississippi, 2010), 77–102; Bianca Nielsen, "'Something's Wrong, Like More Than You Being Female': Transgressive Sexuality and Discourses of Reproduction in *Ginger Snaps*," *thirdspace* 3, no. 2 (2004): 55–69.

47 Timothy Corrigan, *A Cinema without Walls: Movies and Culture after Vietnam* (New Brunswick, N.J.: Rutgers University Press, 1991), 103, 108.

48 Mathijs, *Ginger Snaps*, chap. 3.

49 Landekic, "Ginger Snaps."

50 Although some elements did not appear in the original script, such as suicide notes.
51 Landekic, "Ginger Snaps."
52 Landekic.
53 Landekic.
54 Landekic.
55 Landekic.
56 Steven Maras, *Screenwriting: History, Theory and Practice* (London: Wallflower, 2009), 116.
57 Maras, 109–110.
58 Staiger, "Authorship Approaches," 50.
59 Gaines, "Genius of Genre," 26.
60 Richard Dyer, *Pastiche* (London: Routledge, 2007), 176, 180.

10

The Feminist Art Horror of the New French Extremity

MADDI MCGILLVRAY

The "New French Extremity" was first coined in 2004 by critic and programmer James Quandt to describe the growing presence of extreme violence and sexual brutality in French-language films at the turn of the millennium.[1] The moniker was initially meant to be a derogatory one, as Quandt describes the body of films as "a cinema suddenly determined to break every taboo, to wade in rivers of visceral and spumes of sperm, to fill each frame with flesh, nubile or gnarled, and submit it to all manner of penetration, mutilation, and defilement."[2] Although Quandt initially wrote about the New French Extremity as an art-house movement, in the years that followed, the term became synonymous with horror films and earned a reputation for eliciting heightened affective responses from audiences, including mass walkouts, fainting, and vomiting.[3]

For all that has been written about the excessive nature of the New French Extremity, little attention has been paid to women's foundational contributions. This chapter aims to remedy this gap in the literature by examining women's authorship in the New French Extremity in the early 2000s. In a close analysis of Claire Denis's *Trouble Every Day* (2001) and Marina de Van's *In My Skin* (*Dans ma peau*; 2002), I examine the ways in which both filmmakers combine European avant-garde aesthetics with horror genre tropes. Denis and de Van were crucial in spearheading the movement's art-house lineage with conventions of the horror genre, which arguably motivated a surge in horror film productions in France, including *High Tension* (*Haute tension*; 2003), *Calvaire* (2004), *Them* (*Ils*; 2006), *Sheitan* (2006), *Inside* (*À l'intérieur*; 2007), *Frontier(s)* (*Frontière[s]*; 2007), and *Martyrs* (2008).[4] I propose that Denis and de Van's integration of "high" and "low" cinematic forms establishes a unique approach to film authorship, one that I define as feminist art horror.

Feminist Art Horror

Much of the early critical outrage surrounding the New French Extremity stemmed from what Martine Beugnet describes as "a disregard for genre boundaries."[5] Quandt detested the disparity between the elite art meant to be achieved by European filmmakers and the shock tactics associated with "lower" cinematic genres. As he proclaims, "Images and subjects once the provenance of splatter films, exploitation flicks, and porn . . . proliferate in the high art environs of a national cinema whose provocations have historically been formal, political, or philosophical."[6] This paradox between the high and low has come to define the films of the New French Extremity, yet their hierarchical distinction is not as straightforward as Quandt posits. In *Cutting Edge: Art Horror and the Horrific Avant-Garde*, Joan Hawkins illustrates how lowbrow cinema (such as paracinema catalogs) can elide the boundaries between high and low art, resulting in a cinema she labels "art-horror."[7] Hawkins's art-horror fusion can be explored profitably by considering the work of women filmmakers who also circumvent such polemics. Where Quandt frames the sensationalism of low cinematic genres as oppositional to the movement's high avant-garde principles, I contend that the intersection of the two is indispensable to the feminist sensibility of Denis and de Van's art horror.

Feminist art horror is composed of multiple juxtapositions. First, it stands between two conflicting systems: genre and art-house cinema. This duality is informed by cultural hierarchies, which assert that some forms of art are "higher" than others. Despite being one of the oldest systems used to classify creative works, there has been a substantial devaluation of genre over the years. Thomas Schatz unpacks this hostility by distinguishing between "film genres" and "genre films."[8] On one level, films can be quantified into categories known as genres and based on "familiar formula[s] of interrelated narrative and cinematic components."[9] Schatz then explains that understandings of genre films also rest on mass-market cinema and its processes.[10] This emphasis on commercialism is seen as a threat to artistic creativity, and the resulting criticism, developed in France by creators of the *politique des auteurs*, reinforced an opposition between high art and mass entertainment. Here, "low" is associated with not only genres favored by the majority but also those belonging to the so-called lowbrow.[11] For instance, horror cinema (up until recently) has often been considered to be very low. As Carol J. Clover states, "On the civilized side of the continuum lie the legitimate genres; at the other end . . . lie horror and pornography."[12] This contempt stemmed from attitudes toward genre films but also toward horror being "beyond the purview of the respectable."[13] These considerations, whether intentional or not, also reinforced a gendered hierarchy whereby horror was viewed as "less suitable for women filmmakers."[14]

Feminist art horror also makes up the contrasting positions in feminist studies of female authorship. Since the 1970s, feminist scholarship has looked to women filmmakers for alternatives to the patriarchal language of cinema.[15] Discouraged by Hollywood's ideological and formal treatment of women, feminists aimed to articulate a women's cinema that would counteract the hegemonic nature of mainstream structures. Writing as both a theorist and filmmaker, Laura Mulvey contended that women's cinema was to be an avant-garde practice that would "free the look of the camera into its materiality in time and space and the look of the audience into dialectics, [and] passionate detachment."[16] As noted in chapter 5, such a cinema aimed to disrupt the visual pleasures produced by mainstream films and relied on experimental forms and styles. While Mulvey's model is perhaps the most influential call for an alternative women's cinema, it also reinforced a neglect of popular genre films made by women.[17] To mend this fissure, Claire Johnston conceived of a women's countercinema informed by a "two-way process" between film as a political tool and as entertainment.[18] According to Johnston, "In order to counter our objectification in the cinema, our collective fantasies must be released: women's cinema must embody the working through of desire: such an objective demands the use of the entertainment film."[19] This intertextual approach guides Denis and de Van's feminist art horror.

Traditionally, the dichotomy between high and low has not benefitted women. As Brigitte Rollet stresses, "It has indirectly reinforced male predominance over culture."[20] Denis and de Van's films resist this discourse by subverting the boundaries between high and low institutions. While *Trouble Every Day* and *In My Skin* merge with the horror genre, they are also marked by a particular art-house style. This corresponds with Johnston's countercinema strategy, which recognizes feminist value in women who use the codes of mainstream cinema to challenge them from within. As Johnston asserts, "We should seek to operate at all levels: within the male-dominated cinema and outside of it."[21] Examined from this perspective, Denis and de Van's films are significant not just because they are written and directed by women but also because they encourage us to consider female authorship outside of rigid cultural hierarchies. Their distinctive art-horror synthesis opens up multiple forms of feminist transgression, not least the assumption that horror is only suitable for men.

Trouble Every Day

Trouble Every Day, the third title in Denis's expansive filmography, gained a dubious reputation as a *film maudit* upon release.[22] Unlike Denis's previous critically acclaimed films *Chocolate* (1988) and *Beau Travail* (1999), *Trouble Every Day* was greeted with boos and mass walkouts during its Cannes Film Festival premiere in 2001. Much of the anger surrounding the film was attributed to "the fact that Denis, a respected and revered filmmaker, had made a horror film."[23] Critic Derek Elley scolded the film in *Variety*, proclaiming, "Hannibal gets the French arthouse treatment in Claire Denis' *Trouble Every Day*, a resolutely silly movie, largely shot in English, that plays like 'An Existential American Cannibal in Paris.'"[24] *Trouble Every Day* presents parallel (and at times intersecting) stories of two couples. The film begins with Shane and his wife, June, supposedly traveling to Paris for their honeymoon. In reality, Shane is actually trying to find neuroscientist Dr. Léo Sémeneau and his wife, Coré. Léo's former colleague provides Shane with the couple's address and explains that Léo now works as a general practitioner so he can care for his ailing wife. Coré suffers from a mysterious disorder that triggers cannibalistic impulses when sexually aroused. Shane, as we will discover, is experiencing similar carnal urges.

If one were pressed to assign a generic category to *Trouble Every Day*, it would likely be that of horror. Yet these generic conventions transition into something more abstract as the film progresses. At first glance, *Trouble Every Day* might fit within the horror subgenre concerned with biological disease and contagion. The film opens with the haunting soundtrack, written and performed by Tindersticks, with the lyric "It's on the inside of me . . . I get on the inside of you." Parallel editing is then employed to depict Shane's and Coré's similar violent behaviors. The first half of the film follows the typical story of a male protagonist trying to find a cure for the virus. Even so, Denis keeps the dialogue to a minimum and provides little context for the viewer. This was particularly frustrating for Quandt, who raged, "An enervated Denis barely musters a hint of narrative to contain or explain the orgiastic bloodletting."[25] In a loose backstory, the film reveals that Shane once worked with Léo, who led an experimental bioprospecting mission in Guyana in the hopes of curing neuroses and problems of the libido. Denis offers further hints of a scientific explanation through repeated visuals of spiraling beakers and references to botany. While it is implied that Léo's previous work with Shane is connected to the disease, its direct origin is never made explicit. In turn, key events and character motivations are left to audience interpretation.

Although the word *vampire* is never mentioned, Denis also references elements of the archetype,[26] which Douglas Morrey summarizes: "The blood smeared around Coré's mouth after a kill; the camera that, from Shane's point of view, lingers in close-up on the neck of a chambermaid; Shane's complaint about the bright lights in a laboratory; a shot in which Coré raises her coat like bat-wings behind her shoulders."[27] That being said, Denis is less concerned with vampire mythos than the internal conflicts of her characters. During the newlyweds' flight to Paris, Shane experiences a vivid daydream of June writhing around in a pool of blood. As their plane touches down, he whispers to her, "I will never hurt you." Coré, on the other hand, experiences a more advanced stage of the malady. Unlike Shane, who tries to repress the effects of the disease, Coré acts on her cannibalistic desires. To satisfy her urges, she lures men into remote fields where she seduces them and then feasts on them. Moments after, her eyes fill with tears, and she is overcome with remorse. This postcoital melancholy is further sympathized in Coré's only line of dialogue, wherein she whispers to Léo, "I don't want to wait anymore; I want to die."

Narrative cohesion is secondary to artifice in *Trouble Every Day*. Far from providing the usual build-up of suspense associated with horror, *Trouble Every Day* moves in an unhurried and matter-of-fact progression.[28] Laura McMahon outlines the formulaic unfolding of horror narratives, "whereby the viewer agrees to be terrified of the film in return for the clear unfolding of the plot."[29] This contrasts with Denis's own philosophy, which she describes as "about exploring the formal design with which no one is familiar, the film itself offering a sort of immersion within aesthetic designs, taking us towards a more profound, mysterious place."[30] This juxtaposition is exemplified in the scene where Shane and June visit the Notre-Dame cathedral. Following a series of close-ups on gargoyles, Shane imitates Boris Karloff's Frankenstein by stretching his arms out and lunging toward June. This reference might actually provide valuable insights into the film's biohorror plot, and yet Denis's interest lies elsewhere. She focuses on June's bright-green scarf, blown off her neck by the wind. The camera lingers at length on the fabric as it flutters against the Parisian skyline. This moment is typical of the defamiliarizing qualities of Denis's feminist art horror, as she references one of horror's most infamous figures, only to abandon such allusions for a more lyrical experience.

This approach extends to the way Denis portrays bodies. Aware of his wife's condition, Léo locks Coré inside their home every day before leaving for work. Two young men observe this routine and break into the home in search of drugs. One of the intruders discovers Coré, who then seduces him. Unlike most erotic scenes that illustrate two bodies engaged in sexual acts together, the camera favors extreme close-ups of skin, offering a slow-crawling movement encompassing pores, goose bumps, and small clumps of hair. This makes it nearly impossible for the viewer to detect whose body they are looking at, let alone what body parts are being shown. Coré licks the man's neck and chin, playful movements that become threatening as she begins to gnaw at his flesh. The intruder's moans of pleasure become cries of pain, and he pleads with her to stop. The camera focuses on Coré's mouth as she bites deeper into his neck and then keeps to this close gaze as Coré playfully explores the new orifices she has opened on the boy's body. In the final, arresting image, Coré is in a delirious haze, stumbling past a blood-soaked wall and bearing a striking resemblance to the vampiric figure of Count Orlok in the film *Nosferatu* (1922).

Moments later, Shane rushes home and discovers Coré setting fire to the house. He strangles her and leaves her to be consumed by the flames. The narrative then shifts to focus on his medical condition, which accelerates in intensity. He tries to hide his affliction from June, who grows increasingly suspicious. He goes on solitary long walks, leaves June alone for days on end, and unable to climax during sex, resorts to masturbation in the next room. Eventually, Shane relieves himself by raping a hotel chambermaid. At first, Shane's overtures are consensual, and the maid reciprocates. When Shane becomes increasingly aggressive, the maid tries to pull away, but he forces himself on her. The remainder of the scene is framed through an extreme close-up of the maid's face, emphasizing her displeasure and fear. Shane performs oral sex, which is visibly painful for her, and as he moves his head into frame, he exposes his mouth, covered in blood and bodily tissue. He then drags the maid's lifeless body out of frame, and the camera remains focused on the blood-soaked ground. Shane showers in his hotel room, and the film ends on June's wide-eyed stare as she agrees to go back to America with her husband. A single streak of blood remains on the shower wall, suggesting that June may be conscious of the atrocities Shane has committed.

Coré's and Shane's mirrored scenes both begin in ways that feel carnal and romantic. However, Denis uses the language of the horror film to blur the boundaries of desire. As she remarks, "It's actually a love story. It's about desire and how close the kiss is to the bite."[31] Denis does not represent female desire in an idealized way but instead plays on societal fears about sexuality, creating a slippage between eroticism and agony. Most important is the way Coré transgresses boundaries of socially and sexually acceptable female behavior, also evident in the later scene in which Shane kills the chambermaid, where what begins as a consensual sex act descends into a horrific violation. This "troubling" of desire is made possible by Denis's "troubling" of cinematic traditions. She makes horror's most fundamental features strange through high-art provocations. Nevertheless, Denis's art horror blend was not intentionally created in response to feminist theory. As Denis made clear in an interview for the *Irish Times*, "When you say 'female director' I already want to stop this conversation! . . . Female director? I feel like I am an animal. I am a female director like this is a female bird. No, I am a director—good or bad I don't know."[32] Rather, this chapter argues that the feminist value of Denis's art horror comes from the transgressive interventions it espouses.

In My Skin

In My Skin was inspired by an event in de Van's childhood when a car ran over her leg. As she recalls, "I felt no sense of panic, no pain, even though I should have passed out. I saw my leg just as another object. . . . Later, at school my scars became a kind of game. My friends and I amused ourselves by sticking them with needles, because my skin had become numb there. I felt proud, but at the same time this insensitivity was frightening."[33] This corporeal fascination prompted de Van to directly insert herself as the writer, director, and lead actor for *In My Skin*. The film centers on Esther, a young marketing professional. While at a party with colleagues, she goes out to the hosts' dark garden and falls. Esther does not realize she has been hurt until much later. She visits a doctor, who asks her jokingly, "Are you sure it's your leg?" This comment seems to set into motion the beginning (or initial evidence) of a radical shift in Esther's relationship with her own body. From this point, Esther becomes fixated on mutilating her body. She starts by reopening her wound with knives, scissors, and other sharp household objects. Her boyfriend Vincent and her best friend/coworker Sandrine are both concerned and repulsed by her behavior. Despite their multiple interventions, Esther's condition becomes so severe that she stages a car accident to explain away her lacerations. Her curiosity accelerates, and she eventually experiments with self-cannibalism. Esther withdraws from her loved ones and, in the end, rents a hotel room where she violently explores her body.

According to Alexandra West, *In My Skin* can be described as "a mediation on body horror."[34] Made famous by the early oeuvre of Canadian filmmaker David Cronenberg, body horror is a subgenre concerned with graphic violations of the human body, including transformations, decompositions, mutilations, or unnatural movements.[35] In accordance with the subgenre, *In My Skin* focuses on Esther's bodily deterioration. That being said, whereas most body horror films tend to offer a medical or technological explanation for the corporeal phenomenon, de Van provides few narrative motivations. Esther's doctor tests her for neurological damage but does not find anything. Vincent repeatedly questions Esther about her behavior. For instance, when he first notices a number of new scars on Esther's body, he expresses his concern (and judgment). In lieu of confiding in her partner, Esther laughs off the incident, simply replying, "I did it without thinking. It just came over me." As Esther's grip on reality disappears, the audience grows as confused as Vincent. The plot may center on Esther, but the viewer has a minimal grasp of her interior life or how her self-harm will intensify. The narrative breaks apart during Esther's isolation in the later stages of the film, creating a complete transgression of dominant narrative film practices.

Esther's fixation is not merely the opposite of normal, sanctioned behavior. Her self-destruction overlaps with, responds to, and emerges from the normality that surrounds her. From the outset, Esther seems to have a lifestyle that many women strive for. She is a professional businesswoman who has just received a coveted promotion in her office and has also found herself in a stable relationship. However, this perfection is merely an illusion. She also displays an abnormal fascination with harming herself. For example, when Esther returns to work after her initial leg injury, she is asked by her employer to correct a mistake she made on a product report. She goes into the office supply closet and finds the nearest sharp object and begins to cut into her skin, seemingly offering her a feeling of release. As such, Esther is torn between two worlds. She practices her self-cutting in private (at least initially) and continues to excel in her professional and personal life.

Although *In My Skin* is horrific at times, de Van knowingly distances herself from definable body horror conventions. As such, generic references become reinterpreted through her avant-garde style. One night, at an important business dinner with clients, Esther consumes too much wine and suddenly sees her left arm as separate from her body. Her imagination drifts, and she hallucinates, seeing her forearm lying immobile on the table next to the silverware. She attempts to reattach it, and when all her efforts fail, she begins to stab her arm with a steak knife to regain some sentience. The scene bears a striking resemblance to the classic surrealism of *Un chien Andalou* (1929), in which a hand becomes disembodied and moves on its own.[36] In 1924, Andrew Breton described surrealism as "the future resolution of these two states, dream and reality, which are seemingly contradictory, into a kind of absolute reality, a surreality."[37] De Van adopts a dream-like aesthetic that stylistically overturns the film's narrative. In most body horror films, blood would spurt out of the wound, emphasizing her suffering. Instead, there is almost no blood or visible gore. De Van is more concerned with showing the knife writhing around inside Esther's skin and the pleasure she experiences from it.

Much like Denis, de Van depicts female desire but portrays it going in unexpected directions. Early in the film, Esther and Vincent discuss purchasing an apartment together. The milestone would typically be a celebratory occasion for most couples, yet Esther and Vincent seal their confirmation with a kiss devoid of any passion or romance. *In My Skin* does not include sex scenes per se; rather, Esther's titillating relationship is with her flesh. Esther rejoices in hurting herself, and she kisses the wounds on her arm with more emotion than she offers Vincent. Moreover, de Van's art horror deconstructs the meanings that are commonly attached to representations of the body in pain. As de Van claims, "I wanted the audience to be affected strongly, but with Esther I didn't want them to feel violence, to be frightened or uncomfortable. What was most important for me was the emotion in her curiosity."[38] Esther is filmed in a strangely seductive fashion; images of her self-harm are filmed with a heightened level of sensuality, the camera slowly tracking up her legs. Through the combination of close-up shots and subjective camera angles, the viewer comes to look at Esther's body with (and through) her.

Unlike most horror films that typically unfold on one side of the normal/abnormal dichotomy, something else happens toward the end of *In My Skin*. Esther does not return to her prior normal self before her accident, nor does the film end with her abnormal death or despair. Instead, Esther's self-harm allows her to reach a new state of being. In the final moments of the film, she isolates herself in a hotel room and, in a series of split-screen tableaus, takes her brutal practice to a new extreme. With a calm, detached stare, Esther performs gruesome acts such as cutting her face, attempting to tan a piece of skin she has removed from herself, and eating her own flesh. She cuts her upper thigh and maneuvers her leg close to her head, allowing the blood to pour out of her wound and onto her face. For the first time, she uses a camera to photograph the damage she has done to her body. These images are extreme close-ups revealing the full extent of her lacerations. Esther seems to have reached a new state, but we do not have a sense of what she might be seeing. Instead, she appears to be calmed (and even satisfied) by the process of cutting.

In My Skin ends ambiguously. In the morning, Esther is alone in the hotel room in an unresponsive state. Her body is maimed, but her face is devoid of emotion. She wakes and inspects her piece of skin that she attempted to tan. It has gone hard and shriveled, and she lovingly places it inside her bra. She then fixes her hair, grabs her coat, and leaves the hotel room. Her acts are deliberate and goal oriented and, for a brief moment, suggest that the horror is over. However, the subsequent shot shows Esther lying on a bed, unmoving and staring vacantly into the camera. Unlike the directional pan that was used to illustrate Esther leaving the hotel room, *In My Skin* concludes with a tracking shot of Esther's face, framed in close-up as she stares into the camera. The right side of Esther's face appears normal and engaged, but the left side is slightly "off," and her left eye is bizarrely squinted. The camera holds on Esther's face for several seconds until the image fades to black.

The feminist art horror of *In My Skin* is somewhat different than *Trouble Every Day*. Denis was already a well-regarded filmmaker (even bordering on auteur) when she wrote and directed *Trouble Every Day*, whereas *In My Skin* was de Van's feature film debut. Furthermore, the narrative of *In My Skin* is told entirely from a female point of view. For a year in advance, de Van carried out actor exercises designed to increase her objectivity and self-detachment, which included walking around in uncomfortable shoes, buying and wearing clothes she disliked, and growing her fingernails to awkward lengths.[39] By removing the structures that are commonly relied upon in genre filmmaking, we are left to the mercy of Esther and her violent desires. When Esther's bloody face gazes into the camera, de Van produces a startling moment of feminist art horror, a portrayal of female fantasy that causes a series of distortions within the very structures of cinematic form.

Conclusion

In this chapter, I propose a theory of feminist art horror in order to explore the hybrid nature of Denis and de Van's New French Extremity films. I've argued that not only did *Trouble Every Day* and *In My Skin* evade the boundaries between high and low cinematic forms, but they can also be seen as art horror films with feminist objectives. However, they are not alone in their transgressive style, especially in France. Denis and de Van's feminist art horror combines two trends distinguishable in the work of French women directors.[40] On the one hand, they can be situated alongside a wave of contemporary filmmakers—including Josiane Balasko, Daniele Dubroux, and Marion Vernoux—who contribute to popular, male-dominated genres including comedies, crime films, and road movies.[41] At the same time, Denis and de Van's films also harken back to the avant-garde work of Agnes Varda, Chantal Ackerman, and Marguerite Duras, in particular their desire to renew the cinematic language itself. This chapter has suggested that considering these films in terms of women's authorship offers an opportunity to integrate high and low cultural forms in shocking ways. As Hawkins asserts, "Both high art and low culture have the capacity to . . . rattle the cage."[42] If we can accept this, we are able to move beyond the scholarly dichotomy of high/low, experimental/mainstream, and art/horror and can instead consider the possibilities of their crossover. Ultimately, the concept of feminist art horror suggests a fascinating and exciting plurality of cinematic forms available for women filmmakers.

Notes

1   James Quandt, "Flesh and Blood: Sex and Violence in Recent French Cinema," *Artforum*, February 2004, http://www.artforum.com/inprint/id=6199.
2   Quandt.
3   Alexandra West, *Films of the New French Extremity: Visceral Horror and National Identity* (Jefferson, N.C.: McFarland, 2016), 17; Tanya Horeck and Tina Kendall, *The New Extremism in Cinema: From France to Europe* (Edinburgh: Edinburgh University Press, 2011), 7.
4   West, *Films*, 17.
5   Martine Beugnet, *Cinema and Sensation: French Film and the Art of Transgression* (Edinburgh: Edinburgh University Press, 2007), 15.
6   Quandt, "Flesh and Blood."
7   Joan Hawkins, *Cutting Edge: Art-Horror and the Horrific Avant-Garde* (Minneapolis: University of Minnesota Press, 2000).
8   Thomas Schatz, *Hollywood Genres: Formulas, Filmmaking, and the Studio System* (Philadelphia: Temple University Press, 1981), 14.
9   Schatz, 16.
10 Schatz, 16.
11 Brigitte Rollet, "Women Directors and Genre Films in France," in *Women Filmmakers: Refocusing*, ed. Jaqueline Levitin, Judith Plessis, and Valerie Raoul (Vancouver: University of British Columbia Press, 2003), 128.
12 Carol J. Clover, *Men, Women, and Chain Saws: Gender in the Modern Horror Film* (Princeton, N.J.: Princeton University Press, 1992), 21.
13 Clover, 21.
14 Katarzyna Paszkiewicz, *Genre, Authorship and Contemporary Women Filmmakers* (Edinburgh: Edinburgh University Press, 2018), 4.
15 Hilary Neroni, *Feminist Film Theory and Cléo from 5 to 7* (London: Bloomsbury, 2016), 60.

16 Laura Mulvey, "Visual Pleasure and Narrative Cinema," *Screen* 13, no. 3 (Fall 1975): 18.

17 Anneke Smelik, "Feminist Film Theory," in *The Cinema Book*, ed. Pam Cook, 3rd ed. (London: BFI, 2007), 494.

18 Claire Johnston, "Women's Cinema as Counter-cinema," in *Notes on Women's Cinema*, ed. Claire Johnston (London: SEFT, 1973), 31.

19 Johnston, 31.

20 Rollet, "Women Directors," 129.

21 Johnston, "Women's Cinema," 31.

22 West, *Films*, 94.

23 West, 94.

24 Derek Elley, "Review: *Trouble Every Day*," *Variety*, May 2001, https://variety.com/2001/film/reviews/trouble-every-day-1200468352/.

25 Quandt, "Flesh and Blood."

26 Douglas Morrey, "Textures of Terror: Claire Denis's *Trouble Every Day*," *Belphégor* 3, no. 2 (Spring 2004): 2.

27 Morrey, 2.

28 Morrey, 3.

29 Laura McMahon, "The Contagious Body of the Film: Claire Denis' *Trouble Every Day* (2001)," in *Transmissions: Essays in French Thought, Literature and Cinema*, ed. Isabel McNeill and Bradley Stephens (New York: Peter Lang, 2007), 78.

30 Isabelle Regnier, "Les Pensionnat des épouses dociles," trans. Tim Palmer, *Le Monde*, January 2005, 28.

31 Samantha Dinning, "Claire Denis: Great Directors," *Senses of Cinema*, April 2009, http://sensesofcinema.com/2009/great-directors/claire-denis/.

32 Donald Clarke, "Claire Denis: 'We Are Normal People. Even Though We Are French,'" *Irish Times*, April 2014, https://www.irishtimes.com/culture/film/claire-denis-we-are-normal-people-even-though-we-are-french-1.3457322.

33 Philippe Piazzo, "Le film vient de mes émotions, pas d'un principe," *Le Monde*, trans. Tim Palmer, December 4, 2002, 35.

34 West, *Films*, 97.

35 Ronald Allan Lopez Cruz, "Mutations and Metamorphoses: Body Horror Is Biological Horror," *Journal of Popular Film and Television* 40, no. 4 (Fall 2011): 160–168.

36 Adam Lowenstein, "Feminine Horror: The Embodied Surrealism of *In My Skin*," in *The Dread of Difference: Gender and the Modern Horror Film*, ed. Barry Keith Grant, 2nd ed. (Austin: University of Texas Press, 2015), 473.

37 André Breton, "Manifesto of Surrealism," in *Manifestos of Surrealism*, trans. Richard Seaver and Helen R. Lane (Ann Arbor: University of Michigan Press, 1994), 14.

38 Tim Palmer, "Don't Look Back: An Interview with Marina de Van," *French Review* 83, no. 5 (Spring 2010), 1060.

39 Palmer, 84.

40 Rachel Ritterbusch, "Anne Fontaine and Contemporary Women's Cinema in France," *Rocky Mountain Review* 62, no. 2 (Fall 2008): 69.

41 Rollet, "Women Directors," 127.

42 Hawkins, *Cutting Edge*, 215.

11

Women-Made Horror in Korean Cinema

MOLLY KIM

The Korean horror films *The Uninvited* (*4 inyong shiktak*; 2003), *Whispering Corridors: Wishing Stairs* (*Yeogo goedam 3: Yeowoo gyedan*; 2003), *Roommates* (*D-day*; 2006), and *Shadows in the Palace* (*Goongnyeo*; 2007) are produced by first-time female directors and are critical and commercial successes. The films explore the place of women in Korean society, employing female characters not only as protagonists but also as key narrative drivers, as opposed to the marginal, passive, or nonexistent female characters depicted in many popular genre Korean films. Given their commercial success, these films have demonstrated and encouraged a new prominent role for women within the Korean film industry. For example, *Shadows in the Palace*, set during the Joseon dynasty (1392–1910), serves to cinematize female experience by focusing on the lives and duties of *goong nyeo* (palace women). Horror emerges through the silence of the *goong nyeo*, as the women were forced to be witnesses and victims of brutal crimes committed by (male) royal authorities. This approach can also be linked to the wider global trend of horror indies made by women. Julia Ducournau, director of *Raw* (2016), has commented that women make "interesting, different horror films because when [they] make horror, it's the expression of a form of violence [they] feel inside. . . . [And] it's important we recognize that women feel violence and anger."[1]

There has been a considerable amount of Korean- and English-language academic work dedicated to Korean horror films, of which much relates to the representation of women. Eunha Oh and Kim Yoon-hee both examine the representation of maternity in Korean horror films, while Baek Moon-im historicizes the cinematization of the *gwisin* (ghost) in classic horror films.[2] In a similar context, Park Ju-young analyzes Korean horror films after 1998 to demonstrate how the technical development and industrial changes of Korean cinema influenced the mode of representation of *yeogwi* (female ghosts) and *cheonyeo gwisin* (female virgin ghosts).[3] These studies illuminate how women are represented in the horror films of a particular historical period and how the cinematic representation of women has (not) changed over time. Nevertheless, these works do not consider how these issues were or could have been addressed and delivered from the perspective of women filmmakers. In fact, no in-depth study (in either Korean or English) has yet been done on women-made Korean horror films.

In this chapter, I analyze *The Uninvited* and *Shadows in the Palace* as examples of "women's cinema," following Alison Butler's definition as films "made by, addressed to, or concerned with women, or all three."[4] As Butler states, the notion of women's cinema should be considered as "neither a genre nor a movement in film history, it has . . . no filmic or aesthetic specificity, but traverses and negotiates cinematic and cultural traditions and critical and political debates."[5] Through this analysis, I demonstrate how Korean women filmmakers have utilized the horror genre to work within and/or against cultural restrictions in popular genre cinema.[6]

Korean Horror Cinema

The golden era of Korean horror cinema was in the 1960s, beginning with cult director Kim Ki-young's *The Housemaid* (*Hanyeo*; 1960). The film, with its themes of infidelity and murder, was inspired by the real-life event of a young housemaid killing a newborn baby. Due to the scandal of portraying a recent, sensational murder case, when the film opened in a single theater—Myung-bo Geuk Jang in Seoul—more than one hundred thousand people attended.[7] *The Housemaid* initiated the first cycle of modern Korean horror cinema and inspired several domestic thrillers and horror films, including *A Devilish Homicide* (*Salinma*; 1965), *Beauty with No Neck* (*Mokeomneun minyeo*; 1966), and *A Public Cemetery under the Moon* (*Wolhaui gongdongmyoji*; 1967). In 1967, seven horror films were released in Korea, which was the highest amount in one year up until that date.[8]

However, the heyday of the genre did not last long, as the Korean film industry's success declined following the popularization of television in the 1970s. Adding to this pressure, Park Chung-hee's military government imposed various restrictive regulations on the film industry. In 1973, the fourth revision of the Motion Picture Law mandated film companies to acquire an official government license, which was only given to studios with a high level of facilities and conditions.[9] Under these circumstances, from 1970 to 1975, some midsize film studios declared bankruptcy, and the number of companies decreased from twenty-three to fifteen. Overall, between 1970 and 1979, the number of films in production plunged from 231 to 96.[10]

Despite the industry recession, until the mid-1970s, horror films continued to be made, and the genre enjoyed success in regional, second-run theaters, where horror films tended to be cheaper to exhibit. However, by the end of the 1970s, the horror genre gradually faded out of popularity. Studios were encouraged by state policy to exclusively support "literary films" (adaptations of respected Korean novels) and government-sponsored propaganda films. If studios engaged in such productions, they were rewarded with a permit to import lucrative foreign films for domestic exhibition.[11] As a result, after the release of *Suddenly at Midnight* (*Gipeunbam gapjagi*) in 1981, the horror genre more or less disappeared until 1995.[12]

Restrictive film laws continued to affect filmmaking practices throughout the 1980s. Chun Doo-hwan's military regime, established in 1980 by coup, maintained the same rigid regulations as the Park regime but also offered more liberalized policies in order to appease an increasingly malcontent public. One of the initiatives enacted during Chun's rule was the "3S policy," through which the government promoted sex, sports, and (the cinematic) screen in an attempt to lead public concerns away from political issues. Under the 3S policy, Chun established professional baseball leagues, semiofficial prostitution parlors, and late-night movie theaters and, in 1984, within the fifth reconstitution of the Motion Picture Law, notably relaxed the censorship of sexual representation in film.[13] Consequently, Korean cinema was swamped with soft-core erotic films, particularly the subgenre of *ero-sageuk* (erotic historical dramas). The *ero-sageuk* then dominated the box office while most other genres, including horror and action, were marginalized, if not disregarded entirely.[14]

In 1987, a democratic government was established, and in the mid-1990s, the Korean film industry underwent a revival. Ironically, the expansion of the film industry coincided with the Korean International Monetary Fund crisis in 1997, as investors began to look for new avenues for their funds beyond the unreliable stock market.[15] Many financiers considered film production a relatively safe investment. From 1998 to 2005, the total financial outlay in film production reached $535 million, and new, independent production companies, including Shin Cine and Myung Film, joined the domestic market.[16]

Empowered by these industrial changes, the number of productions increased, and more diverse types of films were made. Horror was preferred by many independent film companies due to the relatively low production costs associated with the genre.[17] In 1998, the low-budget comedy horror *The Quiet*

Family (*Joyonghan gajok*), the fantasy horror *Soul Guardians* (*Toemarok*), and the high school horror *Whispering Corridors* (*Yeogo goedam*) were all released and were financial successes that generated profits far exceeding their break-even point (BEP).[18] In terms of domestic box office, *Whispering Corridors* became the highest-grossing Korean horror film in the history of the genre and has generated four sequels in the eleven-year period. The rising popularity of horror film reached its apex in 2003 in terms of commercial success. Five horror films were released in 2003, and two of those were directed by women, half of the total number of films directed by women in that year.[19] Lee Soo-yeon's *The Uninvited* and Yun Jae-yeon's *Whispering Corridors 3: Wishing Stairs* recorded audience numbers in excess of five hundred thousand in Seoul.[20]

These postclassical Korean horror films are significant not just because they are representative of the changing landscape of the Korean film industry but also because they highlight the emergence of female filmmakers specializing in genre films, particularly horrors and thrillers. This was a remarkable development in Korean horror film, as, until this point, the genre had been monopolized by male directors. Perhaps not coincidentally, this period also marked the rise of female producers associated with horror films, including Lee Yoo-jin on *The Uninvited* and Cheong Seung-hye on *Shadows in the Palace*. The successful teaming of these directors and producers also indicates greater ramifications for the diversification of the larger professional landscape of the Korean film industry.

History within History: "Herstory" of Korean Cinema

The history of Korean female filmmakers is not short, but it is thin. The first Korean female director was Park Nam-ok, whose first feature, *The Widow* (*Mimangin*), was released in 1955. *The Widow* tells the story of a war widow in postwar Korea, addressing sensitive but critical women's issues such as sexual desire and remarriage. Park did not portray the widow as either a war victim or a morally fallen woman, the two most common tropes of popular Korean films and novels of this period. Instead, Park represented her heroine as an independent and modern woman, able to balance her work and desires while seeking new opportunities for the future. Perhaps this depiction of women was too intimidating or progressive for the era; *The Widow* did not do well at the box office and was removed from theaters just three days after its release. No investors and producers were prepared to support a second feature, and unfortunately, *The Widow* became Park's first and only film.

Hong Eun-won worked as a scripter and an assistant director for fifteen years before directing her debut film, *A Woman Judge* (*Yeopansa*; 1962). It received substantial attention, as it was inspired by actual events: the unsolved mystery of the death of Hwang Yoon-seok, the first female judge in Korea. Under the pen name Hong Eun-hee, Hong also wrote several articles and personal essays about being a (woman) filmmaker and in one article revealed that she endured occasional sexual harassment in order to work as a film director.[21] Hong portrays Jin-sook as a "superwoman" who holds a high-position job and somehow still manages to fulfill her traditional familial responsibilities. In some ways, Jin-sook mirrors Hong's own idealized notion of a modern woman and reflects the director's personal struggle and the negotiations she had to make in order to further her career. As Joo Jin-sook points out, Hong's films conceptualize the potential of a new woman in the new postwar generation but also reveal clear gendered limitations.[22] In subsequent decades, Hwang Hye-mi, director of *First Experience* (*Cheot gyeongheom*; 1970), and Lee Mi-rye, director of *My Daughter Rescued from the Swamp* (*Sureongeseo geonjin naeddal*; 1984), assumed the "female filmmakers in Korea" mantle, but they continued to lead a lonely march. Their films were often primarily marketed as a novelty, "rare films made by female directors," a label that served only to emphasize the scarcity of women directors within the industry. By the 1990s, more female directors began to emerge, including Im Soon-rye, Byun Young-ju, and Jeong Jae-eun, all of whom created films that delivered a more explicit critique of social and gender inequality in Korea.

According to Kim Sun-ah, eight female-directed films drew more than one million moviegoers between 2000 and 2012, and four of these productions were horrors and thrillers.[23] Horror was a viable option for first-time directors, as, due to the fact that they did not require big-name stars and costly spectacles, they were considered low-budget, low-risk productions. Therefore, studios were often willing to hire directors and actors with little experience. According to Choi's interview with Lee Chun-yeon, the production head of Cine 2000 who produced the *Whispering Corridors* series, every installment was directed by a first-time director using a cast of emerging actors, which significantly lowered the production costs.[24]

As Kim has indicated, for young female directors, the horror film is a fertile space where issues of social oppression and inequality can be effectively discussed through genre conventions, a comment that parallels Paszkiewicz's remarks that women "working in Hollywood demonstrated what genre can do with women filmmakers and what they can do with genre through their commercially and culturally impactful texts."[25] Kim mentions *Shadows in the Palace* as an example that utilized the popular tropes of horror to illustrate the history of women's oppression in a familiar and effective manner. The film sold 1,430,000 tickets in Korea and enjoyed the highest domestic booking rate for any Korean film in its opening week, making it one of the most popular films to date in Korea directed by a woman.[26]

The Dread of Motherhood in *The Uninvited*

The Uninvited (not to be confused with the U.S. remake of *A Tale of Two Sisters*, also titled *The Uninvited*) is the directorial debut of Lee Soo-yeon. She wrote the original script based on real events that happened in Bucheon in 1996, in which a distraught mother threw two children from the top floor of an apartment building: one of the children was her own, one was her neighbor's. *The Uninvited* received a positive critical reception for its sophisticated camera movement and nonlinear storytelling, and the film earned international recognition at numerous film awards and festivals in and outside of Korea, including the Baeksang Arts Awards and the Sitges International Fantastic Film Festival.[27]

The film follows the story of Jung-won, an ordinary young architect who has no memory of the first seven years of his life. One day, he sees two girls on the train and discovers that they were the ghosts of two children who were poisoned and killed by their desperate, poverty-stricken mother. Jung-won then sees the ghosts sitting at his dining table and discovers his neighbor Yeon also has the ability to see spirits and people's pasts. Sharing their mysterious abilities, the two grow close, and Yeon helps him uncover his lost memories of childhood, only to discover the horrific truth that he killed his own father and sister. Jung-won also learns how Yeon's child was killed by her best friend, Jung-sook, who murdered her own child as well.

Throughout the film, motherhood is challenged and desanctified. Lee's portrayal of the female characters rejects the traditional notion of motherhood as the sacred duty of women. Instead, she portrays it as a dreadful burden, foregrounding the pain that women go through to become a mother instead of paying tribute to the maternal process. This perspective is particularly evident in the portrayal of Jung-sook. During her trial, Jung-sook's husband testifies that she never breastfed her child, accusing her of negligence. In her defense, she responds that she could not breastfeed, as she feared that the baby might eat her breast. The film juxtaposes the trial sequence with Jung-sook's flashback from her own childhood. After being trapped in a well with her dead mother, Jung-sook survived by feeding on her mother's flesh. Traumatized ever since, the experience in the well is revealed as the root cause of her mental illness. Here, the idea of the mother's womb parallels the space where Jung-sook's initial traumatic experience took place, where the bond between a child and mother is horrifically reconceived, a place of survival for the child but death for the mother.

As such, the film defies the norms of maternal discourse that conceptualize motherhood as an inherent sacrifice. Discussing Patrice DiQuinzio's account on the construction of "essential motherhood," Sarah Arnold argues that essential motherhood requires the mother to sacrifice herself, "sacrifices she endures to maintain wholeness with the child. . . . [M]othering is a function of women's essentially female nature, women's biological reproductive capacities, and/or human evolutionary development. Essential motherhood construes women's motherhood as natural and inevitable. It requires women's exclusive and selfless attention to and care of children based on women's psychological and emotional capacities for empathy, awareness of the needs of others, and self-sacrifice."[28] In *The Uninvited*, motherhood is defined not by self-sacrifice but instead by the horror that the mother feels, elicited by her child's persistent need for survival. At the end of the film, Jung-sook is acquitted because of her mental state, but as soon as she leaves the trial, she jumps from the court building and kills herself in front of Yeon and Jung-won. Soon after, Yeon follows Jung-sook's tragic path. Both women contest the idea of motherhood as "natural and inevitable," and both end their lives in an extreme way.

Lee Soo-yeon herself has claimed that motherhood is overly idealized in and outside of cinema. She argues, "Motherhood that has been fantasized and sanctified is like a 'bridle' to women. People conceptualize motherhood with selflessness at the same level as that of a god. When you are a mother, you are not a human, you need to be a god. Through my film, I wanted people to perceive motherhood in terms of what it really means for women."[29] Therefore, Lee's representation of motherhood is distinctive from the cinematic representations of such in most Korean maternal dramas. For instance, *Marathon* (*Mal-a-ton*; 2005) and *Barefoot Gi Bong* (*Maenbaleui Gibong*; 2006), released around the same time as *The Uninvited*, feature a mother with a disabled adult child and highlight the mother's endless responsibility for the caretaking of her children. Such films normalize and solidify the notion of a good, true mother based on selflessness and the utter devotion to her child.[30]

The Uninvited also critiques the idea of motherhood as inevitably dependent upon and relative to the patriarchal ideals of family. In the first instance, this is shown through Jung-won's hidden childhood memory that he killed his tyrannical and alcoholic father after prolonged abuse. Lee's critique of the ideals of the patriarchal family is further indicated through the recurring symbol of the two dead children of Yeon and Jung-sook. The two children represent the ideal model for the Korean nuclear family, reflected in the original Korean title for the film, "A [Dinner] Table for Four." As maternal horror, *The Uninvited* is an antithesis to the culturally sanctioned concept of maternal self-sacrifice and how this is bound up with the dominant discourses of the idealization of the patriarchal nuclear family.

Silencing Women in *Shadows in the Palace*

Shadows in the Palace is the directorial debut of Kim Mi-jeong, who worked as an assistant director on Lee Joon-ik's successful historical drama *The King and the Clown* (*Wang-ui namja*; 2005). Like Lee, Kim also wrote her own script, this time based on her extensive research into the role and history of palace women, who were royal attendants ranging in rank from courtiers to domestic workers during the Joseon dynasty.

Set during the rule of King Jeongjo in the eighteenth century, the film traces the mysterious death of Wol-ryung, one of the palace servant women. The case is disguised as a suicide, but Chun-ryung, a royal medic, finds out that Wol-ryung was murdered. She also discovers evidence from the autopsy that Wol-ryung had given birth before she died. Ignoring orders from her superiors to close the case, Chun-ryung continues her own investigation. Not only does she find out about a conspiracy to provide an heir set up by the royal family and their subordinates, but she also learns about countless other sacrifices that have been made to silence palace women whom the royal court finds problematic.

Apart from the dreadful death of Wol-ryung, the film generates horror through the many rules and punishments that palace women endured. They were forced to help conceal the wrongdoings and crimes of officials, particularly in relation to frequent sexual abuse committed by royal authorities, and they were secretly tortured and killed to ensure their silence. Perhaps the most spectacular example of this in the film is *jui-bu-ri-geul-ryeo* (the torch ritual), an event held to persuade the newly recruited palace women of the importance of maintaining a code of silence in relation to any events they might witness.

The film offers a visceral, highly elaborate visualization of an actual event, with hundreds of extras playing palace women and professional drummers and sword dancers. The ritual starts with the performance of an executioner who emulates burning a person's tongue with a huge torch, symbolizing the punishment of "tongue cutting." The executioner then steps forward toward the girls to threaten them with his sword and torch. The newly recruited palace women are visibly terrified but are forced to watch the ritual until the end. The climax of the sequence is a gory execution scene in which an innocent palace woman is wrongly and brutally executed for the murder of Wol-ryung. The woman's hands and head are cut off in an attempt to conceal the conspiracy surrounding the birth of the new prince, and the ritual serves its purpose: to warn all the newly recruited palace women to witness the fate that will befall them if they fail to maintain their silence.

The character Ok-jin, a mute, young *goong nyeo*, is another example of how *Shadows in the Palace* configures horror through female silence. Ok-jin not only suffers bullying due to her disability but is also sexually exploited by one of the royals, Lee Hyung-jik, who has harassed other palace women, including Chun-ryung. Ok-jin can't speak out for herself when she is framed by her bullies as a thief, and she is then tortured as a result. During the torture, the film depicts a flashback that documents all the unjust treatment Ok-jin has endured. Even after enduring excessive punishment and torture, Ok-jin declines to give her tormentors any information about Wol-ryung and also stays entirely silent about Lee's sexual exploitation of her. She represents the idea that women's silence is to be kept at any expense.

Through her investigation, Chun-ryung then learns the truth: Wol-ryung was chosen to bear a prince by the king's infertile concubine, Hee-bin. When Wol-ryung delivered this son, she was killed by Hee-bin's subordinates. Yet Chun-ryung doesn't attempt to avenge Ok-jin. Nor does she attempt to achieve justice by revealing the evidence that implicates the (male, hegemonic) royal family in Wol-ryung's death. Rather, when the ghost of Wol-ryung returns to the palace for her revenge, Chun-ryung simply stands by, and the ghost massacres all the palace men and women involved in her murder.

In traditional *yeogwi* films such as *The Story of Jang-hwa and Hong-ryeon* (*Jang-hwa Hong-ryeon jeon*; 1972) and *A Public Cemetery under the Moon*, the male protagonist fulfills the female ghost's postdeath wish generated through her *han* (a Korean word referring to pent-up anger and sorrow). In these films, the male character seeks out justice for the female ghost. However, when Chun-ryung solves the mystery, she chooses to remain silent and let Wol-ryung complete her revenge herself. As such, women's silence once again is called for, but this time, for the first time, to make things even for the victimized women. The theme of "silence" dominates *Shadows in the Palace*, not just in relation to the murder case but also in multiple episodes involving the palace women. Throughout the film, the silence of women is not glorified as a virtue but presented as a troubled norm that costs women's sacrifice. The film is full of women's personal anecdotes that testify to how they were forced to remain silent and acquiescent at any time when they might be perceived as a threat to the system of royal dominance. As a vengeful ghost, Wol-ryung can be considered not just as a single victim but the reincarnation of all the abused palace women. She returns to allow them to voice their pain and to emerge from their hidden existence. In this respect, *Shadows in the Palace* offers a dynamic twisting of genre conventions, bridging the traditional female ghost horror with a feminist rereading of women's silenced history. Arguably, both women-made horror films discussed here have demonstrated how the structural and social limitations faced by women filmmakers can be overcome, and they show that when women are able to make horror films, they enable women's perspectives to be more widely received within the language of genre.

Conclusion

The 2000s was a pivotal moment for Korean women filmmakers working in the horror genre. The films of Lee Soo-yeon and Kim Mi-jeong addressed the experiences and concerns of women in contemporary Korean society in a way that parallels the work of the prior generations of female directors. However, their films also demonstrate a strategic way of working "with and against" genre conventions in a successful fashion. Kim Mi-jeong's *Shadows in the Palace* transforms the classical Korean female ghost into a much more empowered character, while Lee Soo-yeon's *The Uninvited* rejects the traditional norms of motherhood and debunks the idea of a mother's role as defined by self-sacrifice. These female directors have managed to address women's issues as well as satisfy the popular appetite, and their critical and commercial success points to a growing level of female creativity within Korean cinema.

After this first wave of women-made Korean horror film in the early 2000s, Korean women filmmakers made commercially successful feature films across various genres, including writer-director Lee Jung-hyang's family film *The Way Home* (*Jibeuro*; 2002), writer-director Bang Eun-jin's thriller *Princess Aurora* (*Orora Gongju*; 2005), and writer-director Park Hyun-jin's romance *Lovers of 6 Years* (*6nyeonjjae yeonaejung*; 2008), all of which created profits far exceeding their BEP.[31] Horror then took a downturn in Korean filmmaking from the mid-2000s, and the numbers of women directing horror films accordingly reduced.

While this was occurring in horror though, the number of films made by female filmmakers in Korea has gradually and steadily continued to increase, and as of 2019, women-made films occupy 13 percent of the entire range of Korean films released (excluding independent films) and 31 percent for films with female leads.[32] Though this number might seem insignificant in terms of increase, there are two important tendencies to note here. First, the type of films that women directors are making is becoming far more diverse. If we look back over the past year, we can see diversity in genre with Kim Bo-ram's documentary *For Vagina's Sake* (*Piui yeondaegi*; 2018), Lee Eon-hee's action comedy *The Accidental Detective 2: In Action* (*Tam-jeong: Liteonjeu*; 2018), and Kim Bo-ra's family drama *House of Hummingbird* (*Beol-sae*; 2019). Second, the career prospects for this new generation of women directors seem to be more credible and consistent in the longer term, particularly in comparison to their historical predecessors such as Park Nam-ok. In 2017, Lee Soo-yeon returned with the thriller *Blue Beard* (*Haebing*), and Kim Mi-jeong is currently in production on *Maze*, another historical drama.[33]

This chapter is the first academic publication (in either Korean or English) dedicated to examining the perspective of the woman filmmaker in Korean horror cinema. It is hoped that my work will remind the filmmakers of their cinematic achievements and, from a larger perspective, stimulate new thoughts for women-made films, which (I believe) will eventually provoke more women to direct films themselves. By strategically utilizing "the generative force of genres" to inscribe their work with feminist politics, the films discussed here have become culturally and commercially significant productions that I hope will influence women filmmakers for many years to come.[34]

Notes

1 Elena Nicolaou, "22 Unmissable Horror Movies Directed by Women," Refinery29, October 31, 2017, https://www.refinery29.com/en-us/2017/10/179049/horror-movie-directors-female.
2 Eunha Oh, "Monster Mothers and the Confucian Ideal: Korean Horror Cinema in the Park Chung Hee Era" (PhD diss., Southern Illinois University Carbondale, 2012); Kim Yoon-hee, "Hankook gongpo younghwa sok byunhwa haneun moseong-seong" [The changes of maternity in Korean horror films] (master's thesis, Dongkook University, 2003); Baek Moon-im, *Wolha-eui yeogoksong: Yeogwi-ro ingneun hanguk gongpo yeonhwasa* [Sorrowful screaming: A history of the female ghost in Korean films] (Seoul: Chaeksesang, 2008).

3 Park Ju-young, "1998 nyeon hu Hankook guishin younghwa e-seo eui yeo seong jae hyun" [The representation of women in Korean horror films since 1998] (master's thesis, Yonsei University, 2005).

4 Alison Butler, *Women's Cinema: The Contested Screen* (London: Wallflower, 2002), 1.

5 Butler, 1.

6 See Katarzyna Paszkiewicz, "When the Woman Directs (a Horror Film)," in *Women Do Genre in Film and Television*, ed. Mary Harrod and Katarzyna Paszkiewicz (London: Routledge, 2018), 39.

7 "KTV Horror Films," Yonhap News Agency, accessed June 17, 2019, https://www.yna .co.kr/view/AKR20160803068000033?input=1195m.

8 Park, "1998," 31.

9 Jin-hee Choi, *The South Korean Film Renaissance: Local Hitmakers, Global Provocateurs* (Middletown, Conn.: Wesleyan University Press, 2010), 16; Jeong Joong-heon, "1970 nyeon dae Hankook younghwasa yeon gu-Yushin sidae reul joongshim eu ro-" [A study on Korean film history of the 1970s: Focusing on the yusin regime period] (PhD diss., Sungkyunkwan University, 2009), 23–25.

10 Jeong, "1970," 12–25.

11 Kim Hoon-soon and Lee So-youn, "Korean Modern Horror Films and the Transformation of Genre Conventions," *Korean Women's Communication Studies* 6 (2005): 10–13.

12 Park, "1998," 32.

13 Molly Kim, "Whoring the Mermaid: The Study of South Korean Hostess Films (1974–1982)" (PhD diss., University of Illinois, Urbana-Champaign, 2014), 156; Min Eun-jung, Joo Jin-sook, and Kwak Han-joo, *Korean Film: History, Resistance, and Democratic Imagination* (Westport, Conn.: Praeger, 2003), 58.

14 Kim and Lee, "Korean Modern Horror Films," 9.

15 Choi, *South Korean Film Renaissance*, 19.

16 Choi, 31.

17 Choi, 40.

18 Choi, 3.

19 Kim Sun-ah, "Analysis of Performances of Korean Female Directors in the Thriller Genre Focusing on the Cases, *Helpless* and *Perfect Number*," *Korean Journal of Contents* 14 (2014): 77.

20 Lee Min-ho, "Hankook gongpo younghwa saneop eui byunhwa wa hyanghoo baljeon ganeung seong" [A study of the Korean horror cinema industry] (master's thesis, Dong Guk University, 2008), 8.

21 Hong Eun-hee, "My Grief as a Female Filmmaker," Sookmyung Women's University Library, accessed March 3, 2019, http://e-lumiere.sookmyung.ac.kr/sookmyung/ user/class/sub3_2-1.htm.

22 Joo Jin-sook, "(A) Study on Women Directors in Korea: Women in the Scenario *Affection and Apathy* by Hong Eun-won," *Journal of Image and Film Studies* 7 (2005): 80–85.

23 Kim, "Analysis," 78.

24 Choi, *South Korean Film Renaissance*, 125.

25 Kim, "Analysis," 78; Paszkiewicz, "When the Woman Directs," 39.

26 Yun-mi Hwang, "Heritage of Horrors: Reclaiming the Female Ghost in *Shadows in the Palace*," in *Korean Horror Cinema*, ed. Alison Peirse and Daniel Martin (Edinburgh: Edinburgh University Press, 2013), 75.

27 Brian Yecies and Richard Howson, "Korean Cinema's Female Writers-Directors and the Hegemony of Men," *Gender, rovné příležitosti, výzkum* 16, no. 1 (2015): 17.

28 Sarah Arnold, *Maternal Horror Film: Melodrama and Motherhood* (Basingstoke, U.K.: Palgrave Macmillan, 2013), 39.

29 Maengmodangi, "The Interview with the Director, Lee Soo-yeon," *Yeonghwa-in*, July 7, 2004, https://m1005m7575.blog.me/40003957527?Redirect=Log&from= postView.

30 Han Mi-ra, "Hankook younghwa eseo eui gajok jaehyun: 1990 nyeon dae hooban eseo hyunjae ggaji younghwa reul joongshim eu ro" [Representation of family on Korean cinema: Centering on the cinema from the end of 1990s to the present] (PhD diss., Chung Ang University, 2002), 60.

31 Kim, "Analysis," 77.

32 Kim, 77; Kim Jin-soo, "We Need More Films Directed by Females," *Women News*, February 20, 2019, http://www.womennews.co.kr/news/articleView.html?idxno= 185932.

33 Nam Hye-yeon, "Interview with Won Dong-yeon, a Producer of *Along with the Gods*," Sports Seoul, January 8, 2018, http://www.sportsseoul.com/news/read/ 587873.

34 Paszkiewicz, "When the Woman Directs," 32.

The Stranger With My Face International Film Festival and the Australian Female Gothic

DONNA MCRAE

The state of Tasmania is situated at the bottom of the world. From this point of geographic extremity, its capital city, Hobart, hosts the Stranger With My Face International Film Festival (SWMFIFF). Run since 2012 by writer-director Briony Kidd, this festival brings together female writer-directors interested in the horror genre. Dina Iordanova observes that a film festival "becomes a participant in many other aspects of the creative cycle," and in this way, SWMFIFF focuses on female perspectives in storytelling and aims to fill a gap that has been largely ignored by other Australian film festivals.[1] The festival is influenced by its geographical positioning: Tasmania is haunted by its volatile history of colonization and treatment of the first peoples and convict settlers, and SWMFIFF builds upon this to influence and shape the thinking of participating female writer and directors. Tom O'Regan states that "Australian cinema serves as a vehicle of popular socialisation and as a forum for telling uncomfortable truths about its society," and this chapter will address the way in which the Tasmanian landscape and the curatorial premise of the festival combine to create a particular conceptual style that I term the *Australian female Gothic*.[2]

The chapter also considers the influence of a female-centric genre film festival on the promotion and production of a particular type of women's genre filmmaking in Australia today. While other women's film festivals are now operating in Australia (e.g., Women in Film Festival, Melbourne, and For Film's Sake, Sydney), SWMFIFF is the only festival to focus solely on horror, thriller, and fantasy narratives and offers festival "add-ons," such as short filmmaking and screenplay competitions, industry guests, retrospectives, workshops, readings, and sidebars. These add-ons, Russ Hunter suggests, are "a key part of genre programming strategy."[3] In short, SWMFIFF provides an abundant resource for practitioners of the Australian female Gothic.

Australia has a short but important history of women's film festivals. In 1975, the Women's International Film Festival was born from a submission to the Film and Television Board of the Australian Council of the Arts "to provide an historical and cultural context of women's cinema"; "to explore our own creativity through films"; and "to counteract the reluctance of distributors to women's films in Australia," which resulted in an investment of $20,000 to stage events in Melbourne, Sydney, and Canberra with smaller capital city screenings.[4] This was successful, but momentum was not sustained, and women's filmmaking went on to feature in sidebars and focus events at the more established film festivals, including Melbourne International Film Festival and Sydney Film Festival. However, in the 1990s, according to Kirsten Stevens, "film festivals with increasingly specialised programmes aimed at particular communities and identity groups multiplied quickly . . . producing women's events such as *Women in Motion* and *Out of the Frying Pan*."[5] Nevertheless, a film made by a woman programmed in an event or sidebar does not have the same impact as one presented in an opening night slot or in a festival dedicated entirely to women's filmmaking: "The value of a film becomes coded by where in the programme the work appears—the likelihood of it being seen and the expected audience that it will attract ultimately informing the reception and possible interpretations that might be generated."[6] With genre films rarely programmed within these types of festivals (with the possible exception of a midnight screening), Hunter notes, "A combination of their popular form and related perceptions about their cultural value means [genre films] are often viewed as niche products at best or being derivative, lacking in depth, and disposable at worst."[7] As a result, a gap emerges in Australia for a film festival that is dedicated to promoting not only women's filmmaking but also the evolving juggernaut of the women's genre film and in a geographical space that does not compete with larger and publicly funded film festivals.

The setting of Tasmania is crucial to the uniqueness of the setting and has a significant impact on the festival. Tasmania is a rugged landscape cut off and separated by water from mainland Australia. The first recorded European sight-ing of the island was made by the Dutch explorer Abel Tasman, who named the island Van Diemen's Land. Early European settlers of this colonial outpost were mainly convicts and their police guards, with several penal settlements built around the island, including one at Port Arthur, the site of a mass shooting in 1996 that catalyzed change in Australia's gun laws. Mount Wellington, a moun-tain of 4,170 feet, presides over the metropolitan environment, its surround-ing mist distilling the city with a cold, European feel, distinct from the sunny outlook of the other mainland capitals. One could almost believe that this city belongs to another era, one that is brutal, fogbound, and unforgiving. Hobart, complete with sandstone houses and a penchant for restoring colonial build-ings, has a tone that sets it apart from the rest of the country. It stands at the foot of Mount Wellington, was founded in 1804 as a penal colony, and was the site of the mass genocide of the local indigenous people in the 1820s and 1830s. Wiping out communities in order to build new, colonial replacements has a lingering and indelible effect on the future inhabitants of Tasmania. It is a place of grief and desolation, even as it provides a rich vein to tap for untold stories hundreds of years later.

The menacing Cascades Female Factory site in Hobart is composed of a group of gloomy and merciless buildings built in 1823 for the sole purpose of incarcerating British women in the first colonies. Here the inmates attempted to survive through unrelenting hours of toil in darkly oppressive and damp condi-tions, penance for trivial crimes and misdemeanors. Now a UNESCO World Heritage site, Cascades Female Factory operated with three classes for women between 1823 and 1856, sorted by police charges or good behavior on board the transport ships from England. These women served long hours of hard labor performing tasks that ranged from rock breaking and laundry to sewing and spinning. Other women were sent to this institution to wait for childbirth or to be trained to become servants to wealthy colonial households. There is an irony here that at the time of the factory's operation, Gothic literature was at its most popular in Britain. Middle-class women were both reading and writ-ing Gothic novels, thrilling to the chilly and clammy atmospheres of abandoned castles, chains, and dungeons while unaware of their less fortunate sisters living out their lives at the bottom of the world in Gothic confinement. As Ross Gib-son notes in *Seven Versions of an Australian Badland*, "Most cultures contain prohibited or illicit spaces but no-go zones are especially compelling within colonial societies. By calling a place ominous and bad, citizens can admit that a pre-colonial kind of savagery lingers inside the colony even though most of the country has been tamed for husbandry and profit."[8]

Tasmania has always been a natural location for both Australian and inter-national filmmaking. The renowned Australian silent film *For the Term of His Natural Life* (1927) was based on a colonial convict story, and there have been three recent films about infamous Irish convict cannibal Alexander Pearce,

Van Diemen's Land (2009), *The Last Confession of Alexander Pearce* (2008), and *Dying Breed* (2008). Set in 1800s Tasmania and shot in the Tasmanian wilderness, *The Tale of Ruby Rose* (1987) focuses on the marginalization of Ruby according to her gender and societal status, and the natural power of the landscape drives her self-imposed banishment from society even further. These films represent a subgenre of Australian filmmaking that we can label as Tasmanian Gothic. Emily Bullock points out that Tasmania has a "dark and troubling past as a brutal penal colony," its stories are grounded in "dramatic and unforgiving natural settings," and the Tasmanian Gothic "has become a by-word for this unsettling combination."[9] The power of these surroundings might be seen to open doors to a particular strand of imagination and artistry. Fueled by the compelling atmosphere of this city at the bottom of the world, a group of female writer-directors with similar interests are thus catalyzed to look into the dark heart of the origins of colonization and create stories that will resonate with a contemporary audience. For SMWFIFF to provide the framework for artistic ideas to flourish, this chapter argues that perhaps the setting needs to be just as Gothic as the content of the film ideas and stories.

After having their short films programmed in the Viscera Film Festival in Los Angeles, California, Kidd and fellow Tasmanian writer-director Rebecca Thomson became involved with the Women in Horror Recognition Month (WiHM) initiative, as discussed in chapter 1. Kidd and Thomson were inspired and wanted to present something similar in their home state in an attempt to join the global conversation, support female filmmakers, and highlight the local inequalities they were experiencing. The inequalities are very real: women writer-directors do not have the same opportunities in Australia as male writer-directors. In terms of government film funding and paid roles on commercial productions, Screen Australia figures from 2015 reveal that the gender imbalance is most notable in traditional film, with women accounting for 32 percent of producers, 23 percent of writers, and only 16 percent of directors.[10] Kidd states, "At first my motivation was purely to provide a platform for under-recognized work by women filmmakers, but of course my taste has influenced its evolution as well, and I gradually have become more interested in the art or craft of film programming for its own sake. . . . It was always a Tasmanian event because we created the event within a fairly impoverished screen culture environment."[11]

For Kidd, the first few years of SWMFIFF were a niche operation, catering to a small network of friends and acquaintances that she had reached out to online, women who were experiencing the same sort of inequities she was trying to counterbalance. These Australian female writer-directors were all working independently in the horror genre and finally had a place to congregate. The Cascades Female Factory stood out to the women who visited the festival, reminding them of the historical harshness afforded to their gender and captivating them with stories of hardship, loss, and the hostility of their environment—in essence, offering the basic building blocks for Gothic imaginations. As the film festival has evolved, Kidd has positioned it to be "strongly Tasmanian" in its outlook. She goes on to say that "Tasmanian Gothic and the perceived exoticism of Tasmania have certainly worked in the event's favor, as it's a point of difference and is a large part of [the festival's] identity."[12] The participants of SWMFIFF have come to expect dark skies, gloomy conditions, and historic stories of severity and punishment. Yet while the "Tasmanian" Gothic has piqued the imagination of female writer-directors invested in horror, is it just Tasmania itself that can provoke this reading? Or could a broader term be used to determine the feel of the festival and the work that emerges from it?

The Australian Female Gothic

For Fred Botting, the term *Gothic* signifies "a barbarous, medieval and supernatural past. Used derogatively about art, architecture and writing that failed to conform to the standards of neoclassical taste, 'Gothic' signified the lack of reason, morality and beauty of feudal beliefs, customs and works."[13] In the context of this chapter, the Gothic has clearly shifted, particularly as the tropes of the genre are played out in a landscape far away from Europe. Gothic has become a "range of thematic, stylistic and political tendencies," a "mode referring to a broader thematic and tonal qualification or colouring of a genre rather than specific and time-bound formal structures."[14] Given this, it is possible to imagine the Gothic to be equally at home among the dark beauty of Tasmania or in the bright daylight of the Australian landscape.

Traditionally, Australian influences have been inevitably associated with colonization, and with stories of settlers trying to tame the wild landscape into something more familiar amid ghosts and unsettling occurrences. The Australian countryside provides a fertile foundation for the imagining of such stories—whether it be modern outback detective stories such as *Goldstone* (2016) or ghostly tales of unexplained disappearances in *Lake Mungo* (2008). Similarly, the short stories of Australian writer Barbara Baynton conjure a landscape suffused with an Australian Gothic sensibility, a sensibility that only locals know of: the sudden failing of the light in the bush or the wilderness, laden with thick eucalyptus trees and emerging nocturnal animals. She writes, "Australian daylight dies with short shrift, and in this mighty scrub the pall of darkness fell with startling abruptness. She knew it would be madness to seek home, so, selecting a sparse spot, she shrouded the dead and laid it beside her."[15] According to Stuart Richards, "The Australian Gothic film does not have a universal, distinctive aesthetic"; however, I would argue that an Australian Gothic film can always be recognized by its unfiltered light and arresting landscape, whether it be the lush green countryside of *Picnic at Hanging Rock* (1975), the harsh yellow outback depicted in *Wake in Fright* (1972) and *Kiss or Kill* (1997), or the stark urban setting of *The Babadook* (Jennifer Kent, 2014).[16] As Ken Gelder suggests, "There is plenty of evidence of the spectralization of the Australian desert landscape by explorers given over to superstitious imaginings. But the explorer himself—so often a foundational and heroic figure for colonial nation-building mythologies—could become ghostly too."[17]

With the exception of *Ruby Rose* and *The Nightingale* (Jennifer Kent, 2018), the Tasmanian Gothic film has a historical absence of female lead characters, so *female* is out of place in the term. The Australian female Gothic film is more inclusive—describing ethereal, female schoolgirls of *Picnic at Hanging Rock* or something eerier, such as the mysterious retirement home deaths in *Next of Kin* (1982). However, both of these films are directed by men, and as Amanda Howell has stated in relation to Roman Polanski's *Repulsion* (1965) and *Rosemary's Baby* (1968), there is an "overpowering and largely misogynist male presence that shapes the realities of female protagonists in domestic horrors and female gothic more generally."[18] Perhaps the *female* in the term *Australian female Gothic* is better signaled by the maker—that is, the Australian female horror practitioner?

A number of Australian genre films are made by Australian female practitioners, including *Broken Highway* (Laurie McInnes, 1993), *The Well* (Samantha Lang, 1997), and *The Nightingale*, of which the latter is a strong example of a female writer-director giving voice to female suffering. *The Nightingale* delves deeply into Tasmanian colonization and the brutality of what it was like for women living in those times. Visceral and uncompromising, the film has been controversial in its reception, especially in Australia, where these atrocities occurred. *Celia* (Ann Turner, 1989) was selected by Kidd for the opening night of SWMFIFF 2014. It was unusual that a repertory title was selected for this coveted slot, but Kidd wanted to draw attention to an underrecognized film and share her love of the film with her audience. This is typical for genre festivals, as Hunter states, which are "run by programmers who are genre fans," and this "becomes doubly important, as the purpose of the festival is first and foremost to share a love of a certain kind of cinema."[19] In programming *Celia*, Kidd elevated the film to become a "festival" film, it would go on to be featured in other festivals, and then the film print received a digital restoration by the Australian Film and Sound Archive.

A sense of unease and dread is frequently fortified in these female-led works that deal with a more subversive side to daily activity and the female experience. Discussing the Australian Gothic cinema more generally, David Thomas and Garry Gillard state that this mode is about "this idea of the perversion of the mundane, the dark undercurrent running through 'ordinary' existence that generally remains undisturbed and hidden from view."[20] Defining the uncanny in this quote, *Broken Highway*, *The Babadook*, and *Celia* then tap into a sensibility that is then uniquely female in the handling of material. Whether it be Celia's adolescent journey into her imagination, the gradual breakdown of family and relationships for Catherine in *Broken Highway*, or the anxiety around single parenting for Amelia in *The Babadook*, these women are concerned with the messy part of life that is defined by their gender and the place that is accorded to them in a patriarchal society. According to Adrian Martin, a guest speaker at SWMFIFF 2012, "Female Gothic films are about women journeying through a tantalizing but menacing dreamscape that is equated with male society. These films are all about women's ambivalence, their attraction to the dark side and to the bad guys—but also every step that they have to take to survive this desire."[21] Placing the word *Australian* in front of *female Gothic* is even more specific. These are genre films made about women by women and from a specific place, both physically and metaphorically: the dark heart of colonization that lies beneath Australian personal and political everyday life. Many of the filmmakers showcased at SWMFIFF draw their stories from this deep well of uneasiness and anxiety of living in modern Australia.

The Australian female Gothic then arguably aligns female writer-directors with this point of view, utilizing horror as a blueprint for examining societal norms and conundrums significant to them. Drawing from the country's colonial history, the treatment of its indigenous people and women, and latter-day political challenges such as the current treatment of refugees, border control, and climate change, Australian female writer-directors can use the genre to suit their own voice, creating region-specific commentary. Female characters are placed in the lead roles, while audiences are offered a narrative experience inside the unhospitable Australian landscape. As Kidd explains, "I've long been interested in the concept of 'female response horror,' meaning women using genre to express personal and deep emotions (rage being one, from within a patriarchal construct). I think that's quite a useful way of thinking about women working in horror, how they tend to use the genre, and so maybe Australian female Gothic is a region-specific version of that."[22]

Curation

Kidd is guided by her own taste as a writer-director in shaping her curation of the festival. She has presented international films such as *XX* (Jovanka Vuckovic, Annie Clark, Roxanne Benjamin, and Karyn Kusama, 2017), discussed in chapter 13; *Evolution* (Lucile Hadžihalilović, 2015), discussed in chapter 16; *The Book of Birdie* (Elizabeth E. Schuch, 2016); *American Mary* (Jen and Sylvia Soska, 2013); *Chained* (Jennifer Lynch, 2012); and *The Love Witch* (Anna Biller, 2016) and Australian titles such as *Crushed* (Jane Sanger, 2014), *Innuendo* (Saara Lamberg, 2014), and my own feature film, *Johnny Ghost* (2013). Kidd's ongoing interest in the short format also includes the curation of Australian titles such as *Butterflies* (Isabel Peppard, 2012) and *Blood Sisters* (Caitlin Koller and Lachlan Smith, 2017), the latter a previous winner of the festival's own Tasmanian Gothic Screenwriting Challenge, and international short-form offerings such as *What Happened to Her* (Kristy Guevara-Flanagan, 2017) and *Wretched* (Leslie Delano and Heidi Honeycutt, 2007).

Australian writer-director Heidi Lee Douglas's short film *Little Lamb* (2014) is a good example of Kidd's curation. *Little Lamb* was the inaugural winner of the SWMFIFF screenplay competition in 2012. After winning the competition, Douglas successfully obtained a small grant to make the short film, which has now spent over four years on the international film circuit. Using the Bluebeard folktale as a starting point, Douglas sets the story in 1829, and the main character Louisa is a convict who swaps prison for kitchen duties in the home of Mr. Black, a mysterious settler. It is there that she finds an even worse situation waiting for her. *Little Lamb* begins in the Cascade Female Factory, with an array of desperate women chained, malnourished, and waiting for orders. Once Louisa is selected to work for Black, the film becomes a cat-and-mouse game of capture and escape through the remote forests of Tasmania. Louisa's only ally is a little lamb picked for slaughter, part of a new colony where indigenous animals were not valued and farm animals were treated inhumanely. The film builds to Louisa's shocking discovery: in a nondescript barn, she finds the bodies of women that had come before her, discarded by Black and left to decay, their destruction mirroring the treatment of the first settlers in Tasmania under colonization. Douglas, who has a close relationship with Tasmania, was inspired by the festival to write this work: "The festival inspired me to write *Little Lamb*. Tasmania has a potent Gothic atmosphere, especially in autumn or winter's twilight. The bare skeletal branches of trees scratch against sandstone walls soaked with the invisible, ghostly blood of the convicts who were forced to build the colony. The architecture, the light, the shadows, and the stories they hold are an inspiring backdrop for a women-in-horror film festival."[23]

The curatorial premise that runs through all these film selections involves a female lead character(s) grasping with an ever-changing landscape of personal, domestic, and workplace anxieties for women. Without exception, these films are independently produced by female writer-directors with varying financial budgets. SWMFIFF brings female writer-directors of SWMFIFF together in one space to not only present their ideas and films but also interact with people who have similar sensibilities and creative impulses. The festival encourages women to seek out stories that may not have been previously told and, in a nod to the pioneer past, stories of women that may have been at the forefront of nation building but have been reduced to mere footnotes in history. In works such as *Little Lamb*, the festival has developed opportunities for women to tell region-specific stories that explore what it is to be female without the constraints of distribution or exhibition pressure.

Mentors

In her quest to escalate the careers of the writer-directors that attend SWM-FIFF, Kidd has engaged international filmmakers such as Jennifer Lynch, Gaylene Preston, Stephanie Trepanier, Sandi Sissel, and Roxanne Benjamin to mentor the festival's aptly named Attic Lab, which aims to highlight new work made by women in the horror and fantasy genres. The lab takes place in a wood-lined room in the top story of the Salamanca Arts Centre in Hobart, adapted from a group of warehouses built in the 1850s. Its atmospheric environs present a suitable setting for the two-day intensive workshop, which consists of filmmaking discussions, screenings, and the development of selected writer-directors' new feature film projects. It culminates in a public pitching session where invited industry guests can provide feedback on each of the projects.

Some of these have gone onto further markets, such as Katrina Irawati Graham's *Raesita Grey*, selected for the Screen Queensland incuBAIT horror initiative, and my 2016 feature film project *Kate Kelly*, which was selected for Frontières Market at Fantasia Film Festival in Montreal in the same year. Other projects have found development partners and collaborators through Attic Lab. Natalie Ericka James pitched the feature film *Relic* at Attic Lab, which then premiered at the Sundance Film Festival in January 2020.; *Siti Rubiyah*, a multifaceted project by Irawati Graham, has since gone on to multiple development rounds and is now under option from Contemporary Asian Australian Performance; and *Morgana* (2019), a feature documentary by Isabel Peppard, had its world premiere at the Melbourne International Film Festival in August 2019. Again, Kidd's curation plays a part in the type of guest that she entices to Hobart: "The person's work and career must be something special . . . but the other crucial criterion is that their personality is a good fit. SWMFIFF needs to operate as an exchange of ideas, fundamentally, so it's important to get the mix right so that that can occur. I'm looking for people who are generous and genuinely interested in meeting our writer-directors and other artists (and audiences, even). They need to understand the nature of the event and support its aims."[24]

Kidd's ambitions to produce fruitful mentor-mentee relationships have been achieved many times. Writer Kier-la Janisse (2016), producer Stephanie Trepanier (2016), and producer-directors Gaylene Preston and Roxanne Benjamin (2017) attended Attic Lab initiatives, while Jennifer Lynch attended in 2013. She not only showed her feature films *Chained* (2012) and *Surveillance* (2008) to the small audience but also participated in mentoring on a one-on-one basis with other writer-directors that attended. Australian filmmaker Isabel Peppard benefited from the size of the gathering; she spent time with Lynch, which led to a month-long writing and directing mentorship in Los Angeles supported by the Director's Acclaim Fund from Screen Australia, the most important film-funding body in the country. Peppard reveals, "[Jennifer] supported and guided me through the writing of my first feature horror screenplay, *Silk*, which went on to garner development funding and won me a prize at Asia's biggest competitive genre market, NAFF BIFAN [Bucheon International Fantastic Film Festival] in South Korea. Working with such an inspiring and powerful creative woman was instrumental in giving me that push I needed to get my first feature script out into the world."[25]

Through Attic Lab, Kidd has produced an environment whereby female writer-directors feel comfortable enough to share their work in development, forge links, and learn from these international filmmakers. Peppard explains, "Attending the festival has opened my eyes to the cultural landscape of Australian female horror directors and the diversity of visions and voices within that community. As a filmmaker, it has given me a sense of connection to a local tribe of women all exploring different aspects of horror from the personal to the political," adding that it provides "a sense of where your personal vision fits into what is happening on a national and international scale." In Attic Lab, SWMFIFF has created a Gothic think tank, a Hobart-set assembly of imaginative and compatible women who can look to each other and internationally in shaping their personal visions for future film projects. Arguably, this is the place where the Australian female Gothic can be found in its purest form.

Conclusion

Can a small festival on a shoestring budget have a lasting impact on film production in Australia? Is it then capable of having international influence? This chapter has revealed that SWMFIFF has met these challenges each year by developing work inspired by Australian history and modern anxieties, work that has the capacity to reach audiences beyond Australia. It has offered a closed and intensive environment reminiscent of the Cascade Female Factory, but rather than being a place of oppression, it encourages women to thrive and to write and direct the stories they wish to tell. In so doing, it has supported the future of female horror filmmaking in Australia as well as globally.

However, as of mid-2019, SWMFIFF is on hiatus, Kidd revealing she intends to bring the festival back "once more stable, ongoing funding is established." She further explains, "I'm motivated to continue the event, not having seen anything else that fills this gap in the market since the last festival. My contact with female filmmakers with great projects leads me to believe something like this is still much needed in the Australian landscape, which tends to be quite narrow in terms of the kinds of films that are lauded and widely distributed."[26] For Australian female Gothic films to flourish, SWMFIFF is crucial, and its importance has been made clear during its temporary absence from the festival scene.

SWMFIFF is more than a film event; it acts as a political barometer and champion of women's filmmaking in Australia. It promotes female-centric works through curation and exhibition, it competes and agitates for change through supporting filmmaker development and mentorship, and it opens up opportunities for a wider range of perspectives from women working in horror. The festival challenges accepted notions of what can be achieved from a small genre festival by presenting types of programs that are "different from other (mainstream) festivals" and "engages in constructing not only a site of exhibition, but also a site for film culture."[27] I have suggested SWMFIFF is best understood as a mode of the Australian female Gothic, not just in the choice of films screened at the festival but as a lively, regionally specific space where female writer-directors are brought together as a small, supportive community to produce their own creative works. In turn, the festival creates important networks that can reach out internationally from the very bottom of the world.

Notes

1   Dina Iordanova, "The Film Festival as an Industry Node," *Media Industries Journal* 1, no. 3 (2015): 7.
2   Tom O'Regan, *Australian National Cinema* (London: Routledge, 1996), 10.
3   Russ Hunter, "Genre Film Festivals and Rethinking the Definition of 'The Festival Film,'" in *International Film Festivals: Contemporary Cultures and History beyond Venice and Cannes*, ed. Tricia Jenkins (London: Bloomsbury, 2018), 90.
4   Suzanne Spunner, "With Audacity, Passion, and a Certain Naivety: The 1975 International Women's Film Festival," in *Don't Shoot Darling! Women's Independent Filmmaking in Australia*, ed. Annette Blonski, Barbara Creed, and Frida Freiberg (Richmond, Va.: Greenhouse, 1987), 94.
5   Kirsten Stevens, *Australian Film Festivals: Audience, Place, and Exhibition Culture* (Basingstoke, U.K.: Palgrave Macmillan, 2017), 84.
6   Stevens, 150.
7   Hunter, "Genre Film Festivals," 95.
8   Ross Gibson, *Seven Versions of an Australian Badland* (St Lucia, Australia: University of Queensland Press, 2002), 15.
9   Emily Bullock, "Rumblings from Australia's Deep South: Tasmanian Gothic On-Screen," *Studies in Australasian Cinema* 5, no. 1 (2011): 72.
10 "Gender Matters," Screen Australia, December 7, 2017, https://www.screenaustralia .gov.au/sa/new-directions/gender-matters.
11 Briony Kidd, interview with author, October 2, 2018.
12 Kidd.
13 Fred Botting, "In Gothic Darkly: Heterotopia, History, Culture," in *A New Companion to the Gothic*, ed. David Punter (Oxford: Blackwell, 2012), 13.
14 Bullock, "Rumblings," 72.
15 Barbara Baynton, *Human Toll* (London: Duckworth, 1907), 139.
16 Stuart Richards, "Reawakening in Yoorana: Glitch and the Australian Gothic Film," *New Review of Film and Television Studies* 16, no. 3 (2018): 221.
17 Ken Gelder, "Australian Gothic," in Punter, *New Companion to the Gothic*, 380.
18 Amanda Howell, "The Terrible Terrace: Australian Gothic Reimagined and the (Inner) Suburban Horror of *The Babadook*," in *American-Australian Cinema: Transnational Connections*, ed. Adrian Danks, Stephen Gaunson, and Peter C. Kunze (Basingstoke, U.K.: Palgrave Macmillan, 2017), 188.
19 Hunter, "Genre Film Festivals," 99.
20 David Thomas and Garry Gillard, "Threads of Resemblance in New Australian Gothic Cinema," *Metro Magazine Media & Education Magazine* 136 (2003): 36.
21 Adrian Martin, email to author, August 31, 2012.
22 Kidd, interview with author.
23 Heidi Lee Douglas, interview with author, October 9, 2018.
24 Kidd, interview with author.
25 Isabel Peppard, interview with author, October 5, 2018.
26 Briony Kidd, email to author, June 13, 2019.
27 Hunter, "Genre Film Festivals," 92; Stevens, *Australian Film Festivals*, 187.

13

Slicing Up the Boys' Club

The Female-Led Horror
Anthology Film

ERIN HARRINGTON

If horror films are like mirrors that reflect our anxieties, then episodic horror films are more like kaleidoscopes: they create complex, often surprising images through the collation, repetition, and reflection of multiple small parts. Episodic horrors have a long and varied history, and they have seen a significant and recent resurgence in popularity, although as a form, they have been almost entirely absent from horror scholarship.[1] This is regrettable: contemporary horror anthology and omnibus films offer viewers a prepackaged smorgasbord of genre-bending shorts from around the world while also giving emerging and established filmmakers alike the opportunity to experiment narratively and formally. As collections that sometimes profess to showcase a diverse "best of the best," these films are an important snapshot of creative and cultural production. However, when considered together, they also expose patterns of inequity in industrial and cultural practice.

In this chapter, I suggest that horror omnibuses and anthologies, despite their self-professed eclecticism, offer an inconvenient cultural barometer that exposes the limits of a frustrating, male-dominated status quo. In particular, some recent omnibus films have been plagued by tired, sophomoric clichés that emphasize the objectification and victimization of women—patterns that are all the more obvious, even cringeworthy, when multiple shorts are presented en masse. This predicament is addressed by *XX* (2017), a horror omnibus that offers itself as an exemplar of female-led horror. The film features stand-alone female-centric horror shorts by four female directors—Americans Roxanne Benjamin, Annie Clark (also known as the musician St. Vincent), and Karyn Kusama and Canadian Jovanka Vuckovic. These are couched within a dreamy Gothic frame narrative by Mexican stop-motion animator Sofia Carrillo. Industrially, the producers XYZ Films indicate the collection serves two underrepresented sectors: female-led films generally and female-led horror films specifically.[2] Additionally, the film raises provocative questions about how we might analyze hybrid work through the lens of gendered authorship and textuality. We can connect (in)equity in terms of women's on-screen representation with production and creative direction by investigating patterns in narrative, characterization, and aesthetics. We can also consider how the term *female centric* might be (cynically?) leveraged as a specific category or genre of horror rather than a plain descriptor of authorship, which in turn implies that male authorship is universal and diverse and female authorship specific and narrow. This chapter teases out these issues through a comparative discussion of *XX* and other omnibuses while also problematizing the film's marketing, which leans on sexualized, essentialized femininity. *XX* offers a challenge to a male-dominated cultural and industrial environment, but as a commodity, the film uncomfortably celebrates difference while further marginalizing female-centric creative practice.

The Attack of the Horror (M)anthology

Episodic horror films are broadly defined as feature-length films designed to be watched in a single sitting that present a collection of (usually) self-contained segments connected by a theme or specific narrative conceit. The terminology we have for episodic films is as fragmented as the form itself, which poses challenges for robust formal and textual analysis.[3] For example, the horror films I discuss here have been popularly termed *anthologies*; *The ABCs of Death* (2012), which features twenty-six shorts, boldly describes itself as "perhaps the most ambitious anthology film ever conceived."[4] For clarity, I follow David S. Diffrient, who defines feature-length, multidirector episodic films as "omnibuses" to emphasize their transauthorial nature and single-director episodic films as "anthologies."[5] Diffrient's taxonomy clarifies formal strategies for unpacking these films' complex arrangements of moving parts. Individual segments may interlock, or they may be "freestanding." They may be embedded within a frame narrative or connected by interstitial sequences. They may be internally consistent or profoundly disjointed. The films may also be analyzed as aggregate entities or assemblages in which each segment can then be read on its own or in necessary intratextual and intertextual conversation with the other episodes. Additionally, we may also consider paratextual features or framing tools (such as title cards) or interrogate the interpretive lens of the films' organizing conceit.[6] This heterogeneity makes these films fascinating, multifaceted, and hybridized genre texts.

The motley, international genealogy of episodic horror opens up further spaces of inquiry. Episodic horror draws from a cultural history that connects radio drama, vaudeville, theater, television, comics, pulp fiction, and short fiction forms that lean on twists, surprises, and sometimes gimmicks for narrative and emotional effect.[7] These films are also commercial, industrial, creative products that invite complex reception and interpretation strategies. As omnibuses feature multiple directors and writers, they lend themselves well to analyses of gender, because patterns of representation—and inequity—are quickly rendered visible, much as production and curatorial decisions make space for an interrogation of inclusions and exclusions. However, as Diffrient notes, episodic horror films have "been marginalized to the point of near oblivion," perhaps due to the critical hostility that has characterized their reception and their persistent status as cultural marginalia.[8]

Nonetheless, despite this lack of critical attention, episodic horror films have been a persistent part of the development of what we now think of as horror, at least as far back as German director Richard Oswald's silent anthology *Unheimliche geschichten* (*Uncanny tales*; 1919), which featured segments based on fantasy, mystery, and Gothic short fiction. Interest in the form has endured, although its mainstream popularity and success have ebbed and flowed. Influential British supernatural horror film *Dead of Night* (1945) sparked serious interest in the form, but many notable omnibus films have leaned toward humor and even self-parody; consider the schlocky, lurid "portmanteau" films produced by British studio Amicus Productions from 1965 to 1974.[9] This playfulness is similarly present in a cluster of wry American feature film adaptations of "vintage" episodic media, including *Creepshow* (1982), *The Twilight Zone: The Movie* (1983), *Tales from the Dark Side: The Movie* (1990), and *Trick 'r Treat* (2007). Important titles outside the Anglosphere include the celebrated Japanese folk tale anthology *Kwaidan* (1965) and the transgressive East Asian omnibus *Three . . . Extremes* (2004), both of which resonated strongly with domestic and international audiences alike. In a dynamic example of ongoing cross-platform hybridity, the American cable series *Masters of Horror* (2005–2007) in turn featured twenty-six stand-alone episodes directed by predominantly American horror film directors. None of these titles has featured the work of a female director.

Two multidirector films herald the recent reemergence of mainstream interest in the form: abecedary *The ABCs of Death* and found-footage omnibus

V/H/S (2012). These films and their sequels—*The ABCs of Death 2* (2014), *The ABCs of Death 2.5* (2016), *V/H/S 2* (2013), and *V/H/S: Viral* (2014)—are the most prominent of this recent bubble. They offer a fertile site of initial inquiry, giving important and frustrating insight into *XX*'s specific cultural, representational, and industrial contexts. *The ABCs of Death* is an explicitly transnational endeavor: twenty-seven directors (including one duo) from fifteen countries were given $5,000 and a letter of the alphabet upon which to base a short "tale of death." The resulting collection, which includes brief animated intertitles, is an eclectic, carnivalesque miscellany of films that emphasize the plasticity of "horror" as a category. *V/H/S* updates a well-known horror trope—that of a collection of terrible tales that have been brought together by a group of storytellers, a narrator, or other such conceit. The film's frame narrative features a group of young criminals who are offered money by an anonymous client to retrieve a specific VHS tape from a decrepit house. Upon entering the house, which is filled with unmarked tapes, they find a room in which a decomposing man is "watching" a wall of televisions, all set to static. As the men ransack the house, they take turns viewing the tapes, each of which features a self-contained found-footage film. The tapes are presented as a form of haunted media; they are mysterious, originless snuff flicks that transmit death like a contagion. Needless to say, by the end of the film, the criminals have all been dispatched by the (un)dead man, who flits about the house like a glitch in a recording.

Significantly, both films and their sequels sit within a space marked by the intersections of fandom, production, consumption, and cinephilia, which complicates how we might position them as creative hybrid texts. *The ABCs of Death* and its sequels were coproduced by Drafthouse Films, founded in 2010 as the distribution arm of the Alamo Drafthouse Cinema chain. The chain, through its family of events and subsidiary companies, has a privileged position within genre, cult, and exploitation film fandom, news, preservation, and distribution. It hosts the annual international genre film festival Fantastic Fest in Austin, Texas; it publishes entertainment website Birth.Movies.Death; and it is one of the drivers behind the American Genre Film Archive, the largest non-profit genre film archive in the world. Coproducer Ant Timpson is a notable New Zealand–based film festival programmer and film producer who specializes in "incredibly strange" films. His company, Timpson Films, maintains the Exploitation Film Archive, a collection of three thousand rare 16mm and 35mm prints. *V/H/S* and its sequels were coproduced by Brad Miska in association with the successful American horror genre website Bloody Disgusting, which he cofounded in 2001. Bloody Disgusting ventured into film production in 2010, including a distribution partnership with entertainment company AMC Networks called Bloody Disgusting Selects.

The films' association with noted genre film proponents situates them within the context of a fan-oriented, genre-savvy cinephilia that is highly gendered. Female spectatorship and subcultural practice have been increasingly recognized as a dynamic, rich site of consumption and contestation.[10] Nonetheless, traditional horror, exploitation, cult, and genre film (fan) spaces are hegemonically masculine, even while female representation becomes more prominent. "Paracinematic" communities, which are catered to by those organizations above, are subcultural spaces of oppositional cultural taste dominated by young, straight, white men, whose celebration (and sense of ownership) of the marginal functions as a way of expressing cultural deviancy that sits in tension with their cultural privilege.[11] Additionally, producers of omnibus films take on the role of creative directors; they commission eclectic films that are often created in isolation and merge them into a hybrid product that attempts to find coherence in heterogeneity. "Authentic" fan producers thus act as auteur-curators, inferring a sense of in-spirit consistency even within wildly inconsistent products. The films' producers, therefore, bring horror-centric cultural capital and cult value to the projects, which are coupled with a sense of discerning "taste making." This validates the projects and offers an impression of authority that inadvertently positions women as, at best, marginal and, at worst, invisible or abjected.

This is evident in the makeup of directors and writers in recent horror omnibus films. Consider the seven post-2010 omnibus films listed as Box Office Mojo's top-grossing horror anthologies: *V/H/S*, *V/H/S 2*, *V/H/S: Viral*, *Holidays*, *Southbound*, *The ABCs of Death*, and *The ABCs of Death 2*.[12] Between them, they contain seventy-seven segments, three frame narratives, two animated interstitial sequences, and the work of eighty-nine individual directors (some of whom work in teams), of whom only seven are female.[13] A mere eight of the ninety-two credited writers are female. No female directors or writers feature at all in the *V/H/S* franchise, although filmmaker Roxanne Benjamin, who also directs shorts in *Southbound* and *XX*, works as a coproducer. Poor levels of female representation in filmmaking personnel persist in *The ABCs of Death 2.5*, a straight-to-video on-demand collection of the best worldwide competition submissions for the letter *M*. The twenty-six finalists were selected by Timpson and coproducer Tim League out of 540 entries. The finalists feature four female directors out of a slate of thirty—a paltry 13 percent. This also raises questions about how many women submitted shorts at all.

Consider, first, the low levels of female participation in feature filmmaking: in 2017–2018, only 27 percent of independent narrative feature films that screened at high-profile American film festivals featured a female director, and 26 percent featured a female writer.[14] In 2017, women accounted for 18 percent of directors of the five hundred top U.S. domestic grossing films; similarly, female directors accounted for 18 percent of horror films featured in that top five hundred.[15] Female representation in horror omnibus films is even lower. Hypothetically, the do-it-yourself nature of microbudget short filmmaking mitigates some of the structural and discriminatory barriers to production that female filmmakers face in the production of feature films, even though they must still find ways to finance and practically support their activities and to "break into" traditionally male cultural spaces. Poor participation at all levels of production leads to a cycle of poor visibility and the perpetuation of an assumption that female directors just aren't there. In fact, it is a lack of opportunities or access, not a lack of women, that is the problem.

Paratextual positioning of these omnibus films further reiterates women's peripheral status. We must, of course, take the gleeful hyperbolic marketing hype long associated with horror films with a grain of salt.[16] After all, the sense of anticipation that is generated by outlandish marketing copy can be a key part of the affective, participatory, and spectatorial pleasures of horror.[17] Nonetheless, when *The ABCs of Death* markets itself as "the definitive vision of modern horror diversity" featuring "the world's leading talents in contemporary genre film," and when *The ABCs of Death 2* positions itself as "another global celebration of next generation genre filmmaking," we must ask who is being included in this next generation of masters and what exactly is meant by "diversity."[18]

A lack of behind-the-scenes diversity leads to a lack of diverse stories, characters, and representation. In top-grossing Hollywood films, women are significantly less likely to appear on screen than men and less likely to be protagonists, more likely to be in younger roles or to be described as "attractive," *much* more likely to be sexualized, less likely to be portrayed as leaders, and less likely to even speak at all.[19] Rates of representation improve in independent features, but horror is far from intersectional: across the board, women of color and queer women are even less visible and active than heterosexual white women.[20] Significantly, if a film has at least one female producer, female characters are less likely to be sexually objectified and are more likely to be protagonists and to have speaking roles, even though the prevalence of women in *all* speaking roles is never higher than a third.[21] No comparable, detailed research has been undertaken on female representation in horror specifically, although two quantitative studies of fifty slasher films (predominantly directed and written by men) indicate that women are far more likely than men to be victimized in scenes of sex, violence, and suffering.[22] Simply put, when women are underrepresented as writers and directors, female representation is limited, female objectification is more prominent, and female perspectives are marginalized.

Horror omnibus films are fascinating sites of inquiry in this regard, for this inequity is significantly amplified because of the sheer number of shorts available. One of the fascinating and (in this case) unfortunate quirks of the form is the cumulative effect of the juxtaposition of multiple short texts. These texts are designed to be watched in a single sitting, and negative patterns of representation are intensified through persistent repetition. This is exacerbated by the intersection of the affective and narrative demands of the horror genre, with its intention to horrify, and the constraints of the short film format, which doesn't offer much time for the generation of suspense, character development, or atmosphere. As I have outlined elsewhere, a significant portion of the twenty-six microshorts in *The ABCs of Death* lean on sex and violence as means to generate quick shocks, often at the expense of female characters.[23] Given that the films were made in isolation, it offers a perturbing picture of the place of women on screen in horror (there are also a surprising number of shorts that feature toilets, which perhaps reveals the overall tone). Many of the microshorts present women's bodies in a derogatory or hypersexualized manner: more than half feature explicit sexual content, a quarter feature rape or sexual coercion, and at least twelve explicitly objectify women for an implied heterosexual male gaze or character. The accumulative effect of such representations is pronounced. Only one of the films—the abstract, artful fantasy "O for Orgasm," directed by French duo Hélène Cattet and Bruno Forzani—centralizes female sexuality and eroticism. The shorts in the follow-up *The ABCs of Death 2* are far less reliant on casual misogyny as a narrative and aesthetic strategy and far more diverse in their address. Even though this film, like the first, states that directors were given total artistic freedom, one can't help but wonder if the producers had given everyone a quiet word about the (mis)use of sexualized violence and female objectification as shock tactics.

It is facile to suggest that the presence of violence and sexual content in horror is inherently misogynistic or lacking in ideological complexity. Nonetheless, when considered together, *V/H/S* and its sequels grapple with an intermittent seediness that infers that we, as viewers, are privileged voyeurs watching illicit, sometimes highly sexual and objectifying footage of unsuspecting individuals. We might also feel discomfort at how we are implicated in the action through our alignment with the shifting gaze of multiple cameras, especially as many of the diegetic amateur filmmakers are men whose homosocial posturing uses casual misogyny as a part of its lexicon.

We might ask ourselves, who is the intended viewer? The obnoxious delinquents who appear in the frame narrative of *V/H/S* ("Tape 56") film sexual assaults for money and make their own (nonconsensual) reality porn. Part of our pleasure in their comeuppance—death by video zombie—is in seeing them punished for their transgressions. The frame narrative of *V/H/S 2* ("Tape 49") similarly starts with someone illicitly filming a naked woman who is having her breasts groped by a man, in what we learn is a sleazy sextortion scam. The frame narrative of *V/H/S: Viral* ("Vicious Circles") opens with the cameraman repeatedly filming his girlfriend's buttocks and breasts without her knowledge. Afterward, she indulgently strips, performing for him and his camera. Later, another young woman undresses and begins to masturbate in the back of a taxi cab for a man who is making salacious amateur porn before attacking and attempting to blackmail him. The women in *V/H/S*'s "The Sick Thing That Happened to Emily When She Was Younger" and *V/H/S 2*'s "Phase I Clinical Trials" show a pronounced enthusiasm for spontaneously undressing for the camera.

Only one short in the three *V/H/S* films—"Second Honeymoon"—troubles this gendered scopic regime. It reveals that a violent voyeur who has broken into a couple's motel room and killed the sleeping husband is actually the secret lesbian lover of the wife. The film's twist is that the two women have been complicit in the entire homicidal endeavor. The short offers some ambivalence in terms of its gender politics, for it hinges on, and draws attention to, the viewer's presumed assumption that the voyeur is a heterosexual male. However, using lesbian desire as a "gotcha!" punchline is a pitch-perfect example of "killer queer" and "psychotic lesbian" tropes that do little to destabilize the films' sexual conservatism. Instead, it pathologizes and demonizes queer sexuality by linking same-sex desire with murderous and vengeful violence.[24]

The more subversive, complex, or ambivalent shorts in the *V/H/S* series are often recontextualized and undermined by patterns of representation and expression that foreground the misogynistic objectification and dehumanization of women as well as violence against them—although it is worth noting that the shorts in *Holidays* and *Southbound* fare remarkably better. Nonetheless, the majority of shorts in omnibus horror films treat women as sex dolls, sophomoric fantasies, vessels, or punching bags. When juxtaposed against these images and themes, a socially minded but grim short that highlights the terrible rates of femicide in Mexico (*The ABCs of Death*'s "I Is for Ingrown") or a film that critiques the male sexual entitlement behind the creation of nonconsensual point-of-view porn (*V/H/S*'s "Amateur Night") start to look a little like films that are just further reveling in the victimization and exploitation of women. While omnibus films may be formally and narratively varied, and while their component shorts may stand alone as complex or even progressive texts, together they offer a depressingly reductive picture that excludes women as authors and significantly constrains women's representation.

Staging an Intervention

XX is a female-led, female-centric omnibus that explicitly positions itself as a necessary, even overdue intervention within the horror genre: as segment director and coproducer Jovanka Vuckovic noted in an interview, "the horror genre is badly in need of a new perspective."[25] Its intention is to elevate the work of female directors and writers who might otherwise be marginalized within an industry that takes for granted the centrality (and neutrality) of male perspectives. This is a fascinating rejoinder to the established gendered patterns of inequity and objectification in many horror omnibuses. From here I outline how *XX* attempts to achieve these goals and the extent to which its success might be measured. The film's intention to provide a female perspective also opens up important questions about how this might function beyond personnel and narrative. I suggest that the individual segments of the film, when read independently and together, tentatively offer a hybrid text that positions itself as not just female centric in its perspective but also feminine in its form and aesthetics.

Although the shorts in *XX* were produced independently, three demonstrate a significant thematic consistency. Roxanne Benjamin's economical creature short "Don't Fall" is the most traditional horror narrative but perhaps the odd one out. Four friends traveling in the desert discover some sinister petroglyphs, but being young and dumb, they fail to take their warning seriously. Carnage ensues. The short film taps directly into a tradition of campfire tales about unheeded warnings in liminal spaces, which connects it to episodic horror's long history of morality tales. The other three shorts, though, cohere strongly in their varied explorations of maternal ambivalence, domestic horror, and female alienation.

Jovanka Vuckovic's "The Box" is an adaptation of Jack Ketchum's Bram Stoker Award–winning short story of the same name. In the lead-up to Christmas, Susan and her children travel home via train after an idyllic day shopping and skating in New York City. A peculiar-looking man sits next to them, holding a large, red present, and he lets Susan's son Danny have a peek inside. The box is a horrific MacGuffin, for whatever Danny sees changes him. His demeanor remains pleasant, but he refuses to eat anything: he is no longer hungry. The family's evening dinners become a quiet battleground. The short, which contains an overt critique of materialism and consumption, emphasizes bird's-eye shots of the lavish shared meals. They become grotesque first in their over-abundance and then in their rejection and implied waste. Attempts to reverse Danny's lack of appetite fail, and worse still, he quietly passes on his secret to his sister and then his father. The gaunt family shares a loving, laughter-filled Christmas before the three slowly starve to death. Susan spends her days on the train, hoping to see the man with the box, hungry for his dark knowledge. The protagonist of Ketchum's story is the father, whose sense of alienation seems to insulate him from whatever quiet, terrible knowledge has claimed his otherwise tight-knit family. In placing the mother in this detached position and her increasingly distraught husband as the more attentive parent, the short renders the nuclear family's seemingly catalog-perfect dynamic as Gothic, even vulgar. The short's most gruesome image comes as Susan dreams that she's lying on the dinner table, smiling while her family members happily carve away at her flesh, enjoying every dripping morsel. In this macabre, ambivalent moment, Susan is able to finally sustain and please her family, but only through her destruction. "The Box" thus explores complex, gendered issues relating to the women's ideologically sanctioned social roles, especially as it highlights the alienation of a woman with a "perfect life" who clearly does not embrace the trappings of motherhood.

The two remaining shorts also explore maternal ambivalence, though using different tonal palettes. Clark's "The Birthday Party," cowritten with Benjamin, is a macabre comedy of errors. Mary, an anxious upper-class housewife, prepares for her daughter's lavish birthday party but discovers that her businessman husband has died in his home office. Mary is under relentless pressure from other voraciously competitive mothers and from the sleek, disdainful nanny, who circles the beautiful home like a shark. Her panicked response to the death is to hide the body inside a giant panda costume, turning the birthday party into a bleak take on the cadaver comedy *Weekend at Bernie's* (1989). Mary stares, glassy-eyed, into the camera as the chaotic party unfolds around her in slow motion, before the corpse slumps into the birthday cake. The punchline is the short's title—"The Birthday Party, or, the Memory Lucy Suppressed from Her Seventh Birthday . . . That Wasn't Really Her Mom's Fault (Even Though Her Therapist Says It's Probably Why She Fears Intimacy)"—which serves to reinscribe Mary's maternal fallibility.

Karyn Kusama's contribution, "Her Only Living Son," is a revisionist take on *Rosemary's Baby* (1968): it explores what might have happened had Rosemary absconded with her Antichrist child. Cora has spent years in hiding, but dark satanic forces begin to close in upon her as her son, Andy, approaches his eighteenth birthday. Cora is exhausted, working multiple, menial jobs and existing in a state of financial precarity and personal isolation. She is also overwhelmed by the increasingly horrific conduct of her child: Andy has spent years belittling and humiliating her, and now his disturbing behavior has escalated into acts of sadistic violence. Andy's demonic father arrives to claim him, and as Andy is forced to choose between his apocalyptic destiny and the protective mother he resents, the short reflects upon the nature of maternal self-sacrifice and the myriad ways that mother figures are abjected. The thematic consistency of these three shorts reiterates how well the horror genre interrogates the complexities of maternal ambivalence—much in the same way as contemporaneous, high-profile, mother-centric art-house horror films such as *Hereditary* (2018), *mother!* (2017), and Jennifer Kent's *The Babadook* (2014) have mined grief, entrapment, and cycles of trauma. This perhaps typifies the female-centric perspective that *XX* showcases—or at least *a* perspective, if we are not to be too reductive about the scope of women's authorship.

And yet it is in the film's interstitial scenes (which have received little attention within its marketing and reviews) that most explicitly consolidate a specifically *feminine* aesthetic. Sofia Carrillo's Gothic stop-motion animated sequences follow the explorations of a walking doll's house. This uncanny domestic hybrid creature wanders through a tattered, abandoned family home on its four chubby doll legs, followed and tended to by skittering little doll hands. The house has a benign, blinking doll face in place of one of its windows, which spins so that it might look inside itself or out into the world. The melancholy vignettes, which echo Carrillo's notable 2013 short *The Sad House* (*La Casa Triste*), give the sense that we are in the quiet, forgotten space left after some sort of trauma. The creature moves up and down spiraling staircases, collecting discarded remnants of the previous inhabitants. It tucks these treasures inside of itself, in tiny internal rooms that echo the larger house's spatiality. It traps and "eats" an insect; a pin cushion pulses; fabric embroiders itself; a rotting apple throbs like a heart; dead moths flicker and scratch; tiny baby teeth line a door. Shadows move swiftly across the floor, just as storm clouds build and dissipate: temporality is unmoored. The abstract narrative concludes as the creature approaches what appears to be a sleeping, pale girl and places a small dead bird into a little door that sits in her chest. The creature's act of generosity and the bird's miraculous revival bring the girl back to life, and the creature and girl smile at one another.

This frame sequence evokes a domestic, distinctly feminine horror that intertwines recognizable representational, affective, and aesthetic Gothic markers. These include abandoned spaces; the grotesque, uncanny dolls; ancient houses; irrationality; anxiety; isolation; figurative hauntings; echoes of trauma; the diffractions of history; and a feeling of melancholy and ambivalence. Additionally, the four shorts' formal and aesthetic features overlap significantly with the "feminine aesthetic" identified by Brigid Cherry in her studies of female horror fans' self-professed preferences. They combine psychological horror, strong female characters, morbid fascination, melodrama (and its subversion), and a sense of suggestion and anticipation with limited, strategic doses of gore and special effects.[26] XX's relative consistency, especially when compared to other omnibuses, offers provocative questions as we study women-made horror films: do female directors and a so-called female perspective result more often in a feminine aesthetic? And is this even an appropriate question?[27] Do we connect female filmmakers because they are perceived as other or because of genuine shared patterns of representation and expression? Are there other areas of (perhaps underserved) female preference that may be catered to by female filmmakers more successfully than their male peers? Might there be alternative feminine aesthetics that are yet to be articulated or explored? And how might we consider the work of female filmmakers who reject this model?

Does *XX* Mark the Spot?

Questions remain about the extent to which *XX* acts as a robust "alternative" perspective, for its industrial and paratextual positioning place it in an uncomfortable space: the film's difference becomes marketed as a niche, othered product, not just a much-needed expansion of horror's terrain. The film succeeds in amplifying the voices of five female filmmakers, but the film's marketing and emphasis upon auteurism lean on a performative, narrow type of femininity that both emphasizes and exoticizes sexual difference. The film's title refers (of course) to the XX chromosomal pairing that generally differentiates human female biological sex from (XY) male. The "XX" logo is roughly scrawled in hot pink, accompanied by a bold-pink lipstick print that resembles a stylized skull; this pink-on-black color scheme persists through the film's marketing. The first, widely quoted tag line—"Four deadly tales by four killer women"—alludes to the sexualized figure of the *femme fatale*, although the film's current promotional material describes the directors more moderately as "four female filmmakers."[28] The film is distributed by Magnet Releasing, who is also the distributor for *The ABCs of Death* and *V/H/S* series, and its promotional material describes the directors as "fiercely talented women."[29] Again, it is hard to imagine a similar descriptor being applied to their male counterparts. Yes, the film is a commodity that is being positioned within a crowded marketplace. But this indirectly reveals the dismal position of female filmmakers, if the most effective way of promoting women's artistic work is by leveraging essentialist, biologically determinist (albeit tongue-in-cheek) signifiers of stereotypical femininity that present femaleness and feminism "as a unified and one-dimensional entity."[30] This is also entirely symptomatic of the myriad ways that female horror directors have long been dismissed, patronized, or treated as exceptions.[31] *XX* is therefore caught in tension: the promotion of its point of difference becomes a reiteration of its fundamental otherness and the perceived otherness of its filmmakers.

This provokes further questions about how we might strategically amplify and support historically excluded voices in a manner that opens up opportunities within the mainstream while also protecting spaces on the (relative) margins. We must find better ways to support difference and diversity without fetishizing it. Additionally, female filmmakers, as well as creatives from other marginalized groups, have long been plagued by the damaging supposition that their individual work is representative of their entire community, so it is also vital that female-helmed films such as *XX* are allowed to potentially fail without dragging female authorship as a whole into disrepute. Finally, producers and audiences must not be allowed to inadvertently see female-authored films as demographic box-ticking exercises—that in their creation, "women's stuff" is handily taken care of. *XX* stands on its own as a competent and comparatively coherent omnibus, but it needs to be one of many—one of a *diverse* many—and not a lone voice in a field that remains persistently, stubbornly, something of a boys' club.

Notes

1   It is difficult to find a definitive list of horror anthologies, although one user-generated list on IMDb identifies forty-four titles released between 2010 and June 2018. See IMDb, "The Horror Anthologies Collection [1912–2018]," June 23, 2018, http://www.imdb.com/list/ls074993025/. Notable published work has focused on individual titles or the output of specific production houses rather than episodic horror as a form; see David Scott Diffrient, "Narrative Mortality: The 'Fragmented' Corpse of the Horror Anthology Film," *Paradoxa: Studies in World Literary Genres* 14 (2002): 271–301; Peter Hutchings, "The Amicus House of Horrors," in *British Horror Cinema*, ed. Steve Chibnall and Julian Petley (London: Routledge, 2002), 131–144.

2   Jen Yamato, "Magnet Springs for Femme-Driven Horror Anthology *XX*," *Deadline*, October 8, 2014, https://deadline.com/2014/10/magnet-female-horror-anthology-xx-848156/.

3   Mark Betz, "Film History, Film Genre, and Their Discontents: The Case of the Omnibus Film," *Moving Image: The Journal of the Association of Moving Image Archivists* 1, no. 2 (2001): 56–87.

4   "*The ABCs of Death*: 26 Directors, 26 Way to Die," Drafthouse Films, accessed May 1, 2019, https://drafthousefilms.com/collections/the-abcs-of-death/.

5 David S. Diffrient, *Omnibus Films: Theorizing Transauthorial Cinema* (Edinburgh: Edinburgh University Press, 2014), 14.

6 Diffrient, 26–29, 32, 81–82.

7 See Richard J. Hand and Michael Wilson, "Transatlantic Terror! French Horror Theatre and American Pre-code Comics," *Journal of Popular Culture* 45, no. 2 (2012): 301–318.

8 Diffrient, *Omnibus Films*, 131.

9 Betz, "Film History," 81.

10 See Brigid Cherry, "Refusing to Refuse to Look: Female Viewers of the Horror Film," in *Horror, the Film Reader*, ed. Mark Jancovich (London: Routledge, 2002), 169–178; Amy Jane Vosper, "Film, Fear and the Female: An Empirical Study of the Female Horror Fan," *Offscreen* 18, nos. 6–7 (2014), http://offscreen.com/view/film-fear-and-the-female.

11 Jeffrey Sconce, "'Trashing' the Academy: Taste, Excess, and an Emerging Politics of Cinematic Style," *Screen* 36, no. 4 (1995): 375.

12 "Horror Anthology Movies at the Box Office," Box Office Mojo, accessed May 1, 2019, https://www.boxofficemojo.com/genres/chart/?id=horroranthology.htm.

13 Production information is taken from IMDb.com.

14 Martha M. Lauzen, *Indie Women: Behind-the-Scenes Employment of Women in Independent Film, 2017–2018* (California: San Diego State University, Center for the Study of Women in Television in Film, 2018), https://womenintvfilm.sdsu.edu/wp-content/uploads/2018/07/2017-18_Indie_Women_Report_rev.pdf.

15 Martha M. Lauzen, *It's a Man's (Celluloid) World: Portrayals of Female Characters in the 100 Top Films of 2017 Center for the Study of Women in Television and Film* (California: San Diego State University, Center for the Study of Women in Television in Film, 2018), https://womenintvfilm.sdsu.edu/wp-content/uploads/2018/01/2017_Celluloid_Ceiling_Report.pdf.

16 See Ben Kooyman, "How the Masters of Horror Master Their Personae: Self-Fashioning At Play in the Masters of Horrors DVD Extras," in *American Horror Film: The Genre at the Turn of the Millennium*, ed. Steffen Hantke (Jackson: University Press of Mississippi, 2010), 193–220.

17 See Eric Schaefer, *"Bold! Daring! Shocking! True!" A History of Exploitation Films, 1919–1959* (Durham, N.C.: Duke University Press, 1999), 104–119.

18 Drafthouse Films, *"ABCs of Death"*; *"The ABCs of Death 2,"* Magnet, http://www.magnetreleasing.com/theabcsofdeath.

19 Stacy L. Smith, Marc Choueiti, and Katherine Pieper, *Gender Inequality in Popular Films: Examining On Screen Portrayals and Behind-the-Scenes Employment Patterns in Motion Pictures Released between 2007–2013* (Los Angeles: University of Southern California Annenberg, 2014), https://annenberg.usc.edu/sites/default/files/MDSCI_Gender_Inequality_in_600_films.pdf; Lauzen, *It's a Man's (Celluloid) World*.

20 Lauzen, *Indie Women*.

21 Smith, Choueiti, and Pieper, *Gender Inequality*, 5, 17n19.

22 Andrew Welsh and Laurier Brantford, "Sex and Violence in the Slasher Horror Film: A Content Analysis of Gender Differences in the Depiction of Violence," *Journal of Criminal Justice and Popular Culture* 16, no. 1 (2009): 1–25; Andrew Welsh, "On the Perils of Living Dangerously in the Slasher Horror Film: Gender Differences in the Association between Sexual Activity and Survival," *Sex Roles* 62, nos. 11–12 (2010): 762–773.

23 Erin Harrington, *Women, Monstrosity and Horror Film: Gynaehorror* (New York: Routledge, 2017), 271–273.

24 Harry M. Benshoff and Sean Griffin, "General Introduction," in *Queer Cinema: The Film Reader*, ed. Harry M. Benshoff and Sean Griffin (New York: Routledge, 2004), 10–13; Christine Coffman, *Insane Passions: Lesbianism and Psychosis in Literature and Film* (Middletown, Conn.: Wesleyan University Press, 2006).

25 James Roberts, "Mistress of Horror Jovanka Vuckovic Talks *XX* and the Female Perspective," *Glide Magazine*, February 15, 2017, https://glidemagazine.com/180058/jovanka-vuckovic-xx-interview/.

26 Brigid Cherry, "Gothics and Grand Guignols: Violence and the Gendered Aesthetics of Cinematic Horror," *Particip@tions* 5, no. 1 (2008), http://www.participations.org/Volume%205/Issue%201%20-%20special/5_01_cherry.htm.

27 See Katarzyna Paszkiewicz, "When the Woman Directs (a Horror Film)," in *Women Do Genre in Film and Television*, ed. Mary Harrod and Katarzyna Paszkiewicz (London: Routledge, 2018), 45.

28 Derek Anderson, "New *XX* Featurette Explores the Horror Anthology's Four Deadly Tales," Daily Dead, February 16, 2017, https://dailydead.com/new-xx-featurette-explores-the-horror-anthologys-four-deadly-tales/; "*XX* Official Movie Site," Magnet, accessed December 8, 2018, http://www.magnetreleasing.com/xx/.

29 Magnet, "*XX* Official Movie Site—Synopsis," http://www.magnetreleasing.com/xx/synopsis/.

30 Paszkiewicz, "When the Woman Directs," 48.

31 Paszkiewicz, 43–45.

14

The Transnational Gaze in *A Girl Walks Home Alone at Night*

LINDSEY DECKER

Iranian American director Ana Lily Amirpour's *A Girl Walks Home Alone at Night* (2014) tells the story of a vampire (the Girl) who wears a chador (a large circular cloth, usually black) as she stalks Bad City, Iran, dispensing rough justice on behalf of the city's downtrodden while pursuing a gentle romance with the quiet Arash. The film has been celebrated as a feminist take on the vampire and contemporary Iran. *Bitch* and *Jezebel* called it "the feminist vampire movie that teaches 'bad men' a gory lesson" and praised its "vampire vigilante."[1] Amirpour, though, seems particularly averse to feminist interpretations of her work. When asked about critics labeling *Girl* as feminist, Amirpour demurred, telling interviewer Rich Juzwiak, "I think people tend to see themselves in films."[2] When pressed, she added, "I find that these philosophies [feminisms] are the disease for which they claim to be the cure. . . . I'm more interested in asking questions than finding a specific answer." These comments certainly discourage the sort of auteur-focused approach common in both popular discussions and academic studies of women directors. Films are complicated, polysemous productions, created collaboratively. Amirpour's stated, conscious intent should shape but cannot be the sole frame of meaning for the film any more than we can claim the film as feminist solely based on Amirpour's gender.

Amirpour has been vocal, though, about the film's and her own transnationalism. In a *Vice* documentary on *Girl*, she talks about her identity to Sheila Vand, the Iranian American actress who plays the Girl, stating, "It's not really an Iranian film, and it's also not an American film. But, like, what are we? Am I Iranian? Am I pure?"[3] Juxtaposing tropes from different national cinemas thus enables the film to pose questions about cinema and gender that culminate in a metacinematic feminist critique. This chapter traces the relationship between transnationalism, the gaze, and women's representation in *Girl*. The film's transnational hybridity manifests in part through its Persian-language dialogue and in part through its eclectic genre influences, including the Iranian new wave, 1950s Hollywood teen films, and Italian spaghetti westerns. Equally important is the film's regime of gazing, which eschews the assaultive and reactive gazes common in American horror. Instead, the gaze in *Girl* operates in complex and subversive ways by playing with the averted gaze of postrevolutionary Iranian cinema, rejecting the normative gazes of the Iranian and American genres that it hybridizes. This rejection allows the film to critique the gender politics within both countries' cinemas. It also allows for a reevaluation of the dominance of accepted Western academic theories of the gaze prevalent in horror studies in light of other, more transnational modes of gazing.

Feminist horror criticism has operated under the basic premises of Laura Mulvey's theory of the male gaze for the last forty years.[4] Even Steven Jay Schneider's otherwise provocative 2004 edited collection *Horror Film and Psychoanalysis: Freud's Worst Nightmare*, meant to assess the subfield and take it in new directions, does not present a new take on feminist psychoanalysis or the gaze.[5] The theory has been productively applied and extended by scholars to a number of American horror films and cycles, particularly those made by directors and in industries openly fascinated with psychoanalysis. However, in part because of Amirpour's self-described hybrid nationality as well as that of *Girl*, I take up Hamid Naficy's Islamicate gaze theory, an alternative theorization of averted gazes specific to Iranian cinema after the 1978–1979 Islamic Revolution.[6] The Islamic Revolution put into place many rules governing women's on-screen representation and, by extension, the gaze of the camera. Naficy, one of the preeminent scholars of Iranian cinema, argues the Islamicate gaze theory is both "an undertheorized engine of cinematic looking and storytelling in today's Iran" and "radically different from Western feminist gaze theory."[7] Here, I extend Naficy's theorization to examine how *Girl* challenges this now-hegemonic style of gazing without slipping into the Hollywood "male gaze."

I begin by discussing the film's transnational genre hybridity, situating *Girl* with regard to its myriad generic references and exploring how those references position the film as explicitly transnational. In particular, the film's hybridization of Iranian new wave influences with visual tropes from classic Hollywood teen films points toward *Girl*'s concern with these cinemas and their modes of gazing. This leads me to discuss Western feminist psychoanalytic analyses of the gaze, particularly those that have become canonical within horror studies. Next, I flesh out Naficy's notion of the Islamicate gaze theory as it relates to Iranian cinema. I contend that *Girl* constructs a transnationally hybrid gaze that eschews the negative patriarchal assumptions of both Hollywood and postrevolutionary Iranian cinema. In doing so, the film critiques both gazes, illuminating new ways in which contemporary horror studies can understand the gaze.

Iranian Cinema and Hollywood Nostalgia

Scholars have written little about Amirpour, in part because she only came to prominence as a horror director with *Girl* in 2014. Much of the scholarship focuses on the possibilities presented by an Iranian vampire. Shadee Abdi and Bernadette Marie Calafell argue *Girl* represents the possibility of queer utopia, wherein connections between the Girl, Arash, and Atti can be seen as "moments of queer potentiality and Othered belonging."[8] Dale Hudson uses the figure of the Girl to discuss the changing ethnic representation of the vampire in transnationally inflected American vampire films.[9] And Zachary Cheney discusses the film's indebtedness to Chantal Akerman's long-take aesthetic and how that indebtedness leads *Girl*, like Akerman's *Jeanne Dielman, 23 quai du Commerce, 1080 Bruxelles* (1975), to demonstrate an investment in "unsettling audience . . . gender biases."[10]

However, scholars have not addressed Amirpour's work with sustained attention to gaze or genre. Abdi and Calafell address the film's relation to Iranian feminisms but not Iranian cinema itself. Hudson discusses the film's links to Iranian culture and diasporic audiences but, again, not Iranian cinema. The exception is Katarzyna Marciniak, who reads the film as addressing itself to a "*foreign* female" spectatorial gaze, drawing on Teresa de Lauretis's work on the defamiliarized and delocated spectatorial gaze.[11] Marciniak reads the Girl as one of a wave of migrant women protagonists in post–2000s women-directed films that unsettle the U.S. discursive link between migrant women and waste or disposability. However, her brief reading of *Girl*, in an otherwise compelling essay, depends on conflating the film's fictional setting in Bad City, Iran, with its production location in California and reading the Girl as a U.S. migrant.[12] Marciniak is partly correct nonetheless: Bad City's hybrid identity—simultaneously Iranian, American, and neither—helps reinforce the film's concern with transnationalism, which also comes out in its genre hybridity. *Girl* addresses itself to a *transnational* spectatorial gaze, in that the film can reward American, Iranian, and Iranian diasporic audiences in different ways. And it is this transnational genre hybridity, signaling a metacinematic concern with both Iranian and American cinemas, that allows the film to critique normative gazing regimes.

As noted in the film's press kit, *Girl* has many connections to the Iranian new wave. Most simply, as with Iranian new wave films, the director is presented as an auteur: a singular author-director with a particular vision, whose skill allows for the expression of her worldview. The Iranian new wave started in 1969 with Dariush Mehrjui's *The Cow* (*Gaav*; 1969) and Massoud Kimiai's *Qeysar* (1969). These films brought Iranian cinema to the attention of the international festival circuit. The movement ended in 1978 with the revolution.[13] As Naficy notes, while much of the style of new wave films is heterogeneous and varies from director to director, the films tend to use high-contrast black-and-white cinematography with rural settings that avoid large cities like Tehran.[14] The films' gritty social realism and concern with serious social problems in Iran combine with a visual lyricism, a "poetic vision of the world" emphasized in part by a scarcity of dialogue. This combination results in what Naficy terms a "poetic realist style" that is linked to a kind of surrealism that comes about through the alienating effects of fundamentalism and patriarchy.[15]

Arguably, Amirpour's film includes all of these qualities. The stark, high-contrast black-and-white cinematography in *Girl* is a visual link to the Iranian new wave, followed by the film's setting in Bad City. The film avoids the city center, focusing instead on the outskirts of the city and the suburban area where Shaydah lives and Arash works. The film clearly signals its concern with depicting serious Iranian social problems by centering on socially marginal characters, from vampires to sex workers and heroin addicts. The film's poetic realism is achieved through depicting the daily realities of the marginalized in combination with sparse dialogue, evocative use of music—much of it drawn from Iranian club culture—and haunting long takes.[16] Negar Mottahedeh reads the film's silences as illustrative of Amitav Ghosh's "muteness of the Oil Encounter," or, as Mottahedeh discusses it, a silencing of those marginalized by the myriad disruptions caused by Iran's relationship to oil. While this reading is compelling, particularly as oil derricks haunt the background and edges of the frame in *Girl*, the sparse dialogue is also a clear film nod to the Iranian new wave.

And as with new wave films, *Girl* presents viewers with a variety of narratively and aesthetically surreal moments. There is the strange, hallucinatory cinematography when Arash takes drugs at Shaydah's party or the scene where Hossein badgers Arash's cat, convinced it is the reincarnation of his dead wife. Or consider when the Girl meets Arash properly: he is clothed in a Dracula costume, high and staring into a streetlight. This uncanny meeting of real and cinematic vampires only becomes more bizarre when they hug. Then there is the floaty, slow-motion scene where Rockabilly (whom Amirpour has noted is a gay man in drag) dances with a balloon in an abandoned dirt lot to the opening bars of Federale's "Sisyphus," a semioperatic song reminiscent of Ennio Morricone's western scores. Of these scenes, Rockabilly's is easiest to link to the alienating effects of fundamentalism and patriarchy. As Amirpour puts it, "It's not OK to be gay in Iran."[17] Rockabilly's surreal dance acts as a moment of unpoliced queer joy. We can also see the surrealism of Arash and Hossein's hallucinatory scenes as rooted in the normative pressures that patriarchy places on even ostensibly straight men, pressures that can lead to drug use or abuse when those men do not or cannot conform.

However, the Girl's interactions with her victims are more surreal. In one dreamlike scene, a clueless Saeed, high on cocaine, attempts to seduce her with drugs and dancing. Using his exposed, undulating abdominal muscles, he attempts to hypnotize the Girl (and the viewer), even as her gaze hypnotizes him. Similarly, when the Girl kills Hossein, she leaps into the room in slow motion, dragging Hossein from the bed and throwing him to the floor. A percussive sound builds, like an army of women synchronously stomping their feet in anticipation. This sound ends as the Girl pounces, replaced by biting, tearing, and slurping sounds. The attack is, in turn, intercut with plain black images and unearthly, howling wind sounds. The Girl arrives as an avenging angel, but the jarring cuts and sounds emphasize her terrifying unknowability, exceeding the representational powers of the film itself.

Here, the surrealism is linked directly to the Girl's subversion of patriarchy. Saeed treats the Girl as prey when she is the superior predator, and she kills Hossein for drugging Atti against her will. Significantly, the Girl uses her chador as a vampire's cape, and it cloaks her. A more traditional covering popular in Iran, it covers the hair, as mandated by modesty laws, but also the majority of the body down to the ankles. The chador is open in front and must be actively held closed by the wearer, making it a limiting garment. The Girl uses it as a vampire's cape, and it cloaks her in the illusion of compliance. With her chador draped around her as she stalks the streets of Bad City, it is hard not to read the Girl's subversiveness as directed at what the film envisions as Iranian Islamic patriarchy.

Beyond its touchstone links to the Iranian new wave, *Girl* also references 1950s Hollywood teen films, including the teen melodrama, the juvenile delinquent film, and the hot-rod film. These subgenres were popularized by *Rebel without a Cause* (1955) starring James Dean. Beyond being called the "Persian James Dean" in the film's press kit, Arash's character is costumed and styled to look like Dean, from the blue jeans to the white T-shirt and pompadour, mirroring Dean's look in *Rebel*. Cigarettes and a 1950s Ford Thunderbird complete the linkage. As with Jim, Dean's character in *Rebel*, the Girl and Arash are lonely social outsiders; Arash is also angry over his father's parental inadequacies. Indeed, *Rebel*'s visual iconography links *Girl* more broadly and Arash more specifically to "the sense of alienation from society and distrust of authority," of "powerlessness and purposelessness in an adult-dominated world."[18] Given that contemporary Iran seeks to legally and culturally disallow Western cultural influence, Arash seems to be at odds with his own nation, seeking to express his masculinity in alternate ways that separate him from both the Iranian male ideal and the men of Bad City. Unlike the other men in the film, he does not seek to dominate or coerce the Girl or any other woman. Even if we reduce their relationship to the basic terms of the penetrative economy of heterosexual desire, we must note that while Arash pierces the Girl's ears, he only does so at her explicit bidding.

The Canonical (Western, Feminist) Gaze of Horror

Given the vampire's obvious connection to penetration, how might traditional feminist approaches to horror apply to *A Girl Walks Home Alone at Night*? In a Freudian feminist psychoanalytic reading, a la Laura Mulvey's early work in the 1970s on classic Hollywood cinema, we might discuss the camera's masochistic gaze. The woman vampire is invested with both lack and phallic power via her fangs as well as her role as an active subject who propels the narrative and eschews traditional "to-be-looked-at-ness."[19] This renders the Girl a powerful source of fear, simultaneously reminding the gazing male (camera and spectator) of the castration threat posed by female lack and the threat of female usurpation of male phallic power. Her cross-sex appropriation of power could also be read as sadomasochistic.

In the 1980s and 1990s, several scholars took up Mulvey's work and extended it to horror films, most notably Linda Williams, Barbara Creed, and Carol Clover. Following Williams's work, *Girl* could appeal to spectators because its female monster, her appropriated phallic power, and her male victims "repeat the trauma of castration as if to 'explain' . . . the originary problem of sexual difference."[20] The Girl, then, is a double threat of physical and psychological castration. We might also read the Girl via a Kristevan feminist psychoanalytic lens, as in Barbara Creed's work. She could be seen, as female vampires often are, as a representation of voracious female sexual appetite, abject in her liminal state between "living and dead, . . . human and animal."[21] She fulfills the male spectator's "sexual death wish" while simultaneously "point[ing] to the perversity of masculine desire" and "the male imagination."[22] The danger the Girl represents, then, is a threatened confrontation between the male audience and the sexually voracious female monster, whose attacks on men like Saeed can be read as a form of sexualized violence. The Girl's escape from Bad City, then, accompanied by Arash, could be seen as the film's containment of that sexual excess within the bounds of a heterosexual relationship. Or taking up Carol J. Clover's foundational work, one might be tempted to read the Girl as akin to the violent heroines in rape-revenge films, who turn the assaultive gaze back on their (male) assaulters.[23] While the Girl was not assaulted by either of the men she kills, both men have coercive sexual relations with Atti, so the Girl's revenge could be communal rather than individual.

And yet a feminist psychoanalytic reading of *Girl* does not satisfy. The Girl's threat is not nullified through sexual objectification by the camera or the men in the film, nor is her threat demystified via the gaze of camera or man and then contained through punishment. The Girl does not signal her threat by gazing in sympathy at the monster. She is no Final Girl. The Girl is the monster.

Feminist psychoanalytic readings push toward a universalizing theory of gender psychology rooted in a patriarchal conception of sexual difference, whereas *Girl* goes out of its way to signal its concern with the specific (the national, the historico-cultural, etc.).

Theorists like Cynthia Freeland and Toril Moi have persuasively criticized feminist psychoanalysis. For Freeland, feminist psychoanalytic approaches to horror are flawed for a number of reasons, including the fact that psychoanalysis is not widely accepted within psychiatry, and even within psychoanalysis, there is no consensus around Freud's, Lacan's, or Kristeva's theories.[24] Also, psychoanalysis is not widely accepted within feminist scholarship outside of film studies, particularly non-Western and anticolonial work.[25] Freeland also notes that feminist psychoanalytic approaches tend to be somewhat reductive, privileging a male fear of castration over other categories of difference like "social class, sexual orientation, age, race," cis- or transness, and so on while also presuming that castration fears are not "radically culture- and era-bound."[26] This is why the feminist psychoanalytic work on the gaze done by Mulvey, Williams, Creed, and Clover is so persuasive for the texts they chose but often feels shallow when extended to other texts not created during a historical moment when the culture, industry, or creative forces behind the texts under examination were fascinated with psychoanalysis.

Toril Moi and other feminist theorists have critiqued psychoanalytic feminism for its foundational equation of sexual difference with castration and female inferiority. For Moi, children's discovery of the different sexes "doesn't have to lead straight to the claim that when a little girl discovers that her brother has a penis, then she will instantly feel inferior. Yet that claim grounds the whole theory of castration and lack for Freud."[27] Instead of a universalizing theory that fundamentally reinforces men as "the norm" and women as "the problem to be explained," Moi advocates for "a more nuanced, historically and culturally specific account of the many different psychosexual options" available.[28] As she notes, to reject Freud's "story" of sexual difference "is not to reject psychoanalysis" entirely, because other psychoanalysts "have tried to develop a better story ever since Freud first launched his."[29] Moi's critique and proposal seem particularly poignant as trans, genderqueer, and intersex narratives and characters become more visible in films.

What is particularly disappointing about psychoanalytic feminist theories is their inability to account for the visceral, invigorating thrill of watching a woman vampire mete out bloody justice to men who treat women as objects rather than subjects while she also forms tender, protective relationships with other characters. Indeed, Brigid Cherry's landmark study of women horror fans, originally published in 1999, showed that they often experience a "subversive affinity" with and "empathy for the monster" based on their shared status as social outsiders.[30] Rather than "refusing to look" (per Williams), "adopting a male gaze," or "colluding with the male oppressor," women horror fans take pleasure in gazing at, identifying with, and even loving male monsters as well as horror heroines who are "strong, intelligent and resilient," even "masculine."[31] The Girl embodies both of these figures valued by women horror fans; she is complexly drawn to be monstrous and heroic, harsh and gentle, a level of sophistication traditionally reserved for men characters. Audiences must decide for themselves how to interpret and reconcile, say, her unmotivated murder of a homeless man or her dire threats to the little boy with her sweet slow dance with Arash. Early in the film, as the Girl skateboards toward the camera, her chador billowing behind her like bat wings, her progress toward the camera is less a threat than a building sense of promise. The sound of the skateboard's wheels on the pavement feels like an auditory tidal wave, rushing forward to sweep away tired clichés of women's representation and the gaze in not only Iranian and Hollywood film but also studies of horror film.

The Transnationally Hybrid Gaze as Critique

Rather than using the classically theorized assaultive male gaze, *A Girl Walks Home Alone at Night* subverts the tropes and assumptions of Naficy's Islamicate gaze. In this way, the film functions as a critique of the classic Hollywood and horror gaze as well as the postrevolutionary Iranian gaze. During and after the 1978–1979 Islamic Revolution in Iran, the incoming government targeted cinema because of its perceived ties to the West. Around one-third of Iran's cinemas were destroyed, and the Islamic Republic instituted rules to make women a "desexualized and veiled presence" on screen.[32] As Mottahedeh argues, Iran's film censorship stems from fears about "media technologies . . . transport[ing] the bitter seeds of westernization to Iran." Officials fear that film technologies' fundamental relationship to sight and sound can warp Iranians' "sense perception." This could alienate "the national body" from its physical senses and create an estrangement from "correct" religious practices.[33]

Because of the government's interpretation of Islamic modesty codes, postrevolutionary Iranian cinema has had to assume a male camera and spectator and specifically a man not related to the women on screen. Gender norms had shifted toward allowing more legal and social empowerment for women during the Pahlavi era (1925–1979). However, as Naficy notes, the revolution returned the country to an older mindset, wherein Iranian women must "be protected from unrelated males by following rules of modesty in architecture, dress, behavior, voice, touch, eye contact, and relations." All social spaces and art "must be gendered and segregated by some sort of veil or barrier inscribing the fundamental separation and inequality of the sexes."[34] On film, this has meant reducing women's screen time; keeping them veiled at all times, even when they would not be veiled within the diegesis; restricting their presence to spaces where they would be veiled to preserve verisimilitude; or risking censorship (or worse). Mottahedeh similarly notes that "the ever-presence of the veil reflexively points to . . . the presence everywhere of an unrelated male viewer."[35]

The theory of gendered difference underlying the gaze in postrevolutionary Iranian cinema is not based on men's fear of women's lack (or castration) but on the idea that women are "a constitutive part of the core self of the males to whom they are related, and they must, therefore, be protected."[36] This leads to the Islamicate gaze regime, which, Naficy argues, is based on several further assumptions. First, the "eyes are active, even invasive organs." Second, women possess an extraordinary sexual desire that must be contained through modesty to prevent it from corrupting men because, third, they are weak and unable to resist "women's powerful sexual allure."[37] These assumptions lead Naficy to conclude that "power relations in the relay of gazes in the Islamic world seem the obverse of those posited in Western feminist gaze theory: the aggressive male gaze supposedly affects not the female target but the gaze's male owner."[38]

Instead of an aggressive gaze, then, through which men can fetishize or punish women, the dominant regime of gazing in postrevolutionary Iran centers on the averted gaze. As Naficy notes, in practice this means that "many people avoid looking at others directly," regardless of the gender of the looker or looked-upon, instead looking down, to the side, or at the person in "an unfocused way."[39] Cinematographers tend to use long shots to hide women's bodies, gazes, and, in turn, subjectivities.[40] And yet because of modesty laws around veiling, women's eyes and gazes become even more important as expressive tools. This is bolstered by the traditional use of the chador, especially when it is held to cover the lower face, creating a theatrical, proscenium arch for the eyes. Thus the woman's gaze in Iranian cinema is much more powerful than the passive or reactive gaze of the objectified victim conceived of by Western feminist psychoanalytic film criticism—but powerful in terms of expressivity, not in terms of the threat of lack or appropriated phallic power. Also, a sense of surveillance permeates Iranian gazing, because segregation and veiling are imperfect. An averted gaze creates an opportunity to gaze at that person both directly and openly.[41] As Naficy notes, women's hidden gazing and eavesdropping are less about the "desire to control the other" in Iranian cinema and more a function of their "subsidiary social position."[42] Women gain knowledge and power to "equalize their situation" through distanced gazing.[43]

These rules were most strictly followed by filmmakers in the 1980s in the years directly after the revolution. However, restrictions were relaxed somewhat starting with President Khatami's rule in 1997, "in the form of physically active women . . . , their mobility in vehicles . . . , and their active narrative agency."[44] In the 1990s and 2000s, Iranian women filmmakers created a significant number of films, including directors like Tahmineh Milani, Manijeh Hekmat, Samira and Hana Makhmalbaf, Marjane Satrapi, Marzieh Meshkini, Rakhshan Bani-E'temad, Pouran Derakh'shandeh, and Nikki Karimi. Many of these women directors have also been nominated for or won prizes at prestigious international film festivals. Indeed, women make up a higher percentage of the total number of directors in the Iranian film industry than in Hollywood. And yet even in more contemporary Iranian films, despite these gains in front of and behind the camera, women's voices and gazes are still often absent on screen.[45]

Yet *Girl* privileges women's gazing. The Girl watches Saeed as he meets Atti to collect money from her, the moment captured through the car's small, circular rear side windows. The camerawork, combined with a reveal shot that pulls back over the Girl's shoulder, evokes the surveillance culture encouraged by the Islamicate gaze. The kill scene starts with Saeed walking down a dark street where he and the Girl make sustained eye contact. He interprets her direct, unabashed gaze through the lens of the Islamicate gaze, seeing a signal that she is willing to use the sexual power of her gaze to corrupt him. After they return to his apartment, it takes him several minutes and a great deal of cocaine to look at her again, while the Girl stares at him openly. Saeed starts lifting weights but, after a few moments of sustained eye contact, stops and begins to dance toward her in a sexual manner, chest and abdomen exposed, as though inexorably drawn by her look. The intimate close-ups and shallow focus combine with Saeed's loud, pulsing techno to give a feeling of dizzying claustrophobia and inescapability. For Saeed and viewers, everything blurs into the background under the Girl's powerful gaze.

Unblinking, the Girl allows Saeed to play his finger around her mouth. The techno fades low and disappears as the Girl bites his finger off and backs him against the wall. A handheld, weaving camera captures her playing his severed finger around his mouth for a few seconds as he whimpers and screams. This gesture mimics his earlier actions with the Girl as well as his coercion of Atti and the fear that likely compelled her to comply with his sexual demands. As the Girl attacks Saeed's neck, the camera follows his gaze as it transitions into the aimless gaze of the dead. His belief in the ideology behind the Islamicate gazing regime gives the Girl power over him. And yet she does not use her gaze to fulfill the insatiable sexual desire that this gazing regime and Saeed presuppose. Instead, she subverts the gaze's normative rules as well as uses the knowledge afforded to her through the surveillance the regime enables. The Girl uses that power to murder Saeed as vengeance for his sexual coercion and violence.

While Saeed is punished for buying into the negative, patriarchal assumptions behind the Islamicate gaze, Arash earns the Girl's trust because he does not. Like with Saeed, the Girl's first sustained interaction with Arash comes about when she passes him on the street. After he stumbles up to her, openly and directly returning her gaze, the Girl pursues him, staring into his eyes with the same expression she used on Saeed. Despite being framed in the same intimate style of close-ups, Arash is unaffected. The sound, too, remains consistent through the scene. There is a low howl of wind, but neither the audience nor Arash becomes so hypnotized that the Girl's powers affect what is heard. When the Girl takes Arash back to her room, where she discards her chador and plays her music for him, the sound level again remains unaffected, even as the Girl stares longingly at Arash's neck. The music only begins to fade at the moment it appears the Girl decides not to kill Arash. Instead, she closes her eyes and rests her head against Arash's chest, listening to his heartbeat as the music fades out, as though she is the one hypnotized. When they meet again over hamburgers, their gazes are mostly averted. No longer on drugs, both Arash and the Girl tend to stare forward as they stand side by side; they look at each other directly only when the other is looking away, looking down, or gazing in an unfocused way. As the Girl and Arash play with the codes of Islamicate gazing, she develops a closer relationship with him that is more based in equity. His rejection of the gaze's patriarchal foundations protects him, as it negates the Girl's hypnotic powers, but it also allows her to step outside the role of avenging murderess to pursue a tender relationship that she obviously also desires. Both cede a kind of power to embrace connection.

Conclusion

In her 2004 essay "Why I Did Not Want to Write This Essay," Linda Williams criticizes ahistorical psychoanalytic feminist approaches that continue to uncritically restage arguments made in the 1970s and 1980s, in part because it has "become boring and repetitive to see all the sensationalism of cinema motivated by castration anxiety."[46] Indeed, Williams seems frustrated with scholarship that eschews an intersectional focus that gets outside of "heterosexual feminism" or ignores later work done by key theorists, like Williams herself, to revise their most famous claims.[47] I would add that we must also examine issues of nation and, when appropriate, transnationalism. In *Girl*, the Girl has been a vampire since 1899, a fact disclosed via paratext.[48] Her vampiric "birth" took place a year before the birth of Iranian cinema. She would have seen the entirety of cinema history in Iran, likely developed her affection for American popular culture during the Western-influenced Pahlavi monarchy, and seen the massive changes of the 1978–1979 Islamic Revolution. She would also have witnessed the more recent changes in the country, including the cultural rebellions and underground bootleg practices that have allowed young Iranians to access Western culture and films like *Girl*. Having seen all this history and been exposed to different types of cinematic gazing, all prefaced on patriarchal frameworks that disallow women pleasure while objectifying them or denying their autonomous subjectivity, it is unsurprising that the Girl subverts these gazes.

Furthermore, in blending historically and nationally specific aesthetics from the Iranian new wave and classic Hollywood teen films, *Girl* signals its concern with the cinematic, which supports the film's critique of those cinemas. In drawing upon and subverting the classic Hollywood and horror gaze as well as what Naficy terms the Islamicate gaze of postrevolutionary Iranian cinema, the film posits a gaze that is not based on female lack (and male castration anxiety) or the sexual power of a woman's gaze to corrupt nonfamilial men. This dual subversion critiques the gender politics within both countries and both countries' cinemas while also depicting something rare in either cinema: a complicated woman and man who are able to look at each other with intimacy and trust. The Girl and Arash eschew any so-called battle of the sexes to instead work together, to leave Bad City and their social marginalization there behind.

Notes

1   Laura Barcella, "The Feminist Vampire Movie That Teaches 'Bad Men' a Gory Lesson," Jezebel, November 25, 2014, https://jezebel.com/the-feminist-vampire-movie -that-teaches-bad-men-a-gory-1662788544; Kamelya Youssef, "The Vampire Vigilante," *Bitch Media*, December 10, 2014, https://www.bitchmedia.org/a-girl-walks -home-alone-at-night-feminist-film-review-farsi-iran.

2   Rich Juzwiak, "The Iranian Vampire Tale of *A Girl Walks Home Alone at Night*," *Gawker*, November 21, 2014, https://gawker.com/the-iranian-vampire-tale-of-a-girl -walks-home-alone-at-1661607676.

3   VICE, "Behind the Scenes of *A Girl Walks Home Alone at Night* (Part 2)," December 4, 2014, video, 12:11, https://www.youtube.com/watch?v=WC0LFR_1BwA.

4   Laura Mulvey, "Visual Pleasure and Narrative Cinema," *Screen* 16, no. 2 (1975): 6–18. See also Mulvey, "Afterthoughts on 'Visual Pleasure and Narrative Cinema' Inspired by *Duel in the Sun* (King Vidor, 1946)," *Framework: The Journal of Cinema and Media* 15/17 (1981): 12–15.

5   Steven Jay Schneider, ed., *Horror Film and Psychoanalysis: Freud's Worst Nightmare* (Cambridge: Cambridge University Press, 2004).

6   See Kaleem Aftab, "Ana Lily Amirpour Has Created a Completely New Film Genre—the Iranian Vampire Western," *Independent*, May 20, 2015, https://www .independent.co.uk/arts-entertainment/films/features/ana-lily-amirpour-has-created -a-completely-new-film-genre-the-iranian-vampire-western-10265538.html.

7   Hamid Naficy, *A Social History of Iranian Cinema*, vol. 4, *The Globalizing Era, 1984–2010* (Durham, N.C.: Duke University Press, 2012), 106.

8   Shadee Abdi and Bernadette Marie Calafell, "Queer Utopias and a (Feminist) Iranian Vampire: A Critical Analysis of Resistive Monstrosity in *A Girl Walks Home Alone at Night*," *Critical Studies in Media Communication* 34, no. 4 (2017): 367.

9   Dale Hudson, *Vampires, Race, and Transnational Hollywoods* (Edinburgh: Edinburgh University Press, 2017).

10   Zachary Cheney, "Stylish Politics: Long Takes in Post-1945 Cinema" (PhD diss., University of Oregon, 2017), 156.

11   Katarzyna Marciniak, "Revolting Aesthetics: Feminist Transnational Cinema in the US," in *The Routledge Companion to Cinema and Gender*, ed. Kristen Lené Hole, Dijana Jelača, E. Ann Kaplan, and Patrice Petro (New York: Routledge, 2017), 386.

12   Marciniak, 392–393.

13   Richard Tapper, *The New Iranian Cinema: Politics, Representation and Identity* (London: I.B. Tauris, 2002), 3.

14   Hamid Naficy, *A Social History of Iranian Cinema*, vol. 2, *The Industrializing Years, 1941–1978* (Durham, N.C.: Duke University Press, 2011), 336–341.

15   Naficy, 342.

16   Negar Mottahedeh, "Crude Extractions: The Voice in Iranian Cinema," in *Locating*

the Voice in Film: Critical Approaches and Global Practices, ed. Tom Whittaker and Sarah Wright (New York: Oxford University Press, 2017), 240.

17 See Angela Watercutter, "Meet the Woman Who Directed the World's Only Iranian Vampire Western," *Wired*, February 5, 2014, https://www.wired.com/2014/02/girl-walks-home-alone-at-night/.

18 Doug Owram, *Born at the Right Time: A History of the Baby-Boom Generation* (Toronto: University of Toronto Press, 1997), 141 196.

19 See Mulvey, "Afterthoughts on 'Visual Pleasure.'"

20 Linda Williams, "Film Bodies: Gender, Genre, and Excess," *Film Quarterly* 44, no. 4 (1991): 10.

21 Barbara Creed, *The Monstrous-Feminine: Film, Feminism, Psychoanalysis* (London: Routledge, 1993), 61.

22 Barbara Creed, "Dark Desires: Male Masochism in the Horror Film," in *Screening the Male: Exploring Masculinities in Hollywood Cinema*, ed. Steven Cohan and Ina Rae Hark (New York: Routledge, 1993), 130, 132.

23 Carol J. Clover, *Men, Women, and Chain Saws: Gender in the Modern Horror Film* (Princeton, N.J.: Princeton University Press, 1992), 182–191.

24 Cynthia A. Freeland, "Feminist Frameworks for Horror Films," in *Post-Theory: Reconstructing Film Studies*, ed. David Bordwell and Noël Carroll (Madison: University of Wisconsin Press, 1996), 198–199.

25 Freeland, 201.

26 Freeland, 200.

27 Toril Moi, "From Femininity to Finitude: Freud, Lacan, and Feminism, Again," *Signs: Journal of Woman in Culture and Society* 29, no. 3 (2004): 846.

28 Moi, 844, 846–847.

29 Moi, 847.

30 Brigid Cherry, "Refusing to Refuse to Look: Female Viewers of the Horror Film," in *Horror, the Film Reader*, ed. Mark Jancovich (New York: Routledge, 2002), 174–175.

31 Cherry, 171–172, 176.

32 Naficy, *Social History of Iranian Cinema*, vol. 4, 93.

33 Negar Mottahedeh, *Displaced Allegories: Post-revolutionary Iranian Cinema* (Durham, N.C.: Duke University Press, 2008), 1.

34 Naficy, *Social History of Iranian Cinema*, vol. 4, 102.

35 Mottahedeh, *Displaced Allegories*, 10.

36 Naficy, *Social History of Iranian Cinema*, vol. 4, 102.

37 Naficy, 106.

38 Naficy, 106.

39 Naficy, 107.

40 Naficy, 115.

41 Naficy, 108.

42 Naficy, 108.

43 Naficy, 108.

44 Naficy, 134.

45 Naficy, 128.

46 Linda Williams, "Why I Did Not Want to Write This Essay," *Signs* 30, no. 1 (2004): 1266–1268.

47 Williams, 1270.

48 VICE, "Behind the Scenes."

15

Gigi Saul Guerrero and Her Latin American Female Monsters

VALERIA VILLEGAS LINDVALL

The film begins with black-and-white images of a bathroom and an operatic score. We see a dripping faucet, a selection of blades on a white towel, and a mystery woman sliding into a bathtub. The woman, her eyes framed with wet mascara, reaches out for a blade. She slits her wrist, and the film turns to color as blood gushes out of her body. But then things take an unexpected turn. The music stops, and the fleshy slit she has created in her wrist yells, "About bloody time! Oh, come on, love! I ain't your first bleeding slit to spring a leak, now am I?" This is Gigi Saul Guerrero's short film *O Negative* (2016), the first film in the horror anthology *Women in Horror Massive Blood Drive Public Service Announcement*, an annual collaboration between filmmakers Jen and Sylvia Soska and Women in Horror Recognition Month (WiHM) created to encourage people to donate blood. In *O Negative*, the mystery woman is revealed to be the Mexican Canadian director Gigi Saul Guerrero, and the bleeding slit literally speaks for itself.

Known by her fanbase as *la muñeca del terror* (the horror babe), Gigi Saul Guerrero was born and raised in Mexico City but relocated with her family to Canada at a young age. Saul Guerrero is remarkably proficient in all aspects of film production: she is a director, actor, writer, and editor who has also taught at the Vancouver Film School. She founded Luchagore Productions in 2013 with Luke Bramley and Raynor Shimabukuro and recently collaborated with Blumhouse and Hulu on the horror anthology series *Into the Dark*, directing the feature-length episode "Culture Shock." In 2019, she was acknowledged by *Variety* as one of the Top 10 Latinxs to Watch.[1] While citing admiration for Eli Roth, Quentin Tarantino, and Robert Rodríguez, Saul Guerrero has gradually established her own directorial voice.[2] She describes the Luchagore universe as "tons of blood; probably half-naked babes; lots of gritty, gritty gore and usually our monsters are really nasty and sweaty."[3] She actively integrates her Mexican heritage into her films, stating, "I will continue to bring some of my Mexican background/culture to my films as much as I can. . . . Bringing my heritage into the genre of horror has been so much fun because I am able to give it a dark twist and make it unique."[4] Indeed, in *Dead Crossing* (2011), *El Gigante* (2014), and *The Cull* (2018), Saul Guerrero directly conflates Mexicanness and horror, exploring racialized bodies at the point of "illegal" border crossing to the United States.

However, her interest in representing borders and the exploitation of racialized bodies takes different forms in the female monsters of her films *Testament* (2014), *Día de los muertos* (2013), and *Madre de Dios* (2015). This chapter will argue that Saul Guerrero creates Latin American female monsters in these films who engage in instances of rupture that expose the structures that discipline women by portraying their corporeality or their deviance from the cultural norm as monstrous, noxious, or threatening. Here, monstrosity is explored through the image of the bleeding slit, and I will argue that the construction of the slit occurs in two main ways. First, the slit is considered in terms of sexual difference, as Elizabeth Grosz writes, in "an order that renders female sexuality and corporeality marginal, indeterminate, and viscous that constitutes the sticky and the viscous with their disgusting, horrifying connotations."[5] Second, the slit is considered as a site of pain and fragmentation in relation to nationality, where, following Gloria Anzaldúa, I consider the colonial wound as a reminder of Mexican identity's fraught relationship with its colonial past.[6] Saul Guerrero's films offer unique articulations of national identity, stemming from the liminal space between the filmmaker's Mexican and Canadian identities, which in turn reflects the arbitrariness of borders, both corporeal and territorial. In exploring her work, this chapter understands her monsters as destabilizers and negotiators of hegemonic structures.

Barbarous Latin America in Theory

Gustavo Subero and Gabriel Eljaiek-Rodríguez offer important accounts of the constitution and policing of gender and sexuality in Latin American horror film, exploring the repurposing of Gothic conventions as tools to reinforce or contest hegemonic gender norms and expectations. Both assessments highlight the "tropical Gothic" as a means to articulate repressed passages of a colonial past and its aftermath.[7] However, the allure of the weird is typical of certain literature that insists on Latin American horror film at large as an exotic (even erotic) rarity. A good example is Pete Tomb's book *Mondo Macabro* (along with its documentary miniseries), which champions non-Western horror film as "weird and wonderful, filled with local color as well as odd borrowings from the West."[8]

Another instance of this is Doyle Greene's *Mexploitation Cinema*, which Dolores Tierney problematizes, highlighting the limitations of literature fixed on the cult reception of Latin American films *outside* Latin America.[9] She points out that Greene bypasses the decisive role of specific distribution, editing, and dubbing practices for U.S. television during the early 1960s.[10] For Tierney, works that focus on the "peculiar" features and technical shortcomings of these films position them against Hollywood classical continuity and realism. This eschews national readings and removes the films from their own film cultures. To counter these problematic acts of "cult colonialist appropriation," as Tierney calls them, more recent scholarship such as Tierney and Victoria Ruétalo's edited collection *Latsploitation, Exploitation Cinemas and Latin America* offers a more nuanced understanding of power relations and the way genre film can negotiate, reinforce, or contest such relations.[11] This study embraces the specificities of Latin American filmmaking amid uneven economic development, neoimperialist enterprises, and a troubled relationship with modernity and globalization, approaching "latsploitation" features in context.

More recently, the legacy, iconography, and representation of Mexican monsters are thoroughly illustrated in *Mostrología del cine mexicano* and in *Belcebú*. Additionally, Hernán Moyano and Carina Rodríguez's outstanding edited collection *Manual de cine de género* offers an insider's view of the particularities of financing, distribution, production, and exhibition practices in Latin American countries and includes a contribution from Saul Guerrero herself.[12] Also, in her discussion of Latin American genre filmmaking, Luisela Alvaray recuperates Néstor García Canclini's idea of "hybridity" to account for the negotiation of different symbolic offers as a product of transnational exchange.[13] Here, Eljaiek-Rodríguez's formulations regarding the tropical Gothic coincide with Alvaray's acknowledgment that the representational level sees itself affected by processes of hybridization.[14] Eljaiek-Rodríguez puts Canclini's hybridization in dialogue with Ángel Rama's "transculturation" and Antonio Cornejo Polar's "heterogeneity." Privileging the latter, the author poses the potentiality of the Latin

American monster as an embodiment of a "plurality that sometimes cannot be synthesized," a potential site of resistance.[15]

This literature reveals the reevaluation of hybridity and heterogeneity, which underscore the possibilities of the liminal space from which Saul Guerrero articulates Mexicanness. Here, the articulation of cultural specificities through horror film conventions enables the monster to function as a figurative site of negotiation. The plasticity of the genre allows national identities to be constantly negotiated through the figure of the monster, and the "Tex-Mex vibe" that Saul Guerrero ascribes to her visual and narrative style is a good example of this repurposing.[16] In addition to national identity, the gender of the monster is also vital to Saul Guerrero's films. Consequently, my framework is also rooted in diverse takes on feminist thought, including Luce Irigaray's term "fluidity," Elizabeth Grosz's notion of "seepage," and Erin Harrington's theory of "gynae-horror." As Lindsey Decker's rich contribution to this collection states, drawing on Cynthia Freeland, Toril Moi, and Brigid Cherry, criticism regarding the inadequacy of some feminist psychoanalytic theory points to tendencies toward universalism and their resulting lack of cultural and historical nuance. Hence I seek to overcome these limitations by advancing the possibilities of decolonial thought and its revision by decolonial feminists as a critical tool to address racialized female monstrosity.[17]

Aníbal Quijano is a key reference point on decolonial thought. He poses that the colonization of America prompted the creation of a global model of hegemony and control, referred to as "coloniality of power."[18] Its formation was aided by two key historical processes: the legitimization of the fictive category of race and the establishment of a structure to manage labor and its resources. Thus social relations of domination gave place to hierarchies, later naturalized to justify exploitative practices such as slavery and serfdom. Imperial expansion allowed for this order to take root in other territories and ensured its prevalence under the guise of "modernity," solidifying it throughout time by means of its institutions and practices. This order exercises control in four main interrelated spheres: labor, authority, gender/sexuality, and knowledge/intersubjectivity. As Quijano elaborates, "Thus, in the control of labor and its resources and products, it is the capitalist enterprise; in the control of sex and its resources and products, the bourgeois family; in the control of authority and its resources and products, the nation-state; in the control of intersubjectivity, Eurocentrism."[19]

Though coloniality is succinctly explained by Quijano, the aspect of gender in his matrix is revised by a number of scholars. While decolonial feminisms are the outcome of rich epistemological diversity and have no fixed or unequivocal genealogy, there are key thinkers who can support us here. To illustrate, drawing on Oyéronké Oyewùmi, María Lugones suggests that binary understandings of sex and gender are, greatly, a by-product of the normalization of alleged biological realities based in colonial understandings of gender and sexuality, a detail Quijano's model sidesteps.[20] In contrast, Rita Segato hints, in concurrence with

Anzaldúa, that certain patriarchal understandings of gender were already present in community life before colonial intervention.[21] The coconstitution of race and gender is also present in Nelson Maldonado-Torres's formulations about the "coloniality of Being." He considers how race, gender, and sexuality became undetachable from the rendering of the racialized other as incapable of posing ontological resistance to the universal white male subject implied in René Descartes's *ego cogito* and Martin Heidegger's *Dasein*.[22] Thus while this chapter recuperates previous scholarship regarding female monstrosity, it draws from feminist revisions of decolonial thought in order to provide a more nuanced approach to the Latin American female monsters in Saul Guerrero's work.

Testement: The Menstrual Slit

Testement was created in less than seventy-two hours for the Phrike Film Festival in Vancouver. It opens in a dimly lit garage where a mechanic whistles "Cielito Lindo" as he readies to close up shop. Stepping outside, he is greeted by a young, disheveled woman who suddenly kisses and fondles him. The cadence of an otherwise threatening drone changes to a softer tone as he carries her into the shop and leans her against a stack of tires. Tight shots of their hands reveal them undressing each other, and then two more, half-naked women appear and fondle the mechanic and each other. A fourth woman appears, disturbing the improvised orgy, and nails the mechanic's hands to the tire stack. Giggling and licking her lips, one of the women reaches between her legs. She then uses her blood to draw a *13* on the man's forehead. One of the young women requests that they get "Mama," and another leaves, then returns with an elderly woman in a wheelchair, placing her in front of the sobbing man. One of the women flashes a box cutter. The camera remains fixed to the man's face, and we are spared the sight of the tearing of his scrotum, which is instead conveyed by sound and his sweaty, pained expression as he vomits. A close-up reveals two bloody testicles then being ground in a *molcajete*, a volcanic rock mortar where salsas are traditionally prepared. In tight, flickering shots, the four young women chant as the testicle pulp is injected into the elderly woman as an elixir of life. The ritual is consummated with a horrific kiss as the elderly woman rises and sucks the color from the mechanic's skin, claiming his life as her own.

These events reveal two crucial ways in which the female characters transgress expectations. On the one hand, menstrual blood rejects its classification as filth and is deliberately highlighted, vindicating the alleged horrors of the female body's fluidity.[23] In making this "rejected element" noticeable, the character emphasizes the interaction with the forbidden.[24] The alleged uncleanliness of menstrual blood is negated, as it prepares for life-giving magic. Smearing the blood on the man's forehead is akin to anointing one with holy water, which can also be read as a reaction against the ontological determination over female bodies under patriarchal languages of representation. Menstrual blood is redefined here as a generative fluid, challenging an order that conceives of menstruation as a process that should be hidden. On the other hand, the *molcajete*'s cultural specificity points toward women's domestic labor, which in turn resonates with Segato's work on the separation of the public and domestic as a manifestation of the colonial and patriarchal policing of female bodies. Under this arrangement, female bodies are placed in the allegedly apolitical realm of the home and its unwaged labor, such as child rearing, cooking, and household work.[25] In *Testement*, domestic work becomes the forceful extraction of life performed in a garage, a space of waged labor performed by men.

This gesture also jettisons the solidity attributed to the male corporeality as a point of departure to the writing of female corporeality. Turning the testicles into a viscous paste, these female bodies reject the idea of semen as a fluid that is displaced conveniently toward solidity and snub its characterization as never polluting, always contained, and responsible for fertilization.[26] As Luce Irigaray formulates, "We might ask (ourselves) why sperm is never treated as an object *a*? Isn't the subjection of sperm to the imperatives of reproduction alone symptomatic of a preeminence historically allocated to the solid (product)? And if, in the dynamics of desire, the problem of castration intervenes—fantasy/reality of an amputation, of a 'crumbling' of that solid that the penis represents—a reckoning with *sperm-fluid* as an obstacle to the generalization of an economy restricted to solids remains in suspension."[27] In line with Irigaray's formulations, *Testement* depicts a *literal* amputation of the solid and allows the fluid to prevail. This gesture underlines the importance of questioning the very languages from which these ontological restrictions on the body are articulated, insinuating that the mutability of the female body requires its own set of vocabularies. Here, transgression ensues to question the very hierarchies it disrupts for our visual pleasure.

Día de los Muertos: The Vengeful and Colonial Slit

Welcome to Bordertown, Mexico. A jangly guitar accompanies a close-up of a derelict merry-go-round followed by traveling shots that glide alongside the streets, depicting street vendors, dogs, cows, taxis, pedestrians, and food carts. Santa Muerte is depicted on a wall, surrounded by text offering tarot, voodoo, and non-Christian spiritual practices as paid services. Here, the visual reconciliation of urban and rural, Christian and non-Christian gives meaning to the border as a space where cultural tension and simultaneity are common currency. Later, a series of close-ups of a Día de Muertos altar take us to closed quarters: candles, *cempasúchil* flowers, *calaveritas* (sugar skulls), and a portrait of a woman. A female voice recites a monologue over the shots, creating intimacy. This ceases to be comforting though, as the image opens up to reveal six young women in their underwear, shivering and crying. Doña Luz, a middle-aged woman, berates them, and the oppressive atmosphere is heightened when another woman enters the scene. Doña Luz brushes her hair away from her beaten face, and a flashback shows the woman being raped in an alley. But now it is time to get on with the Día de Muertos celebration, and the women are ordered to make themselves look beautiful for their work.

Overlapping images of the women working as pole dancers take us to La Candelaria strip club. Their breasts, buttocks, midriffs, and legs are in close-up; their faces are drawn in sugar-skull makeup; they are bathed in neon lights. Doña Luz wanders wearing sugar-skull makeup and a black dress with colorful flower embroidery and golden necklaces, reminiscent of a traditional garb from the Isthmus of Tehuantepec. She solemnly explains this celebration as one of "heritage, culture, and race" over guitar riffs and then sits on a leather armchair, smoking and assuming the position of spectator. The scene evolves into passages of cumulative aggression: a man slaps a dancer's backside, a group of patrons harasses a waitress for not speaking English, and then the pace changes suddenly. Saul Guerrero has confirmed that *Día de los muertos* is an homage to Robert Rodríguez's *From Dusk till Dawn* (1996), and in a wink to his iconic sequence where Salma Hayek performs as Satánico Pandemonium, a woman, also in sugar-skull make up, appears on stage.[28]

As she dances, the camera fixes on a man with piercing green eyes that stare at her. We lock eyes with Doña Luz, then with the man, then with the dancer's steely blue look. Returning to the earlier flashback, we confirm that the dancer is facing her assailant. Suddenly, she hurls herself at the man and bites his nose off. Extensive gore ensues, and the bleeding slit is literally relocated from female to male as one dancer cuts the patron's throat. Another pokes out a man's eye, exercising literal punishment of the gaze. This brutal scene conflates the object of desire and the object of horror, presenting the transition of the female gaze; the woman shifts from the punished to the punisher. Thus *Testament* gives place to "the expression of women's sexual potency and desire . . . that associates this desire with the autonomous act of looking," which Linda Williams argues is traditionally absent in classic horror film.[29] For a fleeting moment, the logic of "men act and women appear" is reversed, and we revel in the transgression these women undertake, where the male spectator's monopoly over the power of the gaze is displaced.[30]

Traditionally, female spectacle produces profit, and the dancers' behavior vindicates the part that they actively play in the accumulation of capital. However, the slaughter acts as a purge of sorts but remains fodder for the voyeuristic fantasy of women in hot pants slashing bodies. The push and pull between agency and exploitation comes through in Doña Luz's opening lines, "Nadie me dijo que la vida era fácil. Al contrario. Todavía me acuerdo cuando mi madre me decía: mija, la vida es una cabrona . . . pero tú tienes que ser más cabrona que la vida. Porque si no . . . te lleva la chingada. Mírame ahora mami, que la vida no me llega ni a los pinches talones . . . que la cabrona de cabronas soy yo," which translates as "Nobody told me that life was easy. Instead, I still remember when my mother would tell me, '*Mija*, life is a bitch . . . but you gotta be a bigger bitch than her . . . or she will fuck you over.' Look at me now, Mother. Life can't even begin to drag me by the fucking feet."

La Chingada is another name for Malintzin/Malinche, often characterized as the indigenous mother "traitor" said to have led the Spanish to Tenochtitlan.[31] The weight of her alleged vulnerability and transgression of the racial order is essential to the constitution of Mexicanness. With her invocation of "La Chingada" as a reviled presence in this monologue, *Día de los muertos* reveals a second iteration of the slit as a colonial wound.

Mexicanness is an identity discourse of relatively recent invention. By the 1920s, the (already unstable) postrevolutionary political system struggled to sustain its ideological agenda, and a widening economic gap forced rural populations into cities. The disproportionate influence of the Catholic Church in public and political life was questioned, which prompted the Cristero Rebellion (1926–1929) during Plutarco Elías Calles's presidential term (1924–1928). Postrevolutionary corruption showed its face during the Maximato period (1928–1934), when Calles acted as puppeteer by appointing three interim presidents that advanced his interests.[32] The institutional notion of Mexicanness as a reconciliation of indigenous and European roots took form at this time, as exemplified in José Vasconcelos's *La raza cósmica* (1925). Vasconcelos's proposition that Latin American populations were the seed of a cosmic race meant for transcendence underlines the importance of racial organization as constitutive of Mexicanness.[33] While this text is a product of its time and is open to critique, the implication of racial hierarchy as an organizing axis of social, cultural, and economic existence stands at the heart of its formulations. As Walter Mignolo puts it, "Vasconcelos conflates biological *mestizaje* and epistemic purity—people mix biologically but a rigid structure of thought, Christianity in its Ibero-American version, remains in place."[34] This echoes Quijano's argument of Latin American nation-states as projects intimately tied to hierarchies and relations of domination steeped on Eurocentric notions of racial organization.[35]

The formulation of a unifying, normative account of identity became a primary concern in the national agenda after the creation of the Partido Nacional Revolucionario (National Revolution Party) in 1929, and film and radio became instrumental in both reinforcing and challenging normative Mexicanness. Further, *La llorona* (1933), the first Mexican horror film, even centers the presence of a colonial slit as undetachable from Mexican identity, binding together the legend of La Llorona (the Weeping Woman) to the figure of the indigenous mother, Malintzin.[36] I argue here that over eighty years later, this colonial slit is recuperated in *Día de los muertos* and given new life, as the figure of La Chingada introduced by Doña Luz evokes the presence of Malintzin. Her economic independence allows her to go from *la chingada*, the trumped one, to the *chingona*, where she has the upper hand.[37] The interplay between the fucked one and the one who fucks (*chingada*/female vs. *chingón*/male) hints at these entities as binary, gendered, racialized, and hierarchically opposed, which renders any transgression of such an order to be abhorrent.

Madre de Dios: The Colonial Slit

Madre de Dios explores the colonial slit in a more figurative way than *Día de los muertos*. The film begins with an elderly *brujo* (male witch) in the shower, connecting with a shot of blood flowing down a drain. A *bruja* (female witch) appears from behind, pressing her face against his back, and the tenderness of their physical contact is contrasted with the bloody drain and the sound of a piercing, disembodied shriek. We move to another room, where the mise-en-scène integrates disparate indexes: a figurine of the Virgin Mary, animal skulls, candles, charms with little dead animals, a wooden devil mask. We then see a young, white, well-groomed woman bound and gagged, and the *brujos* enter the room. The *bruja* stares at the woman in tenderness, as if in awe, and these two different iterations of femininity come into contact: the older, darker-skinned, and racialized *bruja* and the white green-eyed woman. The *bruja* crushes bugs over a *molcajete* full of blood and smears a cross on the victim's forehead; the *brujo* soaks his hand in the mixture and touches the victim's abdomen with his whole palm. Her abdomen lights up, triggering sinister fecundation, and a fetus moves beneath the skin, suggesting the gagged woman is impregnated.

The ritual peaks with a Christian prayer uttered by the *bruja*, a gesture that deconstructs Marian faith (the adoration of the Virgin Mary) and subverts the dogma of immaculate conception. Anzaldúa characterizes Mexico as a nonmale entity that has been split and condemned, resulting in great trauma of fragmentation, but here the *brujo* slices the victim's abdomen open, enforcing the bleeding slit upon the white woman while laughing exuberantly. The laughter of the *brujos* ends with the only subjective shot in the film: the woman's point of view as a skull mask is placed over her face. Placing the mask on the face marks an ellipsis in time between the ritual ending and its repercussions. In the next shot, the spawn is asleep in a blood-soaked stroller guarded by the woman, who has been turned into a life-size effigy of Santa Muerte, a female saint variously attributed to medieval Catholic practice and to a revisited representation of Mictecacihuatl, the female ruler of the Mexica underworld (Mictlan) alongside her male counterpart, Mictlantecuhtli.[38] Exercised in the margins, her devotion has been aligned with criminality and precariousness, and today her cult thrives in an inbetweenness where it acknowledges Christian dogma and reframes it, seizing it with a renewed spirit of agency.[39]

In exploring pregnancy and horror, the film alludes to what Erin Harrington discusses as the pregnant and birthing body as the ultimate transgression of boundaries of the self: contesting a "dominant ontological framework of the self, which is predicated on autonomous implicitly masculine individuality that is presumed to be a fixed state of being, is incompatible with the subjective and lived state of pregnancy, which draws attention to mutability and modes of becoming."[40] In this context, the female pregnant body is also a vessel where evil can take root. *Madre de Dios* then develops this concept by drawing on the Mexican occult. Saul Guerrero explains, "My Mexican culture is always a huge influence in my filmmaking, and I wanted to create a new version of the Virgin Mary—a different god-like entity with Mexican witchcraft, which has always fascinated me since childhood!"[41] Filtering Christian belief through premodern "witchcraft," the figure of Santa Muerte speaks to the racial hierarchy of belief in the coloniality of intersubjectivity, as addressed in Quijano's matrix. The film also offers a role reversal, where the racialized bodies of *brujos* force reproduction in their discursive colonial opposite—a white female body. This can be read as a form of retribution for the forced impregnation of serfs and slaves in colonial times; their bodies were at the service of imperial expansion.

Moreover, the end product of the ritual on screen suggests cultural resistance in itself, as Catholic faith (instrumental to the discourse of Mexicanness) is challenged by Santa Muerte. Santa Muerte is both saint and pagan, and her inconsistencies are the inconsistencies of Mexicanness itself. Here, Mexicanness is acknowledged as an identity discourse beset by contradiction, though horror still resides with the colonial conception of non-Christian cosmologies as premodern, so-called hocus-pocus. Accordingly, the film illustrates the epistemic racism of the coloniality of knowledge while simultaneously bringing forward the marginalization of non-Christian spiritual practices of the Americas.[42] Once more, Saul Guerrero plays with the simultaneous negotiation and reinforcement of the borders imposed on the female body.

Conclusion

Saul Guerrero's films provide a valuable opportunity to explore and problematize the concept of the Latin American female monster. In *Testement, Día de los muertos*, and *Madre de Dios*, female bodies subvert the expectations weighed upon them corporeally and culturally, and in different ways, each female monster embraces the bleeding slit as an opportunity rather than as a marker of lack. In *Testement*, the women that castrate the mechanic are the monsters, and the bleeding slit reformulates menstrual blood as generative. *Día de los muertos* creates two forms of female monster. On one hand, we have the exploitative Doña Luz, and on the other, the dancers, as they slay all the patrons and torture them. Here, the gaze is recuperated as female, and the wound is relocated to the male body as a dancer slices a patron's throat open. At the same time, this film also explores the colonial wound, as Doña Luz references La Chingada. In *Madre de Dios*, the monsters are the *brujos*, opening up a bleeding slit and forcefully impregnating the white female victim, allegorically enacting what the colonizer did to the original populations of the Americas by exacting revenge on the limiting dogmas of Christianity.

Gigi Saul Guerrero and Her Latin American Female Monsters • 193

As I acknowledged earlier, psychoanalytical methodology has for a long time been a subject of debate in its validity as a methodological framework, given its problematic naturalization of an unequivocal dichotomy of male/female and its bypassing of the cultural, social, and historical factors that inform the depiction of female colored bodies in this particular context. My adoption of feminist reformulations of psychoanalysis, however, recognizes the relevance of its call to rewrite a language within which the ontological constitution of the self is always gauged against a universal male subject. In so doing, I've illuminated how Saul Guerrero's monsters can suggest, in certain instances, a protolanguage of resistance that vindicates fluidity, seepage, and mutability. Crucially, I have also asserted the importance of feminist decolonial thought as a critical approach toward horror filmmaking, arguing that race and gender are co-constitutive spheres in the oppression of the Latin American female body in coloniality. In examining Saul Guerrero's work, I've opened up a way to consider how the restrictions placed upon the Latin American female body can be negotiated and challenged. Saul Guerrero's monsters enact revenge (albeit often brief), which allows them to recalibrate gendered relations of power and how meaning is produced.

Nevertheless, these works do not offer a panacea in terms of representation. By articulating the female body through visual Mexicanness, the Latin American other/monster remains exotic, distant, and threatening, though Saul Guerrero's transgressive female monsters have a dual nature, one that questions the naturalization of colonial vocabularies while also using them. As such, they are simultaneously sites of negotiation of national identity and also responses to the unequal distribution of power that stems from coloniality. By opening up the wound, these works also open up a space for alternative ways of seeing and acting, enabling further steps toward the construction of new languages of representation. Maybe, like in *O Negative*, it is time to let the wound speak for itself.

Notes

1 Shannon McGrew, "Women in Horror Month Interview: Gigi Saul Guerrero," Nightmarish Conjurings, February 5, 2018, http://www.nightmarishconjurings .com/2018/02/05/women-horror-month-interview-gigi-saul-guerrero; Brad Miska, "Celebrate Father's Day and Independence Day with Hulu's *Into the Dark*," Bloody Disgusting, May 15, 2019, https://bloody-disgusting.com/tv/3561157/celebrate -fathers-day-independence-day-hulus-dark; Jordan Moreau, "*Variety* Announces 10 Latinxs to Watch 2019," *Variety*, February 20, 2019, https://variety.com/2019/film/ news/variety-10-latinx-to-watch-2019-1203143225.
2 "Mini MUFF Profile: Gigi Saul Guerrero," MUFF Society, April 21, 2016, https:// muffsociety.com/blog/2016/4/21/mini-muff-profile-gigi-saul-guerrero; Jonathan Sánchez Corona, "Mórbido Fest 2017: Entrevista con Gigi Saúl Guerrero sobre La Quinceañera," 2017, https://mundomorbido.com/morbido-fest-2017-entrevista-con -gigi-saul-guerrero-sobre-la-quinceanera/.

3   Mad Bros Media, "Gigi Saul Guerrero Interview Crypticon Seattle 2016," July 9, 2016, video, 7:58, https://youtu.be/J5zj63IVp8s.

4   "Q&A with Gigi Saul Guerrero, Director of *El Gigante*," Cult Projections, November 25, 2015, http://www.cultprojections.com/interviews/qa-with-gigi-saul-guerrero.

5   Elizabeth Grosz, *Volatile Bodies: Toward a Corporeal Feminism* (Bloomington: Indiana University Press, 1994), 195.

6   Gloria Anzaldúa, *Borderlands / La Frontera: The New Mestiza* (San Francisco: Aunt Lute Books, 1987).

7   Gustavo Subero, *Embodiments of Evil: Gender and Sexuality in Latin American Horror Cinema* (Basingstoke, U.K.: Palgrave Macmillan, 2016), 3–4; Gabriel Eljaiek-Rodríguez, *The Migration and Politics of Monsters in Latin America* (Basingstoke, U.K.: Palgrave Macmillan, 2018), 14.

8   Pete Tombs, *Mondo Macabro: Weird and Wonderful Cinema around the World* (New York: St. Martin's Griffin, 1998), 7.

9   Doyle Greene, *Mexploitation Cinema: A Critical History of Mexican Vampire, Wrestler, Ape Man and Similar Films, 1957–1977* (Jefferson, N.C.: McFarland, 2005).

10 Dolores Tierney, "Mapping Cult Cinema in Latin American Film Cultures," *Cinema Journal* 54, no. 1 (Fall 2014): 129–135.

11 Tierney, "Mapping," 131; Victoria Ruétalo and Dolores Tierney, "Introduction: Reinventing the Frame—Exploitation and Latin America," in *Latsploitation, Exploitation Cinemas and Latin America*, ed. Victoria Ruétalo and Dolores Tierney (New York: Routledge, 2009), 1–12.

12 Marco González Ambriz, ed., *Mostrología del cine mexicano* (Mexico City: La Caja de Cerillos/Conaculta, 2015); "50 filmes del cine mexicano de terror, horror y lo grotesco," special issue of *Belcebú* 4, vol. 5 (Mexico City: Samsara, 2019); Hernán Moyano and Carina Rodríguez, eds., *Manual de cine de género (experiencias de la guerrilla audiovisual en América Latina)* (Mexico City: Samsara, 2017).

13 Luisela Alvaray, "Hybridity and Genre in Transnational Latin American Cinemas," *Transnational Cinemas* 4, no. 1 (2014): 68.

14 Alvaray, "Hybridity," 71.

15 Eljaiek-Rodríguez, *Migration*, 14–15.

16 Izzy Lee, "Luchagore's Gigi Saul Guerrero and Raynor Shima on Inspiration and the Making of *La Quinceañera*," Dread Central, April 3, 2018, https://www.dreadcentral.com/news/270338/interview-luchagores-gigi-saul-guerrero-and-raynor-shima-on-inspiration-and-the-making-of-la-quinceanera/.

17 María Lugones, "Colonialidad y género: Hacia un feminismo descolonial," in *Género y descolonialidad*, ed. Walter Mignolo (Buenos Aires: Ediciones del Signo, 2008), 13–54; Rita Segato, *La crítica de la colonialidad en ocho ensayos y una antropología por demanda* (Buenos Aires: Prometeo, 2013).

18 Aníbal Quijano, "Coloniality of Power, Eurocentrism and Latin America," trans. Michael Ennis, *Nepantla: Views from South* 1, no. 3 (2000): 533–580. Ramón Grosfoguel critiques Quijano's late adoption of the notion of coloniality in "Caos sistémico, crisis civilizatoria y proyectos descoloniales," *Tabula Rasa* 25 (2016): 153–174.

19 Quijano, "Coloniality of Power," 545.

20 Lugones, "Colonialidad y género," 32.

21 Anzaldúa, *Borderlines*, 5; Segato, *Crítica*, 81–96.

22 Nelson Maldonado-Torres, "On the Coloniality of Being," *Cultural Studies* 21, nos. 2–3 (2007): 240–270.

23 Grosz, *Volatile Bodies*, 187–210.

24 Grosz, 192; Mary Douglas, *Purity and Danger: An Analysis of Concepts of Pollution and Taboo* (London: Taylor & Francis, 2002), 44.

25 Rita Laura Segato, "Patriarchy from Margin to Center: Discipline, Territoriality, and Cruelty in the Apocalyptic Phase of Capital," *South Atlantic Quarterly* 115, no. 3 (2016): 615–624.

26 Grosz, *Volatile Bodies*, 199.

27 Luce Irigaray, *This Sex Which Is Not One* (New York: Cornell University Press, 1985), 114.

28 Revista Cinefagia, "Cinefagia programa #3: Entrevista Gigi Saul Guerrero," September 7, 2015, video, 5:57, https://www.youtube.com/watch?v=N9x5Vi5Agfc&feature= youtu.be.

29 Linda Williams, "When the Woman Looks," in *The Dread of Difference: Gender and the Horror Film*, ed. Barry Keith Grant (Austin: University of Texas Press, 1996), 32–33.

30 John Berger, *Ways of Seeing* (London: Penguin, 1972), 47.

31 Anzaldúa, *Borderlands*, 30–31.

32 Ana M. López, "Before Exploitation: The Three Men of the Cinema in Mexico," in Ruétalo and Tierney, *Latsploitation*, 13–33.

33 José Vasconcelos, *La raza cósmica* (Mexico City: Porrúa Editores, 2001).

34 Walter D. Mignolo, *The Idea of Latin America* (Malden, Mass.: Blackwell, 2005), 136.

35 Quijano, "Coloniality of Power," 556–564.

36 Subero, *Embodiments*, 10.

37 See Rolando Romero and Amanda Nolacea Harris, eds., *Feminism, Nation and Myth: La Malinche* (Houston: Arte Público, 2005).

38 Andrew Chesnut, *Devoted to Death: Santa Muerte, the Skeleton Saint* (Oxford: Oxford University Press, 2012), chap. 1, Kindle.

39 Valeria Villegas, "El mero chingón: Mexicanness at Large" (master's thesis, Stockholm University, 2013), 55–59.

40 Erin Harrington, *Women, Monstrosity and Horror Film: Gynaehorror* (London: Routledge, 2018), 87.

41 "Mini MUFF profile."

42 Segato, *Crítica*, 48.

16

Uncanny Tales

Lucile Hadžihalilović's *Évolution*

JANICE LORECK

When Lucile Hadžihalilović released her debut feature-length film *Innocence* in 2004, critics declared her an exciting new auteur. Jonathan Romney described Hadžihalilović as "an audacious talent"; Ginette Vincendeau stated that her work was "testimony to the vitality and diversity of female filmmaking in France"; Vivian Sobchack wrote that Hadžihalilović was "assured," "highly original," and full of promise.[1] Born in France of Bosnian heritage, Hadžihalilović had a relatively small body of work as a director at this point. She had directed three short films: her student thesis, *La premiere mort de nono* (1987); the short drama *La bouche de Jean-Pierre* (1996); and an erotic educational film for French television, *Good Boys Use Condoms* (1998). *Innocence* is an adaptation of Frank Wedekind's novella *Mine-Haha, or On the Bodily Education of Young Girls* (1903), and it tells the story of a mysterious boarding school that instructs young girls in ballet and natural history. *Innocence* is thematically dark and at times unnerving, and industry and critics alike praised the film for its vivid imagery and careful direction. The film won several international awards, including the Fédération internationale de la presse cinématographique Prize, Best New Director at the San Sebastián International Film Festival, and the Bronze Horse for best film at the Stockholm International Film Festival. With

Innocence, Hadžihalilović established herself as an auteur distinguished by the beauty of her mise-en-scène as well as her willingness to unsettle audiences.

Few anticipated that Hadžihalilović would become a horror film director. Released eleven years later, her long-awaited second film, *Évolution* (2015), is set on a remote island within a community of prepubescent boys and their mothers. The story begins as Nicolas discovers the corpse of another boy while swimming in the ocean near his home. Following this event, Nicolas grows suspicious of his mother and the circumstances of his life on the island. There are no adult men or female children, and Nicolas and his friends are routinely admitted to the hospital for mysterious surgeries. Eventually, Nicolas discovers the truth: the women implant embryos into the boys' abdomens and use their bodies to incubate offspring. While the other children grow weak and die, Nicolas escapes with the help of a young nurse, Stella, who smuggles him off the island in a small dinghy. *Évolution* has much in common with *Innocence*. Both tell stories about children trapped in a beautiful but threatening environment, subject to adults' control. Both films pivot on Hadžihalilović's ability to evoke anxiety through striking visual imagery. *Évolution*, however, more explicitly operates as a horror film: it contains malevolent mothers, forced pregnancy, and the spectacle of mutilation and death. Moreover, the presence of maternal impostors and a bold child protagonist also cast *Évolution* in the mold of a dark fairy tale.

This chapter investigates how Hadžihalilović constructs horror in *Évolution*, examining her strategies as a director and how these connect more broadly to women's horror cinema. *Évolution* offers a unique case study for investigating women's horror filmmaking, exemplifying how an individual director—known for her aesthetic skill and distinctive sensory style—engages with the genre. *Évolution* was a difficult project to realize due to its position as both a horror and an "auteur" film. The story is based on an original idea conceived by Hadžihalilović, who enlisted the help of fellow filmmaker Alanté Kavaïté to structure the narrative. With the concept developed, Hadžihalilović initially pitched *Évolution* as a genre piece, thinking that such a label would help secure financing. This turned out to be a mistake given the French funding body's preference for art films. *Évolution* "had to be financed through a system of art house film, and for these people horror, sci-fi, fantasy, is stupid," Hadžihalilović recalls.[2] While Joan Hawkins notes that horror and art cinema are not mutually exclusive—an idea that is now axiomatic in film scholarship—the industry personnel Hadžihalilović encountered enforced a distinction.[3] She tried again, evoking the cachet of art cinema to sell her film: "I tried to say, it's just a *film d'auteur*, but they were very suspicious towards that."[4] *Évolution* eventually did secure support from French, Spanish, and Belgian sources, including the Institute of Cinematography and Audiovisual Arts (ICAA; Instituto de la cinematografía y de las artes audiovisuals) and the National Centre for Cinema and the Moving Image (CNC; Centre national du cinéma et de l'image animée), yet its production history reveals that it has never been easily classified. Both a genre piece and a product of a known auteur, it emerged at the intersection of women's art cinema and genre filmmaking.

This chapter tackles *Évolution* as a horror film operating at this juncture. The first section considers Hadžihalilović's evocative engagement with horror through its use of fairy-tale tropes. Fairy tales are a category of folk story defined chiefly by the presence of magical and wondrous events as well as stock characters such as powerful women (godmothers, stepmothers, and fairies) and bold young protagonists. I therefore consider how *Évolution* draws strongly upon this model, operating within a context of preceding female-authored films that all use folklore to weave horror stories, including those by Agnieszka Smoczyńska, Anna Biller, Angela Carter, Karen Walton, and Karyn Kusama. The chapter's second section further elaborates upon Hadžihalilović's approach to horror, looking specifically at how Hadžihalilović uses folk tale imagery to construct tone and mood. Observing that outdated things can provoke an unsettling sense of familiarity, I link the rich imagery of fairy-tale obsolescence in Hadžihalilović's mise-en-scène to the uncanny. By exploring the connection between tone, genre, and aesthetics in *Évolution*, this chapter not only contributes to the critical understanding of Hadžihalilović as an important director in contemporary cinema but also illuminates women's diverse, evocative, and elegant approaches to horror.

Women, Horror, and Fairy Tale

Although *Évolution* is an original narrative conceived by Hadžihalilović, the film has the distinct aura of a folk tale. The story takes place on an island—it is not clear exactly where or when. It may be a remote community in the present day, but it could also be a place dislocated from time. The women who live there have an otherworldly bearing; their pale faces are angular and their eyes piercing. They also engage in strange rituals. By day they bathe their sons in salt water; at night, they writhe naked on the beach in an act that resembles a sexual orgy, like sea creatures spawning on the sand. It is clear from the outset that the women harbor many secrets and powers, possibly of a malicious kind. When the young protagonist, Nicolas, decides to escape, he can only do so with the help of one of the island women: like the mermaids of folklore, her kiss lets him breathe underwater and escape undetected. With its small boy protagonist; powerful, witch-like women; and faraway setting, *Évolution* thus takes the form of an oneiric and dark fairy tale.

Évolution is not unique in this regard. Fairy tales have a persistent link to women's horror authorship: director Anna Biller reinvents the figure of the enchantress in *The Love Witch* (2016); Agnieszka Smoczyńska appropriates mermaid lore in *The Lure* (2015); Catherine Hardwicke puts a horror spin on *Red Riding Hood* (2011); and Karyn Kusama revisits the folkloric succubus in *Jennifer's Body* (2009). The affinity between women and folklore becomes even more evident if we expand definitions of authorship to include the work of screen-writers: Ester Krumbachová's adaptation of the Czech fairy tale *Valerie and Her Week of Wonders* (1970); Angela Carter's screenplay for *The Company of Wolves* (1984); and Karen Walton's and Megan Martin's screenplays for *Ginger Snaps* (2000) and *Ginger Snaps 2: Unleashed* (2004), respectively. Hadžihalilović has a clear interest in fairy tales too. Her first film, *La bouche de Jean-Pierre* (1996), echoes "Little Red Riding Hood" in its tale about a girl threatened by a preda-tory male. At the time of writing, Hadžihalilović also has an adaptation of Hans Christian Andersen's "The Snow Queen" in development.

Fairy tales offer women revisionist opportunities, the chance to retell old stories from a female perspective. Discussing Angela Carter's influential work, for example, Donald Haase observes that Carter's folktales were "aimed at reas-serting precisely those dimensions of a woman's life—including sexuality—that male editors had suppressed."[5] Such approaches also appear in cinema. Horror-musical hybrid *The Lure*, for example, draws heavily upon Hans Christian Andersen's "The Little Mermaid." Instead of focusing on the mermaid's desire for a soul, however, the film emphasizes the treacherousness of human men and the significance of sisterly love. In a similarly revisionist vein, Anna Biller's *The Love Witch* takes the folklore figure of the witch and reimagines her as a sym-pathetic figure, explaining her violent impulses as a consequence of past mis-treatment by men. Fairy tales also provide an opportunity to tell stories about women's experiences in allegorical form. *Ginger Snaps* and *Jennifer's Body* utilize the folkloric figures of the werewolf and the succubus to explore teenage sexual awakening and the demonization (quite literally) of their desires. In both films, the protagonists' supernatural metamorphosis—into a werewolf and a succu-bus, respectively—operates as a metaphor for the ways that patriarchal culture constructs women's sexuality as monstrous.

In *Évolution*, Hadžihalilović uses the fairy tale in ways that are representative of this broader revisionist and allegorical trend. The film accesses the fairy tale's potential specifically through its emphasis on wondrous transformation in the plot. According to Marina Warner, metamorphosis is the principal trait of fairy tales: "More so than the presence of fairies, the moral function, the imagined antiquity and oral anonymity of the ultimate source, and the happy ending (although all these factors help towards a definition of the genre), metamor-phosis defines the fairy tale."[6] This can consist of shape-shifting, the animation of the inanimate, and the magical conversion of objects. Such events are usu-ally the source of wonder. In *Évolution*, however, the same transformations elicit horror. The boys' ghastly illness and pregnancy mirror the physical changes of adolescence: the "difficulties" of growing up, as Hadžihalilović describes it.[7] *Évolution* emphasizes this through an early conversation between Nicolas and his mother. As Nicolas prepares for bed, his mother administers an inky tincture—something she clearly does regularly. Reluctant, Nicolas asks her why he is "sick" and needs to take the medicine. The mother replies that Nicolas's body is changing and weak, comparing his growth to the transformations of lizards and crabs: "When they molt, they're very fragile," she observes. Her words make a direct analogy between puberty and metamorphosis. It also characterizes adolescence as a dangerous time fraught with sickness, which proves prophetic for Nicolas. He and the other children grow feverish and frail, and their mothers admit them to the hospital for surgical procedures. Yet the boys do not grow up or shed their skins like lizards. Instead, they grow weaker until they "give birth" to the creatures the women implanted inside them.

The birth sequence is particularly nightmarish. Sometime after Nicolas's hospitalization, the women come for him as they have done for the other boys. They wheel Nicolas into the surgical theater; one preps his belly with iodine, another holds a scalpel perilously above his torso. The scene ends as Nicolas loses consciousness. Then a feeble cry can be heard. Nicolas wakes up suspended in cloudy water. Two infants suckle at his abdomen, crunching and nuzzling his flesh. A wide shot reveals that Nicolas is restrained, semisubmerged in a grimy water tank and unable to escape. He panics, but there is no one to help. The scene ends as one of the creatures rises to the surface to look upon Nicolas, mewling from its little mouth.

Here *Évolution* centers on a ghastly transformation in which Nicolas gives birth, an event made horrible by his youth and lack of understanding. In this, the narrative not only repurposes the metamorphoses of fairy tales to evoke anxiety about puberty; the film also undertakes a reversal of folk tales about the impregnation of young women against their will, such as "Rapunzel" and "Sun, Moon, and Talia." Unlike these stories, *Évolution* emphasizes the cruelty and suffering that the young protagonists experience. Importantly, this allegorical interpretation of *Évolution* breaks with earlier readings of Hadžihalilović's films, where commentators usually insist that it is difficult—and even inadvisable—to ascribe symbolic meaning to her work. Sobchack, for example, writes that Hadžihalilović's films give the impression of great significance but should ultimately be experienced rather than interpreted: "The urge they provoke towards interpretation is irresistible," she states, "and yet, if one yields to it, the outcome is reductive, unsatisfying."[8] Nikolaj Lübecker further opines that ideological interpretations of Hadžihalilović's work are necessary but inelegant and "clumsy."[9] Nevertheless, the events of *Évolution* have unmistakable allegorical significance. With this film, Hadžihalilović joins a lineage of women authors who find horror in fairy-tale metamorphoses, who recast fairy-tale transformations as bizarre and grotesque metaphors for menstruation, sexual awakening, and growing up. While such transformations are wondrous in traditional tales, these films render them terrifying and catastrophic.

The Child Perspective

Hadžihalilović does not use the fairy-tale mode in *Évolution* solely for its allegorical potential, however. Intense, aesthetically induced sensations are a distinctive quality of her films. As Sobchack writes, Hadžihalilović's work anchors spectators "in our own intense (and emotionally tinged) sensations of audiovisual texture, color, and atmosphere."[10] Such remarks about Hadžihalilović's work are well taken. A queasy dread hangs over *La bouche de Jean-Pierre*, its claustrophobic mise-en-scène aligning spectators with Mimi's entrapment in her aunt's apartment. *Innocence* is undergirded by a sinister anticipation of the girls' fate after they leave school. In interviews Hadžihalilović also expresses reluctance to pinpoint the meaning of her work, discouraging interpretation and refocusing on the experiential elements. Discussing *Innocence*, she states, "I haven't tried to convey any particular message. Just as there are no answers to the questions, there's no moral to the story either."[11] While Hadžihalilović has been more forthcoming regarding the metaphoric dimension of *Évolution*, she nevertheless emphasizes that the film is a sensuous work: "The horror is more in the mood than the images," she says. "It's a film about sensations, emotions."[12] Such comments insist that tone is the film's key register.

Hadžihalilović's statements ring true. Fairy-tale tropes infuse *Évolution* with anxiety, particularly with respect to the adult women and their secrets. The film achieves this by organizing the narrative around Nicolas's subjectivity as the child hero. On the one hand, this maneuver consolidates the film as a dark fairy tale. Children are regular protagonists of folklore in the Western tradition, and quick-witted boys appear insistently in "Hop-o'-My-Thumb," "Jack and the Beanstalk," and the tales woven around Tom Thumb. Small, dark, and solemn, Nicolas is cast in the mold of such characters. Yet the emphasis on his point of view also produces much of the film's horror. Nicolas's suspicion informs the narrative, and *Évolution* aligns both story and spectator with his point of view. An illustrative example is the pervasively malevolent representation of Nicolas's mother. At several points, she prepares food for her son on the stove in their house. Close-ups reveal a gray slime of unappetizing texture, with viscous sauce and translucent blue noodles. The substance does not resemble any recognizable food, and Nicolas eventually refuses to eat it. Presented differently, the scene could be read as a moment where a stubborn child rejects his dinner. Yet *Évolution* positions viewers to share Nicolas's disgust. Such moments invite suspicion of the mother's caretaking behavior. From Nicolas's point of view, her motives are shadowy and the food she prepares is revolting.

By privileging Nicolas's perspective, *Évolution* constructs anxiety about adults as terrifying and unknowable beings. This approach was an early factor in the film's genesis. Hadžihalilović states that *Évolution* is based on a charged memory from her own childhood in which she was hospitalized for appendicitis. During this event, she found the doctors' attention ambiguous and threatening: "It was the first time in my life when my body was [being] touched by adults I didn't know," she says.[13] The emotional charge of this memory underpins the narrative perspective of *Évolution* insofar as Nicolas perceives grownups as unknowable and sinister. Indeed, the film corresponds to Robin Wood's foundational observations on horror cinema, in which he notes that the genre invokes the fear of society's suppressed Others.[14] Rather than positioning adults as "outsiders," however, the horror of *Évolution* pivots on the child subject's fear of the adult as *radically* Other to her- or himself. Nicolas declares this unbridgeable difference when he rejects all kinship with his mother. While he lies sick in the hospital, the mother discovers her son's cherished notebook hidden under his bedlinen. She is oddly affronted by the drawings of starfish and Ferris wheels inside, refusing to return the book and insisting that Nicolas obey his mother. He retorts emphatically, "You are not my mother!" In this moment, *Évolution* depicts the adult woman's behavior as inexplicable and hostile from the child's point of view, and Nicolas responds by disowning her completely. As Hadžihalilović says, "I have the feeling that maybe as a child you are kind of isolated from the adult world. Not in the physical way, but just because you don't really understand what they're doing, what their purpose is, whether they're good or bad."[15] Such ideas animate *Évolution*. The film foregrounds the imperiled child protagonist of fairy tales, using his point of view to render the adult world sinister. Food is poison, doctors are hazardous, and mothers have ulterior motives.

Hadžihalilović's use of childhood not only produces anxiety in ways that align *Évolution* with the horror genre; it also connects her to trends in women's global art cinema. With the exception of her short films *Nectar* (2014) and *Good Boys Use Condoms*, children and teenagers are always the protagonists of Hadžihalilović's fiction films: young Mimi in *La bouche de Jean-Pierre*, the girls of *Innocence*, the boys in *Évolution*, and more recently, the children of *De Natura* (2017), a short cinepoem about two girls playing in a forest. Hadžihalilović acknowledges her fascination with childhood: "It's kind of against my will that I'm attracted to this time period," she says.[16] Yet childhood is not just Hadžihalilović's personal preoccupation. It frequently appears in films directed by women, particularly those that circulate on the international art-house and film festival circuit, where Hadžihalilović's work predominately appears. Child protagonists populate *The Virgin Suicides* (Sofia Coppola, 1999), *À ma sœur!* (Catherine Breillat, 2001), *She Monkeys* (Lisa Aschan, 2011), *The Fits* (Anna Rose Holmer, 2015), *The Falling* (Carol Morley, 2014), and *I Am Not a Witch* (Rungano Nyoni, 2017), to name a few examples. Carrie Tarr and Brigitte Rollet argue that this tendency occurs because of an affinity between women and children as marginalized subjects. They note that women and children rarely command the film gaze, and their subjectivity seldom guides the plot or shapes the narrative point of view. As such, the depiction of children can be a political act, per Tarr and Rollet: "Foregrounding of the perceptions of child or adolescent protagonists whose experiences are normally marginal and marginalized has the potential to challenge hegemonic adult modes of seeing and displace the fetishistic male gaze of dominant cinema."[17] Childhood perspectives therefore offer women an opportunity for both artistic innovation as well as subversion of dominant representational schemas in cinema.

Hadžihalilović's career thus forms a point of connection between women's art cinema and horror filmmaking. *Évolution* extends the affinity between women's horror and fairy tale, yet the film also bears the hallmarks of Hadžihalilović's earlier work as a writer-director, continuing her interest in child subjectivity. Indeed, the marginalized child perspective is the shared territory between Hadžihalilović's work as a lauded art film auteur and as a horror filmmaker. Wood notes that although children are regularly demonized as Other in horror films, they are, in fact, "the most oppressed section of the population."[18] Hadžihalilović's films—as well as those by Lisa Aschan, Anna Rose Holmer, Carol Morley, and others—acknowledge and investigate that oppression. Children allow a unique perspective for auteurs, and they also provide a means for generating horror. In Hadžihalilović's case, they do both.

Uncanny Tales

Like fairy tales before it, *Évolution* concerns metamorphosis, maternal conspiracy, and imperiled children. Instead of feelings of enchantment, however, the film inspires dread. According to Warner, fairy tales should not be existentially unsettling in this way: "These are not tales of the uncanny . . . they do not leave open prickly possibilities, or enter un-negotiated areas of the unknown, as in fantasy or surrealist literature or ghost stories."[19] Yet *Évolution* is precisely that: a tale about the unnegotiated unknown, the fear of puberty, reproduction, and malevolent adults. It also adopts a conspicuously surrealist aesthetic, another attribute that Warner excludes from fairy tales. Paintings by Giorgio de Chirico, Yves Tanguy, and Salvador Dalí served as visual references for the film's sun-bleached landscapes.[20] Filmed on Lanzarote in the Canary Islands, Nicolas's village rests on a ragged coastline, recalling both Tanguy's *Légendes ni figures* (1930) and Dalí's *Moment de Transition* (1934). Surf breaks relentlessly against jagged rocks; geometric houses gleam white in the sun, like the structures of de Chirico's *Piazza* (1913) and *Turin Spring* (1914). On land, there is little sign of vegetation, but an abundance of seaweed, urchins, and starfish thrive in the ocean. The setting immediately evokes *dépaysement*, the psychic state of dislocation and disorientation when outside of one's own country. Uncanniness also pervades *Évolution*—an uncertain sense that Nicolas's village could be located in the present day, a dream, or another world entirely. Indeed, the intensity of such tones regularly seizes attention above the enigmas of the plot. To use Susan Sontag's words, *Évolution* constructs an aesthetic experience that momentarily "frees us from the itch to interpret" its fairy-tale content.[21]

While *Évolution* does indeed echo tales of maternal impostors and bold children from Western folklore, the mise-en-scène conjures an uncanny rather than wondrous feeling. The term *uncanny* or *unheimlich* refers to an aesthetic experience of a disturbing variety. Sigmund Freud offers one of the best-known accounts of the phenomenon, describing the *unheimlich* as the unsettling sensation produced in encounters with things that evoke repressed memories—hence the perception of uncanny objects as strangely familiar.[22] *Évolution* invokes the uncanny from its opening moments. The film begins as Nicolas discovers a corpse submerged in the ocean near the village. The body lies with its arms raised and eyes open; a red starfish clings to its belly. It is a boy of Nicolas's age. Freud argues that dead bodies are frequently experienced as uncanny because of humanity's inability to assimilate death as a concept.[23] Moreover, the dead boy's resemblance to Nicolas recalls the "double," an uncanny phenomenon that terrifies the onlooker because it uncovers the juvenile psyche's repressed narcissistic replications of itself. The turbulent, muffled roar of the ocean also alludes to this unwelcome return of infantile memory. From Nicolas's position under the surf, the waves pulsate and thud in ways reminiscent of the fetal and maternal heartbeat. Lastly, the double is also a harbinger of death and an unwelcome reminder of the body's impermanence.[24] The corpse that Nicolas discovers serves this precise function—its uncanny appearance ignites his suspicion of the island and motivates his desire to escape.

In *Évolution*, the uncanny is also triggered by its fairy-tale aura of the past: the temporal indeterminacy of the mise-en-scène, the appearance of outdated technologies, and the ahistoricity of the setting. In an essay on the surrealists, Walter Benjamin observes that outmoded things can trigger powerful aesthetic experiences. These can be elicited by obsolete technologies, styles fallen out of fashion, and other objects that retain an air of the recent past.[25] Benjamin ultimately considers the aesthetic experience of outmoded things to elicit revolutionary energies. Producing not only nostalgia, the outmoded can also generate discomfort about the acceleration of commodity culture and capitalism in modernity. In *Évolution*, however, Hadžihalilović's anachronistic mise-en-scène uses the outmoded in a different way. As Hal Foster explains, temporal disruptions can be experienced as uncanny: "The outmoded not only recalls the present to the past; it may also return the past to the present, in which case it often assumes a demonic guise."[26] The reason for this is that the past is "damaged by repression" and thus unsettles the onlooker.[27]

Hadžihalilović's extends and intensifies the discomfort that the outmoded can bring, generating an aesthetic of the temporal uncanny. The production design is integral to this process. *Évolution* gives no indication of the story's location or era. As Hadžihalilović notes, she wanted the film to be "out of time," and indeed, there is little in the film to firmly date it.[28] Scalpels and hypodermic syringes appear in the hospital, but there are no cars in the street or televisions in the houses. The set contains no props that decisively anchor the setting in history. This in turn provides another link to the fairy tale; while the majority of folk stories take place in an imagined approximation of the Middle Ages, they are not strongly historicized. Moreover, Hadžihalilović's mise-en-scène itself is indeterminate in terms of historicity, melding surrealist iconography with classical figures and midcentury modernity. The island women, for instance, resemble living replicas of the nymphs painted by Titian, Sandro Botticelli, and Raphael. Pale with waxy, uniform complexions; fair hair; and heavy eyelids, they appear ferocious, beautiful, and decidedly noncontemporary. Stella, the nurse who aids Nicolas's escape, particularly resembles Botticelli's models that appeared in his religious and classical works, such as *Madonna Magnificat* (1481) and *La Primavera* (1482). Her red hair and prominent bowed lips also recall di Chirico's neoclassical *Bathers on the Beach* (1934), in which nudes recline on a rocky shore. Stella's costume, however, consists of mid-twentieth-century nurses' attire—a tailored white dress, pumps, and cap. Her appearance thus evokes clashing temporalities; her face emerges from a distant past, yet her attire hails from a recent, outmoded modernity.

Évolution also enhances its disorienting historicity by drawing heavily upon science fiction, in terms of both iconography and story events. On one hand, stock fairy-tale characters such as bold children and powerful maternal impostors abound in *Évolution*. On the other, the film substitutes many typical fairy-tale tropes with technologies from a more recent past: surgery rather than magic, ultrasound machines instead of enchanted mirrors, and syringes rather than wands. Moreover, the boy's fate is not the usual kind that befalls children in the Western fairy-tale tradition. Murder, transmogrification, or cannibalism are far more common, appearing in stories such as "Little Red Riding Hood," "Hansel and Gretel," "Hop-o'-My-Thumb," "Jack and the Beanstalk," and "Wild Swans." Instead, the women use the boys as surrogate hosts for offspring. *Évolution* thus reinvents old tales of imperiled children to explore a more contemporary worry about the loss of reproductive autonomy. Nicolas's fate resembles forced commercial surrogacy and the appropriation of the body for its biological value.[29] Such worries are thematic of twentieth- and twenty-first-century science fiction and appear in novels like *Never Let Me Go* (2005) and Eric Garcia's *The Repossession Mambo* (2009) as well as in films such as *The Island* (2005) and *Antiviral* (2012). Fears such as these seem out of place within a traditional fairy-tale cosmology. This, however, is precisely the point. *Évolution* constructs a rich and horrifying imagery of obsolescence and ahistoricity; things are both out of place and out of time.

Critics have produced a substantial body of work on Hadžihalilović's films following the release of *Innocence*. None of this research positions her as a horror film director. Instead, commentators firmly place Hadžihalilović's work within the context of art cinema, varying only in terms of which mode they choose to emphasize. Lübecker includes Hadžihalilović in his book *The Feel-Bad Film*, comparing her to provocateurs such as Gus Van Sant, Lars von Trier, and Yorgos Lanthimos. Lübecker categorizes *Innocence* as a "feel-bad" film because it is "ethically elusive," leaving the spectator unsure of whether his or her gaze sexualizes the young protagonists or not.[30] Matilda Mroz chooses a different art cinema style for Hadžihalilović, locating *Innocence* within the "slow-cinema" movement. She argues that the film's dilated pace corresponds to the "performance of evolution" of the girl protagonists.[31] Davina Quinlivan takes a different approach again. She describes Hadžihalilović's work as part of the French "cinema of the body," saying that, like Claire Denis and Marina de Van (who are discussed in chapter 10 by Maddi McGillvray), she adopts a visual style that arrests dynamic images in tableaux.[32] Such analyses illuminate much about Hadžihalilović's power to manipulate sensation and the logic of her aesthetic. They also define her unanimously as an art film director.

Évolution allows for a different perspective on Hadžihalilović. As Laura Kern observes, *Évolution* can be categorized into several different genres: as "sci-fi allegory, surreal body horror, medical thriller, melancholy coming-of-age tale, or . . . *un film fantastique*."[33] These are all valid classifications. Viewing the film as horror also provides critical opportunities. First, an analysis of Hadžihalilović contributes to a broader project of investigating women's genre filmmaking—to illuminate women's contributions and champion them as "generic innovators," as Mary Harrod and Katarzyna Paszkiewicz put it.[34] Analyzing *Évolution* as a genre piece also consolidates wider trends in women's horror cinema. Like other dark fairy tales by women, such as *The Lure* or *Jennifer's Body*, *Évolution* uses the trope of metamorphosis to discuss the transformations of puberty and female desire. Unlike in these women-focused works, however, it is the male body that undergoes physical change in *Évolution*. Indeed, it is arguable that the film's horror resides in the feminizing of boys through pregnancy and that it is female puberty specifically that is to be feared. Yet the allegorical role of metamorphosis remains consistent across *Évolution* as well as other women's entries in the subgenre. To grow up and acquire an adult body with its full range of sexual and reproductive functions is to be both monstrous and vulnerable to the ill intentions of others.

Approaching *Évolution* as a horror film also provides a fuller understanding of Hadžihalilović's qualities as an auteur and how they have developed. Such an approach reveals that Hadžihalilović need not be viewed exclusively as a genre filmmaker or art film auteur. *Évolution* indicates that she is both, a state of affairs that French funding bodies would not permit when she first approached them for financing (and indeed, one wonders how many other female "auteurs" might also be productively identified as genre filmmakers and vice versa). Dark, unsettling, and over a decade in the making, *Évolution* consolidates Hadžihalilović's signature as an accomplished director of tone. Indeed, an investigation of the film as a horror text confirms this characteristic as well as her status as an auteur. Foregrounding the obsolete and old-fashioned, Hadžihalilović's combines an uncanny surrealist mise-en-scène with fairy-tale horrors. Moreover, like *Innocence* and *La bouche de Jean-Pierre*, *Évolution* continues her interest in children as protagonists, pushing this preoccupation to its full, terrifying potential. *Évolution* installs Nicolas as the organizing perspective of the tale and thus locates Otherness in the shadowy figures of adults. This is the place where Hadžihalilović's has always found darkness, whether in the inexplicable motives of the schoolmistresses in *Innocence* or the predatory behavior of men in *La bouche de Jean-Pierre*. Hadžihalilović's work gives audiences intimate representations of children and their experience. In *Évolution*, however, the price of such intimacy is horror.

Notes

This chapter was completed with the support of the Small Grants Program in the School of Media, Creative Arts and Social Inquiry, Curtin University, Australia.

1 Jonathan Romney, "School for Scandal," *Sight and Sound* 15, no. 10 (October 2005): 36; Ginette Vincendeau, "*Innocence*," *Sight and Sound* 15, no. 10 (October 2005): 69; Vivian Sobchack, "Waking Life," *Film Comment* 41, no. 6 (November/December 2005): 49.
2 Lucile Hadžihalilović, "*Evolution* Q&A | Lucile Hadžihalilović | New Directors/New Films 2016," filmed March 2016 at Film Society Lincoln Center, New York, N.Y., video, 6:17, https://www.youtube.com/watch?v=EFZLotoCj3g.
3 Joan Hawkins, *Cutting Edge: Art-Horror and the Horrific Avant-Garde* (Minneapolis: Minnesota University Press, 2000), 23–25.
4 Hadžihalilović, "*Evolution* Q&A," 6:49.
5 Donald Haase, "Feminist Fairy-Tale Scholarship," in *Fairy Tales and Feminism: New Approaches*, ed. Donald Haase (Detroit: Wayne State University Press, 2004), 9.
6 Marina Warner, *From the Beast to the Blonde: On Fairy Tales and Their Tellers* (New York: Farrar, Straus and Giroux, 1995), xv–xvi.
7 Hadžihalilović, "*Evolution* Q&A," 4:16.
8 Sobchack, "Waking Life," 46–47.
9 Nikolaj Lübecker, *The Feel-Bad Film* (Edinburgh: Edinburgh University Press, 2015), 83.
10 Sobchack, "Waking Life," 49.
11 Vincendeau, "*Innocence*," 69.
12 Colin Crummy, "A Closer Look at Beautifully Perverse New Body Horror, *Evolution*," *i-D*, May 7, 2016, https://i-d.vice.com/en_au/article/nen548/a-closer-look-at-beautifully-perverse-new-body-horror-evolution; Jonathan Romney, "*Evolution* Director Lucile Hadžihalilović: 'The Starfish Was the One Worry,'" *Guardian*, April 29, 2016, https://www.theguardian.com/film/2016/apr/28/evolution-lucile-hadzihalilovic-starfish-worry-boys-mothers.
13 Tara Brady, "Lucile Hadžihalilović: 'The First Idea Was the Male Pregnancy and the Hospital,'" *Irish Times*, May 5, 2016, https://www.irishtimes.com/culture/film/lucile-hadihalilovic-the-first-idea-was-the-male-pregnancy-and-the-hospital-1.2636456.
14 Robin Wood, "The American Nightmare: Horror in the 70s," in *Horror, the Film Reader*, ed. Mark Jancovich (London: Routledge, 2002), 28.
15 Dominic Preston, "'The Adult World Is Something Mysterious,'" *Candid*, May 5, 2016, https://candidmagazine.com/lucile-hadihalilovic-interview/.

16   Hadžihalilović, "*Evolution* Q&A," 4:16.
17   Carrie Tarr and Brigitte Rollet, *Cinema and the Second Sex: Women's Filmmaking in France in the 1980s and 1990s* (New York: Continuum, 2001), 25.
18   Wood, "American Nightmare," 28.
19   Warner, *From the Beast to the Blonde*, xvi.
20   Hadžihalilović, "*Evolution* Q&A," 29:40.
21   Susan Sontag, "Against Interpretation," in *Against Interpretation and Other Essays* (London: Penguin, 2009), 11.
22   Sigmund Freud, "The Uncanny," in *The Standard Edition of the Complete Psychological Works of Sigmund Freud*, trans. James Strachey, ed. James Strachey, Anna Freud, Alix Strachey, and Alan Tyson (London: Hogarth, 1953), 245.
23   Freud, 241.
24   Freud, 235.
25   Walter Benjamin, "Surrealism: The Last Snapshot of the European Intelligentsia," *New Left Review*, no. 108 (March 1978): 50.
26   Hal Foster, *Compulsive Beauty* (Cambridge, Mass.: MIT Press, 1993), 164.
27   Foster, 164.
28   Hadžihalilović, "*Evolution* Q&A," 15:52.
29   See Nikolas Rose, *The Politics of Life Itself: Biomedicine, Power, and Subjectivity in the Twenty-First Century* (Princeton, N.J.: Princeton University Press, 2007).
30   Lübecker, *Feel-Bad Film*, 93.
31   Matilda Mroz, "Performing Evolution: Immersion, Unfolding and Lucile Hadžihalilović's *Innocence*," in *Slow Cinema*, ed. Tiago de Luca and Nuno Barradas Jorge (Edinburgh: Edinburgh University Press, 2016), 287.
32   Davina Quinlivan, "The French Female Butterfly Collector: Hadžihalilović, Denis, de Van and the *Cinéma du corps*," *Studies in European Cinema* 10, no. 1 (March 2013): 38–39.
33   Laura Kern, "The Miracle of Life," *Film Comment* 52, no. 3 (May/June 2016): 36.
34   Mary Harrod and Katarzyna Paszkiewicz, "Introduction: Women's Authorship and Genre in Contemporary Film and Television," in *Women Do Genre in Film and Television*, ed. Mary Harrod and Katarzyna Paszkiewicz (New York: Routledge, 2018), 3.

The (Re)birth of Pregnancy Horror in Alice Lowe's *Prevenge*

AMY C. CHAMBERS

Alice Lowe's directorial feature debut, *Prevenge* (2016), is an antenatal horror film conceived and conceptualized by a pregnant woman. The film offers a new approach to a horror subgenre that has so readily been the preserve of male directors looking to sensationalize the complex experience of pregnancy and childbirth. Unusually for gynaehorror, in *Prevenge* pregnancy is not the result of sexual violence, forced insemination (by aliens, monsters, or scientists), or supernatural intervention. Rather, it is a consensual conception, albeit one that is disturbed by what could be interpreted as extreme perinatal psychosis. Lowe further subverts the pregnancy horror by showing neither the conception nor the birth of "baby," which are so often the sites of performative gore and female pain and powerlessness. In avoiding these images, she places this specifically female-lived experience at the center of a film that unsettles expectations of horror and how (and by whom) it is told, experienced, and resolved. This chapter will analyze the shift in pregnancy-themed horror from being about women as invaded, involuntary hosts to exploring how *Prevenge* represents the agency and subjective experience of the pregnant woman.

Prevenge is a dark comedy horror written, directed, and starring the then-pregnant Lowe. Following the sudden death of her partner in a climbing accident, the central character Ruth goes on a murderous rampage, apparently compelled by her unborn child, whose uncanny disembodied voice (also voiced by Lowe) offers unnerving analysis and encouragement to the events on screen. The killings are a preemptive prerevenge that is seemingly fueled by the victims' apparent and perceptibly harmless attitudes toward women, pregnancy, and children. Perhaps tellingly, Ruth refers to her pregnancy as "a hostile takeover," framing it as a merger, a forced relinquishing of total control in the business parlance rather than a parasitic invasion. By placing an apparently natural event within a horror setting, Lowe makes a domestic experience obscene and disrupts traditional narratives surrounding the "joy" of pregnancy.

Lowe works in a male-dominated industry where there are comparably few women directors and even fewer making their directorial feature debut in their late thirties with young children. The funding for the film came from a company that had released financing for a low-budget, short-shoot feature—colleagues sent the details to Lowe, who initially thought it was unfeasible because she was already well into her first trimester. Pregnancy was not "sitting well with her as a freelancer," as the precarious nature of her work as an actor and writer did not seem to be compatible with pregnancy and child rearing.[1] She also struggled with dealing with the way people responded to the news of her pregnancy and her own perceptions of how other women seemed to change once they became pregnant. As she explains,

> I was going through sort of an existential crisis with my work. I wasn't sure what having a baby was going to do to my career and whether I could afford to take the time out. Also, just in terms of myself I was like: Does it change you completely when you have a baby? Maybe you become this soft, sweet, caring person? I took all of my fears and anxieties about that and put it into the film. Ruth's someone who's quite alienated and detached from her environment because she feels like everyone's making assumptions about her due to her pregnancy, which she's completely separate from. It was quite a personal thing to me.[2]

She started to think about what characters she could play as a pregnant woman, and the idea for Ruth came to her, a woman who "is the opposite of the fluffy mum stereotype, painting the nursery pastel colors—[she is] someone who [is] hellbent on revenge and obsessed with the past and death."[3] She pitched *Prevenge* to the producers, who loved it, but the project needed turning around in a few months, meaning that Lowe and Ruth would go through their final trimester together. In the creation of Ruth, Lowe debuted a new vision of the horror movie mother-to-be: "an anti-superheroine, for whom pregnancy is her special power" that allows her to almost invisibly pass through social situations as a carrier of evil intent rather than as bouncing baby joy.[4]

One of the main difficulties for working women in the film and television industries is childbirth and childcare, even, as Natalie Wreyford argues, "for those who do not choose to have children."[5] In a recent study of 3,452 films in production between 2003 and 2015 in the United Kingdom, it was found that only 14 percent of directors were women, with 1 percent of those women being BAME (black, Asian, minority ethnic).[6] Women may be seen as "inevitable mothers" and thus a risky investment regardless of potential and their actual intentions concerning children.[7] This is not to say that men are not parents, but societally, it is women who are more closely associated with care narratives and the "invisible" emotional labor of family life.[8] The creative industries are built upon a "compulsory sociality" (informal networking and freelancing) that is often not compatible with care responsibilities.[9] Whereas for many pregnancy risks being seen as a stigma that must be overcome or accepted as a career issue / death knell, Alice Lowe was able to incorporate her pregnancy positively within an industry that has often been quick to deny women and their bodies a space and place both on- and off-screen.

Through *Prevenge*, Alice Lowe mediates the biologically female experience of pregnancy, gestating during preproduction and production and becoming a new mother prior to postproduction and then the press tours and premieres. Lowe's daughter, Della, appears as the born "baby" in the closing scenes and made several appearances with Lowe at premieres and in interviews. Lowe's visibility as a pregnant person and a new parent is striking, and Lowe's decision to incorporate her daughter into the press tour and interview process feels as much like a necessity (of a working parent) as it does an opportunity to highlight her relative uniqueness and the issues with the wider creative industries' "systemic inequalities" that disproportionately affect women of childbearing age.[10] Thus the lived experiences and challenges of pregnancy are given a new authority within *Prevenge* because of the director's specific gendered knowledge and bodily experiences that are literally inaccessible to male horror directors. This chapter asks whether a long-established genre that has regularly offered up the woman's body as a fetishized spectacle can be altered when the film is conceived, written, and directed by a woman.[11] *Prevenge* provides a space for discussing the clinicalization and lived medical experiences of pregnancy (loss of bodily control), the perception of antenatal psychosis (loss of mental control) from a woman's perspective, and the existing and persisting cultural and medical narratives where the agency of the mother is lost to the baby who knows best.

The (Re)birth of Pregnancy Horror

Pregnancy horror emerged in British and Hollywood cinema after 1968, following the relaxation and rescinding of censorship rules that had previously deemed stories about birth control, conception, abortion, and birth as morally reprehensible. Although there were "no specific policies addressing science" in the guidelines set forth by the BBFC (British Board of Film Censors, established 1912) and the Hollywood Motion Picture Production Code (1930–1968), there were caveats that ensured that birth control and childbirth were restricted, as they were defined as "repellent subjects."[12] Pregnancy horror then, with its potential for gruesome and graphic medicalized moments, horrific engagements with technology, and metaphors about the liminal female body, emerged from the changes to permissible content. Roman Polanski's psychological satanic horror *Rosemary's Baby* (1968) and its representation of the infantile paranoid mother heralded "both the birth of horror and the horror of birth in modern cinema" and inspired a spurt of films that utilized pregnancy and childbirth as spectacle, including *It's Alive* (1974), *Beyond the Door* (1974), *Embryo* (1976), *Demon Seed* (1977), *The Brood* (1979), and *Alien* (1979).[13] The processes of conception, pregnancy, and birth are made horrific and thus "reflect, amplify, and perpetuate ambivalent attitudes" toward women's bodies and their power within society, which also coincided with the reemergence of a women's rights movement.[14]

This first wave of pregnancy horror was released as second-wave feminism gained momentum and women liberationists "started to mobilize around their own, rather than other people's, oppression."[15] As Barbara Creed claims, horror cinema in the 1970s and 1980s adversely responded to this historical moment of women's liberation and highlighted the "ancient connection between woman, womb, and the monstrous."[16] The pregnant woman and her offspring become terrifying, uncontrolled, insane, and abject. She is wretchedly inscribed with both "biological bodily functions" provoking disgust and discomfort and a "symbolic economy" that takes a private (literal in-body experience) into public and political discussions of how the female body should be controlled and monitored.[17] Thus this first phase of pregnancy horror, created in an era of discussions of women's rights, provided a perceptibly misogynistic and male-directed representation of "the lived, embodied and subjective experience of women."[18] It is not until Leigh Janiak's *Honeymoon* (2014) that a woman directs a gynaehorror, but even this is a film that replicates many of the patriarchal tropes of violent conception, loss of female identity, and gruesome monstrous fetus. *Prevenge* offers a potential turning point in women's horror filmmaking that positions the female experience at its center.

Developing this further, Erin Harrington's term *gynaehorror* gives credence to the "social, cultural, political, and biomedical layers" that are integral to an understanding of the pregnancy subgenre and the broader female-focused horror under discussion. Gynaehorror is a "horror that deals with all aspects of female reproductive horror, from the reproductive and sexual organs, to virginity and first sex, through to pregnancy, birth and motherhood, and finally to menopause and post-menopause."[19] Harrington's term attends to the entire female reproductive cycle and how these experiences have been mediated by horror cinema and television. It is a term that promotes feminist engagement with the representation of the embodied experience of the woman as well as recognizes the horrific ways in which women have been limited to/by images of monstrosity. For this discussion, the distinction between the woman's antenatal experience (relating specifically to pregnancy) and her postpartum role as mother and caregiver is important. In Harrington's work, pregnancy is understood as "its own corporeal state" that can be analyzed alongside and also beyond narratives of motherhood.[20] In *Prevenge*, the focus is the pregnancy rather than the conception, the birth, the baby, or motherhood, and the horror and associated pain is external to the female body rather than being located within it.

Alice Lowe is keen to highlight in interviews that *Prevenge* is the first pregnancy horror to be told "from the female perspective."[21] This is particularly relevant to the recent upsurge in women horror directors as they reclaim a genre that has so often used their bodies as sites of horror. Pregnant women have frequently been framed as a locus of "fascination and repulsion" in a horror cinema that is defined by "doubleness."[22] The horror pregnancy has repeatedly been seen as a threat both to the mother *and* to society because of "*what* [rather than whom] the woman's womb may harbor."[23] The pregnant body is "horrific and abject" and unsettles the boundaries between self and other, presenting the experience as one associated with "permeability, corruptibility, and pollution."[24] Instead of signaling anxieties over or about women's reproductive capacities from the perspective of male filmmakers, *Prevenge* instead focuses on the women's own anxieties about their own experiences of pregnancy.

Horror in the Domestic Space

Prevenge is a horror comedy that lies in stark contrast to the majority of gynae-horror that is often aligned with science fiction or fantasy and the corruption of the conception, gestation, and birth that those generic interventions permit. Ruth's condition is not due to alien insemination (*Alien*, *The Brood*, *Honeymoon*), satanic ritual or demonic possession (*Rosemary's Baby*, *Beyond the Door*), nonhuman monsters (*It's Alive*), or mad scientists' experiments (*Embryo*, *Demon Seed*). The death of the father (Matt) is postconception, and the news of his loss coincides with Ruth discovering that she is carrying his child. Ruth makes no mention of the conception, suggesting that it was just the result of a normal unmemorable sexual encounter with her long-term partner, while the birth after the water breaks is absent from the film entirely.

Despite this rejection of traditional feminized domesticity, *Prevenge* can be defined as a domestic horror that can be aligned with British supernatural horror television comedies such as *Being Human* (2008–2013) and *In the Flesh* (2013–2014).[25] Both dramas place supernatural horror figures into domestic spaces, with a vampire, a werewolf, and a ghost sharing a Bristol apartment

(*Being Human*) and a gay "cured" zombie trying to fit into a rural Lancashire village (*In the Flesh*). As Hannah J. Elizabeth and I have argued, these British domestic horrors "provide social commentaries and interventions by narrativizing the constant definition and redefinition of what constitutes the obscene by placing them in contrast or complicity with the domestic."[26] Pregnancy is not innately horrific, but in a horror film, it can be framed and narrativized as such. Ruth follows a routine: she organizes her supplies in a neat and innocuous doctor's bag and washes and dries her kitchen-knife murder weapon, ready for its next outing. By making the horrific domestic, especially its eschewing of the violent conception and bloody birth tropes, *Prevenge* shows that what we consider obscene is "situationally, temporally and spatially specific, and the way [that] it can be lived or embodied provokes horror."[27]

The home is a key setting in *Prevenge*, although it is never Ruth's own home. The only living space we are presented with for Ruth is a generic and rather grim hotel room. But the homes of others are the scenes of her murders: the apartment DJ Dan shares with his mother; the apartment of Josh and Zac; and the cozy home of Len. She is seen to be "less than"—homeless, sexless, and as one of the film's jokes goes, "Ruthless"—as she unemotionally murders people in their own homes.[28] After killing DJ Dan, she tidies up a bit (but notably not the body or the blood). She does the washing up, cleans the kitchen knife she brought from home, and starts the laundry for her victim's mother, whom she also tucks into bed. It is the only time Ruth performs anything resembling seemingly feminine "nesting instincts" in preparation for the arrival of a baby. The safety of the home is disturbed by a murderous mother-to-be who also sometimes does the dishes, enhancing *Prevenge*'s surreal mix of black comedy and horror.

Baby Knows Best

Ruth follows the adage of "baby knows best" somewhat literally in *Prevenge*, as she believes that the baby is talking to her and that it needs her to kill. Ruth interprets abdominal pain as punishment from "baby" to ensure she remembers "who's the mastermind." Despite Ruth's rejection of what we might expect from someone who is expecting, she diligently attends her scans and meetings with her midwife. The film takes an episodic structure, with the murders—where Ruth encounters her victims and their different interactions and reactions to pregnancy—alternating with sequences of routine prenatal medical checkups. The episodic style is practically due to the restrictions on filming caused by the eleven-day shoot and Lowe's growing and changing body (a film continuity issue)—but the style of each murder, as Lowe explains, shifts "tonally because they represent a different facet of what challenges she thinks she's meeting, in terms of society."[29] She and her fetus travel through these Dantesque layers of hell, which from the outside appear to be regular, albeit infuriating, encounters for a pregnant woman as strangers talk to the bump, touch without asking, and assume that the woman is somehow less capable mentally and physically.

Several of the midwife sequences are perceptively patronizing, revealing the way that pregnant women are told they are secondary to "baby" and that they should listen to "baby," because, as the midwife coos, "baby knows what to do; baby will tell you what to do." The midwife, "Nurse Jennifer," continually talks to Ruth like she is the baby, using a softened, high-pitched, lullaby voice. Once the baby is born, Nurse Jennifer still uses this tone, greeting Ruth with "Good morning, Mummy" and to reiterate that it is "all about what's best for baby," once again reminding her of the sublimation of control. Indeed, control is a recurrent theme in the prenatal appointments, as Jennifer tells Ruth that she is "absolutely not in control over [her] mind and body" and patronizingly pats her belly and remarks that instead, "this one does, she's got all the control now." Ruth's choices and desires are "rejected as irrelevant, or even seen as having been replaced by the fetus' own agency."[30] Ruth believes this literally. She repeats "baby knows best" as she ritualistically paints her face in preparation for a Halloween party where she intends to confront and kill Tom.

Issues of control plague the cultural framing of pregnancy as an individual, medical, and political experience. As Clare Hanson notes in her *A Cultural History of Pregnancy*, if a woman is seen to have no control, "her identity as speaking subject is threatened," yet if she is seen to be in control of the pregnancy, she is still "undermined," as symbolically, her body "acts as both a reminder of our material origins and a signifier of the (uncertain) future."[31] Control over body and mind—or rather the loss thereof—is fundamental to the pregnancy horrors that established the gynaehorror subgenre. The female body is then exposed as simultaneously desirous and monstrous in the horror genre, with the sense of unease and terror being elicited from this tension between woman as either and both mistress and mother.

Prevenge interrogates the tensions apparently inherent in the pregnant body and defetishizes them. It does not provoke horror at the abject representation of the uncontrolled female body and the repellent process whereby new life is painfully dragged into existence "from inside to outside bringing with it traces of its contamination—blood, afterbirth, feces."[32] Instead, *Prevenge* plays the unwieldy pregnant body for laughs. Ruth prepares to murder DJ Dan by trying on clothes in a charity shop. She struggles in a cramped changing room with a pink sequined dress that she has to pair with a stretchy skirt in an attempt to hide and dress up her bump. It is a scene that also highlights her isolation, as there is no one there to help her either get through the day-to-day or exact her revenge. Ruth's attempt to obscure her bump in the darkened nightclub is successful, as DJ Dan sees her as a "fat bird" rather than a pregnant woman. But Ruth's body is not fetishized as either sexual or even grotesque—when Dan takes her back to his flat, his focus is on her "fanny" and not her swelled physique. Ruth has one nude scene after the death of

DJ Dan, but she is in the dingy hotel bath, and her pregnant belly obscures the rest of her body. Her body is not described as a vessel or cocoon but rather as a "crap banged-out car" and "just the vehicle" for her baby. The "inhuman uterine space" of the horror, which Andrew Scahill compares to the Gothic imaginary of the house that becomes haunted by "specters and ancient evils that threaten to emerge," is replaced with images of domestic horrors and secondhand motors.[33]

"I Think Nature Is a Bit of Cunt, Don't You?": Subverting "Trust in Nature" Narratives

The natural birth movement emerged in the 1930s in the United Kingdom and United States and gained momentum in the 1960s and 1970s, around the same time as the emergence of pregnancy horror film. The pregnant woman was constructed as "natural," but this alignment with the biological and the bodily was intended to "undermine her status as rational subject and social agent."[34] The natural birth movement emerged as a "reaction against both 'mass production' and increasing technological intervention in obstetrics"; women distrusted the antenatal care that was bound up with the (predominately male doctors') enthusiasm for new technological interventions and the increasing clinicization and medicalization of pregnancy and childbirth.[35] The 1970s also saw the proliferation and normalization of fetal scans and imagery that literally and scientifically pictured the fetus as Other and as a distinct entity *within* the woman. Yet in *Prevenge*, the scenes in the hospital with the midwife are quite soft, warm (caring/patronizing), and friendly, whereas the murders are clinical. As throats and groins are sliced open, the natural ambient sounds of cutting flesh and dripping and gushing blood are amplified above the synthetic nondiegetic soundtrack. Ruth's murders are, in her mind, procedures that must be enacted for the health and safety of herself and the baby, just as the medicalization of pregnancy was deemed to have standardized and depersonalized the experience and processes of pregnancy.

References to nature and the need to trust "in nature's way" underpin Ruth's first encounter with the midwife. The midwife awkwardly fumbles over her notes and asks about Ruth's partner, only to discover that she has been recently bereaved:

MIDWIFE: Oh. Oh, I'm very sorry. I didn't know. I wasn't aware.
RUTH: Well how would you know, because you don't actually know me, do you?
MIDWIFE: No.

[beat]

It's very important to let the past stay in the past. It's just nature's way.
RUTH: I think nature is a bit of cunt though, don't you?

MIDWIFE: Oh, negativity is not good for the baby's spirit.
RUTH: Do you think?
MIDWIFE: Yes, I think it's good to try to stay positive.

[beat]

> And at the end of the day, you've got this force of nature now inside you. Baby
> knows what to do. Baby will tell you what to do.
> RUTH: I think she already does.

Whereas Ruth's seemingly powerless position as a widowed woman and single-mother-to-be is explained as "nature's way," the baby's connection to nature is a powerful biological phenomenon. In contemporary medical discourses, there persists a "reverence for 'the natural'" despite the "increased medicalization of these events through ART [assisted reproductive technology] and elective C-sections."[36] Natural childbirth and the focus on "nature" is one of a "range of reproductive choices," yet its prevalence suggests that it is the only option. Throughout her pregnancy, Ruth is seemingly unable to avoid narratives of nature, as she is metaphorically and literally framed and reframed as a force of nature—and also nature's bitch.

Throughout *Prevenge*, Ruth is surrounded by nature. This is a visual device that connects the pregnant woman with nature, highlighting the traditional alignment of women with animals and the less-than-human while also highlighting the horror and unnaturalness of Ruth's individual (and murderous) response. As identified by Kelly Oliver, the connection between woman and animal is a key theme of the 1970s and 1980s pregnancy horror.[37] This theme is demonstrated in *Prevenge*'s inaugural murder sequence, when Ruth murders Mr. Zabek. Zabek compares her to a "dangerous" pregnant spider that he keeps illegally—the spider jumps at the glass that encases her, and so Zabek chooses a different spider to look at in a lower terrarium. This gives the film's own black widow her chance to strike: the slice to Zabek's neck is loud and visceral, but his spluttering death knell has to compete with the sounds of the wildlife that surrounds them.

In many of the scenes where Ruth is alone, Lowe chooses to create a frame around her(self) with leaves, grass, and hedges—again using shallow depth of field to place Ruth as the focus of the shot while the flora remains blurred at the periphery. Her interaction with DJ Dan also plays with ideas of the natural and synthetic. The sequence opens with a shot of a mounted stag's head, and both Ruth and Dan (who is dressed in a 1970s-style polyester floral shirt) throw out verbal clichés like "eggs in one basket" and "you know your onions." Dan even tells Ruth that he will "come at [her] like a dog" as he readies himself for coitus. Just prior to Dan's castrated demise, Ruth is once again framed by the natural. This time, it is a through-the-leg shot with Dan's sex-ready loins face-to-face with Ruth's less-than-impressed response. This scene is a subversion of a traditional stance that shows the empowered male gazing upon the sexualized or/and submissive woman. The natural and yet clinical approach that Ruth has toward her victims is reflected in *Prevenge*'s aesthetical and formal style. This in turn contrasts with the way Lowe chooses to show the gestation itself, as she actively avoids the trappings of traditional pregnancy horror and its spectacular portrayal of expectant female suffering.

The horrific birthing that one might expect from a film that focuses on a murderous spawn is notable in *Prevenge* by its absence; instead, Lowe's film centers on the "violence and chaos" of the drudgery of pregnancy.[38] When Ruth's water breaks, we see a tame and medically viable amount of fluid, and then we are presented with the newborn baby clean and dressed rather than bloodied and naked. Despite the clinical focus on the cutting during the murders, Lowe chooses not to focus on the cuts and rips of childbirth. This decision keeps the focus on the pregnancy and frames the murders as consequences of the trauma of gestation and the changed female mind and body.

The loose explanation of Ruth's rampage is disrupted in the final scene, where Ruth is revealed to still be compelled to kill. She goes after Tom, the man forced to cut the climbing safety cord that led to her partner Matt's death. The cutting of the cord is a literal and metaphorical motif throughout the film: the cord that Tom literally cuts that "kills" Matt, the medical cutting of the cord between the baby and the mother, and the metaphorical cut that Tom makes when he says Matt was unhappy in his relationship with Ruth, which severs her from her memories and the apparent justification for the (p)revenge killings. Murder is in her nature rather than a natural (and mentally unbalanced) consequence of the trauma of pregnancy and grief. In a retort to Tom, Ruth snaps, "I'm not grieving; I'm gestating . . . fucking rage," suggesting that her murder spree has not been simply a maternal attempt to please "baby" but possibly one born of feminist rage at the patriarchy.

The final moments of *Prevenge* suggest that Ruth is a female serial killer who has used the pregnancy as an excuse to fulfill her desire to kill. Arguably, her homicidal behavior, which has almost been sympathetically presented as a maternal response to pregnancy, is in fact her true nature, perhaps suppressed until she went through the uniquely feminine experience of gestating new life. It is a fitting close to a film that actively sets up and then subverts viewer expectations. The first two men Ruth kills are overtly creepy (Mr. Zabek and DJ Dan), and Ruth is presented as a victim or at least justified, but once she moves on to female victims (Ellie and Len), the neat confines of the audience's understanding of her motivation are undermined. Lowe has explained that this rejection of the simplistic women-versus-men brand of feminism does not mean that *Prevenge* is not intentionally feminist. For Lowe, Ruth takes revenge against society more generally because "the pressures that women have in society are from society, it's not just men. There are plenty of women supporting that system as well."[39] The ending sabotages the viewers' understanding of *Prevenge* as diegetically justified by antenatal psychosis (however unlikely in reality). Instead, it suggests that it is not the pregnant woman that audiences should be scared of but women (and their suppressed rage) more generally.

Prevenge challenges the traditional approach to gynaehorror by placing the individual woman's experience at its narrative and aesthetic center while also critiquing the ongoing cultural reduction of the pregnant woman as a medical object that needs to be monitored and managed. Rather than being a barrier to opportunity, Lowe's pregnancy gave her the impetus and inspiration needed to make her directorial feature film debut and to develop a unique response to the genre. The resulting film is a subversion of traditional narratives of pregnancy that have been critically framed as being about "patriarchal omnipotence," the "monstrous feminine," and the "excessive, violent, and threatening" nature of reproduction.[40] Instead, it is a potential site of feminist discourse, where male power is either absent (Matt) or symbolically (and literally, in DJ Dan's case) sterilized and where the pregnant woman forges her own (albeit murderous) path with and without the support of other women.

Lowe's personal and thus gendered response to her own pregnancy and the trepidation she experienced during her gestation is a Gothic, comedic, and long-awaited intervention into a horror subgenre that has been too long dominated (almost entirely) by men. The film offers visibility of the lived experience that is biologically unavailable to male directors, and her work has garnered positive responses from other women going through the same experience who appreciate the "cathartic" opportunity to see a "pregnant character in a completely different light," a "relief" in a society where women are bombarded with expectations for the expecting.[41] *Prevenge* demonstrates it is possible to do pregnancy horror without resorting to tired tropes that spectacularize and fetishize the female form and experience.

Notes

1   Alice Lowe, "Delivering Results: How Alice Lowe Wrote *Prevenge* in a Week and Shot It in 11 Days . . . While Pregnant," Moviemaker, March 24, 2017, https://www .moviemaker.com/archives/moviemaking/alice-lowe-pregnant-prevenge/.
2   Simon Bland, "Birth Pangs," *Big Issue North*, February 16, 2017, https://www .bigissuenorth.com/features/2017/02/alice-lowe-birth-pangs/.
3   Bland.
4   Lowe, "Delivering Results."
5   Natalie Wreyford, *Gender Inequality in Screenwriting Work* (Basingstoke, U.K.: Palgrave Macmillan, 2018), 111.
6   Shelley Cobb, Linda Ruth Williams, and Natalie Wreyford, *Calling the Shots: Women Directors and Cinematographers on British Films since 2003*, February 2018, https://s25407.pcdn.co/wp-content/uploads/2018/02/Calling-the-Shots-Report -Feb-2018-Women-directors-and-cinematographers.pdf.
7   Wreyford, *Gender Inequality*, 111.
8   Wreyford, 122.

9 Leung Wing-fai, Rosalind Gill, and Keith Randle, "Getting In, Getting On, Getting Out? Women as Career Scramblers in the UK Film and Television Industries," *Sociological Review* 63, no. 1 (2015): 57.

10 Doris Ruth Eikof and Chris Warhurst, "The Promised Land? Why Social Inequalities Are Systemic in the Creative Industries," *Employee Relations* 35, no. 5 (2013): 495–508.

11 See Carol J. Clover, *Men, Women, and Chain Saws: Gender in the Modern Horror Film* (Princeton, N.J.: Princeton University Press, 2015); Linda Williams, "Film Bodies: Gender, Genre, and Excess," *Film Quarterly* 44, no. 4 (Summer 1991): 2–13.

12 David A. Kirby and Amy C. Chambers, "Playing God: Religious Influences on the Depictions of Science in Mainstream Movies," in *Science, Politics and the Dilemmas of Openness: Here Be Monsters*, ed. Brigitte Nerlich, Alexander Smith, and Sujatha Raman (Manchester: Manchester University Press, 2018), 283; Susan E. Lederer, "Repellent Subjects: Hollywood Censorship and Surgical Images," *Literature and Medicine* 17 (1998): 91–113.

13 Lucy Fischer, *Cinematernity: Film, Motherhood, Genre* (Princeton, N.J.: Princeton University Press, 1996), 75.

14 Kelly Oliver, *Knock Me Up, Knock Me Down: Images of Pregnancy in Hollywood Films* (New York: Columbia University Press, 2012), 12.

15 Alice Echols, *Shaky Ground: The '60s and Its Aftershocks* (New York: Columbia University Press, 2002), 77; see also Sara M. Evans, "Sources of the Second Wave: The Rebirth of Feminism," in *Long Time Gone: Sixties America Then and Now*, ed. Alexander Bloom (Oxford: Oxford University Press, 2001), 189–208.

16 Barbara Creed, *The Monstrous-Feminine: Film, Feminism and Psychoanalysis* (London: Routledge, 1993), 43.

17 Creed, 69.

18 Erin Harrington, *Women, Monstrosity and Horror Film: Gynaehorror* (London: Routledge, 2018), 5.

19 Harrington, 3.

20 Harrington, 97.

21 William Bibbiani, "Interview: Alice Lowe, *Prevenge* and the Horrors of Pregnancy," *Mandatory*, March 28, 2017, https://www.mandatory.com/culture/1238993-interview-alice-lowe-prevenge-horrors-pregnancy.

22 Sarah Arnold, *Maternal Horror Film: Melodrama and Motherhood* (Basingstoke, U.K.: Palgrave Macmillan, 2013), 1; Oliver, *Knock Me Up*, 111.

23 Oliver, *Knock Me Up*, 111.

24 Arnold, *Maternal Horror*, 154.

25 See Lorna Jowett and Stacey Abbott, *TV Horror: Investigating the Dark Side of the Small Screen* (London: I.B. Tauris, 2012), 120.

26 Amy C. Chambers and Hannah J. Elizabeth, "It's Grimm up North: Domestic Obscenity, Assimilation Anxiety, and Medical Salvation in BBC Three's *In the Flesh*," in *Heading North: The North of England in Film and Television*, ed. Ewa Hanna Mazierska (Basingstoke, U.K.: Palgrave Macmillan, 2017), 195.

27 Chambers and Elizabeth, 195.

28 Chambers and Elizabeth, 195.

29 Bibbiani, "Interview."

30 Harriet Cooper, "Alice Lowe's *Prevenge*: A Response," *Studies in the Maternal* 9, no. 1 (2017): 2.

31 Clare Hanson, *A Cultural History of Pregnancy: Pregnancy, Medicine and Culture, 1750–2000* (Basingstoke, U.K.: Palgrave Macmillan, 2004), 149.

32 Creed, *Monstrous Feminine*, 49.

33 Andrew Scahill, "Deviled Eggs: Teratogenesis and the Gynecological Gothic in the Cinema of Monstrous Birth," in *Demons of the Body and Mind: Essays on Disability in Gothic Literature*, ed. Ruth Bienstock Anolik (Jefferson, N.C.: McFarland, 2010): 205, 207.

34 Hanson, *Cultural History*, 12.

35 Hanson, 137.

36 Candace Johnson, "The Political 'Nature' of Pregnancy and Childbirth," *Canadian Journal of Political Science* 41, no 4 (2008): 907.

37 Oliver, *Knock Me Up*, 117.

38 Oliver, 110.

39 Quoted in "In Conversation with Alice Lowe," *Another Gaze*, June 7, 2017, https://www.anothergaze.com/in-conversation-with-alice-lowe/.

40 Arnold, *Maternal Horror*, 156; Creed, *Monstrous Feminine*; Oliver, *Knock Me Up*, 118.

41 Lowe, "Delivering Results."

18

The Rise of the Female Horror Filmmaker-Fan

SONIA LUPHER

In April 2017, Erik Piepenburg of the *New York Times* interviewed a handful of female horror fans about their experience attending HorrorHound Weekend in Cincinnati, the largest horror convention in the United States.[1] While horror has historically been a "boys' club," Piepenburg writes, "devotion runs deep" for female fans; women make up a vital part of the attendance and culture of such conventions. For many horror fans, male and female alike, HorrorHound and the horror family they find there provides a kinder, more welcoming community than they find in their everyday lives. At the same time, with few exceptions, the female horror fan has remained marginalized within the horror community and appeared only sporadically in academic study.[2] In the past ten years, the dramatic increase of women turning to horror filmmaking has been documented journalistically and, more recently, in film scholarship, but the role that female fandom contributes to this surge has not been sufficiently addressed. There is plenty of evidence to show that women have been a primary audience for the horror genre throughout its history despite their marginalization in its fan cultures.[3] This chapter thereby proposes to theorize the role of female horror film fandom in the growing numbers of women directors turning to horror, contending that their films offer a concrete, textual basis for considering how female fandom looks and functions.

I would like to make it clear now that the purpose of this chapter is not to dismiss female horror filmmakers as simply (or complexly) "fans" or to label their work as akin to fan fiction, fan art, or other fan-created artifacts. Rather, this chapter aims to contextualize female horror filmmakers within the independent horror filmmaking community in order to show (1) that studies of fandom and fan communities provide a productive framework for discussing horror filmmakers as a whole and (2) that contemporary independent horror filmmakers are prone to experiment with the genre in similar ways to how fans experiment with their preferred source material. My goal in this chapter is to locate and analyze the work of select female filmmakers within these broader trends in horror production worldwide. If genre is more productively discussed in terms of cycles rather than groupings of films that serve a "traditional 'empiricist dilemma,'" then the current state of horror film production, consumption, and aesthetics must be considered within the rising prevalence of independent horror film production.[4] This subset of horror film production is traceable through established festivals such as London's FrightFest (founded in 2000) and emerging festivals such as Nightmares Film Festival (founded in 2016).

Horror film festivals emerged from and share common ground with horror and genre fan conventions; in a 2009 article, Matt Hills conflates the community and experience of attending both, though he points out that festivals are attended by "fan groups and horror genre professionals" alike.[5] In recent years, the boundary between the two groups has become less rigid. Independent genre film festivals such as Nightmares and GenreBlast (founded in 2016) have rapidly begun to serve the growing community of fans-turned-filmmakers; the discourse at such festivals encourages other fans and interested viewers to "Make Your Own Damn Movie," which was the title of a filmmaker panel at the 2018 iteration of GenreBlast.[6] Independent horror film festivals are therefore among the most visible platforms for the "horror filmmaker-fan," a filmmaker whose artistic output is heavily influenced by and stems largely from their horror film fandom. Film festivals are playing a pivotal role in the transition between fandom and practice within the horror community.

In this chapter, I will draw on interviews conducted with filmmakers at festivals in which they articulate the role of fandom in their work. This will lead me to analyze three films in detail—Aislínn Clarke's *Childer* (2016, Northern Ireland), Norma Vila's *Jules D.* (2016, Spain), and Misty Dawn's *Hooker Assassin* (2016, United States)—in order to demonstrate how female fandom can be "viewed" in their films and contend that the contemporary horror filmmaker at large functions within an intertextual, self-referential fan community. My selected texts are short films, all under twenty minutes long, a choice that reflects the dominant film form in which contemporary independent horror directors work; nearly all if not all women who turn to horror filmmaking make short films, while comparatively few make feature-length films. In some cases, this is an artistic choice, but for the most part, it is due to financial, equipment, or other restrictions.

Finally, I avoid suggesting that there is an inherent progressive "femininity" or feminism present in women's horror cinema. While I have noticed more overt discussions about feminism and issues affecting women and people with other marginalizing markers (such as race, disability, and sexuality) at women-centered horror film festivals than at other genre festivals or settings, I follow Katarzyna Paszkiewicz's lead in arguing that any apparent subversion of the horror genre in female-directed films must be considered first and foremost as natural expressions of "repetition with difference" ascribed to genre trends at large.[7] Paszkiewicz usefully articulates the terms through which female horror directors, involved in the production and circulation of genre and gender, should be seen as creators working in formulaic filmmaking in which innovation is key to advancing the formula.[8] She concludes her article by insisting, "Instead of conceptualizing these filmmakers *a priori* as feminist auteurs who transcend the industrially imposed formats, it seems more useful to draw attention to how they activate the 'generative' force of genres in order to engage with feminist politics."[9] In the introduction to their 2011 edited collection, Kristina Busse and Jonathan Gray refer to Joli Jensen when they call on fan studies "to apply its methods to the study of high-culture fans or 'aficionados.'"[10] Along these lines, I argue that the horror genre is particularly ripe terrain in which to explore the phenomenon of the filmmaker-fan with a focus on the role of women in contemporary horror. I further contend that female fandom plays a crucial role in the way female horror filmmakers activate these "'generative' forces" toward a female-focused end. In this way, many female horror filmmakers turn to the genre because they are fans and because they read horror films as legitimizing women's fears and experiences in a creative and cathartic way.

First Fans, Then Filmmakers

In her 1990s studies of British female horror fans, Brigid Cherry discovered that female viewers find "pleasure . . . in images of terror and gore and, in particular, in the body of the monster" and compared her findings to Janice Radway's discussion of romance fiction readers.[11] Cherry's subjects were more likely to gravitate toward horror films "they took to be imaginative, intelligent, literary or thought-provoking," while "[dislike] was often expressed for films that revolved around excessive or gratuitous displays of violence, gore, or other effects used to evoke revulsion in the audience."[12] Cherry found that female horror fans seek out films in which they form connections with protagonists and villains alike. As one twenty-four-year-old survey responder says, "Monster films always make me cry"; Cherry's interviewees were frequently attracted by films that inspire "empathy for the monster."[13] Ultimately, however, Cherry notes that female horror fans were isolated from one another and the then-burgeoning horror fan community at large. Their responses reveal private—often even erotic—viewing experiences and connections with the characters and monsters on the screen.

Isabel Pinedo counters the seeming incompatibility of her feminist leanings with her horror film fandom, arguing that the genre continually "allowed [her] to exercise, rather than exorcise, emotions of tremendous importance that were otherwise denied legitimate expression."[14] For these writers, the horror film's representation of its female characters can provide a way for women to enjoy genre films as metaphors for everyday female experience. As Alison Gillmor puts it, "For many women, the horror genre is profoundly cathartic: It constructs imaginary spaces where they can work through true-life trauma."[15] These all suggest that women have, in the past, been marginalized from horror film fandom and that their viewership has historically occurred privately, as a cathartic or erotic viewing experience. In recent years, the internet has served to unite female horror fans and to make their fandom more prominent online, at conventions, and elsewhere; the women's horror film festival phenomenon is a recent manifestation of female horror fans' newfound visibility.

Fandom influences women's horror filmmaking in two key ways: first, the filmmakers are fans themselves, and second, the audience heavily support it. Many—if not all—of the female directors of these horror films are fans; like many of the fans interviewed by Cherry, they were exposed to it at an early age. The viewing pleasures of watching horror and the thematic tendencies of the genre resonate with their experiences and fuel their creative visions. Aislínn Clarke recalls that she "got really into horror as a young kid"; Zena Sade Dixon (*Night of the Witch*, 2017) names her mother as a key influence for her love of horror.[16] Prano Bailey-Bond (*Nasty*, 2015) remembers being deeply frightened by one figure in particular: "The first thing that [truly] scared me was the backwards-talking dwarf in *Twin Peaks*. I must have been about seven years old."[17] Caitlin Koller (*Blood Sisters*, 2017) was afraid of horror films as a child but became a voracious fan in her adolescence, in part to help herself overcome the fear, recalling that "it worked, effectively. I think the movies that really helped were slasher movies—I really loved *Nightmare on Elm Street*, and *Halloween* appealed to me especially with a female heroine."[18] Many filmmakers specify the particular aspects of horror that drew them growing up, such as female heroines and complex genre blending, and they actively foreground these aspects in their own work.

The ready-made horror production and fan community is a practical draw for many female horror filmmakers. England Simpson (*Prelude: A Love Story*, 2017) and Mattie Do (*Dearest Sister*, 2016) both isolate the fan community as vital to their decision to work in genre. Simpson says, "You can have a very successful career as a filmmaker just doing horror . . . we have conventions, we have film festivals targeted specifically for this genre."[19] She notes that few other genres have a prominent film festival or convention scene as the horror, science fiction, and fantasy genres, adding, "Horror is the only genre where you can grab your phone, [film something in a weekend,] and find an audience for it the next day." Mattie Do (among the few active female horror directors whose career began with a feature-length film) describes her experience at Fantastic Fest as overwhelmingly positive: "People would go see every kind of film, films that I can barely categorize . . . and they were just so nice, and so respectful. . . . People aren't all that receptive to subtitled films in general. But horror people are! Horror people will watch anything, as long as it's interesting and brings something new to the table."[20] Although Do acknowledges that *Dearest Sister* received positive feedback at other film festivals as well, she felt alienated by the cinephilia pervading nonhorror festivals.

Most female horror filmmakers therefore cite their own fandom as key to their decision to start making films but acknowledge that the audience they find for their work motivates them to remain in the genre. Furthermore, because they are so knowledgeable—the cinematic influences they name include George Romero, David Cronenberg, David Lynch, and Alice Lowe (discussed in chapter 17 by Amy C. Chambers)—their films generally function as a reference to the horror genre as a whole—its various tropes, narratives, and aesthetic tendencies. Coincidentally, all three filmmakers discussed in detail later named Brian De Palma as an influence. Bailey-Bond describes her short *Nasty* as "a love-letter to horror [and] the bonds that we form through films, as well as a tongue-in-cheek look at the fears surrounding VHS horror in the early 80s. . . . I wanted to satirize the idea that Video Nasties were going to turn us all into monsters."[21] Bailey-Bond's intentions with *Nasty* are traceable in many other female-directed horror shorts and features: an affection for and familiarity with genre tropes alongside a broader message or theme, whether relating to women, media, or society at large. Many female-directed horror films exercise familiar horror codes and conventions, while the content of their films elaborate or focus on the specific aspects of the genre that appeal most to individual filmmakers. As Amelia Moses (*Undress Me*, 2017) puts it, "There's a sense of reclaiming the tropes and narratives that are problematic."[22] Moses's statement recalls Cherry's finding that female horror fans pick and choose tropes and narratives of horror cinema; rather than accepting the problematic aspects, they ignore them and focus on the positive. In the following sections, I will analyze three short films in order to foreground how they approach this.

Aislínn Clarke's *Childer*

Aislínn Clarke, who was raised in a working-class Irish family, completed and released her first feature-length film, *The Devil's Doorway*, in 2018. Her short film *Childer* preceded *The Devil's Doorway* by roughly a year; as Clarke explains, it "was developed with Northern Ireland Screen, via the NI Screen/ BFI Shorts to Features scheme . . . [which] allowed me to develop some of the aesthetic qualities of what that would be via a short."[23] *Childer*, therefore, was funded with the express intention of leading Clarke to direct her first feature. The short follows a mother, Mary, and her young son, Mark, who live alone in a rural cottage on the border of a forest. Mary is extremely fastidious and tidy; the perimeter of her property is clearly marked by the contrast between her manicured lawn and the unruly weeds leading to the forest. The interior of their home is bare and clean. In one scene, she even vacuums the backyard grass. Mary perceives that her home is under threat by untidy "childer"—"a colloquial Irish word for children . . . [who] are badly [behaved] or threatening in some way"—who loiter on the borders of her lawn.[24] Mark, alone and stifled by his mother's extreme cleanliness, is intrigued by the prospect of having play-mates his age.

On Halloween, Mary fashions Mark a ghost costume out of a white sheet (despite his preference to go as "a fireman, or a superhero, or a knight, or a sol-dier. Or at least a dinosaur!") and releases him to play in the yard; he runs off with the "childer" whose presence has been tormenting Mary. When he returns scuffed up and filthy, Mary puts him in the bathtub and anxiously scolds him, demanding, "Didn't I tell you not to play with those children? Didn't I tell you not to play with those childer?" She falters as she utters the final word, then abruptly pushes his head beneath the water, drowning him. Crucially, the cam-era pulls away from the scene and retreats shakily backward down the stairs to reveal a ceramic bowl filled with water and apples, presumably a Halloween treat that Mary had prepared for Mark. On the soundtrack, an erratic piano tune accompanies the sounds of splashing and Mary's strangled sobs. After-ward, Mary buries Mark in the backyard cabbage patch, along with his little green tetherball. Then she bathes, puts on a red dress, and carefully brushes her hair in front of the mirror. A thud at the back door leads her to descend and investigate, where she finds the grimy, exhumed tetherball on the porch. The last scene of the film shows the cottage and Mary in a long shot, presumably from the point of view of one of the wild children, the top of the frame shrouded by branches and leaves. On the soundtrack, a child's laugh is heard.

In an interview with *Morbidly Beautiful*, Clarke names a handful of films that were instrumental in concretizing her horror film fandom, including *Rosemary's Baby* (1968), *Nightmare on Elm Street* (1984), and *The Exorcist* (1973).[25] Else-where, she names *Carrie* (1976) as an aesthetic influence for *Childer*. Notably, these are all films with a central mother-child relationship; the latter three, fur-thermore, feature a daughter and single mother. Clarke is drawn to the idea that a mother is expected to be self-sacrificing, selfless, and wholly in service of her child(ren) and seen as a "terrible person" if she falls short. The popular depiction of mothers seen in binary terms, as either good or evil, is particularly reflected in *Rosemary's Baby* and *Carrie*. In *Rosemary's Baby*, Rosemary is eager to become a mother; at the film's close, she accepts her role as the mother of the devil's child, not necessarily rejecting but at least putting aside her Catholic faith in order to assume her maternal duties. Throughout the film, furthermore, she withstands excruciating pain and illness in order to carry the child safely to term. Her concern for the child is paramount, despite the severity of her own discomfort. In *Carrie*, the eponymous heroine's mother, Margaret, more closely reflects Mary: she is forced to live with Carrie, the daughter who reminds Margaret of her vulnerability to nature (and human nature) in the sole breach of marital chastity that she and Carrie's father committed and that resulted in Carrie's conception. Unlike Rosemary, Margaret cannot reconcile her religious beliefs with her maternal duties, and she ultimately attempts to murder Carrie. In certain ways, then, Mary can be seen as the conflation of Rosemary and Margaret; she loves and cares for Mark, but she ultimately cannot stand what he represents. *Childer* also looks back to these films through Clarke's refusal to make it identifiable within a particular time period. Further complicating the film's temporal and realistic grounding, it remains ambiguous whether the wild children are real, ghosts, or figments of her and Mark's imaginations. They appear soundlessly and leave their mark in mysterious ways. In one scene, one of the girls holds a frog while one of her male companions somberly informs Mary that "my sister kissed a frog once, but she's dead now." Although the children are never seen traversing the boundary from the unruly weeds into Mary's manicured lawn, Mary finds a crushed frog between her bedsheets shortly thereafter, suggesting that the children have been there; they therefore function as potentially otherworldly beings that can cross boundaries undetected.

While *Childer* reflects elements of these films, Clarke explicitly brings her own experiences to her work and cites the difficult birth of her son as a frequent thematic cue. Clarke was particularly eager to explore Mary's complex character, a mother who likely did not want to be a mother and whose child affirms and triggers Mary's fear of filth and of nature in its entirety. Clarke is interested in human beings' desire to be "cognizant, logical, [and] rational," which seems at odds with and "inextricable from our organic mess, from nature, from our blood and guts, from dirt."[26] Mary's desire to be clean cannot be fulfilled, because nature seeps in—between her bedsheets, on her floor, and even in her bathtub drain. Being a mother herself, Clarke finds it particularly important to render Mary sympathetic, even as she commits infanticide. She takes recourse from true crime reports of similar crimes, noting that women who kill their children tend to deeply regret their crime; these crimes are often due to momentary lapses of reason in an otherwise ordinary life. Clarke notes that other characters are often rendered as complex, "whereas mothers [are seen as] very binary." She therefore created Mary as "fully human, but also a mother." To Mary, Mark is a symbol of nature's violation against her. He is "an extension of her being, but he is not hers to control, just as we are all part of Nature, but separate from it and from each other. He is a constant reminder that she lost control of her body in his conception, in her pregnancy, and through his whole young life."[27] Importantly, there is no mention of Mark's father; the only adult male character is the postman, whose innocent intrusions into Mary's life motivate her to further isolate her home environment.

Norma Vila's *Jules D.*

In *Jules D.*, the titular school-aged boy (played androgynously by Lucía Pollán and voiced by Izan Maillo) yearns to become a vampire like his hero, Dracula. The film opens ominously, during a storm, with lightning revealing a barbed-wire fence and a forbidding, castle-like structure, and offers in voice-over (delivered by Jordi Brau) an account of the legendary birth of the film's eponymous hero: "He is said to have come into the world with teeth, and he drank blood from his mother's breast." The image cuts to an overhead shot of a pale-skinned, black-haired young boy, clad in a red-and-black cape and staring upside-down at the camera, with a bat clinging to his neck. As the camera zooms into Jules's face, ending with a close-up on his eyes, the narrator continues, "Some said that he spent nights staring at the full moon with his enormous black eyes. That's what they said about Jules." The film cuts to Jules, presumably earlier, sitting in a movie theater seat, as the narrator adds, "But actually, it is safe to say that Jules really saw the light that day at an old cinema." The film cultivates a fantastical tone from the beginning, establishing Jules's "origin story" by suggesting that he—a peculiar child with piercing black eyes and a pale face—was introduced to what would become his obsession, Dracula, in a movie theater; the story of Jules's "birth," therefore, is related as a cinephilic moment in which Jules sees himself in the figure of Dracula. The remainder of the film follows Jules as he voraciously reads Bram Stoker's *Dracula* (pointedly adding the *D.* to his name), is expelled from school for biting his teacher (and expressing his desire "to suck girls' blood"), befriends a vampire bat at his local zoo, and finally releases the bat and allows it to bite him in the neck. There follows a lengthy black-and-white sequence in which Jules lies in a grimy puddle of filth and his own blood; the film suggests here that his imagination has run too far and that he might die a tragic death. But then a shadowy figure appears and extends a hand with long, curved fingernails to Jules, hissing, "My son." Presumably, Jules then joins his undead hero and fulfills his vampiric fantasies.

Like *Childer*, *Jules D.* stands outside of time in many ways—Jules is a child, and although he has his own bedroom, his parents are never seen. In school, his teacher is only revealed in fragments—high-heeled feet, red fingernails tapping impatiently, a lock of out-of-focus brown hair—and his classmates only appear in shadow. He goes to school in a modern-day classroom with linoleum floors and electric lights, but his classroom is decorated with taxidermy animals and lit with eerie, greenish lighting that obscures the other children in the class. The film's cinematography and production design are striking, with vibrant color contrasts and period costumes. Jules seems attracted to the vampire in erotic terms, as he expresses through poetry his desire to suck girls' blood and let "stolen blood flow in his veins." In a *Filmlab* interview, Vila comments on seeing the Universal monster movies decades after their release: "The sensation I had was deliciously paradoxical, those monsters provoked in me what could be called a harrowing tenderness, the passing of time had transformed what was terrifying in its day to something that, without ceasing to be macabre, today can be understood as endearing. Today, when you see Tod Browning's *Dracula* or James Whale's *Frankenstein* you don't know whether, when faced by the monster, to run or give it a hug."[28] Like Clarke, Vila is drawn to the Gothic—its tonal and aesthetic dissonance, the lure of eroticism and affection with monstrosity, and above all, the influence of horror cinephilia and fandom on an innocent and impressionable child who empathizes more with monsters than with his classmates.

Vila cites years of viewing Tod Browning, James Whale, and Jacques Tourneur and reading Edgar Allan Poe as instrumental to her cinematic career; these influences are clear in *Jules D.* She consciously looks back to the monsters of classic horror cinema, saying, "*Jules D.* is a work born from passion and love of cinema, above all love of classic horror cinema, of the Universal monsters, whom I believe are the fathers of horror. *Jules D.* is my small homage."[29] As I noted earlier, *Jules D.* reflects the cinephilic moment equivalent of a horror fan's birth, in which Jules becomes obsessed with the figure of Dracula through its film adaptation and Bela Lugosi's portrayal of him (crucially, Lugosi goes unmentioned in the short—Dracula is, to Jules, the true "star"). In turn, Jules's viewing of *Dracula* leads him to devour Bram Stoker's novel and to infuse his entire young life with the obsession sparked by viewing the film. Jules fabricates his vampiric persona after watching the film, and he is led to cultivate his own particular brand of fandom after seeing the film; the book functions as an extratextual fan-building reference to Jules. He adds the *D.* to his name as an extension of his own identity that can accommodate his fandom. Jules even appropriates the persona of Dracula into his own creative outlet—the poem he reads to the class in which he expresses his near-erotic attraction to the idea of drinking blood. *Jules D.* is in dialogue with classic horror cinema, Vila focusing primarily on the erotic draw of the horror film monster to her young, androgynous protagonist.

Misty Dawn's *Hooker Assassin*

While Clarke's and Vila's films flirt with aspects of the Gothic horror tradition, Misty Dawn's *Hooker Assassin* fits squarely within a very different subgenre: the rape-revenge film. The plot is simple, but Dawn's use of split screen (reminiscent of De Palma) introduces her protagonist Jessi and her double life in striking visual comparisons: attentive mother by day, streetwalker by night. The film follows one day—very likely the worst day—in Jessi's life: after she leaves her daughter at home with a babysitter, she is picked up by a john who knocks her out, rapes her while she is unconscious, and ties her up with the intention to murder her. After a lengthy dialogue between the two of them in which he implies that he kidnapped her daughter, she manages to fight her way out in her bloodstained white dress, slicing his throat with her earring and castrating him with her bare hands. She then runs home barefoot to confirm that her daughter is missing. The film ends with Jessi pulling a baseball bat peppered with haphazardly inserted nails around the cap out of a flowerpot and looking determinedly into the camera. *Hooker Assassin* appears, in certain ways, to be a teaser for a feature-length film in which Jessi goes on a rampage to rescue her daughter and exact revenge on her attacker or other men who get in her way.

Rape-revenge films continually provoke contention among critics and scholars who struggle to come to terms with its apparent contradiction: that the depiction of brutal sexual violence against women appears alongside the justified—in many cases equally savage—depiction of violence they subsequently inflict against men. In the early nineties, Carol J. Clover famously argued that rape-revenge films frequently align the camera's gaze with the female under attack, thereby stripping the sexual violence of anything resembling visual pleasure.[30] More recently, Cate Young pointed out the glaring problem that "most [rape-revenge films] linger on the initial assault, dragging it out as a form of entertainment."[31] Anne Billson suggests, in contrast, that the rape-revenge film can offer a cathartic viewing experience for women in particular who feel disempowered by sexual violence or harassment in their own lives, asking, "What's wrong with a little fantasy wish fulfillment?"[32] In a December 2015 piece for *Medium*, Noah Berlatsky cites a conversation with horror scholar Alexandra Heller-Nicholas in which she suggested that women are (as with horror at large) among the subgenre's most voracious viewers.[33] There is even contention whether rape-revenge is a horror subgenre at all; Jacinda Read, for instance, labels it "not a genre but a narrative structure, which has been mapped over other genres."[34] The "rape-revenge" canon under the umbrella of horror is a problematic concept to Read because of its placement alongside other films that privilege male patterns of pleasurable looking.

Dawn remembers seeing the classic rape-revenge film *I Spit on Your Grave* (1978) as a teenager, falling in love with the heroine's progression into a strong, violent woman who takes matters into her own hands. *Hooker Assassin* fits squarely in this tradition, but it stands apart from key rape-revenge films in two crucial ways. First, it bypasses Young's grievance with "lingering" on the assault by not showing it at all; the film stubbornly maintains subjective alignment with Jessi, who is unconscious during the rape—her attacker tells her about it afterward. Dawn confirms her intention to lead viewers to empathize with Jessi without exhibiting, as she puts it, "that level of extreme suffering."[35] Second, the film thwarts the tendency, in many rape-revenge narratives, to depict the protagonist as enduringly innocent and nonsexual; often, they attempt to obstruct any victim-blaming impulse on the part of the audience, showcasing protagonists who keep to themselves and do not seek out attention, sexual or otherwise

(Thana in *Ms .45* [1981] is mute and painfully shy, while the novelist Jennifer in *I Spit on Your Grave* is expressly seeking solitude in a rural cabin, and although she does wear revealing clothing, it is clear that she does not expect to interact with anyone). Jessi, on the other hand, is overtly seeking men: it is her job to do so. She wears tight-fitting, revealing clothing; she walks the streets alone at night; she is, explicitly, looking for sex, or, rather, selling it. Dawn's decision to center a rape-revenge narrative on a sex worker revises the "she wasn't asking for it" impulse of her cinematic predecessors into an issue of consent and body ownership. Even if Jessi's living depends on sex work, her violent retaliation against sexual assault is no less justified than Thana's or Jennifer's. Dawn's personal friendships with sex workers inspired her to make a film in which a prostitute is not simply defined by her work but could correct societal misconceptions about women in the sex industry and depict them as the "headstrong and determined women" Dawn knows.[36] In turn, the film's political stance refuses to apologize for—or demonize—Jessi's line of work, violently discouraging viewers from defining her only through her sexualized body.

Apart from De Palma, whom she names as a stylistic reference, Dawn mentions Quentin Tarantino and Robert Rodríguez among her cinematic influences for *Hooker Assassin*, both of whom are directors who, despite their popularity, are frequently criticized by feminists. Among the tendencies of postfeminism, Sarah Banet-Weiser describes "a renewed focus on a woman's body as a site of liberation"; at the same time, she notes that postfeminist culture disavows feminism altogether, ignoring or denying "the vulnerability of women in a sexist context."[37] While Tarantino's or Rodríguez's films (particularly their joint 2007 project *Grindhouse*) arguably reflect a postfeminist position—obliterating threats against women through graphic violence rather than addressing them in any meaningful way—Dawn does not align her film with postfeminism, nor does she overtly engage with feminism. *Hooker Assassin* is not a sex-positive film, and it does not glamorize Jessi's occupation as a method of achieving sexual or feminist liberation: in the opening scene, Dawn's camera lingers on Jessi's legs, which are streaked with bruises, scratches, and other physical markers that exhibit the harsh nature of her work. Dawn is invested in sculpting a strong female character, but she finds it equally important to ensure that Jessi's sex work is not the source of her strength. Rather, she must be strong and capable of defending herself in order to work in the sex industry to begin with.

Conclusion

The horror genre is home to many of the most self-referential and homage-ridden films and filmmakers working currently. In some ways, the horror filmmaker functions as a fresh iteration of what Daniel Herbert calls a "video store auteur," a director whose intertextual and referential films serve as movie "recommendations" akin to the erstwhile video-store-clerk recommendations section.[38] In other ways, horror films can be seen as functioning along the same lines as media fandom, where fan-authored texts "[offer] traces of the particular affective engagement and the personalized engagement with the text."[39] For female horror filmmakers, this "personalized engagement" emerges through their stylistic and narrative content, which both recalls and in certain ways restructures aspects of earlier films, thereby specifically highlighting what female fans-turned-filmmakers find most compelling in and crucial to the genre. This mirrors Henry Jenkins's definition of "appropriation and transformation," or "the process of borrowing and reworking cultural materials as resources for the creation of new works."[40] In this case, appropriation and transformation provide insight into how female fans engage with the genre.

In a 2017 article, Matt Hills calls on scholars to "approach contemporary fandom not as a singular or coherent 'culture' . . . but rather as a network of networks, or a loose affiliation of sub-subcultures, all specializing in different modes of fan activity."[41] Here, my focus has been on women's horror shorts, which belong to a broader independent horror filmmaking scene, which in turn is inseparable from the horror fan community on a global scale. The "fan activity" they produce is not always recognizable as such, but observing connections to earlier films reveals the fandom of their makers. As Francesca Coppa puts it, "[Being] in fandom can change a person, who in taking on the identity of 'fan' may also come to take on additional identities—that of a writer, blogger, filmmakers, organizer, activist, etc.—that impact her sense of self and the way she engages the world."[42] Female horror filmmakers frequently express their growing attachment to the horror fan community, in particular the subsection of female-driven horror film festivals and communities. Furthermore, it is striking to see connections between *Childer, Jules D., Hooker Assassin*, and Cherry's discussion of female horror fans in Britain, in particular their fascination and empathy for monstrous figures and strong female characters. Like Cherry's subjects, female filmmakers turn to horror because of its potential for complex emotional or intellectual engagement and ability to blend genres. As Misty Dawn says, "I love a comedy, I love a good drama, sure, I love to cry, but if I can get all of that *and* blood . . ."[43] Cherry's viewers expressed a tendency to ignore certain aspects of horror films "that contradicted their reading of the heroine as strong and independent."[44] Fifteen years later, filmmakers like Clarke, Vila, and Dawn demonstrate that women's turn to horror filmmaking allows female fans-turned-filmmakers to adapt and revise horror film codes and conventions to better fit their readings of the genre.

Notes

1   Erik Piepenburg, "A Sisterhood of Scares," *New York Times*, April 5, 2017, https://www.nytimes.com/2017/04/13/movies/female-horror-movie-fans-horror-hound.html.

2 See Brigid Cherry, "Refusing to Refuse to Look: Female Viewers of the Horror Film," in *Horror, the Film Reader*, ed. Mark Jancovich (London: Routledge, 2002), 169–178; Brigid Cherry, "Screaming for Release: Femininity and Horror Film Fandom in Britain," in *British Horror Cinema*, ed. Steve Chibnall and Julian Petley (London: Routledge, 2002), 42–57; Brigid Cherry, "Stalking the Web: Celebration, Chat and Horror Film Marketing on the Internet," in *Horror Zone: The Cultural Experience of Contemporary Horror Cinema*, ed. Ian Conrich (London: I.B. Tauris, 2010), 67–85; Amy Jane Vasper, "Film, Fear and the Female: An Empirical Study of the Female Horror Fan," *Offscreen* 18, nos. 6–7 (2014), https://offscreen.com/view/film-fear-and-the-female.

3 See Rhona J. Berenstein, *Attack of the Leading Ladies: Gender, Sexuality, and Spectatorship in Classic Horror Cinema* (New York: Columbia University Press, 1996); Brigid Cherry, *Horror* (London: Routledge, 2009).

4 Mark Jancovich, "'A Real Shocker': Authenticity, Genre and the Struggle for Distinction," *Continuum: Journal of Media and Cultural Studies* 14, no. 1 (2000): 23.

5 Matt Hills, "Attending Horror Film Festivals and Conventions: Liveness, Subcultural Capital and 'Flesh-and-Blood Genre Communities,'" in Conrich, *Horror Zone*, 91.

6 Lloyd Kaufman, *Make Your Own Damn Movie! Secrets of a Renegade Director* (Los Angeles: L.A. Weekly Books, 2003).

7 Katarzyna Paszkiewicz, "When the Woman Directs (a Horror Film)," in *Women Do Genre in Film and Television*, ed. Mary Harrod and Katarzyna Paszkiewicz (London: Routledge, 2017), 50.

8 Jane Gaines, "The Genius of Genre and the Ingenuity of Women," in *Gender Meets Genre in Postwar Cinemas*, ed. Christine Gledhill (Champaign: University of Illinois Press, 2012), 16–28.

9 Paszkiewicz, "When the Woman Directs," 54.

10 Joli Jensen, "Fandom as Pathology: The Consequences of Characterization," in *The Adoring Audience*, ed. Lisa A. Lewis (New York: Routledge, 1992), 9–29; Kristina Busse and Jonathan Gray, "Fan Cultures and Fan Communities," in *The Handbook of Media Audiences*, ed. Virginia Nightingale (Oxford: Wiley-Blackwell, 2011), 439.

11 Cherry, "Refusing to Refuse to Look," 176; Janice Radway, *Reading the Romance: Women, Patriarchy, and Popular Literature* (Chapel Hill: University of North Carolina Press, 1991).

12 Cherry, "Refusing to Refuse to Look," 172.

13 Cherry, 174.

14 Isabel Pinedo, *Recreational Terror: Women and the Pleasures of Horror Film Viewing* (Albany: State University of New York Press, 1997), 2.

15 Alison Gillmor, "Feminist Horror: Plotting against Patriarchy," *Herizons*, Summer 2015, 21.

16 Aislínn Clarke, interview with author, September 24, 2017; Zena Sade Dixon, interview with author, December 14, 2017.

17 Prano Bailey-Bond, email with author, October 19, 2017.

18 Caitlin Koller, interview with author, March 17, 2018.

19 England Simpson, interview with author, November 17, 2017.

20 Mattie Do, interview with author, June 13, 2018.

21 Prano Bailey-Bond, email with author, October 19, 2017.

22 Amelia Moses, email with author, October 26, 2017.

23 Francis Quettier and Dora Tennant, "Women CineMakers Meets Aislínn Clarke," *Women CineMakers* 8 (2016): 107.

24 Quettier and Tennant, 107.

25 "Deadly Beauty: Aislínn Clarke," Morbidly Beautiful, February 2018, https://
    morbidlybeautiful.com/deadly-beauty-aislinn-clarke/.
26 Quettier and Tennant, "Women CineMakers," 120.
27 Quettier and Tennant, 113.
28 "Project of the Week: *Jules D.*," Filmlab, November 21, 2016, http://filmlab
    .filmarkethub.com/project-week-jules-d/ (author translation).
29 Norma Vila, email with author, November 16, 2017 (author translation).
30 Carol Clover, *Men, Women, and Chain Saws: Gender in the Modern Horror Film*
    (Princeton, N.J.: Princeton University Press, 1992).
31 Cate Young, "Sadistic Storytellers: Unpacking the Exploitative Violence of Rape-
    Revenge Films," *Bitch Media*, April 24, 2018, https://www.bitchmedia.org/article/
    pixelated/unpacking-the-exploitative-violence-of-rape-revenge-films.
32 Anne Billson, "How the 'Rape-Revenge Movie' Became a Feminist Weapon for
    the #MeToo Generation," *Guardian*, May 11, 2018, https://www.theguardian.com/
    film/2018/may/11/how-the-rape-revenge-movie-became-a-feminist-weapon-for-the
    -metoo-generation.
33 Noah Berlatsky, "The Rape/Revenge Genre's Gender Revelations," *Medium*, Decem-
    ber 29, 2015, https://medium.com/the-establishment/the-rape-revenge-genres
    -gender-revelations-4782a12876b0.
34 Jacinda Read, *The New Avengers: Feminism, Femininity, and the Rape-Revenge Cycle*
    (Manchester: Manchester University Press, 2000), 25.
35 Misty Dawn, email with author, February 24, 2019.
36 Dawn, email with author.
37 Sarah Banet-Weiser, "Postfeminism and Popular Feminism," *Feminist Media Histo-
    ries* 4, no. 2 (2018): 153–154.
38 Daniel Herbert, "Auteurs at the Video Store," in *A Companion to Media Authorship*,
    ed. Jonathan Gray and Derek Johnson (Oxford: Wiley-Blackwell, 2013), 497.
39 Busse and Gray, "Fan Cultures," 435.
40 Henry Jenkins, "The Poachers and the Stormtroopers: Cultural Convergence in the
    Digital Age," in *Les cultes médiatiques: Culture fan et oeuvres cultes*, ed. Philippe Le
    Guern (Rennes, France: Presses Universitaires de Rennes, 2002), 349.
41 Matt Hills, "From Fan Culture/Community to the Fan World: Possible Pathways
    and Ways of Having Done Fandom," *Palabra Clave* 20, no. 4 (2017): 860.
42 Francesca Coppa, "Fuck Yeah, Fandom Is Beautiful," *Journal of Fandom Studies* 2,
    no. 1 (2014): 78.
43 Misty Dawn, interview with author, November 18, 2017.
44 Cherry, "Refusing to Refuse to Look," 172.

Acknowledgments

To Alicia, Alex, Martha, Katia, Tosha, Dahlia, Laura, Kata, Maddi, Molly, Donna, Erin, Lindsey, Valeria, Janice, Amy, and Sonia, thank you for being such a smart, reliable, and well-informed group of contributors. I've learned so much about women and filmmaking from working with you all. Thank you to my editor, Nicole Solano, for commissioning this book, editorial assistant Maggie Tibbitt for supporting its development, Elvis Ramirez and Alissa Zarro for guiding it through production, Daniel Constantino for his excellent copyediting, and Harriet Mathie for preparing the index.

And to those other important people without whom I couldn't have written this book, I say thank you: To Jamie Sexton for your *deep* film knowledge, kindness, and constant support. You are appreciated. To Russ Hunter for getting me out to the Kurja Polt film festival in Slovenia to talk about women horror filmmakers and for being the festival daddy. To Maša Peče at Kurja Polt and Markus Keuschnigg at the /slash Filmfestival in Vienna for being total pleasures to work with. To Annette Kuhn for all the years of film discussion across your dining table in Giggleswick. To Helen Kim for your speedy translations, sarcasm, and always excellent company. To Amy Holdsworth for your wisdom and for instigating our sofa-bound pizza and horror film nights. To Beth Johnson, my fiercest supporter, thank you for always being my girl.

And to Paul, thank you for holding our world together while I finished this book.

Notes on Contributors

DR. AMY C. CHAMBERS is senior lecturer in film and media studies at Manchester School of Art, Manchester Metropolitan University, United Kingdom. Her research examines the intersection of science and entertainment media with specific focus on women and science and discourses surrounding science and religion on screen. Her current book project, *From Star Child to Star Wars: American Science (Fiction), Film, and Religion 1967–1977*, explores how leaders and members of U.S. religious institutions have interpreted and understood science in Hollywood movies in the immediate postcensorship era. She is also developing a major activist/research project exploring the representation and projected futures of women and minority groups within scientific cultures and imagined futures in science fiction since 2000.

DR. LINDSEY DECKER is master lecturer in the Department of Film and Television at Boston University, researching the relationship between transnational horror and film culture. She has articles in the journals *Transnational Cinemas* and *Horror Studies* and coauthored the "Film and Horror" entry in the *Oxford Research Encyclopedia of Communication* with Dr. Kendall R. Phillips. Her book, *Transnationalism and Genre Hybridity in New British Horror Cinema*, is forthcoming from the University of Wales Press.

DR. ERIN HARRINGTON has a PhD in cultural studies and is lecturer in critical and cultural theory in the English Department at the University of Canterbury / Te Whare Wānanga o Waitaha, Aotearoa New Zealand. Her work focuses on horror, popular and visual culture, theater, and gender and sexuality. She is the author of *Women, Monstrosity and Horror Film: Gynaehorror* (2017) and has contributed to the collections *Death and Dying in New Zealand* (2018) and *The Many Lives of* The Evil Dead (2019). She is a regular panelist and host on the podcast *The Nerd Degree* and has appeared on Radio New Zealand National, RadioLIVE, TV3's *Story*, and BBC5 and at events hosted by WORD Writers and Readers Festival, City Gallery Wellington, and the Stranger With My Face International Film Festival.

DR. ALEXANDRA HELLER-NICHOLAS is an award-winning Australian film critic who has written books on *Suspiria* (2015), *Ms .45* (2017), and *The Hitcher* (2018), as well as *Rape-Revenge Films* (2011), *Found Footage Horror Films* (2014), and her 2019 Bram Stoker Award–nominated *Masks in Horror Cinema: Eyes without Faces*. She has coedited collections, including *Cattet & Forzani* (2018), *ReFocus: The Films of Elaine May* (2019), and *Wonderland*, the exhibition catalog for a 2018 Australian Centre for the Moving Image exhibition. Alexandra is a programmer at Fantastic Fest in Austin, Texas; a board member of the Miskatonic Institute of Horror Studies; and a member of both the Alliance of Women Film Journalists and the Australian Academy of Cinema and Television Arts. She holds a PhD in screen studies from the University of Melbourne and is an adjunct professor at Deakin University.

KATIA HOUDE is a PhD student in Cinema and Media Studies at York University in Toronto, Canada. Her research interests include women experimental filmmakers, trauma studies, affect theory, art therapy, and gender politics. Her doctoral research focuses on personal trauma, memory, and its onscreen representations. Katia is a filmmaker and artist whose work has been shown in the United States, Canada, Mexico, Peru, and Spain. Katia has worked for several years at the Toronto International Film Festival and at the National Film Board of Canada.

DR. MOLLY KIM is a film scholar specializing in the history of 1970s–1980s Korean cinema and particularly of film censorship and genre. She is currently teaching early film history and Korean cinematic auteurs at the University of Suwon, Korea. Molly's published articles include "Korean Film Censorship Policy during Park Chung Hee's Military Regime (1960–1979)," "Wedding Eroticism and Horror: The Rise of Erotic Horror Films in the Period of Yushin Regime," and "The Paradoxes of Lois Weber's *Where Are My Children* (1916): Representation of the Eugenics and Birth Control Movement in Early American Cinema." She also works as a film critic contributing a weekly column titled "Erotic Cinema" for *Munhwa Ilbo* and is a programmer for the International Martial Arts and Action Film Festival and Resistance Film Festival in Korea.

DR. ALICIA KOZMA is assistant professor of communication and media studies and the chair of the Communication and Media Studies program at Washington College. Research projects include the intersection of gender and labor in the entertainment industries through a case study of Stephanie Rothman, the role

of gendered labor in the neoart house industry, and an industrial-level investigation into the cultural and economic impact of digital cinema technologies
on contemporary U.S. exhibition practices, their intersections with emerging
media platforms, and the changes they foster across transnational distribution
networks. Her work has been published in several anthologies; in the journals
Television & New Media, *Camera Obscura*, *The Projector*, and *Film Comment*;
and digitally in *Bright Lights Film Journal* and *In Media Res*. She is the series
editor of *New Histories of Women in Entertainment*.

DR. JANICE LORECK is a lecturer in the School of Media, Creative Arts and Social
Inquiry at Curtin University, Australia. Her research focuses on gender and violence in twenty-first-century screen culture. She is the author of *Violent Women
in Contemporary Cinema* (2016) and festival coordinator for the Melbourne
Women in Film Festival. She also works as a film critic for print and radio. Her
forthcoming research considers the female provocateur in global art cinema.

SONIA LUPHER is a doctoral candidate in film and media studies at the University
of Pittsburgh, where she is writing a dissertation on the ties between women's
cinema, women's genres, and women's horror filmmaking. She is the founder/
editor of Cut-Throat Women: A Database of Women Who Make Horror (www
.cutthroatwomen.org), a project that aims to shed light on the role of women
working in horror film production. Her article on Ben Wheatley's *Kill List*
(2011) appeared in *Critical Quarterly*, and she has written for *Jump Cut* and
Ecrans. In 2019, she guest-edited a special issue of *Studies in the Fantastic*. She
has contributed interviews and criticism to *Bitch Flicks*, *Graveyard Shift Sisters*,
and *Grim Magazine*, and she has served as a judge for the Women in Horror
Film Festival since 2017.

MADDI MCGILLVRAY is a third-year PhD student in cinema and media studies at
York University, Canada, where she is completing her doctoral dissertation on
contemporary female horror directors. Her other research interests include
feminist film theory, transmedia studies, and exploitation cinema. She recently
published "To Grandmother's House We Go: Documenting the Aging Female
Body in Found Footage Horror Films" in *Elder Horror: Essays on Film's Frightening Images of Aging* (2019). She is also the editorial assistant for *Rue Morgue*,
the world's leading horror in culture and entertainment magazine.

DR. DONNA MCRAE is a Melbourne-based filmmaker and senior lecturer in screen
and design at Deakin University, Australia. Donna's first microbudget feature,
Johnny Ghost (2012), was screened at the Stranger With My Face Film Festival
and then won seven awards and two special jury prizes at numerous other festivals. Her second microbudget supernatural feature, *Lost Gully Road* (2017),
won best feature at three International Film Festivals and has international

distribution. Her feature documentary, *Cobby: The Other Side of Cute*, is currently on the festival circuit. She is in development with the Acme Film Company on her next project, *Kate Kelly*, a "ghost" western about Ned Kelly's sister that was selected for Frontières coproduction market at Fantasia International Film Festival in July 2016. She was recently nominated for Best Direction in a Feature Film at the 2019 Australian Directors' Guild Awards.

DR. LAURA MEE is senior lecturer in film and television at the University of Hertfordshire, United Kingdom. She is a horror fan with academic interests in the genre, and her work often focuses on adaptation, remaking, and seriality. Her monograph, *Reanimated: The Contemporary American Horror Film Remake* (2019), examines the post-2000 remake trend in U.S. horror cinema. She is also the author of *Devil's Advocates: The Shining* (2017) and coeditor of *Cinema, Television and History: New Approaches* (2014) and has been published in journals and collections on topics including rape-revenge remakes, the critical reception of horror remakes, *Room 237* and cinephilia, Stanley Kubrick and genre, and James Wan's horror franchises.

DR. KATARZYNA PASZKIEWICZ is lecturer in English Studies at the University of the Balearic Islands, Spain, and is a member of ADHUC–Research Center for Theory, Gender and Sexuality at the University of Barcelona. She holds a PhD in film studies (University of Barcelona, 2014). Her primary research is in film studies, cultural studies, and gender studies, with an emphasis on film genres and women's cinema in the United States and Spain. She coedited, with Mary Harrod, *Women Do Genre in Film and Television* (2017), which was the winner of first prize in the British Association of Film, Television and Screen Studies Best Edited Collection competition and has published her monograph *Genre, Authorship and Contemporary Women Filmmakers* (2018). Her latest edited collection *Final Girls, Feminism and Popular Culture* (2020) explores contemporary reformulations of the Final Girl in film, TV, and literature.

DR. ALISON PEIRSE is associate professor in film and media at the University of Leeds, United Kingdom. She is the author of *After Dracula: The 1930s Horror Film* (2013), coeditor of *Korean Horror Cinema* (2013), and editor of a special issue of *Asian Cinema* on cult and horror film. She is also a script editor and scriptwriter specializing in horror and has trained with New Writing North, the Royal Court, and BBC WritersRoom among others. She has contributed her internationally recognized research expertise on horror to media organizations including the BBC and *The Conversation* and through her collaborations with international genre film festivals, including /slash Filmfestival (Austria), Kurja Polt (Slovenia), Offscreen (Brussels), and Etheria Film Night (United States).

DR. DAHLIA SCHWEITZER is associate professor in film and media at the Fashion Institute of Technology, New York City. Her latest book, *L.A. Private Eyes* (2019), examines the tradition of the private eye as it evolves in films, literature, and television shows set in Los Angeles. Her previous works include *Going Viral: Zombies, Viruses, and the End of the World* (2018) and *Cindy Sherman's Office Killer: Another Kind of Monster* (2014) as well as essays in publications including *Journal of Popular Film and Television*, *Jump Cut*, and *Journal of Popular Culture*.

DR. MARTHA SHEARER is assistant professor and Ad Astra Fellow in the School of English, Drama and Film at University College Dublin. She is the author of *New York City and the Hollywood Musical: Dancing in the Streets* (2016). Her work has been published in *Screen* and *The Soundtrack* and the edited collections *The City in American Cinema* (2019) and *The Oxford Handbook of Musical Theatre Screen Adaptations* (2019). She is currently coediting two books: *Musicals at the Margins: Genre, Boundaries, Canons*, with Julie Lobalzo Wright, and *Women and New Hollywood*, with Aaron Hunter.

DR. TOSHA R. TAYLOR is a lecturer at Manhattanville College in New York. She holds a PhD from Loughborough University, United Kingdom, where she studied the captivity of Americans in contemporary horror films. Her recent publications include work on queer bodies in *American Horror Story*, masculinity in the work of the rock band the Killers, and postobject *Walking Dead* fandoms. She is also a Lower East Side–based playwright and performance artist.

VALERIA VILLEGAS LINDVALL is a doctoral candidate in film studies at the University of Gothenburg, Sweden. Her research aims to bring a feminist focus to the understanding of the Latin American female monster. She holds a master of arts degree in cinema studies from Stockholm University, Sweden, and she is on the editorial board of *MAI: Feminism and Visual Culture*. She has also worked in several publications, most prominently as a coeditor, writer, and translator at *Rolling Stone Mexico*, and has been a lecturer at the Department of Communication and Digital Arts at Tecnológico de Monterrey, Campus Estado de México.

Index